PRESIDENTIAL VOICES

Society of Biblical Literature

Biblical Scholarship in North America

Number 22

PRESIDENTIAL VOICES
THE SOCIETY OF BIBLICAL LITEATURE
IN THE TWENTIETH CENTURY

PRESIDENTIAL VOICES

THE SOCIETY OF BIBLICAL LITERATURE IN THE TWENTIETH CENTURY

Edited by

Harold W. Attridge

and

James C. VanderKam

Society of Biblical Literature
Atlanta

PRESIDENTIAL VOICES
The Society of Biblical Literature in the Twentieth Century

Copyright © 2006 by the Society of Biblical Literature

All rights reserved. No part of this work may be reproduced or transmitted in any form or by any means, electronic or mechanical, including photocopying and recording, or by means of any information storage or retrieval system, except as may be expressly permitted by the 1976 Copyright Act or in writing from the publisher. Requests for permission should be addressed in writing to the Rights and Permissions Office, Society of Biblical Literature, 825 Houston Mill Road, Atlanta, GA 30329 USA.

Library of Congress Cataloging-in-Publication Data

Presidential voices : the Society of Biblical Literature in the twentieth century / edited by Harold W. Attridge and James C. VanderKam.
    p. cm. — (Society of Biblical Literature biblical scholarship in North America ; 22)
  ISBN-13: 978-1-58983-259-6 (pbk. : alk. paper)
  ISBN-10: 1-58983-259-0 (pbk. : alk. paper)
  1. Bible—Criticism, interpretation, etc. 2. Society of Biblical Literature—Presidents. 3. Speeches, addresses, etc. I. Attridge, Harold W. II. VanderKam, James C.
  BS511.3.P74 2006
  220.06'01—dc22   2006033699

14 13 12 11 10 09 08 07 06   5 4 3 2 1
Printed in the United States of America on acid-free, recycled paper conforming to ANSI/NISO Z39.48-1992 (R1997) and ISO 9706:1994 standards for paper permanence.

Contents

Preface vii

Introduction ix

The Historical Element in the New Testament (1895)
  J. Henry Thayer 1

Present Tasks of American Biblical Scholarship (1919)
  James A. Montgomery 17

Our Own Future: Forecast and a Programme (1923)
  Max L. Margolis 27

Motives of Biblical Scholarship (1936)
  Henry J. Cadbury 33

The Ancient Near East and the Religion Of Israel (1939)
  W. F. Albright 45

The Society of Biblical Literature and Exegesis (1941)
  Julian Morgenstern 67

The Future of Biblical Studies (1945)
  Morton S. Enslin 75

Scholars, Theologians, and Ancient Rhetoric (1955)
  Amos N. Wilder 83

The Dead Sea Discoveries: Retrospect and Challenge (1956)
  J. Philip Hyatt 95

Parallelomania (1961)
  Samuel Sandmel 107

Form Criticism and Beyond (1968)
  James Muilenburg 119

Whither Biblical Research? (1970)
Harry M. Orlinsky 139

A Reconstruction of the Judean Restoration (1974)
Frank Moore Cross 153

The Watershed of the American Biblical Tradition:
The Chicago School, First Phase, 1892–1920 (1975)
Robert W. Funk 169

"Other Sheep Not of This Fold": The Johannine Perspective
on Christian Diversity in the Late First Century (1977)
Raymond E. Brown 189

The Bible as a Classic and the Bible as Holy Scripture (1983)
Krister Stendahl 209

The Ethics of Biblical Interpretation: Decentering Biblical
Scholarship (1987)
Elisabeth Schüssler Fiorenza 217

The Eighth, the Greatest of Centuries? (1988)
Philip J. King 233

At the Mercy of Babylon: A Subversive Rereading of the Empire (1990)
Walter Brueggemann 247

Jesus the Victim (1991)
Helmut Koester 267

Social Class as an Analytic and Hermeneutical Category in Biblical
Studies (1992)
Norman K. Gottwald 281

Antiquity and Christianity (1997)
Hans Dieter Betz 301

Catholic or catholic? Biblical Scholarship at the Center (2005)
Carolyn Osiek 323

Appendix 1: SBL Presidents and Presidential Addresses 343

Appendix 2: Editors of the *Journal of Biblical Literature* 350

Preface

The preface to Ernest W. Saunders's *Searching the Scriptures A History of the Society of Biblical Literature, 1880–1980,* begins by stating that the volume "is a story of a group of people dedicated to teaching and research." It goes on to acknowledge that the people creating the story "influenced significantly the course of American biblical scholarship." Now, some twenty-five years later, one would need to expand this characterization somewhat, since members of this organization have shaped biblical scholarship not only in America but across the globe.

To supplement and enrich the account told by Saunders, the current volume offers a documentary history of sorts, the "story" of the Society of Biblical Literature through the words of our presidents. Although each presidential address has contributed a chapter to our history, we obviously could not publish all of the presidential addresses given during the first 125 years (1880–2005) of the Society's existence. Therefore, the editors of this volume have selected those addresses that offer noteworthy signposts to the growth, development, and expansion of the Society of Biblical Literature over the past 125 years.

Many of these addresses are, of course, marked by a serious, scholarly tone. But on a lighter note, Saunders ends a chapter entitled "The Voice of Mirth" by recounting that President Robert H. Pfeiffer, who occasionally had "difficulty with the English language," once made an announcement concerning members who had not paid for their registration (room and board): "Please don't go without settling your accounts, if you have slept here, with Miss Aaronson." As Saunders quips, "One man who had remembered the incident offered the appropriate comment, 'It was the best and most successful presidential address ever made!'"

On behalf of the Society, we all give thanks to Harry Attridge, a former president and current chair of the Finance Committee, and Jim VanderKam, current editor of *JBL* and member of Council, for their efforts in bringing this volume to completion even as they lead us and contribute to the shaping of biblical scholarship through their research, teaching, and publications.

Kent Harold Richards
Executive Director
Professor of Old Testament
15 October 2006

Introduction

As it celebrates the 125th year of the *Journal of Biblical Literature,* the Society of Biblical Literature (founded one year earlier, in 1880) is marking the occasion in various ways: through special sessions and events and also through publications. The present collection of presidential addresses is one of those publications. Since 1895, a nearly constant element in the program for the annual meetings of the Society of Biblical Literature (and Exegesis) has been the lecture delivered by the president whose one-year term concludes with that meeting. Those addresses are then published in the *Journal of Biblical Literature* as the first essay in the volume for the following year. Although most presidential addresses are thus in print in *JBL* (the 1908 address by Frank Chamberlain Porter appeared in the *Harvard Theological Review*), it seemed to the organizers of this volume that it would be both appropriate and beneficial to make a selection of them available in a more accessible format.

The president of the SBL is a scholar who has distinguished himself or, more recently, herself through publications and service to the Society. To name just two, Henry J. Cadbury, the 1936 president, served as secretary from 1916 to 1933; Morton Enslin, president in 1945, filled a variety of leadership positions prior to his presidency and edited *JBL* from 1960 to 1969. Because of the stature earned by the presidents, their lectures to the Society have always had the potential to be special occasions, and, as the Society has grown, they are delivered before large audiences of participants and other attendees at the annual meeting. The practice for some time has been that the vice-president of the SBL, who will become the next president, introduces the speaker. The president then gives the address, which, consistent with its special character, is not subjected to questioning and discussion from the audience.

Some of the presidents have observed in their addresses that these speeches could take one of two forms: the scholar could deliver a more technical paper on an aspect of his or her research and perhaps offer a new proposal regarding this specialized subject; or the president could take the opportunity to reflect more widely on the field and the place of the Society in it. The essays selected for inclusion in this volume illustrate both kinds of addresses.

Making a selection from the long list of presidential addresses has proved to be a challenging task. Many are memorable for one reason or another and well worth making more readily available to a wider audience. In choosing the twenty-three addresses included here, we were guided by several considerations.

First, we wanted to include examples of both major kinds described above: the technical contribution as well as the broader reflection on the field. So, for example, the 1974 address of Frank Moore Cross, "A Reconstruction of the Judean Restoration," is a seminal essay whose novel theses were based on the latest archaeological evidence then available for clarifying the early Persian period in Judea. Others have, as it were, stepped back and asked larger questions. Max L. Margolis, for one, in 1923 dealt with "Our Own Future: A Forecast and a Programme," or Henry J. Cadbury treated "The Motives of Biblical Scholarship."

Second, we wished to illustrate important times and circumstances in the history of the Society, to recall the changes through which it has gone as reflected in the presidential addresses. J. Henry Thayer was the first to give a published presidential address, and an interesting one it is. Speaking under the title "The Historical Element in the New Testament," he reflected, even as he urged the importance of reading texts in their ancient settings, the nature of the small society whose members he addressed: they were men, and they were Christian. Of historical note—in addition to it being the first published address—is his proposal near the end of the lecture: "But I am impatient to reach a suggestion which I will frankly confess has with me for the moment vastly more interest and attraction than any other: Is it not high time that an American School for Oriental Study and Research should be established in Palestine?"

The first woman to serve as president, Elisabeth Schüssler Fiorenza, in 1987 offered an important address on "The Ethics of Interpretation: Decentering Biblical Scholarship." She considered the ethics of reading and the contribution (for good or ill) the reader brings to the text: one's social location or rhetorical context (to use her phrases). She also sketched important developments in the history of women in the Society and concluded: "Such a critical-rhetorical paradigm requires that biblical studies continue its descriptive-analytic work utilizing all the critical methods available for illuminating our understanding of ancient texts and their historical location. At the same time, it engages biblical scholarship in a hermeneutic-evaluative discursive practice exploring the power/knowledge relations inscribed in contemporary biblical discourse and in the biblical texts themselves."

As we have selected the first presidential address and the first one delivered by a woman, we have also included the most recent one, Carolyn Osiek's 2005 lecture "Catholic or catholic? Biblical Scholarship at the Center." She focuses her remarks on Catholic biblical scholarship and its place in and contributions to the wider catholic or universal study of the scriptures. "I suggest it is precisely the challenge of holding together ancient text, ongoing history of interpretation, modern science, and postmodern insights, within a conscious participation in a living tradition, that has enabled and can continue to enable Roman Catholic biblical scholarship to make its contribution, so that it can take an important part in the common catholic (small *c*) tradition of biblical interpretation. In this way, catholic can truly mean universal, open to all."

Another sense in which the addresses can be historically significant or even historic is in their reflection of great events in world history. An instance of this kind of lecture is the one presented by James A. Montgomery on December 26, 1918, a little more than one month after the signing of the armistice ending what was then called the Great War. The man who would author the famous commentary on Daniel in the International Critical Commentary series spoke about how the ties between German (the teachers) and American scholars (the students) were now broken and called on American scholars to assert their independence and to supply the basic tools for scholarship on the Bible.

While other presidential addresses could have been selected, we believe that the ones in this book supply a rich sample of the kinds of material in these addresses and the types of issues the presidents have chosen to treat.[1] They also furnish valuable information about much of the 125-year history of the SBL.

---

1. Apart from correcting typographical errors and conforming biblical citations to the now-standard chapter:verse format, the addresses are presented as originally published.

The Historical Element in the New Testament[*]

J. Henry Thayer
Harvard University

When I speak of the historical character of the Scriptures, I beg to be understood as referring to the fact that the truth they convey is couched in history, comes clothed in concrete form, is exhibited, not in abstract and universal propositions, but in specific shape, adjusted to particular times, persons, places, and intended—at least primarily—for definite, contemporary needs and applications.

In making this sweeping statement I do not forget utterances, like the "Golden Rule," which hold good, just as they stand, for all circumstances, all beings, all ages; nor do I overlook the fact that many a particular Biblical direction is apposite as a general maxim. The apostolic statements, "Whatsoever is not of faith is sin," "Let every man be fully persuaded in his own mind," are as wholesome dissuasives to-day from the temptation to disregard conscientious scruples, as they were when addressed to Roman Christians dubitating about observing Jewish feasts and fasts, or about eating flesh that had had some connection with idolatrous worship. Nay, the very circumstance that not a little of the Biblical language admits with facility diverse applications, emphasizes the importance of the exegete's noting narrowly and weighing carefully the specific conditions under which it was first spoken—so far as those can now be ascertained.

That our sacred records have a strong national and local cast is as undeniable as that the Greek in which the New Testament is written is a species of that language current in the Levant during the first century. But both facts are easily forgotten. Language with which we have been familiar from childhood takes on a homelike sound. The full recognition of its foreign quality requires that the attention be concentrated for a moment on this particular aspect of it.

---

[*] The following paragraphs are taken from the President's Annual Address, delivered at the meeting of the Society in Hartford, June 13, 1895. This circumstance will explain alike their somewhat disjointed character, and their popular and unscientific style. After considering briefly the various senses in which the epithet "historic" is applied to the Christian revelation, the speaker proceeded as above.

For this purpose let us open the New Testament, almost at random, and read a considerable extract:—

> Take heed lest there shall be any one that maketh spoil of you through his philosophy and vain deceit, after the tradition of men, after the rudiments of the world, and not after Christ: for in him dwelleth all the fulness of the Godhead bodily, and in him ye are made full, who is the head of all principality and power: in whom ye were also circumcised with a circumcision not made with hands, in the putting off of the body of the flesh, in the circumcision of Christ; having been buried with him in baptism, wherein ye were also raised with him through faith in the working of God, who raised him from the dead. And you, being dead through your trespasses and the uncircumcision of your flesh, you, *I say*, did he quicken together with him, having forgiven us all our trespasses; having blotted out the bond written in ordinances that was against us, which was contrary to us: and he hath taken it out of the way, nailing it to the cross; having put off from himself the principalities and the powers, he made a show of them openly, triumphing over them in it.
>
> Let no man therefore judge you in meat, or in drink, or in respect of a feast day or a new moon or a sabbath day: which are a shadow of the things to come; but the body is Christ's. Let no man rob you of your prize by a voluntary humility and worshipping of the angels, dwelling in the things which he hath seen, vainly puffed up by his fleshly mind, and not holding fast the Head, from whom all the body, being supplied and knit together through the joints and bands, increaseth with the increase of God.
>
> If ye died with Christ from the rudiments of the world, why, as though living in the world, do ye subject yourselves to ordinances, Handle not, nor taste, nor touch (all which things are to perish with the using), after the precepts and doctrines of men? Which things have indeed a show of wisdom in will-worship, and humility, and severity to the body; *but are* not of any value against the indulgence of the flesh.—*Colossians* 2:8–23.

Now it is difficult for an intelligent reader of these sixteen consecutive verses not to feel embarrassed by the air of historic remoteness which overhangs them. Over and above a misgiving which assails him here and there whether he quite understands the allusion on which the thought turns, the evident oriental and first-century air of the whole passage renders it almost ineligible for public reading, without comment, to a miscellaneous audience.

And what is true of this passage holds good of many others: for example, the extended discussions of the gift of tongues; of the relation of the sexes; of the dress and behavior of women in the Christian assemblies; the discipline of the incestuous church member; the collection for the needy believers at Jerusalem, —which make up so large a part of the Epistles to the Corinthians; the precepts relative to ecclesiastical administration, given in the Pastoral Epistles; the elaborate vindication of the rejection of the Jewish nation, which occupies the 9th, 10th, and 11th chapters of the letter to the Romans; nay, in one or two instances, the greater part of entire books, —as, for example, the contrast between Judaism and Christianity composing the bulk of the Epistle to the Hebrews, and the mystic imagery, the dimly intelligible, and, according to modern taste, uncouth symbolism that fills so much space in the last book of the Canon.

Here perhaps I ought to thrust in a caveat. I am only saying that the New Testament is an antique, not an antiquated, book—ancient, not obsolete. I have no sympathy with those who think that because it is old-fashioned it is quite out of date. Just as, a generation or more ago, there were certain wiseacres who held that, because Christianity had superseded Judaism, the Old Testament ought to be discarded; so we occasionally meet advanced spirits at the present day who would shelve the New Testament among the "Records of the Past." I do not agree with them—as I hope will be evident before I close.

Nor would I seem to overlook the fact that there are whole stretches of the sacred text which are as fresh and apposite to the spiritual needs of the generality of men as though they were written yesterday. The twenty-five verses immediately following the extract just read from the Epistle to the Colossians furnish a capital example, making up, as they do, that effulgent third chapter, which begins: "If then ye were raised together with Christ, seek the things that are above, where Christ is," etc. With the exception of an incidental mention of "Greek and Jew, circumcision and uncircumcision, barbarian and Scythian," there is almost nothing in the entire chapter indicating when, where, or to whom it was written. The encomium on Love in the 13th of 1 Cor., the vindication of the resurrection in the 15th, the exhortation to bodily and spiritual consecration in the 12th of Romans, are other conspicuous specimens. But the very fact that they start at once to our thought, and linger so in our memory, is an indirect attestation of their exceptional character.

Nor, in calling fresh attention to the historical, i.e. the national and local, character of our New Testament Scriptures, would I be thought to be insensible to the added charm which a slight touch of archaism lends to certain passages— like the quaintness which enhances the beauty of some mediaeval picture, or the occasional fascination of our vernacular on the tongue of a foreigner.

Still less would I be thought to lose sight of the accession of power which individualization lends, when it sets forth that which is or may be common to man. The personal then concentrates and localizes the universal. Thoughts and experiences gain incalculably in interest when they attach themselves to one whom though not having seen we love. When the apostle to the Gentiles recites his perils, or tells what things he counted to be loss for the sake of Christ, or gives that golden catalogue of experiences in which through evil report and good report he strove in everything to commend himself as God's minister, —no one needs a commentator to help him catch the heartthrobs. It is PAUL who is speaking: the intervening centuries are but his witnesses, catch up, corroborate, reverberate his words.

For still other passages the feeling of historical remoteness is neutralized by the modern or spiritual sense they have been *made to bear*. The current application, in their case, veils the primary intent. The ordinary Christian as he reads in the Prophets the descriptions of Israel's captivity and return, gives little thought to Israel after the flesh; to him they portray the coming triumph of the Israel of God. To such a reader many of the technical terms and phrases of Jewish speech would seem to have a kind of violence done to them if they were reproduced in their historical import. I allude of course to such terms as "the kingdom of heaven," "inherit the land," "see God," "the day of the Lord," "the wrath to come." So thoroughly transfigured have some of them become under the sublimating and spiritualizing influence of Christianity—which influence, by the way, pertains to its very genius and glory—that they are thought to refer solely to the *life beyond;* and certain persons in our day are winning a momentary distinction as great religious discoverers, because, forsooth, they have found out that the "Kingdom of Heaven" may begin to materialize here on earth!

Perhaps the most signal illustration in the New Testament of the power of the spiritual uses of Scripture to swallow up the primary and outward significance, is furnished by the Apocalypse. What cares the average Christian for your theories about its composite structure or historic reference! What matters it to him whether 666 stands for Nero, or Gladstone, or the Sultan! The edificatory use of the Book looks with scorn upon the uncertainties of the critic; yes, even triumphs at times over the natural force of language. At a funeral last winter, when the thermometer stood below zero, the clergyman read to a little shivering company of mourners gathered in a very humble dwelling the familiar words: "They shall hunger no more, neither thirst any more; neither shall the sun strike on them, nor any heat"—and hardly a person seemed conscious of any incongruity.

Let me not be supposed to take exception to this spiritualizing process. It was one great and ever-present aim of the Great Teacher. When he taught his Jewish followers to say "Thy kingdom come," he sought to defecate their mundane expectations by the appended petition, "Thy will be done, as in heaven so on earth." And they shew that they at length learned the lesson. With splendid distinctness does the apostle Paul insist that the true Jew is not the Jew by birth, that the genuine circumcision is of the heart, that the Gentiles become by faith the sons of Abraham, who is thus "the father of all them that believe." So thoroughly has the terrestrial in their thought been swallowed up by the heavenly, that a Peter and a James leave us in uncertainty whether, when they address the "Dispersion," they have in mind merely expatriated Jews, or all those who, having citizenship in the heavenly Jerusalem, are while here on earth far away from home. A James can give commentators a pretext for doubting whether by law he means the Hebrew Torah or that eternal ordinance whose seat is in the bosom of God; and with beautiful unconsciousness does the writer to the Hebrews, within the compass of a single section, use the term "rest" to signify the end of Israel's wanderings in

Canaan, the rest promised in David's day, the divine completion of the creative works, and the everlasting sabbath-tide awaiting believers in heaven.

So far am I from objecting to this elasticity, this varied application of Biblical language, that I beg to call attention to it as to a characteristic which has received abundant recognition by the sacred writers themselves, and the oversight of which has hampered many a modern expositor. It is in the New Testament itself that we find, for instance, our Lord's prediction that he will rebuild the Temple, taken now outwardly, of the material structure, now typically of that body in which the Eternal Word became incarnate, now ideally of that habitation of God through the Spirit in which He will forever tabernacle with men. It is in the New Testament itself that the eucharistic meal is depicted now as a Passover, now as the fellowship of commensality, now as the physical incorporation of the believer and his Lord. And how neatly does the Fourth Evangelist give us the substance, yes, more than the substance, of many voluminous discussions about the manifold sense of Prophecy, when he finds, on the one hand, a fulfilment of the Redeemer's declaration, "Of those whom thou hast given me I lost not one," in the exemption of the disciples from arrest in Gethsemane; and on the other hand—anticipating the irony of history—lifts the ignoble suggestion of the time-serving Caiaphas into a "prophecy" that the death of Jesus was not for the good of the nation only, but of all the scattered children of God.

Paul, too, as I hardly need remind you, once and again breaks through the trammels of a rigorous historic interpretation when the needs of his didactic purpose so require. Let it suffice to recall his procedure in contrasting the Mosaic dispensation and the Christian. The veil which the earlier record represents Moses as putting on his face in order to abate the fear caused by its unearthly brightness, the apostle does not hesitate to say was put on in order that the children of Israel might not see distinctly the evanescence of the glory; and a moment after, he represents the same veil as lying on Israel's heart.

Nevertheless, such Biblical precedents for diversity of reference we shall all admit, I think, are over-pressed when they are made the warrant, for instance, for ascribing to the apostle the very maxims he combats: the "Handle not, nor taste, nor touch," of the Colossian ascetics.

A far more common and more defensible procedure is that which allows one Biblical precept and another to lapse through desuetude. The historical limitations in such cases are recognized, and made the reason for the practical abrogation. In many of them Christianity itself has wrought the change which has nullified the precept. The number of particulars in which Biblical usage has become antiquated is larger, probably, than we are apt to suppose until we set out to reckon them up. Beginning with those early days when "not one of them that believed said that aught of the things which he possessed was his own, but they had all things common," the mind runs along through precepts about the wearing of veils, the treatment of unmarried daughters, the prohibition of braided hair and gold and pearls and costly raiment, the injunctions relative to clerical monogamy, washing the saints' feet, the holy kiss, and I know not how many others.

This admission, that some of the Biblical precepts are at least obsolescent by reason of their historical form, is a scandal in the judgment of the Tolstois, "Joshua Davidsons," and all that ilk; but most of us—with the great body of Christian believers—remain tranquilly acquiescent until perhaps some obtrusive advocate of "Seventh Day" observance, or of immersion as the only valid mode of baptism, forces upon our attention the transientness of the historic form in which the permanent spiritual truth is embodied. Even then our acknowledgment may restrict itself to the issue of the moment, and carry us no farther.

For example, one does not have to look far among the popular commentaries on the Fourth Gospel to find our Lord's words to Nathanael, "Verily, verily, I say unto you, Ye shall see the heaven opened, and the angels of God ascending and descending on the Son of Man," spoken of as referring to the scanty hints of angelic appearances at the transfiguration, in Gethsemane, at the ascension, or on some otherwise unrecorded occasion even. So completely do these interpreters stick in the bark. Stript of its national and local, its historic, costume, what is the saying but the declaration that in the Son of man free intercourse between heaven and earth has been re-established? That which of old was the exceptional privilege of him who strove with God and prevailed, is now the common and constant prerogative of all believers. In reference to this whole subject of the agency of higher beings there still lingers, I suspect, not a little misapprehension, due to failure to discriminate between the Biblical thought and the language in which it is clothed. The thought has come to us in national costume, and we mistake that costume for the livery of heaven.

Few intelligent persons, indeed, nowadays would be disposed to maintain that "waterless places" are the favorite haunt of demons: the accompanying features, of the house put in inviting condition for a new tenant, and the symbolic "seven," compel even a dim perception in this instance to look through the imagery to the underlying thought. So, too, the "fall of Satan, as lightning, from heaven" figures only in poetry and art. But, on the other hand, to call attention to the fact that the language, "There is joy in the presence of the angels of God over one sinner that repenteth," does not give express warrant for the talk about "angels rejoicing over repentant sinners," but is—as the whole tenor of the chapter (Luke 15) shews—a beautifully reverent oriental way of picturing the joy of the Heavenly Father himself at the return of a single wayward child, would be generally thought to savor of exegetical officiousness. To question the statement that the Bible teaches that "angels are sent forth to minister to the heirs of salvation" would strike many minds as audacious unbelief—in spite of the endeavor of the Revision to guide a reader to the Biblical writer's thought. And to assert that what the Sacred Volume is reputed to teach about the "guardian angels" of "little ones" rests merely upon a misapprehension of expressive oriental symbolism, would give not a few persons positive pain. Yet the key to the true thought here, viz., the high dignity belonging to the humblest believer, is given in Scripture repeatedly—from the exclamation of the queen of Sheba, "Happy are these thy servants which stand continually before thee," down to the angel of the annunciation, "I am Gabriel that stand in the presence of God," and the reiterated promise of the vision of God to be granted to the pure in heart and the redeemed. Indeed, one wonders at the persistency of such literalism among modern Christians, in the face of the acknowledged currency among Gentiles and Jews alike of a belief in attendant spirits, whether styled genii, or δαίμονες, or "angels." What do such readers make of the exclamation of the Christians at Jerusalem, who, after interceding with God for the liberation of Peter, were so surprised that their prayer should be answered, that, sooner than believe the literal truth when it was confidently affirmed by Rhoda, "they said, It is his angel"?

And speaking of Peter, what but inattention to the present and personal reference of the Biblical language has caused so many readers to stumble at the only natural interpretation of the Savior's commendation of the "Man of Rock"?—corroborated as that interpretation is by the post of primacy assigned him in all four lists of the Twelve, by the special responsibility laid upon him with reference to his brethren after the "sifting," by the pastoral charge given him to "feed Christ's sheep," by his prominence in the early history of the church as that is recorded in the opening chapters of the Acts.

The accompanying or kindred utterances about "the keys of the kingdom," "the binding and loosing," "the gates of Hades," "the sitting on thrones," are only so many additional exemplifcations of the national and local, the historic, cast of Biblical speech.

The same characteristic of the Biblical language appears, if I mistake not, in passages which have been held to be of cardinal importance in reference to systems of theology. Take, as a specimen, the recognition by Paul of Adamic headship and the unity of the race. But for his rabbinical theological training, it is more than probable that we should have never had that effective contrast of type and anti-type, the man of earth and the man of heaven, the living soul and the life-giving spirit, which sets the radiant crown upon his portraiture of the resurrection in the 15th of Corinthians; or that long perspective of the ages past and the ages to come given us in the 5th of Romans, and which Schlegel is said to have called the grandest philosophy of history that had then entered the human mind. But what doctrinal burdens, what basal significance, what overwrought systems alike of theology and of anthropology, have these two passing references by a single apostle to a contemporary Jewish tenet been made to bear!

We may find an illustration of the principle we are considering in another momentous topic: the Parousia of Christ. This is a topic, indeed, which stirs a hopeless feeling in many minds; a topic on which sober and reserved exegetes have now and then gone so far as to admit that the apostles are chargeable with inextricable confusion—an admission from which they have not allowed themselves to be deterred by the remorseless logic of Strauss, who says[1] (for substance), "The only trouble in the case is, that the event did not agree with the prophecy. Now, Jesus either made these predictions or he did not: if he did, he is thereby proved to have at times lost his mental balance, and hence must be taken with reserve as a teacher and religious guide; if he did not, his disciples, who put such things into his mouth, are not to be trusted in their reports of his teaching."

A full exposition of this intricate subject of course cannot be attempted here and now. At the most I shall endeavor merely to suggest a few particulars tending to show that the key to it is found in the recognition of the historical, i.e. the local and national, cast of our Lord's language.

But I cannot refrain from saying at once, that, as between man and man, the modern interpreter is quite as likely to be under a misapprehension as the original writer. For, not only was the record made by those (whoever they were) who stood so near the prime source as presumably to be tolerably correct in their statements, but those statements were put in circulation at a time when every reader could bring them to the actual test of history. Nevertheless, there they have been allowed to stand, in all their palpable and reiterated erroneousness—if many modern exegetes are right!

Surely, one would think that such language as, "*from this time forward* ye shall see the Son of man sitting at the right hand of power, and coming on the clouds of heaven" (Matt 26:64), or this, "For the Son of man shall come in the glory of his Father with his angels; and then shall he render unto every man according to his deeds. Verily I say unto you, There be some *of them that stand here,* which shall *in no wise taste of death,* till they *see* the Son of man coming in his kingdom" (Matt 16:27, 28), must have seemed to the readers of the first century rather an extravagant description of anything their eyes witnessed. For notice: we have in this last passage an explicit announcement of (a) his coming; (b) his coming as king—in divine glory and with angelic attendants; (c) his coming to universal judgment and requital—("every man according to his deeds"); (d) yet some of those on whose ears the words first fell should live to see their fulfilment. What room for faith in him as a prophet after that! Why did not the early Christians stumble at language which strikes us as extravagant to the verge of bombast?

Because they accepted it in the symbolic significance which current Jewish usage largely gave it. The prevalent Messianic expectations in our Lord's day were in the main confused, earthly, out of harmony with the spiritual kingdom which he aimed to establish. The task which confronted him was, how to lift his hearers from that which was secular to that which was spiritual, —from thoughts about *locality* to aspirations after *quality;* how to transform a kingdom of this world into the kingdom of God. And it was achieved, as his entire work was achieved, by first stooping to their level; by using their language ; by adjusting his teaching so

---

1. *Der alte und der neue Glaube.* Sechste Aufl., p. 80.

far as he truthfully could to their conceptions; by lodging the power of an endless life in local and temporary forms, and trusting to its expansive and transforming energy for the triumphant result.

The Bible is its own interpreter in this matter. An apocalyptic appearance on the clouds was one of the distinctive notes of the Messianic advent, as the Book of Daniel shews. Christ's appropriation of that description was merely an unequivocal avowal of Messiahship.

Readers slow to accept guidance in this matter from the Old Testament's employment of sublime and appalling natural phenomena to typify judgments upon Egypt, Babylon, Edom, and the rest, —judgments that had then passed into history, —may at least listen to the official interpretation of our Lord's eschatological discourses as that interpretation is given by the apostle Peter in his comment on the phenomena at Pentecost (Acts 2:16): "This is that which hath been spoken by the prophet Joel (τοῦτό ἐστιν τὸ εἰρημένον)....

> And I will shew wonders in the heavens above,
> And signs on the earth beneath;
> Blood, and fire, and vapour of smoke:
> The sun shall be turned into darkness,
> And the moon into blood,
> Before the day of the Lord come,
> That great and notable *day*.
> And it shall be, that whosoever shall call on the name of the Lord shall be saved."

Rather a grandiloquent description, *we* should say, of the Pentecostal occurrences! But surely Peter and his contemporaries are competent witnesses as to how such language was used and understood at that time.

As warrantably might we cavil when all three Synoptists find the verification of Isaiah's lofty predictions in the preaching of John the Baptist: "This is he that was spoken of by the prophet:

> Make ye ready the way of the Lord,
> Make his paths straight.
> Every valley shall be filled,
> And every mountain and hill shall be brought low;
> And the crooked shall become straight,
> And the rough ways smooth;
> And all flesh shall see the salvation of God."

The expositors talk to us about diverse "comings": the "eschatological," "historical," "spiritual," "dynamic," "individual," and the rest. But it may be doubted how far sharp lines of demarcation are warranted or helpful. The Biblical representations favor quite as much the conception of *a period and a process,* as of particular epochs and events; lay stress on moral and religious *laws,* rather than prognosticate *external occurrences.* Not that I would deny here or anywhere the indications of development embedded in the sacred record itself. The whole stretch from Judaism to consummate Christianity is measured for us in the twofold use of the term "Son of God" in the first chapter of John. But I question whether, for instance, the Apostle Paul would have been as much embarrassed as some of us are, when attention was called to his intimations in writing to the Thessalonians that the parousia was at hand, and on the other side to the assumption underlying his elaborate theodicy in Rom 9–11, namely, that the consummation of the gospel's work lies in an indefinitely remote future. For the very same writers who put into Christ's mouth these predictions of his impending advent, represent him as also carrying his hearers' thoughts into the indefinite future: "while the bridegroom *tarried,* the foolish virgins slumbered and slept" (Matt 25:5); it is because "My lord *delayeth* his coming" that the self-indulgent servant engages in revelry (Luke 12:45) ; "after *a long time*" the man who went into a far country returns and reckons with his servants (Matt 25:19). In short, the New Testament on this subject exhibits the educative method, the divine reserve, which characterizes the procedure of Providence. And the apostle shews that he was not an inapt pupil under its schooling. The growing spirituality of his conceptions—or at least of his mode of presenting them—discloses itself in his later Epistles. Nay, this very letter to the Romans which assumes the kingdom to be a remote realization, also defines it to be peace and righteousness and joy in the Holy Ghost—the Christian's *present possession.* And if at one moment he speaks of the advent as an event which he and his living associates may expect to witness, some ten years later (Col 1:13) he describes himself and his fellow-Christians as already "delivered out of the power of darkness and translated into the kingdom of the Son of God's love." And in his last recorded utterances on the subject, he can charge Timothy by Christ's appearing and *kingdom* (2 Tim 4:1), and at the same time express his personal assurance that he himself will be "delivered from every evil work and brought safe into the *heavenly* kingdom" (2 Tim 4:18).

In fine, a due recognition of the necessity of employing concrete imagery, material symbols, the current dramatic phraseology, to convey spiritual truth to the first generation of believers, and a parallel recognition of the evolutionary and educative method of the divine administration, will do much, I believe, to relieve of its difficulties a subject still regarded as one of the most perplexing in the domain of exegesis. And it is a subject not to be evaded. In its underlying principles it is central and cardinal, as I have endeavored to indicate. For it turns upon the question, "What was the idea held by *Jesus himself* respecting the nature and destiny of his kingdom, and the mode of its establishment?" The answer to that question our earliest Christian records leave in no manner of uncertainty. The experience of the church through the ages affords that answer historic comment and elucidation. Very interesting and instructive is the process by which the Spirit of Christ in his church has little by little been liberating it from Jewish and secular trammels, and lifting it into the liberty of his "mind," and of the true sons of God. In the kingdom of grace, as in nature, "the nest is emptied by the hatching of its eggs"; and the process of incubation requires patience and time. Mingled fulfilment and deferment, verification and transformation, old hopes blossoming into new surprises, —these are some of the steps in the procedure of Him who "moves in a mysterious way His wonders to perform."

These random illustrations of the historical cast of the language of the New Testament might be indefinitely multiplied; and did time permit, it would be interesting to notice the service which the recognition of this truth can be made to render in the treatment of the wider questions, alike of Criticism and of Biblical Theology. The entire sacrificial conception of the work of Christ, for instance, finds elucidation in, and furnishes corroboration of, our principle; a conception repudiated by many at the present day as factitious and obsolete, and which it must be confessed Christianity itself, by its "one offering once for all," has done much to render antiquated to the average modern mind.

But let me turn to one or two suggestions which this general characteristic of the volume starts.

1. It emphasizes the importance of studying the New Testament writings in their relations—literary, national, local. Much is said in these days about studying the Bible as literature. But what would be thought of the student of English who should assume that the matter of five hundred years or so (say from Chaucer to Lowell) is of small account in its effect on the language? Yet our college boys jump from Thucydides to the New Testament at a bound; and take it for granted that the language of the latter is as much easier to understand than that of the stately historian, as its structure is simpler.

Shakspere, like the Bible, has a certain intrinsic isolation; constitutes by itself a body of literature unique and apart; may in large measure be understood, enjoyed, and profitably used, without preliminary training or attendant comment. But what would be thought of a man who aspired to be a *student* and *expositor* of Shakspere while he remained contentedly in native ignorance of the Elizabethan drama, the growth and characteristics of 16th century English, the social usages of the period, the sources and history of the materials which this peerless master has appropriated and transfigured! Yet not more than one or two theological institutions in the land, so far as I know, offer to their students thorough courses of study in the extant literature—Jewish, Heathen, and Christian—immediately preceding and following that embodied in our sacred volume.

An intelligent treatment of many prominent topics is quite impossible to these future expounders of the Word without some share in the broad outlook here advocated, some first-hand acquaintance with the contemporary life and thought in which our Biblical writings lie embedded. Witness the floundering which has been going on for a decade over the contents of the term "kingdom of heaven"; take up almost any book professedly treating of the Messianic notions current in our Lord's day and his relations to them. True, our present knowledge of these and similar important topics is fragmentary, meagre, conflicting. But what excuse is that for remaining ignorant of what *is* to be known? And how shall knowledge be increased except by study and research? True, again, this desiderated knowledge has but a collateral and incidental bearing on the homiletic and devotional uses of our sacred writings; which uses must and ought to remain paramount with the mass alike of ministers and of people. But I am speaking to *scholars,* or those who aspire to become such; and thus qualify themselves to bring out more and more the inherent truth and power of that volume which under God is the hope of the world.

It must be confessed, further, that the claims, alike respecting inspiration, and the formation of the Canon, which the Protestant theologians of the 16th century thought themselves forced to set up over against the arrogant pretensions to infallibility of the church with which they had broken, have somewhat fettered for many of their modern successors freedom of speculative thought, and enterprise in historic research.

Moreover, it is undeniable that the Christian literature is the product of the Christian religion; and that the Christian religion had its birth with the one solitary and transcendent personality whose name it bears. What *He* did and said, therefore, how *He* was understood and preached by his personal followers, is given us in the earliest extant Christian writings, and nowhere else. These writings make up our New Testament. Hence, it is sometimes argued, we have no need of anything further. Nothing is to be gained by recourse to outside literature, Jewish or Christian. The veil is upon the heart of the Jew even in reading Moses and the Prophets; the later Christian gets his illumination, if he have any, from the same central sun that gilds our sacred page.

But let us not confound the substance of the New Testament with the interpretation of the New Testament. Let no one think that it is proposed to supplement the sacred record from either the puerilities of the Rabbins or the dicta of the Fathers. But how are our Scriptures to be understood? is the question. And without conceding any the least claim to final expository authority to outside individual or church, ancient or modern, the Christian student may eagerly welcome the help to the elucidation of language, customs, opinions, which comes from any quarter; and that much may be expected, is shewn by the progress in the portraiture of Christ himself which the last generation has witnessed.

The visionary and mystical materials which these writers of the second and subsequent generations mingle with the Biblical do not nullify the evidence their works afford in attestation of our New Testament documents on the one hand, and in elucidation of them on the other.

2. Again: The recognition of the historical cast of our sacred records will lend new value to all geographical and archaeological information relative to the country of their origin.

Thanks to the occasional generosity of a missionary or traveller, we have in this country here and there an embryonic museum of Biblical or Semitic antiquities. But such collections are in general but little appreciated and little studied.

Further: how many of the public teachers of religion have any definite knowledge of the mountains and plains, the rivers and highways, of that land which witnessed and shaped the characteristics and history of the ancient people of God, from the Father of the Faithful to the Crucifixion? The "Fifth Gospel" it has been styled; rather might it be called the illustrator and expositor of all Four, yes, and of the entire Hebrew history.

Shortly after the outbreak of the Rebellion, it occurred to a pastor that he might turn to account the prevalent interest in military affairs by attempting with his people a detailed study of the Old Testament wars. He had at command the invaluable works of Robinson and Stanley and the standard encyclopaedic equipment of the average minister's library. But after a few experiments he was forced to abandon his undertaking. The topographical knowledge requisite for an intelligent understanding of Israel's decisive battles was not accessible. Professor George A. Smith's recent work puts a student in a very different position. It is one of the happiest and most stimulating signs of the times for the friends of the Bible, that at length students whose primary interests at least are not religious are beginning to study and test its records from their own point of view. At a recent meeting of the Academy of Inscriptions—as the newspapers tell us—M. Dieulafoy (the well-known Persian traveller) read a paper in which he "reconstituted the principal phases of the battle between David and the Philistines in the Valley of Rephaim, after a detailed study of the exact theatre of operations." He reaches the result that "the plan of the battle is very clearly described in the Bible," and David's complicated and bold strategy on the occasion gives evidence of the highest military capacity, being in striking analogy with the movement executed by "Frederick II. at the battles of Mollwitz and Rossbach, and by Napoleon at Austerlitz."

3. But I am impatient to reach a suggestion which I will frankly confess has with me for the moment vastly more interest and attraction than any other: Is it not high time that an *American School for Oriental Study and Research* should be established in Palestine?

This is no new idea. Others besides myself, no doubt, have been cherishing it as a secret hope for years. Indeed (as many of you know) an attempt was made some ten years ago to lay the foundation for something of the sort at Beirut. A scholarly and interesting article in advocacy of the enterprise, written by Professor Henry W. Hulbert, now of Lane Theological Seminary, was published in the "Presbyterian Review" for January, 1887. Whether because of the somewhat restricted organization and relations of the proposed establishment, or the limited constituency to which it primarily appealed, or other reasons, unknown to me, the project failed to attract the attention and secure the support which such an undertaking merits.

But I have been unable to discover anything which should deter us from renewing the undertaking under better auspices. Indeed, so alluring are enterprises of this sort at present, so great their promise of usefulness alike to Biblical learning and missionary work, that—as you are aware—a French Catholic School of Biblical Studies has established itself already in Jerusalem, whose quarterly "Revue Biblique," printed in Paris, is in its fifth year and deserves the respectful attention of scholars; while the journals tell us of a projected "Church College" in the Holy City, and a School of Rabbinical Learning (with ample library) at Jaffa. As Dr. Smith pithily puts it, "We have run most of the questions to earth: it only remains to *dig them up*." Shall the countrymen of Robinson and Thomson, Lynch and Merrill, Eli Smith and Van Dyck, look on unconcerned? Shall a Society, organized for the express purpose of stimulating and diffusing a scholarly knowledge of the Sacred Word, remain seated with folded hands, taking no part or lot in the matter?

Let it not be supposed that we students, in our poverty, must wait upon the generosity of some liberal friend of sacred learning to fulfil our heart's desire, by blessing the enterprise I am urging with an ample endowment from the start. I will not deny that it stirs one's wonder that somebody with wealth, and the ambition to use it in a way that shall ensure his own renown as well as large and lasting benefits alike to learning and religion, does not seize upon the waiting opportunity. To be sure, of the two classes of "finds" which tempt to exploration—those, namely, of intrinsic value, like jewelry and statuary, and those of archaeological and historical importance—it is mainly the latter which promise to reward oriental research. And yet (to say nothing of the Sidon sarcophagi), the Sendjirli inscription, the Mesha stone, the Temple tablet, the Siloam inscription, the Tel-el-Hesy cuneiform, and countless coins, would made a creditable return, as investments run, if rated in dollars and cents. But we, who cannot look upon the enterprise from this angle, are fortunately not debarred from seriously considering it. The plan I would venture to suggest is simple and modest, but not ineffectual. Can we not take a hint from the School at Athens ? There are, if I am not mistaken, at least two score institutions of learning represented in the list of our "Active Members." Let but half that number, let but twenty or twenty-five of the leading theological seminaries in the land pledge their support to the enterprise for five years to the amount of $100 a year, and the greatest obstacle is overcome. For two thousand or twenty-five hundred dollars, annually, it is believed that modest but adequate accommodations for the School can be secured, and a suitable Director. The general management of the School—which of course should be wholly free from denominational connection—might be lodged in the hands of a Committee chosen by the co-operating Institutions, which should further have the right to be annually represented at the School, in turn, by a resident Professor, while the $500 or less which residence would cost a student, he himself would pay.

The achievements of Dr. Frederick J. Bliss shew how easily a competent Director can be found, while for explorations in the field the efficient co-operation of

Americans long resident in the country as missionaries or teachers can often be secured at a merely nominal cost: men thoroughly acquainted with the language and habits of the people, as well as with the formalities of official etiquette, and whose presence would render exploration vastly less dangerous and expensive, as well as more promising, than it could be apart from such intelligent expert cooperation.

As I have alluded to Beirut, I may perhaps be permitted to say to those who may never have had the privilege of visiting the place, that in addition to its regular connection by steamers with Europe, it possesses already an educational plant, if I may so style it, of exceptional value for our purpose, which—under proper safeguards—I have reason to believe could be rendered serviceable to the School: for example, *there* may be found what is held to be the finest collection in existence of the flora of the country, a respectable museum of local mineralogical and geological specimens, more than 1500 coins from the age of the Seleucidæ down, a library of more than 5000 volumes, including many of the most valuable works relating to Syria and Palestine. Moreover, there are resorts, to be reached in three hours, which are 3000 feet above the sea-level and where the average temperature during the hottest months does not exceed 72° Fahrenheit, thus permitting the results of winter exploration to be worked out comfortably during the warm season.

Whatever results the School may achieve, whether by way of study or of exploration, can at once be spread before the world, free of expense, in the pages of our JOURNAL.

But, dropping details, I beg to commend the project to your most serious consideration before this present meeting of the Society closes.

[NOTE.—It may be added, that the closing suggestion above received the consideration of a special Committee, with whose approval a Circular setting forth a plan for the establishment of the desired School was prepared. After receiving the endorsement of many leading scholars, it has been sent to the theological and other institutions of learning in the hope that some such school may be instituted without much delay.]

Present Tasks of American Biblical Scholarship[*]

James A. Montgomery
University of Pennsylvania

Duty always spells the present task, and the tasks crowd naturally so close upon each other's heels that we do not often enough raise our heads above the routine and take stock of new problems and fresh opportunities.

But upon the whole world the Great War has brought stupendous duties with the compulsion of thinking out grand programs of action never before dreamed of. If in the past four years many of the nations have been compelled to think hard and fast and then turn to the grinding material duty in order to save themselves from a shameful despotism, now a breathing space has come. This might be given to fatigue and repose, but rather it is required for collecting our sadly disturbed minds, boldly prospecting the future, and realizing at least the outlines of its duties and responsibilities.

Yet such a group as this, composed of students of the Bible, might think itself detached from the onward course of the world. If we are personally alive to this detachment and feel at all keenly our place first as citizens of the human polity and not as professional dilettanti, we must be keenly touched by the apparent vanity of much of that in which we have been engaged. As professionals we have been able to contribute nothing to the salvation of the world, and some of us have chafed at the reins, that while almost every other profession has been called on to do its part in the wonderful organization of differentiated functions whereby the war has been won, we, along with similar groups of academics, have been exempted, exempt because we had nothing to give. In the S. A. T. C. courses we have not been wanted, and in the seminaries Hebrew and Greek and Latin have not appealed to men who as ministers of religion felt the war also to be a crusade in which the things of the spirit might be potent as well as the arms of the flesh. With what mind will they come back to their books? At best we can flatter ourselves that as Bible students and teachers we have made some contribution,

---

[*] Presidential Address at the annual meeting of the Society of Biblical Literature at Columbia University, December 26, 1918.

however impalpable, to the nobler humanity that has fought out this war. Yet the evidence is very indirect. Have we even purposed that object?

There may be those among us whose attitude towards the Great War has been one of impatience over the disturbance to our scholarly ease. We have not been able to correspond with foreign scholarship, to publish, or even to study with repose of mind. Such men may sigh a sigh of relief, and think that now it is all over, they may return to their accustomed tasks, to find them the same and to pick up the broken but still identical thread of their ways. It is such an attitude as this, which in the after-war enervation may affect the most patriotic scholar, that threatens grave danger to Biblical and similar sciences. While indeed their groups have been exempt from the great operations of the world in the past four years, I can see no greater peril lying before our studies and our very professions than the vain imagination that our paradise is to remain unchanged after the War.

We academics flatter ourselves on what we call our pure science, and think we are the heirs of an eternal possession abstracted from the vicissitudes of time. We recall Archimedes working out his mathematical problem under the dagger of the assassin or Goethe studying Chinese during the battle of Jena. But we dare not in this day take comfort in those academic anecdotes nor desire to liken ourselves to the monastic scholars who pursued their studies and meditations in their cells undisturbed by the wars raging without. The world has been unified, it is calling upon all to pool their interests and capitals, and those causes which can show no worth-value, spiritual or material, will no longer be quoted in the world's market. This is particularly true of Bible Knowledge. Despite all skepticism and varieties of religious belief, the world has fostered and propagated Bible study because of its assumed value to humanity. For the science of the Bible—an un-English phrase, by the way—it has little care, as little care as for the mediaeval scholasticism, unless the technical study keeps the interpretation of the Bible up to modern needs as well as standards and vivifies it for the ever-changing life of society. We might be a polite group of students of the Koran or the Chinese Classics, and, as far as pure science goes, contribute more than can be drawn from the trite study of the Bible, but we may doubt whether our patrons would agree to such demands of science so-called.

Merely as professional students of the Bible—for the majority of the active members of this Society are salaried teachers in colleges and seminaries—we must weigh with some misgivings the present economic status of our case. Dr. John P. Peters has sketched in a recent paper[2] the remarkable development of Biblical and Semitic studies in this country in the past thirty years and exhibited a record of which Americans may well be proud. But the conditions in the

---

2. In *Thirty Years of Oriental Studies,* issued in commemoration of the thirty years of activity of the Oriental Club of Philadelphia, edited by Dr. R. G. Kent, University of Pennsylvania, 1918. Compare Prof. R. W. Rogers' appended "Discussion" with its pessimistic outlook on the future of Hebrew studies.

latter part of this period are rather ominous. The promise given by Dr. Peters' own Babylonian enterprise of American capacity for great things has not been sustained by American vigor and finance. And at home the shifting of the centre of interest in the seminaries from the Biblical to the sociological studies has severely affected the demand for Biblical scholarship. Hebrew is passing from the seminaries, a *fait accomnpli* in some of the greatest of them; the exemption from Greek is being vigorously discussed, it is chiefly the conservatism of the Churches that has kept it from being consigned to the scrap heap as a requisite of the minister's education. And this debacle of the philological sciences which lie at the base of Biblical study is but the toppling of the upper story of the whole fabric of the ancient classical education. With Greek and Latin out of the schools, or discounted by popular opinion and arrogant pedagogical theory, it becomes increasingly impossible to raise up a scholarship which is worthy of the Bible. There is even the danger of developing a pseudo-Semitic scholarship which has not the solid substratum of the old education in the humanities, the result of which would be a narrow onesidedness which durst not face the scholarship of the past generations. This falling off in the students fitted in the "Sacred Languages" is already having its effect upon the upper classes of scholarship. Chairs are left unfilled, or when they are to be supplied it is difficult to find the man. I fear that the splendid band of Biblical scholars which dates back to the era of the new Biblical scholarship inaugurated by Dr. Harper, and which has made its mark, despite the limitations circumscribing American scholarship, is not leaving behind an adequate progeny. We have been going on an elder momentum which seems to have spent itself, while adverse forces are further disintegrating our cause.

There is a possibility which may check the present trend of our lower and so, higher education. This possibly may come as a consequence of the Great War. The world has not been saved by science, so the man in the street is coming to observe. It was nigh to being ruined by the science of that nation which arrogated all science to itself and which by that token cast down the gage to humanity. At awful cost to the world but more than worth all the blood shed and money spent, has been the pricking of this conceit of science. Not only has the German Terror collapsed, but also—for all modern education has been tarred with the same stick—some of the bubbles of our own conceit have been exploded, more quietly but we may hope with equal effect for good. The world has shaken off its scientistic prepossession and has denied on the field of battle that humanity is merely a scientific specimen, to be studied, experimented upon and exploited by professors, diplomats, despots and spies. The supposed cadaver has risen from its bed and smitten a deathblow to its tormentors. And this discovery may lead us back to the recognition of the discarded humanities, back to, the notion the ancients had, and even uncivilized races still have, that life is something more than a mechanical unit to be expressed in known terms. The old humanities held this view of man, the Bible and its religions have enforced it, in long periods replacing the classic humanities, and there may be a reaction to those studies, if the thinking men in those departments know how to deflect and guide the tide.

For after all—and I venture to speak of the philosophy of the Bible before a Biblical Society without offence—the Bible stands for just those things for which we and our Allies have fought and triumphed. From the story of the Tower of Babel to the Christ on the White Horse of the New Testament there is the constant challenge to every human thing which would set itself in the seat of God, be it force or despot or civilization. It has given guidance and inspiration to the souls groping after the Kingdom of God, held before them the ideals of right and peace as indissolubly related, of a natural humanity and a sane democracy, of an idealism always presented in its contrast to the realities, yet ever seeking realization. Its transcendentalism, long unsympathetic to the modern world, finds an awakened echo in the present world of woe. The classicists make similar arguments for their studies, we Biblical students must not fail in presenting our claims. For our very livelihood's sake we must inquire how effectually we are commending our wares and wherein we have erred. For any cause whose champions cannot present it as worth while, must perish.

In this connection I mark that our American Biblical scholarship has been in danger of drawing too hard and fast a line between what we call the scientific and the popular presentation of the Bible. The latter as the line of greatest demand and also of profit has deflected some scholarship from possible firstrate work, while the former duty has been assumed with too much self-consciousness, and hence the proper appeal has not been sufficiently made by the best equipped to even the intelligent public. It cannot be said that we American scholars have shown up as well as those of Great Britain, France and Germany in the production of ripe work, thought out on large lines, based not merely on a technically correct philology but also on a thorough education and humane sympathy. Our scholarship has been too much content to stand apart by itself, leaving what it calls the graces, which rather are as spirit an essential part of the living organism, too much to the popularizer and the preacher. This is a sophomoric attitude which might be corrected if there were in our community a greater mass of well-educated people, or more centres of positive intellectual breeding. But then all the greater reason why in our very democratic and not broadly educated circles the very best and most profoundly educated of our scholarship is needed to present the Bible in a congenial and sympathetic spirit. If it be only a volume of philology and archaeology, I doubt if appeal can be made for it, except to small groups. We are in danger of falling into the same educational fallacy which has injured the classical studies, where at the hand of so-called scientific students, often just out of college, the classics have been reduced to philological themes. They no longer appeal as humanities, and if we wonder how our forefathers were educated and grew great on those studies, it was not because they were simple-minded; to the contrary, our failure is due to our teaching, to the shifting of the centre of gravity to new but too often minor centres of gravity. Philology, criticism, history of religion, are necessary introductions to the study of the Bible and independent as its by-products, but can never replace the higher introduction, that by which the teacher leads his student *con amore* into the spirit and charm of the Bible. Mere flippancy of treatment of the greater issues of the Bible, a sorry kind of stage effect, has its own reward; the world takes such a scholar at his quip and leaves him and his subject severely alone.

In regard to Biblical criticism our American scholarship is itself to be criticized for remaining too long by the old baggage. It has often been said that British and American scholarship lags a generation behind that of Germany, and I believe that the reproach is true in comparison with Europe in regard to the advanced steps we need to take beyond the critical elements. These are not the *ne plus ultra*. It can hardly be said of us that we have contributed much to the reconstruction of the Biblical history and life. On the historical side our scholarship has been meagre. We have carried on, often parrotwise, our analyses, but when we come to the reconstruction of the original picture, where the criticism should go into the footnotes, we have fallen short. American archaeology has indeed made important and striking historical contributions, this often without reck of criticism or even in defiance of it. But we have not been pliable enough to change the habit of mind from that of analysis to that of synthesis. Whether we are too much under the spell of our schoolboy masters, whether our mind fatigues and runs out early, whether we are afraid of results which will offend whether the radical or conservative, I know not. Here again we have to reckon with our patrons who employ us for their guides and teachers. They are not interested in the laboratory methods which so engross us, absolutely essential as these are. But they do, and rightly, inquire of us the products we have gained. If you have taken away our old views of the Bible; they ask, and these were faiths, what fresh organism of flesh and blood can you recreate for the history which we fondly imagined once beat under these fragments? The world does not care for the Bible as a pursuit of the ingenious mind, but it wants to be assured whether it once fitted into the web and warp of human history and still has something to say to human life. If we cannot prove that, the day of the Bible is over, at least its teaching will pass into other hands and conditions.

To this I venture to add a word on the religious valuation of the Bible. We have essayed to treat it as philology, as archaeology, as history, as literature, and as many new and fascinating phases of study have developed. But the Bible remains primarily a religious book, and the student must approach it with religious sympathy. As it is absurd to think of a student of art approaching his subject without the aesthetic sense, so it is equally absurd for the student of the Bible to handle it without some reaction upon his religious sensibilities. There is the danger of the scientific fetish of mind deadening this sensibility, as if the student of Greek art should think he has accomplished his task when he has minutely and painfully measured an Attic vase, while in spirit he falls infinitely behind the untutored soul that is ravished by its beauty. The mere measurements of the Bible must not deter us from the appreciation of it as that which it claims to be, a book of religion. And none can fully interpret it who is not possessed by that prepossession. Not the childish fear of the appearance of faith or confessionalism should keep us from this full approach to the Bible. It is after all, on the whole, those who have believed in it who have been its greatest interpreters. And the duty lies upon us Biblical scholars to show the world that we believe in its worth and assert its value with an enthusiasm that is tinged by emotion as well as moderated by reason.

Such are some of the internal conditions of our American Biblical scholarship and the criticism that may be applied to it in the present circumstances. But there is also a foreign relationship to whose bearings upon our subject we cannot shut our eyes. Germany has been our mistress in Biblical scholarship, we have gone to school to her, her textbooks have been ours. Now the moral ties binding us with her have been broken, and with that has snapped the intellectual relationship. If it were otherwise, we were pedants, not men, no better than mummies.

We can no longer go to school to a nation against which we feel a moral revulsion. It is not for us a question of politics, whereby we might try to distinguish between the military class and the so-called people. But the Intellectuals of Germany, including the men of our science, sided unanimously and with brazen effrontery with the despotism, through its scientific relations with us tried to pull the wool over our eyes, have misinterpreted facts and history, the realm in which they were professed masters. It is not a question of forgiving but of forgetting. It will take a long time before our natural psychology can again go to school to Germany. As a prominent member of this Society wrote me in 1914, when I was in Jerusalem, "we can no longer accept an ethics made in Germany." And this revulsion must apply also to philosophy and theology and historical science. The men who prostituted their science to the Terror, even deceiving some among us, cannot easily be taken as guides even in pure science. The past is a closed chapter, to be slowly opened and continued by the long hand of time.

We have hardly yet realized the results of this catastrophe, but it has vast implications for us. To begin with, the very social and educational relations are broken. There is a popular hatred of Germany which will condemn for long all things bearing its hallmark. The break in the teaching of German in our schools will have its material effect upon the study of German theology. For this taboo on a glorious language the possessors have themselves to blame.

A break in long and cherished political and academic associations such as we have experienced is a sad disaster. Many of us feel it deeply, because personally. For compensations there are the opportunities offered by the closer academic ties now presenting themselves with Great Britain and France. Negotiations have already been entered into between the American Oriental Society and the Societe Asiatique, looking forward to mutual cooperation among the learned societies of the Allies.[3] We have still much to learn from those countries, which are racially, politically and intellectually our nearest neighbors, bound to us now by a brotherhood knit in blood, and a change of schooling may bring its compensations. But more than these fresh attachments, the opportunity has come for American scholarship to assert its independence and to attempt to work out its equality with that of other nations of the earth. In this competition we have hitherto been, like the Greek before the Egyptian priest, a little too modest, if not as to our deserts at least as to our capabilities. We have no reason to be ashamed of what has been done in certain monumental ways, from Edward Robinson down. We can claim as particularly our own the Great English dictionaries of the two Testaments, ours is in large part the International Commentary, ours the undertaking of the Polychrome Bible. It is impossible to give even a summary view of the work done by individual scholars, much of it of a calibre equal to any done abroad.[4]

Yet there are many deficiencies in our learned encyclopaedia, to which we have resigned ourselves, but which the new spirit of our independence must make us keenly alive to. Before the War the writer felt it was unnecessary for us to attempt to reduplicate the excellent elementary works so cheaply procurable in German; the student should be required to learn the language. But now I am coming to hold that we should make ourselves self-sufficient in all essential literature. This ought to be deemed an integral part of the training of our scholarship that it be required to produce the necessary apparatus. We have at present, for instance, to go to Germany for our elementary textbooks in Biblical Aramaic, Syriac, Arabic. We have no adequate Hebrew grammar or dictionary for school use. We have not supplied ourselves with anything like the Short Commentaries of the German scholars. As scholars we ourselves have not felt the need, but it is to be expected that if the popular interest is to, be maintained and a native substratum of learning is to be accumulated, we must develop a Biblical literature of our own make. Cosmopolitanism in science is a fair ideal for the upper strata, but it must be based upon deep-rooted national foundations. There are stirrings of this sense among us, provoked by the War, and we may hail the program of an Opus of Semitic Inscriptions which has been planned by our colleague Professor Clay. And as an asset to our American scholarship we must mark with great interest the establishment of the new Jewish Learning in our country. America may become the new home of Rabbinic studies; we shall watch with expectation for the enrichment that should come from this foundation to all our Biblical study.

The scholarly lack in our output is conditioned by the mechanical and economical lack of proper printing facilities in this country. This fact may be focussed by recalling that up to the time of the Great War our own Journal and

---

3. For these negotiations see the current part of the *Journal of the American Oriental Society,* 1918, p. 310.

4. See the paper by Peters cited above and the accompanying paper by Jastrow in the same volume.

that of the Oriental Society had been printed for a few years in Germany. This business has come back to our shores, never I hope to return abroad. But the high rates of American printing have gone up steadily in the past four years. The *Jewish Quarterly Review,* now American, is still printed in England. The printing of scholarly books on this side of the Atlantic faces the tremendously high cost of bookmaking, which is aggravated by the lack of a sufficient corps of trained typesetters when it comes to the matter of Oriental types. Again, when such books are published they do not find the local demand to warrant them as in the more intensely educated lands of Europe.

Further there is no national support for our kind of literature and its auxiliaries, and while individual academies and museums have munificently published scientific series, the means for these have been generally supplied by private contributions, in many cases painfully secured through the solicitation of the indefatigable scholars concerned. Our School in Jerusalem has suffered because it has never possessed the means to publish its memoirs, and so has nothing to show comparable with the learned and popular publications and journals of the European schools. It is an eternal credit to President Harper that he demanded that the Press should be part of his University.

This tremendous drawback must be recognized in the first place by us scholars, and the duty lies upon us of forming initial resolutions to abate the evil. We might, for instance, following the trades-union-like rules of certain practical professions, insist that gifts, endowments, academic extensions, should always provide for proper publication, and rather refuse them if their purposes are really to be made useless, if there is to be the process of gestation but no bringing to birth. We might collectively bring pressure to bear upon our schools to induce their patrons to recognize this need, as also upon the large funds that are being given to the cause of education in this country, but which ignore the humanities. The layman fails not in generosity but in imagination, and this it is our professional duty to stimulate. It is a pleasure in this connection to refer to a movement undertaken by our fellow member, President Cyrus Adler, looking towards an endowed Hebrew Press.

One particular desideratum in our literature may be noticed: a current Biblical Bibliography and Review. This want has been supplied to us from Germany, and the necessity of our own operation in that line has been brought home to us by the famine of the past four years. Our journals have not the means to supply this need, at least apparently so, or else they have not duly weighed the matter, and we have been thrown upon the mercies of the national weeklies and dailies or ecclesiastical journals for the learned reviews of learned books. The result is that in general the art of such reviewing has become a lost art in this country. The art may not make an appeal to many minds, but all agree that if it is practised at all it should be of the same calibre as the objects of criticism. Either such a Review for Biblical or general Semitic lines (but the latter would squeeze out the New Testament) should be financed as a separate venture, or to avoid the expense of a new undertaking, the present existing journals should be enabled to supply the need. It might be that this task could be simplified by parcelling the work out among the journals related to our cause, of which we have a highly meritorious list: those of our Society and the Oriental Society, *the Journal of Semitic Languages and Literatures,* the *Jewish Quarterly Review,* the *Harvard Theological Review.* In our present poverty some form of syndicalism may be necessary.

Our American scholarship has taken its part in the duty of Biblical criticism, in some cases notably, but it may be asked whether this labor has not become too much an ingrowing process, tending to deaden spirit and petrify work. None can pore too long over the same material without losing the long sight and wide prospect. What we need is fresh raw material. In this Europe has the advantage over us.

In the first place I would refer to the absence in this country of the materials of the Lower Criticism, the manuscripts. What American scholarship can effect in this line is demonstrated by the admirable work done by our own men, where chance has brought the original documents to our shores; I think particularly of the publication of the Freer manuscripts, done by a classicist whom we gladly welcome as also a Biblical scholar. But in general the absence of the visible, tangible material, at hand in a nearby museum, has impoverished our scholarship. We have a secondhand knowledge of the sigilla representing the Greek manuscripts; a comprehension of a group of manuscripts like the nebulous Lucianic family, is in general void. It puts us in good society to name these things, but our talk is often jargon. Now this stuff is in Europe, we cannot loot it like the treatment of the Belgian churches and museums. And future finds will naturally remain in Europe or gravitate thither. There is, however, one practical thing we can do, which would enable us almost to see and touch those precious things themselves, stimulate our direct knowledge of the sources of text criticism, and give us materal for original work. I refer to the procuring of copies by the photostat process of all important Biblical manuscripts, the so neglected cursives, etc. This is a work that might be undertaken through common understanding and cooperation by our academic and general libraries, with a distribution of the material through the country. I would suggest that the Library of Congress is the proper institution to lead in this work, and I believe it would be worth while to present the matter to the authorities of that Library. In the past years of war we have been made painfully alive to the destruction which barbarians can still work in the world's literary treasures, and it is the duty of booklovers to secure the permanence of the world's treasures by procuring and distributing their facsimiles. For the Bible this Society should take the initiative.

But there is another field of raw material, lying still in its original beds of deposit, for which we can compete with the Europeans on equal, or even, considering our vigor and financial ability, on superior terms. I mean the raw stuff of archaeology. When we look back upon the history of American Biblical scholarship we see, if none else, Edward Robinson, who gave a glory to our name which none will ever dispute. As a great philologist, such as he was, his name would endure only as one of many in the course of learned bookmaking. No Higher Critic, but a devoted adherent to the canonical text of the Bible, and impatient of all which conflicted with it, he might have soon been dismissed from memory as antiquated. But he had the inspired idea of taking scholarship back to the home of the Bible, and opened to the world a new book, even though we have been remiss in perusing it through to the end.

In the eighties one of our own number, still hale and active among us, conceived the expedition to Nippur and put the undertaking through undaunted. Its results are not strictly Biblical, and yet his finds, as the quarry of our American Assyriology and the school of a band of scholars whose names are known worldwide, have directly enriched the philology of the Bible. One other American has followed in the footsteps of Robinson, Dr. Frederick J. Bliss. The great experiment at Nippur has not been duplicated, although it has had a worthy successor in the Harvard Expedition to Samaria, the results of which unfortunately still remain unpublished. It is the labors of the past alone to which we can point with peculiar pride. If first we took the leadership, our competitors have outstripped us. Yet America has the capacity, the means for still greater things.

This or that large-minded institution, this or that beneficent patron, may be induced to revive such works. But I would remind you of an institution which, as a child of this Society, founded by its revered onetime President, Dr. Thayer, has a special claim upon us. I refer to the School in Jerusalem. Its work must primarily appeal to Biblical scholarship, its support must principally be drawn from those who love and care for the Bible. Its results have been outwardly small. But its possibilities of enrichment to our scholarship have been experienced and in some cases notably demonstrated by the scholars who have gone to school at Jerusalem. An enlarged field of activity lies before it now. May I commend it to, your corporate as well as individual interest? In this day of unrest and stimulated energy such a field of archaeology may attract men of practical ability and exploring genius, and so save for us a type of student whom booklearning cannot satisfy.

Duty implies action on the part of men and human organizations, its spirit must have a body. The duties of American Biblical scholarship must be realized by us individuals, or in the mass by some corporation composed of us. This Society meets annually, a sympathetic group of students, feeling more than rewarded by contact with like-minded men. We are known to the world through our scholarly Journal. But might we not do more as a corporate body, following the example of some of our European sisters? Instead of resigning ourselves to our hard conditions, complaining of the American world's neglect, might not the organism of this Society be made to work more efficiently and concretely towards the aims of our quest? None can attain these by himself alone, but only through the union in which is strength. And for what purpose else exists the union?

OUR OWN FUTURE: FORECAST AND A PROGRAMME[*]

Max L. Margolis
Dropsie College

The subject to the consideration of which I would invite your attention has been dealt with by Kittel[1] and Sellin[2] in Germany and earlier still by our own Professor Montgomery in a Presidential address delivered before this Society.[3] If I venture to discuss the same subject, it is because I have carried the thoughts with me for some time and should like to express them in my own way. The German discussion was precipitated by Friedrich Delitzsch's "*Great Deception*" and Harnack's plea for the casting out of the Old Testament from the Protestant canon of Scriptures, followed by an agitation which proposed to eliminate or at least to reduce to modest proportions the teaching of Hebrew and the Old Testament Scriptures in the theological faculties. Germany, it would seem, is awaking to a situation which is new there; in this country we have had the malady in a chronic form and we have had ample leisure to think about it.

Years ago, a young professor in charge of New Testament Exegesis in a divinity school, showed me his copy of Tischendorf's edition of the New Testament closely packed with exegetical notes in the finest writing. I am certain that nothing was left untouched: the force of an aorist, the exact meaning of a particle, the reading supported by the best authorities, and the like. But, alas, in the new field of his activities none of the students knew or was required to know Greek. His duty was to interpret the Gospel or Epistle in the English translation, presumably the American Standard Edition. All the good notes were to no purpose; they simply could not be used. Just then a student turned up at the University who had been trained by an eminent scholar known for his studies in the Grammar of New

---

[*]Presidential address, delivered at the annual meeting of the Society at the Jewish Institute of Religion in New York City, December 27, 1923.

1. *Die Zukunft der Alttestamentlichen Wissenschaft*. Address delivered in the Old Testament Division of the First German Orientalist Congress at Leipzig, September 29, 1921. Printed in *ZAW*, 39 (1921), 84–99.

2. *Das Alte Testament und die evangelische Kirche*. Leipzig, 1921.

3. *Present Tasks of American Biblical Scholarship*. Delivered December 26, 1918. Printed in this JOURNAL, 38 (1919), 1–14. [See pp. 17–26 in this volume.]

Testament Greek; I advised him to take up the study of Syriac, which he found rather difficult. Since then Hellenists and Semitists have contested the possession of the New Testament domain; one such contest was witnessed at a previous meeting of our Society. One might think that now that Torrey has carried the discussion into Acts, and Burney and Montgomery into the Gospel of John, students would be crowding our lecture rooms during a course in Aramaic. It is no longer the Septuagint student alone who operates with "translation Greek." Behind the most uncommon Greek word or idiomatic turn of expression there lurks a Semitic equivalent which it is our business to get at by laborious and painstaking retroversion. The clue is found when the translator errs, when he misconceives, when he is abnormal; when he is normal, when he covers the original, he quite successfully covers it up. There is no reason on earth why a translator should not render one Hebrew or Aramaic word by a multitude of Greek synonyms and, conversely, unite in one Greek word a number of Semitic synonyms. Both phenomena may be witnessed in the English Bible. A glance at any Concordance will reveal how one and the same English word is used for sundry Hebrew and Greek synonyms; and as to foregoing uniformity of phrasing in the English, the Revisers of 1611 are quite explicit on this point: "That we should express the same notion in the same particular words; as for example, if we translate the Hebrew or Greek word once by *purpose*, never to call it *intent*: if one where *journeying*, never *travelling*; if one where *think*, never *suppose*; if one where *pain*, never *ache*; if one where *joy*, never *gladness*, etc. thus to mince the matter, we thought to savour more of curiosity than wisdom, and that rather it would breed scorn in the atheist than bring profit to the godly reader." Just so, to bring profit to the godly reader, and not to facilitate retroversion for latter day students, was the aim of those good men of antiquity, whether it was the Hebrew law and the prophets and the other writings or the Aramaic narratives concerning the new dispensation that they wished to make accessible to those without, Jews or Gentiles. Naturally in the process of translation many an element of the original underwent modification; but this very angle of deflection can be measured only by the aid of the original extant or philologically reconstructed. It ought therefore be clear that to comprehend Torah or Gospel adequately we cannot rest content with substitutes in Greek or in any other language, but must have recourse to the wording in the original tongues, and that can be done only by industrious application to Hebrew and Aramaic and kindred languages.

The trouble, it would appear then, is with our students who are unwilling to study these very languages, and if this unwillingness continues we may anticipate the time when our own usefulness will come to an end. Not that we are thought of as of much use even now. Teaching faculties are at best a necessary evil; what matters is a governing board and a student body and possibly also a library! Jesus said, "Freely ye received, freely give." Or, as the rabbis make Moses to say, "As I was taught freely, so teach ye freely." The world sees to it that we teach for next to nothing and thereby expresses its estimate of our worth. A student in a theological institution once referred to the faculty as but misfit pastors. Students are quite keen on the subject of values; as someone observed, when the other professions are overcrowded, they flock to the schools of divinity, just as they desist when there is room in the other professions or when these pay better. As a matter of fact, our students are largely paid for attending. But, however the path of learning is made smooth for them, they will not go in for heavy work. As undergraduates in the colleges, they have been fed up on "snap" courses, they have remained strangers to philology and the philological method. I am frequently amused by the notion that grammar ought to be an elective course, since not all minds take to it. I am rather of the opinion that grammar should be made obligatory upon all of our students. Of course, grammar cannot be an end in itself; it is far more important that one should know Hebrew for example, the Hebrew language. But grammar is a means not only to the end of mastering a language; by its aid preeminently can that philological method be apprehended without which independent judgment is impossible in the higher branches of exegesis and criticism. It is on the subject of independent judgment that we and our students clash. They prefer to sit back while we do the work for them; they expect at our hands results which they may neatly take down in their notebooks, while we would fain convince them that all we have and hold for transmission is a bundle of questions and that for every problem which a new find disposes of there arise fifty new ones to solve. The student will say that it is not his business to become a specialist or expert; that he leaves to his teacher. But there is one specialty that the churches do or should expect of him, an understanding of the thing Religion and more specifically of a given, positive, revealed religion, which, whether committed into the keeping of the Church or embodied in the Scriptures, involves in one form or another the study of documents. But perhaps it is the case that certain denominations have cut themselves loose from their historical antecedents, that the Scriptures are just tolerated as venerable expressions of discarded notions, that the ancient texts when at all used as the foundation of discourses serve only as a peg upon which to hang the clap-trap that happens to be in vogue at the moment, and that the modern clergyman, a marvel of versatility and ubiquity, exhausts himself in multitudinous doing by which religion is secularized and piety externalized and conscience immersed into dead works away from the service of the living God. However, it is not our province to cast aspersions on the churches and the clergy, when the fault is perhaps largely our own.

Let us search our hearts collectively. It is unnecessary to recall flippancy and downright coarseness of expression, as when one pokes fun at the Jew God enjoying his roast veal in Abraham's tent and revealing himself to Moses *a posteriori*, or when another describes Jahveh as an "uncanny Titan," and a third speaks of him as immorally wicked. Often enough a growth in moral stature is noted, as he rouses himself from slumber in warfare with the Philistines and comes to differentiate himself through his conflicts with the Baals; imparticipative, jealous of his honor, exclusive, intolerant, sternly judicial, he nevertheless develops a strain of tenderness, for he is God and not man and he will not utterly destroy. This God of the Old Testament has his grip on the realities of life: when kingdoms are moved and nations are interlocked in deadly combat, in the hour of dire national distress, the cathedrals of Christendom resound with psalms and prayers which in times of peace are declared to be un-Christian. So at least according to our commentaries. To the Christian conscience the new dispensation is the fulfilment of the old, its flower and fruition; an un-Christian conscience will concede originality to the Gospel; but this originality will be enhanced by illuminating the background rather than by darkening it. We should have learned this lesson from the history of religions, that religious bodies cling to ancient Scriptures when certain details have been outgrown and when the bald literalism has been eclipsed by a spiritualizing interpretation. That progress had been consummated when the Gospel arrived. We do not underestimate the power of a great personality; it has been the besetting sin in our past treatment that personality was resolved into the mere factors of time and place. Much, however, was found prepared; the way had been paved along the lines of internal growth, we need not go far afield in the search for the roots, least of all to "the prophet of Iran." It is a one-sided historicism which, over the regress to beginnings, forgets to register the advance in meaning which just as surely came to be and forms a part of the historical process. According to the letter, the Old Testament held in veneration by latter-day Judaism had not changed in jot or tittle; but it was a transfigured body of Scriptures in which the heights dominated the depressions and the lofty expressions of undying hope and faith raised to their own level the notions and incidents of lower planes. A presentation of the Old Testament religion which winds up with the skepticism of Koheleth fails signally in insight. And, worst of all, neither Jahveh nor his word seem to be able to live down their past. So we have passed on the word to the facile popularizers and through them to the reporters—sometimes we take down copy to them in person—that the Old Testament as seen in the light of today is decidedly not worth while. As to the New Testament, or at least certain parts thereof, we have the word of the Fundamentalist that it has been weighed in the balances of modernism and found wanting. If the Scriptures lack in worthwhileness, why then study them?

For, we must come to realize it, the students of the Scriptures will always be their friends, not those that are hostile to them or even indifferent. But we have profaned the holy, yielding to the unrest which has loosened what was bound and dishallowed what was hallowed. We have furthermore brought our own work into disrepute by indulging in pseudo-science. On the one hand we are beset by a traditionalism which sits tight on the lid, or else by deftly misinterpreting the evidences of archaeology would prop up untenable positions; and on the other hand by a criticism hardened into a tradition and woefully lacking in self-criticism. All scientific questions may be reopened, and the truer solution is not necessarily the straight-line account. Things, I believe, will right themselves. Neither the church nor the synagogue can long continue Scriptureless. After straying in the byways, the ancient paths will once more be trodden. Every age, from its new perspective and angle of vision, must re-interpret for itself the past. And so must every country. We here in America are determined to become self-sufficient in our Biblical studies. Not that we intend to shut ourselves off from contact with other minds. But we have a distinct outlook upon life, itself formed upon the Scriptures, the Old Testament no less than the New. The American conscience will brush away finespun quibblings and, purged from all insinuating motives of the present, apply itself to a renewed apprehension and appraisal of that which abides forever. If we pursue the quest of the historical Jesus or Isaiah, the American public will demand to know what we ourselves have to say. We shall vouch for our findings with all of our own labor and all of our scholarly reputation. If we must needs go abroad, Jerusalem and Bagdad are quite near. In all gratitude to past stimuli from without, in all earnestness bent upon developing our own strength, "with malice toward none, with charity for all," with unswerving fidelity to truth and with infinite love for the object of our studies, we shall dedicate ourselves anew to the task in which our fathers found a worthwhile occupation. An American Biblical science, the corporate contribution of American scholarship, mature, competent, veracious, reverent, this is the vision I see arising before my eyes, this the forecast by which I set out to banish our fear for our future, expressed somewhat apocalyptically—but the wise will understand.

But the fulfilment is conditioned by our own determination to mend our ways. The student of the Bible must fetch his raw material from many quarters, there are any number of auxiliary sciences which furnish him with data, geography, history, archaeology, and the like; they all have a bearing on that which is central in his work, but they cannot take its place. For a generation or so we have lost sight of our central occupation. Let us penitently return to it. Criticism has been overdone, the higher and the lower. Investigations as to date and composition may lie fallow for awhile. Nor shall we go on rewriting the ancient documents in such manner that their authors would exclaim, "Well done, but it is not what we wrote!" Rewriting is not at all our business. We may take it for granted that Isaiah knew his Hebrew quite well. Nor did he consult us as to the arrangement of his thoughts. Let us concentrate on exegesis. It is so easy to break up a text into atoms. It is far more difficult to discern relevancy, continuity, coherence. We should model ourselves upon the inimitable Ewald. What made him so eminently successful as a commentator was his sympathetic attitude: he took on for the time being the personality of the author. Personality is unique, elusive of grammar and lexicon, but revealing itself to intuitive absorption, to that love which "vaunteth not itself, is not puffed up, doth not behave itself unseemly, seeketh not its own ... but rejoiceth with the truth." It is our privilege to interpret the greatest of all ages; their thoughts were of the deepest, and we must not be abashed to own ourselves vanquished by obscurity of expression or obscurity of thought. We shall strive, of course, with all power to recreate the lost context, not the context of a paragraph or chapter, but the context of pulsating life in which these men stood and from which their hope and their faith emerged, touching that of their contemporaries at every point, and yet transcending it so as to focus itself upon eternity. All new finds must be welcome; yet the old material has unexplored mines awaiting the sturdy digger below the surface who is unafraid of the grime and the grind. Away with the multitude of our little publications in which we frequently repeat ourselves! Let us address ourselves to monumental works which will require the cooperation of a large number of us and provide useful occupation beyond the present generation. Need I single out such undertakings as a critical edition of the Masoretic Text (which neither Baer nor Ginsburg have provided), or the assembling of the complete material for a study of the ancient versions? And if we are to recover the Semitic original of Gospel word or Gospel phrase, must we not with infinite toil construct Greek-Semitic Indexes? Here is a programme which, though sketched in its merest outlines, is comprehensive enough: "the people are many, neither is this a work for one day or two, for we have greatly transgressed in this matter."

Motives of Biblical Scholarship*

Henry J. Cadbury
Harvard University

A phenomenon commonly known to students of religious history like ourselves is the long persistence of individual actions or customs while the meaning of these actions is forgotten or reinterpreted. Frequently a cultic act established by habit is given new meaning or is continued long after the considerations which made it once seem important are obsolete.

I think it is Höffding who tells in one of his books of a Lutheran church somewhere in Northern Europe in which by an immemorial custom the worshippers walking up the aisle bow at a certain place, and pass on to their seats. The interior is plainly severe and only by accident was the origin of the custom discovered. Underneath the heavy whitewash opposite the bowing place was found in ancient fresco going back to pre-Reformation times a crude picture of the crucifixion.

It is perhaps fair that we should turn upon ourselves the kind of inquiry which we make professionally of historic religious movements, and compare the study of religious history as we carry it on in the present time with the same activity of earlier times. Harvard is in its 301st year, Union Seminary in its 101st, the neighboring Jewish Theological Seminary in its fiftieth. All of us recognize that in our preoccupation and interest in the history of certain religions and of their classic and most primitive texts we are carrying on a behavior which was observable in these institutions fifty, one hundred and three hundred years ago. Or, if we wish to stretch our imagination to a landmark a century further back, those of us whose interest is in the New Testament may fix our thoughts for comparison on the probable mental and religious outlook of those two men who died in 1536, Erasmus, the humanist, and Tyndal, the martyr, —the first men to produce a printed New Testament in Greek and in English respectively. Can we not contrast any concern we may have today for the Scriptures with that which we may believe was felt by the heroes of these anniversaries?

---

* The Presidential Address delivered at the meeting of the Society of Biblical Literature and Exegesis, December 29, 1936, at Union Theological Seminary, New York City.

I would not attempt to compare or contrast either the methods or the results of such study now and then. There are differences, striking differences, between Biblical scholarship now and in earlier centuries. These are not hard to analyze. But more like the illustration that has been used from our own profession and more subtle is the problem of the changed presuppositions of our age-old occupations. We are used to asking, with what thought do later generations continue to observe ancient rituals or taboos? How do the very same words change their meaning as we compare the prehistoric with the historic, the primitive with the late, in the several stages of religion? Familiar to many of us are such examination questions as these:

What was the motive for sabbath keeping in primitive Semitic religion, in each of the codes of the Hebrew law, and in the age of the Tannaim?

Contrast the motives of the earliest Christian mission with those of some modern missionary that you know.

Let us ask ourselves, what is the present rationale of the time honored profession of Sacred Scripture as compared with the motives of our predecessors.

It is the more necessary to ask the question and to make it quite conscious in that the change itself has been exceedingly gradual and unintended. Revolutions of thought, no matter how complete, are easily overlooked when they occur unconsciously as the result of influences which work slowly and unperceived. These influences are of course in part the results of a different type of Biblical scholarship. But the results, too, are doubtless partly caused by the different underlying attitude to the subject. It would be a mistake to suppose that merely their own new discoveries have changed the scholars' attitude to the Bible. Beginning with different general conceptions they have come to the Bible with questions differently posed, and the new answers have depended on the new approach. This approach is often due to factors quite outside their profession, to political and economic changes not to mention theological or ecclesiastical patterns. The best histories of Biblical scholarship have duly recognized how at every stage the scientific pursuit has been affected by the vogue of contemporary philosophy in a larger sphere.

The history of Biblical science has more than once been written. The influence of contemporary thought, the changes in method, and particularly the various results of study of various parts of Scripture are matters that have all been recorded. But in none of these books, as far as I know, nor in any special monograph, has the *motive* of Biblical study been analyzed. Here is a chapter of our past to which I would call your attention, or rather, a series of unwritten chapters extending back through the whole story of Bible reading and interpretation.

One need not remind this audience that a change of attitude to the Scriptures is not unique to our later generations, but is something that has happened time and time again from the beginning. We speak often of the canonization of the Scriptures and we do well. But what lies behind that word in any official or ecclesiastical sense is a changed presupposition with which the casual products of an earlier age come to enjoy a different regard from their readers. What the special treatment of the Bible books has done for the understanding or misunderstanding of them is a subject that would take long to summarize. It has affected even the transmission of their text, perhaps more for the better than for the worse. It meant a predetermined expectation on the part of the reverent reader. And what the reader sought he often found. He expected unity, consistency, accuracy; he expected authority, regulation and prediction. He expected timelessness, universality and finality. How far the first readers or hearers of Amos or of Jesus, Ezekiel or Paul, expected the same qualities, I do not precisely know, but I am confident that their expectation was rather different.

Let me remind you of the spirit and feeling with which much earlier study of the Scriptures was informed. I describe the attitude without criticizing it, realizing that much of it still continues today. A god now largely incommunicado had once dealt directly with men. He had spoken to the fathers through the prophets. He had revealed his whole will face to face to Moses. He had incarnated himself in Jesus of Nazareth. But the Bible was not thought of as merely a record of revelation. That is one of the stages by which we ease ourselves away from the stricter view. The Bible was the Revelation. Judaism and Protestantism both, I take it, regarded the actual text as inspired, —verbally inspired, —literatim et punctatim, as well as verbatim. This inspiration applied to the original language and to the autograph copies in that language. With some exceptions it was not extended in theory either to translations or to subsequent codices, though as a matter of fact supernatural control of translators and scribes was so naturally assumed, that versions like the Septuagint and the Vulgate were treated as though equally inspired, and standard texts whether Massoretic or Textus Receptus were treated as though they were autographs.

This attitude alone would account for most of the interest and devotion of Biblical study. The motive of a literary scholarship was recognition of the unique religious value of the books. Textual criticism had every reason then for aiming to determine as nearly as possible the original reading of every verse, the *verba ipsissima* of God, and philological acumen had every reason for the most minute study of the dead languages in which the Bible had been inspired or dictated.

I can recall George Foot Moore, who was no conniver at ignorance, explaining apparently without regret the modern trend away from Hebrew and Greek in the training of ministers. The study of these languages, he said, had been justified and required a generation or two ago on the conviction that divine revelation had been made in those tongues, and that no one whose business it was to interpret that revelation could do so successfully if he could not read it in the original. But modern liberal protestantism had abandoned that assumption. There was accordingly less need for first-hand acquaintance, which had often been in practice a bowing acquaintance, with *pi'el* and *pu'al*, with εἰς and ἐν and all the refinements of grammar so dear to the older theologians.

Archaeology as ancillary to Bible study is experiencing a similar change of rôle. Originally I suppose the identification of Biblical scenes was inspired by reverence and piety. With sentiment and emotion pilgrims sought the sites of sacred history and biography, much as we commemorate with tablets of bronze today the sites of secular history and biography. But with the first mutterings of scepticism orthodoxy had recourse to archaeology to confirm the Bible. The discovery of the Babylonian flood tablets was first most generally hailed as proving that the Biblical flood was historical. The literary and cultural implications of the find were only an afterthought. The same apologetic value was claimed of the Egyptian store cities and indeed of nearly every discovery that could be brought into comparison with the Bible. Even today excavators and their sponsors are often motivated by a hope of confirming the Bible.

The rationale of this apologetic if analyzed is briefly this. The Bible is either all true or all false. To prove that Ur was a great city in the time of Abraham, that the four kings mentioned as his contemporaries are the names of real persons like Hammurabi, shows that Abraham himself is no myth, and that all that is said of him in the Bible deserves complete confidence. The proved accuracy of one part of a book proves the accuracy of it all, and the accuracy of one book in the Bible carries the accuracy of others. The exponents of such a view often are consistent enough to admit that a single proved inaccuracy in the Bible would invalidate it all, and in both their positive and negative totalitarianism they do not distinguish between historical fact and religious truth, nor of course between grades of historical probability.

For many of us today archaeology and indeed all study of ancient history has a different value. It helps us to understand rather than to defend the Bible. It provides in a much wider area than in absolutely overlapping data what I like to call "contemporary color." If it dovetails with Biblical statements well and good; but even when it does not, it enables us to recover the life and particularly the mentality of the ancient world, the Biblical environment in the largest sense of the term. Our research is motivated by a concern neither to validate nor to invalidate the narrative, but merely to illustrate and enrich its meaning.

In this way even lexical study has its importance. A better apprehension of the probable force of a single Greek or Hebrew word in the Bible is after all these years of study an achievement to be welcomed and acclaimed, but not as a new insight into the message of the Divine but as a clearer understanding of what a famous and significant author intended to convey. The modern scholar is modestly content to have promoted sound knowledge in this field as his colleagues are in other fields of history and literature without any sense of the unique importance of his findings.

For a more rapid and revolutionary example of changed attitude to the scriptures and one whose psychology deserves more study than it has to my knowledge received I would mention a much older process: —the retention of the Jewish Bible in the early Christian church. The latter included former disciples of the Jewish rabbis, former Jewish Hellenizers, and even Gentiles who had never heard before of Moses and the prophets. In an extraordinarily short time the Christian acceptance and use of the scriptures in Greek was an established and practically universal fact. Marcion is, I take it, not representative of an older Church without the Scripture, but the protester against what was already by 150 C.E. a *fait accompli*.

The novelty of the early Christian use is as striking as its rapidity. We are probably wrong in supposing that it all centered about Messianic prophecy or that it allegorized after the Alexandrian pattern. Hellenistic Judaism as revealed in Philo is only partially a bridge between rabbinic and Christian use of the Old Testament. While Jews then and now may well regard the Christian appropriation of the Old Testament as brazen robbery or perversion, both they and Christians must admit that it illustrates the power of new presumptions to revolutionize the treatment of the Scriptures.

I have spoken thus far of the aims of Biblical scholarship as differing with time, and changing with the passage of the years. There is also, I believe, a contrast in aims at one and the same period and even within the mind of an individual scholar. We are few of us one track minds, though our multiplicity of motive or intention is due more to variety inherited or ill-composed rather than to a well articulated breadth of aim. Even today, as all through earlier history, two principal motives (as far as conscious motivation may be predicated at all) have been at work.

Biblical scholarship has nearly always had as its end some goal of usefulness or service. A study of prefaces in works of scholars would give the clearest picture of this motive over the centuries, differently expressed at one time or another, often with the pious quotation of Hebrew or Greek texts of Scripture, but always, even today, with the hope and anticipation that the labor would result in the spiritual welfare and enlightenment of the reader. Even the most technical and remote fields of study, like textual criticism, have been inspired not merely by a reverence for the subject but by a hope that true religion might be promoted thereby.

Such ulterior ends were combined, however, with what today might seem to us a conflicting standard, the search for pure truth. Fact as an end in itself is very different from fact as an edifying phenomenon. It is remarkable that purely scientific aims have so long played an important part in our profession. Indeed their presence demands some explanation, no matter how natural they seem to us today.

Perhaps some of you had already answered for yourselves the problem of my title by saying to yourselves: The motives of Biblical scholarship are no whit different from the motives of all scholarship, motives sufficient and satisfactory in themselves, the loving, curious search for truth wherever truth should lead. You would resent the idea that you have any special or less scientific aim. Yet I fancy that even today much of the best scholarly work in our fields is combined with a strong religious, not to say apologetic, prepossession. It may not be the prepossession of the past, it may be a prepossession that is itself the result of independent and untrammeled and unorthodox scholarship, but it is a prepossession none the less. If it does not claim from the sacred page direct and authoritative proof of religious standards, it still labors under a protecting confidence that in the end some remote spiritual utility will accrue from the minutest contribution to truth. "Ye shall know the truth and the truth shall make you free."

In brief, the motive of scholarship in this field is still as it has been a combination of search for pure truth and, at least frequently, an expectation of religious serviceableness. The former ideal may seem to us more conspicuous in our day, due perhaps to the growth of conscious scientific method and to the influence of secular standards in the study of other history, literature or religion. Yet it would be quite unfair to our predecessors to fail to recognize their often extraordinary anticipation of the most unbiased processes and most objective techniques of pure scholarship. While we may gratefully acknowledge what we owe to the example and participation of scholars from other fields, we also recognize that Bible study has itself been a pioneer in thoroughness and in progressive methods of dealing with the truth. Many a teacher of the Bible must have been often surprised to find how novel to college students of the best literary and historical training are the everyday methods and standards of scholarship in our own classrooms.

If therefore we are to think of a change of underlying motive as between the older periods and our own, it cannot be described as a change from the purely apologetic to the purely scientific, since both elements both now and then have entered into the profession. It has been rather a change in consciousness accompanying the continuance of the dual aim. For a dual aim implies occasionally at least conflict of aims or tension between them. This tension may be either conscious or unconscious. If the conflict of aims is unobserved, or if the aims are somehow assumed to be inherently harmonious, the scholar is quite otherwise situated than if he is aware of the conflict and deliberately puts, or tries to put, one aim above the other.

Many scholars have completely identified objective truth with religious value. The Bible being the inspired word of God, whatever it actually said was bound to be the ultimate truth and of supreme value to men. Hence one need not hesitate to let text criticism or lexicography or grammar take their natural course. If the Bible said and meant so and so, what it said was the truth in every sense of the word. Thus by hypothesis the two aims of study coincide. If the result of textual and philological study involved apparent contradictions within the Scriptures, or the recording of events apparently denied by external criteria, or the promulgation of sentiments lacking in apparent rationality or morality, plenary inspiration required one to deny the evidence or assumption or standard which interfered with its own inferences. Sometimes it was the text itself which was interpreted to meet the facts of experience, with the midrashic work of the rabbis and with the allegorical work of the commentators. So unity was retained on the surface, but a secret and unacknowledged tension remained, and if we may trust modern psychology unconscious repressions are more volcanic than open doubts.

Equally satisfactory on the surface is the most naive modern view which finds no conflict between religious value and rational results of Bible study on the ground that rational results themselves belong to God and religion must be squared at every point to meet them. If the findings of scholarship upset older or cherished religious ideas, if they seem positively to interfere with religious motivation, so much the worse for the latter. The reckless method which results is prepared to leave all consequences to God, much like the news editor who when criticized for the scandalous doings reported in his paper remarked self-righteously, "What God allows to happen, why should I refuse to print?"

More often the modern scholar assumes, much like his predecessors, that truth in the non-religious sense of the objective findings of scholarship has in itself a kind of religious value. Loyalty to truth becomes his first aim, quite sincerely. But he promptly supplements the negative or prosaic or uninspiring results of his honest inquiry with some vague generalities that after all the same religious values can still be obtained in another way, or at least something else equally good.

The various methods by which the two aims have been combined and reconciled in history would make a somewhat lengthy story, too lengthy for the present occasion. It is only another testimony to the incurable desire of man to find unity and rationality everywhere.

The danger of attempting to combine pure scholarship with an edifying motive is apparent to all of us, at least in others whether of the past or of the present. The examples where presuppositions no matter how commendable have interfered with the untrammeled search for truth are familiar. A slight compensation is perhaps to be found in the fact that without the religious motive, even the partisan and controversial, much of the progress in scientific development would have been lost. Archaeology, inspired first by a desire to defend the faith as in the British support of George Smith, has enriched our knowledge of the environment of every period of Biblical history. Literary criticism inspired by controversial intentions both radical and conservative has led to results both secure and illuminating. Was not the authenticity of Philo's *De Vita Contemplativa* established by the controversies between Protestants and Catholics? If Judaism in the end gains some knowledge of its past through Christian controversy as well as through disputation among its own parties, there is some compensation for all the bias and distortion to which partisanship has subjected the truth. Indeed the religious motive at its worst has often led, though through zig-zag routes, to understandings which without that motive would never have been achieved. Not unlike the scientific process of trial and error has been the unscientific process of dogmatic assertion and defence.

If we agree that less oblique approaches to truth are desirable we do well even in the assurance of our modern age to inquire humbly into our own shortcomings.

The fact that the causes vitiating our work are largely quite unrealized by us is only a partial excuse. The perversions of past scholars were rarely deliberate perversions. We are adepts in identifying and allowing for subjective prejudices in workers of the past. It ought not to be difficult to do the same with ourselves. One object of psychoanalysis is said to be auto-psycho-analysis. "Physician, heal thyself."

If the simple analysis I have made is not beneath the dignity of the presidential address of such an august body, it will not be inappropriate either for me to name briefly what seem to me the besetting sins of our present procedure:

1. One is an Athenian-like craving for something new. It is a fallacy to suppose that the new is more worth saying or hearing or reading than the old. Additions to knowledge are certainly a legitimate aim of each of us. In a field so fully worked as our field is they must perhaps be rather circumscribed. They will come more often from new evidence than from new theories. Perhaps in the history of trial and error it is probable that even the wildest fancy no matter how erroneous will somehow show new facets of truth. But new theories ought at least to be first tested in the relative retirement of scholarly discussion and exchange rather than introduced first to the general reading public in popular form and liable to the extravagant publicity of the salesmanship methods of unscrupulous American publishers. As experts we have some responsibility to help curb the morbid tastes of so many superficial lay book readers who prefer to hear from us some new guess than some old fact.

2. Another bias of our procedure is the over-ready attempt to modernize Bible times. This tendency—which I have elsewhere dealt with extensively in the case of a single Biblical figure—arises partly from taking our own mentality as a norm and partly from a desire to interpret the past for its present values. To regard ourselves, our standards, our ways of thinking, as normative for the Bible is nearly as unscientific and superstitious as to treat the Bible as normative for ourselves. I have heard of modern people that think the world is flat because the Bible says so. I know of modern scholars who almost assume that Bible characters believed in evolution because we do. Though our whole discipline tends often quite successfully to the training of the historical imagination there remain areas where the nuances of the ancient mind escape our notice because of our quite modern and contemporary presuppositions.

The modernizing is in many cases, I am persuaded, due to an even less pardonable defect, the overzealous desire to utilize our study for practical ends. Wishing to short cut the roundabout processes of knowledge we desire to find an immediate utility and applicability in the ancient documents. Our minds as in the older days of prooftexts are more anxious to find what answer the Bible gives to our own perplexities than to hear what seemingly useless and irrelevant information the book itself chooses to volunteer.

3. A third defect that I would mention arises not from a modernizing but from a conservative tendency. When new conceptions force us from old positions

we substitute for the old positions imitations or subterfuges which are no better supported than their predecessors but which we hope are less vulnerable. The discovery of new proof leads to a reluctant retreat which we attempt to cover up by a kind of camouflage or rearguard action. The history of Biblical scholarship is marred by the too fond clinging to the debris of exploded theories. We are afraid to follow the logic of our own discoveries and insist that we are retaining the old values under a new name. The reluctance of our recession is intelligible even if it is not intelligent. Typical was the first early suggestion in Biblical criticism that Moses was the editor rather than the author of the Torah. In other books we hold on to the traditional author by the most tenuous connection rather than abandon the work to complete anonymity. Oftentimes such survivals are due not so much to religious conservatism as to an instinctive repugnance to scientific agnosticism. To paraphrase a modern phrase we prefer to guess a lot than know so little.

But in other cases we are anxious to retain the old values under new conditions. If we surrender the plenary inspiration of the Scriptures we must find, we think, a kind of inspiration that will seem to carry equal assurance. If we doubt the crassly miraculous we must invent some theory of some other way of the special intervention of God in history. If the words of Scripture cannot be assigned absolute authority we must claim for them some other peculiar or exalted merit, or some less literal and more general validity. I am not concerned so much to deny our favorable appraisals of the Bible material, as to regret that they seem to me to come from the attempt to salvage from what we have lost. They ought to come rather from the fresh, independent and original statement of what we have found.

But to return to the motives of our work. If there are two of them, the pursuit of truth and the loyalty to religion, which shall we choose? That we are dealing here with a fundamental philosophical enigma of the relation of fact and value must be evident to all of us. You will not be surprised if I beg leave not to deal exhaustively with such a problem. The cultivation of truth without fear or favor is certainly the nominal ideal of all scholarship today, reinforced by what we like to call the scientific approach to knowledge. I take it that most of us are in sympathy with it, and are horrified by the perversions and prostitutions of learning to partisan or prejudiced ends, whether these illustrations be taken from the past history of our own profession or from the modern inroads on scholarship by the extremes of political theory and control.

But are we equally aware of the responsibilities of scholarship? Since we deal in the area which we should be the first to admit has been so influential for human good and ill, are we not under special obligations to the field of spiritual life and value traditionally associated with the Old and New Testaments? Can we be indifferent to the social consequences of our career? Has the single minded pursuit of truth any limitations on its side, as serious as is the irresponsible and unscientific use of the data of history in propaganda for one's own chosen ends or standards?

Two episodes this summer not especially connected with our own profession illustrate the extremes I have spoken of. One was at the five hundred and fiftieth anniversary of the University of Heidelberg where the ideal of scholarship was definitely renounced as the aim of a great academic tradition in favor of partisan propaganda. According to the official words of the minister of Science and Education, "The old idea of science based on the sovereign right of abstract intellectual activity, ... the unchecked effort to reach the truth," has been forever banished.[1] The figure of Athena was to be replaced by the swastika. The tragedy is not so much that you or I may not sympathize with the special party or policy in power. Even for a more congenial religious or political objective the conscienceless abandonment of honest and open-eyed quest for truth should seem to us tragic.

The other occasion was the September meeting of the British Association for the Advancement of Science. To these expediters of progress there came from their own members a challenge which many an outsider has long been feeling. Are the men of science not responsible for the social consequences of their discovery? Some of them resent being blamed for overproduction and technological unemployment and the destructive use of scientific discoveries. "Pure science," said one of them, "has nothing to do with ethics, she recognizes no moral obligations whatsoever." But others have accepted a new responsibility for the results of their laboratory labors. Said Professor J. C. Philip, president of the chemical section, "Impelled by patriotic motives, most scientists have put themselves freely at the disposal of the state in time of need. But many are hesitating to admit that patriotism must always override considerations of humanity. Whatever be our individual attitude in this matter, it is time for chemists and scientists in general to throw their weight into the scale against the tendencies which are dragging science and civilisation down and debasing our heritage of intellectual and spiritual values."[2]

Here is the kind of challenge which I suppose few of us have really faced. Though our science is quite a different one, and though partisan religion is not often nowadays an excuse for holy wars or the inquisition, there is a sense in which fidelity to the strictest standards of scholarship about the Bible demands all the more from us a responsibility for constructive forces that would counterweigh any destructive, unspiritual results of our labors. No more than the inventor of poison gases in his laboratory can the Biblical scholar remain in his study indifferent to the spiritual welfare which his researches often seem to threaten or destroy. He may be in his processes faithful to the cold standards of history and literary criticism, he must not be indifferent to moral and spiritual values and needs in contemporary life. His own work may seem irrelevant and remote, a luxury hard to justify in a practical age. Whether as irrelevant or as seemingly destructive he

---

1. *New York Times*, June 30th, 1936, p. 14, col. 6.
2. British Association for the Advancement of Science. *Report of the Annual Meeting*, 1936, pp. 146 and 49.

must realize that no less than the unimportance or actually deleterious character of other sciences his own profession carries grave responsibilities. I am not sure that we critics have fully faced our duties along these lines. Each aspect of our motives has its own dangers or defects and its own appropriate safeguards or correctives.

In the end the motives of such scholarship are bound to be various. One could scarcely think of more variant characters than the two quater-centenary figures mentioned at the beginning of this paper, —Erasmus the cool and judicial neutral, the rational and dispassionate humanist; Tyndal the passionate enthusiast, the untiring devotee of a single viewpoint. Yet both men expressed themselves in similar ways and both aimed solely at helping their contemporaries to a better knowledge of the Bible. The well known words of the English martyr about the vernacular understanding of the Scriptures are only a paraphrase of what the Dutch humanist expressed as the hope of the consequences of his labors. The same diversity of temperament prevails in our present Society.

The same general end and aim—a better knowledge and understanding of the Bible—is probably the immediate motive of all of us, often without much further thought of why we wish this result. As we pursue our labors the study of the Bible becomes an end in itself. No doubt many rabbis have quoted as the motive of their labor the command of Joshua: "Thou shalt meditate therein day and night." No further reason is quoted by the Pentateuchal writer. By us also, not so much by divine injunction as by the habit and intrinsic interest of the task, ulterior or self-conscious aims are forgotten. Under these circumstances in our generation as before we can feel ourselves laboring in fellowship with scholars we know today of different lands and creeds and races, as well as carrying on the tasks which our predecessors in the past have passed over to us to complete. Fidelity to the best in our professional tradition, both of piety and of open-minded, honest quest for the truth, may prove in the end one of the most satisfying motives for us all.

The Ancient Near East
and the Religion Of Israel*

W. F. Albright
The Johns Hopkins University

I

Before we can advantageously compare the religion of Israel with the religions of the ancient Near East, we must appraise the state of our knowledge in both fields. Moreover, we must ask ourselves whether our interpretation of the data is affected by extrinsic considerations, such as preconceived theories of the evolution of religion. Each field has its own pitfalls. In dealing with the ancient Near East we must carefully estimate the degree of assurance with which we can translate our documents and interpret our archaeological materials. In approaching the OT we must reckon not only with textual corruption but also with the elusive problem of dating. All our efforts to reconstruct the chronological order of events and documents, and to deduce a satisfactory scheme of historical evolution from them, are inevitably influenced more or less strongly by our philosophical conceptions, as will be pointed out briefly below.

II

There are four main groups of religious literature from the ancient Near East which are of particular importance for the light they throw on the origin and background of Hebrew religion: Egyptian, Mesopotamian (Sumero-Accadian), Horito-Hittite, and West Semitic (Canaanite, Aramaean, South Arabian). In every case it is much more important to know whether a translation is philologically reliable than whether the translator is a specialist in the history of religions. Comparative treatment is relatively futile until the texts on which it is based have been correctly explained as linguistic documents. It is quite true that a trained student

---

* The Presidential address delivered at the meeting of the Society on December 27th, 1939, at Union Theological Seminary, New York City.

of religions may divine the true meaning of a text before philological confirmation is available. In such instances comparative religion has a definite heuristic value. An excellent illustration is furnished by Julian Morgenstern's happy interpretation of a passage in the Gilgamesh Epic as somehow connected with widely diffused stories of the theft of the divine gift of immortality from man by a serpent.[1] However, this remained only a plausible hypothesis until the present writer corrected the reading *qulultum*, supposed to mean "curse" to *quluptum* (*quliptum*), "slough of a serpent."[2] The writer would not have stumbled upon this correction, now accepted by all Assyriologists, without having read Morgenstern's paper.

For convenience we may distinguish three main periods in the history of the interpretation of ancient Near-Eastern documentary sources: 1. decipherment and rough translation; 2. the development of grammatical and lexicographical study, accompanied and followed by much greater accuracy in interpretation; 3. detailed dialectic and syntactic research, accompanied by monographic studies of selected classes of documents.[3] In Egyptology the first phase may be said to have begun with Champollion's famous *Lettre à M. Dacier* (1822) and to have come to an end with the appearance of Erman's *Neuägyptische Grammatik* (1880). The second phase includes the principal grammatical and lexicographical work of Erman and Sethe and was brought to a close by the publication of the grammatical studies of Gunn and Gardiner (1923–27) and of the main part of the great Egyptian dictionary of the Berlin Academy (1925–31). The third phase began in the middle twenties and is still in progress; notable illustrations of its achievements are the publication of detailed documentation for the words listed in Erman's *Wörterbuch* (since 1935), the publication of Sethe's translation and commentary to his edition of the Pyramid Texts (since 1935), the Egyptological publications of the Oriental Institute of the University of Chicago (since 1930), Gardiner's publication of the Chester Beatty papyri (since 1931), the appearance of the *Bibliotheca Aegyptiaca* of Brussels (since 1932), etc.

Assyriology has passed through a similar cycle. The first phase may be said to have begun about 1845 and to have closed with the establishment of the Delitzsch school of trained philological exegesis about 1880. The second phase saw the solid foundation of Assyrian philology through the work of Delitzsch, Haupt, Zimmern, Jensen, Meissner, and Ungnad and of Sumerian through the work of Delitzsch and Thureau-Dangin. With the emergence of the Assyriological school of Landsberger in the early twenties and the appearance of Poebel's *Sumerische Grammatik* (1923) the third and current phase began. This phase is characterized by intense activity in detailed grammar and lexicography, especially among the members of the now scattered Landsberger school and at the Oriental Institute,

---

1. *Zeitschrift fur Assyriologie*, XXIX, 284–301.
2. *Revue d'Assyriologie*, XVI, 189 f.; *Am. Jour. Sem. Lang.*, XXXVI, 278 ff.
3. Cf. the general discussion of the progress and present state of Near-Eastern studies in *Jour. Am. Or. Soc.*, LVI, 121–144.

where it centers about the great Assyrian dictionary which is being prepared by Poebel and his associates. Goetze and Speiser are developing important schools of Accadian linguistics. It is also marked by monographic activity in all important fields of Assyriology, continuing and supplementing the work of the second phase, which was synthesized by Meissner in the two volumes of his *Babylonien und Assyrien* (1920–25).

The story of the recovery of the Horito-Hittite languages is not yet finished. The decipherment of the Hittite hieroglyphs was begun in 1877 by Sayce and was successfully launched by Meriggi, Gelb, Forrer, and Hrozny between 1928 and 1933; it is still under way and no translations of these enigmatic texts can yet be relied on. The decipherment of Horite (Hurrian, Mitannian) was successfully begun by Jensen and Brünnow in 1890; it has been facilitated since the War of 1914–18 by the discovery of new documentary sources at Boğaz-köy, Nuzu, Ugarit, and Mari, and is now making very rapid progress, thanks especially to the work of Friedrich, Speiser, and Goetze; Speiser has a grammar of the language nearly ready for publication. However, great care must be exercised in dealing with questions in the field of Horite philology; translations of unilingual texts are still very precarious. Cuneiform Hittite was deciphered by Hrozny in 1915; progress in its philological interpretation has been rapid and continuous, and good grammars and glossaries are now available. Recent advance has been due largely to the efforts of Friedrich, Ehelolf, and Sommer in Germany, and of Goetze and Sturtevant in America. The first stage of progress in this field may be said to have been surmounted as early as 1925, but we are still far from aspiring to the third stage. Translations by the best authorities in the field may, however, be followed with considerable confidence.

In this connection we may briefly refer to the tremendous advance in our knowledge of Anatolian and Aegean religion which may be confidently expected from the impending decipherment of Mycenaean and Minoan script. The 1600 tablets from Cnossus in the cursive script known as Linear B, excavated by Sir Arthur Evans forty years ago, would probably have been deciphered already if any appreciable part of them had been published. Blegen's sensational discovery of 600 more tablets in this same script in Messenian Pylus (spring of 1939)[4] renders decipherment merely a question of time and effort, since these documents are almost certainly in archaic Greek and many phonetic values are probably deducible from the Cypriote script. Once the phonetic values of the syllabic characters of Linear B have been obtained in this way, it will only be a matter of time and availability of material until the Cnossian tablets are also deciphered. To judge from the evidence of place-names, their language may be only dialectically different from cuneiform Hittite, Luvian, and proto-Lycian. In short, many vexed

---

4. See *Am. Jour. Archaeol.*, 1939, 564 ff. I have extremely interesting information from oral sources with regard to the progress of research on these documents, information which justifies optimism.

problems connected with the relation between Mycenaean and later Greek religion may soon find their solution, at least in part. Since the Cnossian tablets date from about 1400 B.C. and the Pylian ones apparently from the thirteenth century, their decipherment will cast direct light on the sources of Homer, thus perhaps enabling us to decide the question of the extent to which the Iliad and Odyssey reflect the Late Bronze Age.

The fourth of the main groups of documentary material to which we referred above is the West Semitic. This term we use here in a wide sense, to include both Canaanite and Aramaic inscriptions in Northwest Semitic and South Arabic, as well as the rapidly increasing number of documents in early North Arabic. After many more-or-less abortive attempts, Phoenician was finally deciphered by Gesenius in 1837 and South Arabic yielded almost simultaneously to Gesenius and Rödiger about 1840. Since their time the number of known inscriptions has increased vastly, especially in South Arabic. In 1868 the discovery of the Mesha Stone pushed the date of the oldest "Phoenician" document back to about 850; in 1923 discoveries at Byblus carried this date back to before 1100; since then miscellaneous finds have taken it back still farther to the sixteenth century or even earlier.[5] Because of their close linguistic resemblance to Biblical Hebrew, practically all "Phoenician" inscriptions from the twelfth century or later can be read with general certainty; the obscurity of older ones, including the proto-Sinaitic inscriptions from the late Middle Bronze Age (partially deciphered by Gardiner in 1916),[6] is due solely, we may suppose, to the paucity of texts on which to work.

The sensational discovery of tablets in a previously unknown cuneiform alphabet at Ugarit (Râs esh-Shamrah) on the North-Syrian coast in 1929, followed by their decipherment through the joint efforts of Bauer and Dhorme in 1930, has opened up a new phase of Canaanite literature. Successive finds of documents by the excavator, C. F. A. Schaeffer (1929–39), have now brought so much material, still only partly published, that we may confidently expect the major difficulties of interpretation to be solved within a few years, if Virolleaud's yeoman work in editing is not stopped by the present war. The first detailed grammar of Ugaritic is about to be published by C. H. Gordon in *Analecta Orientalia*. The use of current translations of the Ugaritic religious texts requires great caution, since the pioneer work of Virolleaud cannot be regarded as definitive and much of the interpretative work of others is either fanciful or is already antiquated by

---

5. For recent accounts of this material see the divergent treatments by the writer *(Bull. Am. Sch. Or. Res.,* No. 63, pp. 8 ff.) and by Obermann *(Jour. Am. Or. Soc.,* LVIII, Supplement; *Jour. Bib. Lit.,* LVII, 239 ff.). Flight has given a very judicious survey in the *Haverford Symposium on Archaeology and the Bible* (1938).

6. The writer's proposed decipherment *(Jour. Pal. Or. Soc.,* 1935, 334 ff.) remains the only one which fits the linguistic situation in Syria and Palestine as we now know it from Ugarit and Amarna. This does not, of course, prove that it is correct, since our material is inadequate.

the progress of investigation. The best recent work has been done by H. L. Ginsberg, with whom the writer finds himself generally in agreement.

In their present form the Ugaritic documents carry us back only to about 1400,[7] but the syllabic inscriptions on stone and copper which have been excavated at Byblus and in small part published by Dunand seem to date from the late third millennium B.C. That they are in early Canaanite seems highly probable, and most of them presumably have religious significance.[8] Their decipherment may some day enable us to penetrate into an early stage of Canaanite religion, comparable in antiquity to the Pyramid Texts and the contemporary Sumero-Accadian documents from Babylonia.

After being successfully launched by Gesenius and Rödiger about a century ago, the interpretation of South Arabic made little progress until the number of accessible documents had been greatly increased by subsequent explorations, especially those of Glaser. The first stage of their interpretation was brought to a close by the publication of Hommel's *Süd-arabische Chrestomathie* in 1893. Owing to the uniformity of the material and to the fewness of investigators, the progress of the past half century has been disappointing. By far the best man in this field is Rhodokanakis, to whom we are indebted for nearly all real advance in the field. To him and to his pupils, especially Miss Höfner, we also owe substantial improvement in our grammatical knowledge. Aside from the commonest formulae and from clear narrative passages, there is still wide divergence in the translations offered by leading scholars in the South-Arabic field. Consequently the reconstructions of South-Arabian religion offered by Nielsen and Hommel are not to be taken too seriously.

Thanks to the recent work of F. V. Winnett, the early North-Arabian inscriptions written in South-Arabic script are becoming intelligible and are beginning to yield reliable material for the historian of religion.[9] The work of Grimme, though stimulating and sometimes brilliant, is erratic and undependable. It is now clear that the earliest Dedanite inscriptions go back as far as the Minaean, perhaps even farther than the latter. If we date the earliest documents in the South-Arabic script, whether North Arabic or South Arabic, to about the seventh century B.C. we can hardly be far off. A date in the eighth century is possible only for the earliest Sabaean texts. All treatment of proto-Arabic inscriptions must be

---

7. For this date see *Bull. Am. Sch. Or. Res.*, No. 77, pp. 24 f. and the references there given. Several colophons show that the tablets containing the mythological texts of Ugarit date from the reign of Niqmêd.

8. Cf. *Bull. Am. Sch. Or. Res.*, No. 60, pp. 3–5; No. 73, p. 12.

9. See Winnett, *A Study of the Lihyanite and Thamudic Inscriptions* (Toronto, 1937) and the writer's discussion of it, *Bull. Am. Sch. Or. Res.*, No. 66, pp. 30 f.; "The Daughters of Allah," *Moslem World*, April, 1940, 1–18. A letter from him dated April 3rd, 1940, reports that he has made important further progress in his decipherment and interpretation of the Lihyanite inscriptions.

affected by the fact that they generally belong to an age when native South-Arabic culture had been long influenced, not only by Assyro-Babylonian, Persian, and Aramaic culture, but also by Hellenistic and Nabataean.

III

Progress in the field of OT criticism, whether textual, literary or historical, has been incomparably less marked during the past century. Moreover, practically all important forward steps in the historical criticism of the OT since 1840 fall in the generation from 1850 to 1880, that is, at a time when the interpretation of Egyptian, Mesopotamian, and South-Arabian documents was still in its first stage, and before there was either sufficient material or philological foundations strong enough to bear a reliable synthesis of any kind. The greatest Semitic philologian of modern times, Theodor Nöldeke, stubbornly disregarded the young field of Assyriology, though after he had passed his sixtieth year he expressed regret that he had not mastered it. For all his profound control of Arabic, Ethiopic, Hebrew, and the Aramaic dialects, he was helpless, as he candidly confessed, in the terrain of Assyrian, Egyptian, and Sabaean.[10] What was true of Nöldeke was true *a fortiori* of the great founders of modern OT science: Wellhausen, Kuenen, Robertson Smith, Budde, Driver, etc. No less a man than Wellhausen, great Semitist though he was, neglected the new material from the ancient Orient with a disdain as arrogant as it was complete. In his invaluable work, *Reste arabischen Heidentums* (second edition 1897) he does not even apologize for his total disregard of the newly revealed South-Arabic sources. Nöldeke at least had the grace to apologize. Of course, one cannot help sympathizing with the suspicion which the greatest Semitists showed toward the new disciplines of the ancient Orient when one thinks of their parlous state at that time. Nor can one fail to recognize that the adventurous expeditions of a Winckler or of a Hommel into the *terra incognita* of historical synthesis were not calculated to win the approval of masters of exact method in the older disciplines. At the same time, there can no longer be the slightest doubt that neglect of the ancient Orient, whether justified at that time or not, could result only in failure to understand the background of Israel's literature and in consequent inability to place the religion of Israel in its proper evolutionary setting.

No great historian or philologian is likely to construct his system in a vacuum; there must be some body of external data or some exterior plane of reference by the aid of which he can redeem his system from pure subjectivity. Since no body of external data was recognized as being applicable, men like Wellhausen and Robertson Smith were forced to resort to the second alternative: the arrangement of Israelite data with reference to the evolutionary historical philosophies of

---

10. See Nöldeke, *Beiträge zur semitischen Sprachwissenschaft*, I (1904), p. v, II (1912), p. v.

Hegel (so Wellhausen) or of the English positivists (so Robertson Smith). Graf, Kuenen, and Wellhausen, the joint creators of the so-called Wellhausenist system, were all Hegelians, and Wellhausen, who was the greatest thinker of the three, avowed his allegiance in unmistakable terms when in the introduction to his famous *Prolegomena* (1878) he wrote (p. 14): "Meine Untersuchung ... nähert sich der Art Vatke's, von welchem letzteren ich auch das Meiste und das Beste gelernt zu haben bekenne." Now Vatke was, we must remember, an ardent disciple of Hegel, who was one of the first and certainly the most successful exponent of Hegelianism among German Protestant theologians; his most important work appeared in 1835. This Hegelianism, more implicit than explicit with Wellhausen, became even clearer with his followers, especially in the books of Marti, whose influence was much greater than his scholarly merit would seem to warrant. OT literature was now divided into three phases: early poetry and saga, prophetic writings, and legal codes. The religion of Israel exhibited three stages: polydemonism, henotheism, monotheism. To Wellhausen the fully developed religion of Israel was latent in its earlier stages, spirit and law replacing nature and primitive freedom from fixed norms, all this development following strictly Hegelian dialectic: thesis (the pre-prophetic stage), antithesis (the prophetic reaction), synthesis (the nomistic stage).

Robertson Smith was no less a positivist because he nowhere described his theory of the evolution of Israel in formal positivistic terms than Wellhausen was a Hegelian because he failed to reduce his system to explicitly Hegelian language. The historical chain of students of comparative religion formed by Tylor, Robertson Smith and Frazer was largely dependent on the philosophical temper of the age in England, a temper which was powerfully influenced by the work of John Stuart Mill and Herbert Spencer, through whom the positivism of Comte passed into the history of religion and related fields. It is quite impossible to understand the development of Robertson Smith's thought without understanding the nature of English positivistic philosophy. English OT scholarship subsequently fell even more completely under the domination of the positivist tradition, as is particularly evident in the writings of S. R. Driver and S. A. Cook, to name only its most prominent representatives in the two generations that have elapsed since Smith's death. In France the positivist tradition has also been dominant, except in Catholic circles, as is clear from the recent work of such Protestant scholars as Lods and Causse.[11] With the latter we move into a new stage, which has been deeply influenced by the sociological schools of Durkheim and Lévy-Bruhl. It is historically

---

11. I take this opportunity to correct the erroneous emphasis I placed on the Hegelian atmosphere of Causse's work in my review (*Jour. Bib. Lit.*, LVII, 220), where I wrote: "The sociological determinism of the author is thus essentially Hegelian." In a recent letter to me Professor Causse protests against this statement, insisting that he is actually opposed to Hegelianism. The "rigid Wellhausenism" for which I tax him later does, in fact, give his picture of Israelite evolution a Hegelian appearance. However, direct philosophical influence on his work is mostly

important to stress the fact that, in spite of the far-reaching resemblances between the conclusions of the German and of the Anglo-French schools, they go back to essentially different philosophical horizons. Accidentally, however, it happens that there is a striking superficial resemblance between the evolutionary religious schemes of Hegel and of Comte, since the latter also thought in triads as illustrated by his progressive sequence: fetishism, polytheism, monotheism. On the other hand, Comte's triple hierarchy of modes of thought (theological, metaphysical, and positivistic or scientific), which was in some respects diametrically opposed to Hegelian doctrines, has led Anglo-French and more recently American Biblical scholarship into more and more drastic evolutionary materialism. Under the influence of current instrumentalist philosophy, American Biblical scholarship tends to construct unilateral schemes of evolution, oriented either toward some form of socialism or toward ethical humanism. In these systems mechanical progressivism competes with a remorseless meliorism to produce increasingly artificial results. Whenever doubts arise they are quickly suppressed by appeal to the authority of Biblical criticism, which by establishing the chronological sequence, early poems and sagas, prophetic writings, legal codes, appears *superficially* to confirm the evolutionary schemes in question.

The reaction against these suspiciously aprioristic constructions came first in Germany, where they originated. The first competent scholar to give formal utterance to the new attitude was none other than Rudolf Kittel, in his historic address, "Die Zukunft der Alttestamentlichen Wissenschaft," delivered at the first German Orientalistentag in Leipzig, September 29th, 1921: "Es fehlte dem Gebäude (d.h., der Schule Wellhausens) das Fundament, und es fehlten den Baumeistern die Massstäbe."[12] In this address he stressed, as we have, the fact that the founders of modern OT science had no idea of the great world of the ancient Orient, which was just then opening up, and that their successors also failed to reckon with it, in spite of the vast increase in our knowledge. There were two weaknesses in Kittel's presentation. In the first place, he was premature. The past twenty years have enormously extended and deepened our knowledge of the ancient Near East; in fact they have brought the first real syntheses, which were still absolutely impossible when Kittel spoke. Even nine years ago, when I wrote my first partial synthesis of the results of Palestinian archaeology for Biblical scholarship,[13] the time was not

---

of neo-positivistic character (Frazer, Durkheim, Lévy-Bruhl), and Max Weber, whom he often quotes, was as much of a positivist as he was a Hegelian.

12. *Zeits. Alttest. Wiss.*, 1921, 86.

13. *The Archaeology of Palestine and the Bible* (New York, 1932-5). For an accurate foreshadowing of my present attitude see "Archaeology Confronts Biblical Criticism," *The American Scholar*, 1938, 176–188, with W. C. Graham's reply, "Higher Criticism Survives Archaeology," *Ibid.*, 409–427. In the latter article Principal Graham makes so many concessions that in some respects the difference between our stated views becomes a matter of terminology. However, he continues to maintain a theory of the development of Israelite religion which I cannot accept,

ripe for a successful effort to reinterpret the history of Israel's religion in the light of archaeological discoveries. Such a reinterpretation I hope to offer in two volumes which should appear in the coming two years; the present article contains a greatly condensed abstract of certain chapters of them. Kittel's second weakness was that he lacked the perspective from which to judge the philosophical tendencies inherent in the development of Biblical research, especially in Germany. It is all very well to declare that the historico-religious edifice of Wellhausen lacked a solid foundation and to point out his ignorance of the historical and cultural background of Israel, but conviction can come only after an exposition of the intrinsic reasons for the artificiality of this edifice and a synchronous demonstration of a better structure, founded on solid historical material.

Since 1921 there have been sporadic attempts, mainly in Germany, to shake off the yoke of a rigid Wellhausenism, but it cannot be said that any has succeeded, though there have been numerous partial successes and many correct observations. However, voices are more and more often heard decrying the artificiality of most modern theories of the religious evolution of Israel. The important and influential school of Albrecht Alt has performed exceedingly valuable services for Israelite history as a whole, but it is clear that it is weak in the sphere of religious history. Meanwhile the crisis of religious faith in Central Europe which heralded the victory of National Socialism in Germany, has brought with it a violent reaction against historicism (*Historismus*) in all its manifestations, a reaction almost as pronounced among foes of the movement as among its friends. The great work of the Swiss scholar, Walther Eichrodt, *Theologie des Alten Testaments* (1933-39), expresses the author's conviction in emphatic words: "In der Tat ist es hohe Zeit, dass auf dem Gebiet des Alten Testaments einmal mit der Alleinherrschaft des Historismus gebrochen und der Weg zuruckgefunden wird zu der alten und in jeder wissenschaftlichen Epoche neu zu lösenden Aufgabe, die alttestamentliche Glaubenswelt in ihrer strukturellen Einheit zu begreifen."[14]

IV

This is hardly the place in which to present my philosophical credo, but a few observations are in order, since one's philosophical position is inseparably bound up with one's efforts at synthesis—perhaps more in the field of this paper than in most essays at historical interpretation. In the first place, I am a resolute positivist—but *only in so far as positivism is the expression of the modern rational-scientific approach to physical and historical reality*. I would not call myself a positivist at all if it were not for the insistence with which National-Socialist theorists have rejected the rational-scientific approach to reality, calling it "positivism."

---

while I adhere to the standard critical position with regard to the order and chronology of J, E, D, P, though he is ready to abandon it.
14. I, 5.

I am even in a sense an instrumentalist, but only to the extent that I acknowledge the truth of an instrumentalism *sub specie aeternitatis,* in complete opposition to the metaphysical system of the Dewey school. Men can judge the value of a movement or of a method only by inadequate criteria, and to set up such criteria as absolute guides is the most dangerous possible procedure, both in science and in life. I am an evolutionist, but only in an organismic, not in a mechanical or a melioristic sense. All such aprioristic evolutionary systems as those of Hegel and Comte are so artificial and so divorced from physical or historical reality that they cannot be safely used as frames of reference, though they have undoubtedly possessed real heuristic value—a partially erroneous classification is generally better than no classification at all. Subsequent evolutionary philosophies are so unilaterally determined that they can at best reflect only one facet of a polyhedron. Favorite forms of determinism in our day are socio-economic, ranging all the way from the brilliant and often correct work of Max Weber[15] to the plausible but factitious reconstructions of orthodox Marxists.

The most reasonable philosophy of history, in my judgment, is evolutionary and organismic. Evolution is not unilateral progress, it is more than a series of abrupt mutations; yet, like organic development, it falls into more or less definite forms, patterns, and configurations, each with its own complex body of characteristics. In recent years we have been made familiar with "Gestalt" in psychology, with "patterns" in the history of religions and sociology, with "cultures" in archaeology and ethnography. A comparison of successive organismic phenomena discloses definite organic relationships, which cannot possibly be accidental and which require some causal or purposive explanation, whether it be some latent or potential entelechy or whether it be interpreted teleologically. But the task of the historian, as distinguished from the philosopher or the theologian, is to study the phenomena as objectively as possible, employing inductive methods wherever possible. My task is restricted as far as possible to historical description and interpretation, leaving the higher but less rigorous forms of interpretation to others. Though I am, as will be clear from the above sketch, essentially an historicist, my point of view remains very different from that of the older representatives of *Historismus,* whose interpretation was distorted by erroneous postulates and false frames of reference, and who sinned grievously in subordinating structural and organismic considerations to sequential relationships.

Broad classifications of historical phenomena are inevitably inadequate, yet if they are planned with sufficient care they can be illuminating. I have found the following classification of mental operations very useful in the study of the history of religions. The late R. Lévy-Bruhl[16] introduced a happy new term into

---

15. I do not wish to give the impression that all Weber's work was characterized by socio-economic determinism. Far from it. I wish here only to emphasize the relative soundness of this phase of his work.

16. See especially Lévy-Bruhl, *La mentalité primitive* (1922).

current terminology: "prelogical" thought. In other words, primitive men and modern savages share a type of thinking which never rises to the logical level, but always remains more or less fluid and impersonal, not distinguishing between causal relationships and coincidences or purely superficial similarities, unable to make precise definitions and utterly unconscious of their necessity. Most ancient mythology goes back to the prelogical stage of thinking. Next above this stage is what I would term "empirico-logical" thought, in which sound, though unconscious, observation and simple deduction from experience, subconscious as a rule, play an important part. This stage, in which most of the fundamental discoveries and inventions of primitive man were made, was to a large extent contemporary with the prelogical stage, but it assumed the dominant role during the third millennium B.C. and continued until the dawn of logical reasoning in sixth-century Greece. Empirical logic became self-conscious in the systematic "science" of the Babylonians and Egyptians, at least as early as 2100 B.C.; it is best illustrated by the elaborate systems of magic and divination developed in Babylonia during the following centuries, where we find a "proto-inductive" method of gathering data and methodical deduction from these "inductions" as well as from empirically developed or mythologically conditioned postulates. Empirical logic survived long after the discovery of logical reasoning by the Greeks, even in some dominant intellectual circles. It goes without saying that prelogical thinking has never become extinct among savages and children, and that a disconcerting proportion of contemporary adult thinking is essentially prelogical, especially among uneducated people, in the most civilized lands. Empirico-logical thinking is still commoner. However, since we must classify modes of thought according to their best examples and since chronological progress in dominant types of thinking is certain, our classification is just as instructive, *mutatis mutandis,* as the archaeologically useful (but culturally somewhat misleading) series, stone—bronze—iron.

V

After these preliminary remarks, whose apparently disproportionate length is required by the nature of our theme, we may turn to consider the subject of our paper. The space at our disposal is, however, too short to allow a full treatment of so extensive a topic, and we shall restrict ourselves to a brief comparison of the conceptions regarding the nature of deity among the peoples of the ancient Near East between cir. 2000 and 1000 B.C. with those prevailing in Israel between cir. 1200 and 800 B.C. Since the national and cultural evolution of Israel shows an inevitable lag (which must not be exaggerated!) when compared to that of the surrounding peoples this apparent chronological disparity is quite justified. When we remember that Israel was situated in the middle of the ancient Near East and that all streams of influence from the richer and older centers of culture percolated into Palestine, when we recall that Israelite tradition itself derived both its ancestors and its civilization from Babylonia, Egypt, and Canaan (Phoenicia), then our chronological postulate is not only justified but becomes inevitable. Incidentally, it has the practical advantage of scrupulous fairness, since we are not retrojecting ideas which are expressed in documents of—say—the seventh century B.C. into the middle of the second millennium, following the example of many members of the *Religionsgeschichtliche Schule,* who did not hesitate to relate the Gospels and the Pauline Epistles to the Mandaean liturgies and the Corpus Hermeticum, though the latter cannot antedate the third century A.D., and the former can hardly be earlier than the sixth century A.D. Slight chronological uncertainties must remain: it is by no means always certain that a given religious text from the ancient Orient (including the Bible) actually reflects the period when it was ostensibly compiled; it may belong to a considerably earlier period, being handed down orally or in writing and then adapted to a special purpose, with no change in its religious atmosphere. Moreover, in dealing with Biblical literature unusual care must be exercised in dating and interpreting our material, both because of its complicated transmission and because of frequent textual and lexical uncertainty.

Among the most serious methodological fallacies of most current OT scholarship is the tendency to telescope an evolution that actually took many thousands of years into the space of a few centuries.[17] This is a direct result of adherence to a unilateral evolutionary scheme which requires a definite succession from simpler and cruder to more complex and more refined forms, and which tries to eliminate the latter from early stages and the former from later stages of a given development. Actually, of course, the order of evolution is, in the main, correct, but we must go back several thousand years to find prelogical thinking dominant in the most advanced circles. The religious literature of the ancient Orient is mainly empirico-logical and there is little evidence of true prelogical thought except in such bodies of material as the Pyramid Texts, unilingual Sumerian religious compositions of the third millennium, and other documents transmitted to later times but redolent of their primitive origins. Even in magic and divination after the beginning of the second millennium, there was increasing tendency to restrict the prelogical element to inherited elements (very numerous, of course) and to employ empirico-logical methods to innovate and develop. The mythological substratum of fertility cults and ritual retains its prelogical character longest, but after 2000 B.C. there is an increasing tendency to explain away inconsistencies and to turn the originally impersonal, dynamistic figures of the "drama" into definite forms with tangible personalities, fitted into a special niche

---

17. This tendency is by no means the exclusive property of OT scholars. An example of it, though much less drastic, is Breasted's brilliant book, *The Dawn of Conscience* (1933), in which he seems to date the effective emergence of social conscience in Egypt in the Old Empire. However, since he defines "conscience" in social terms, his conclusion is not without some historical justification.

in an organized pantheon. On the other hand, of course, empirico-logical thinking generalizes by intuitive "induction," and reasons by intuitive analogy, so we cannot be surprised to find the highest religious thought of the late third and the second millennia B.C. engaged in modifying the fluid dynamism of early religious expression in two directions: pantheism and monotheism. Both in Egypt and in Babylonia pantheistic tendencies appear clearly but remained in general abortive. After the middle of the second millennium B.C. monotheistic tendencies also appear in our sources, but were also repressed by the standard pluralistic polytheism of the age—except in Israel, where monotheism flowered. In India, on the other hand, primitive dynamistic ideas persisted and were transformed into pantheistic conceptions by the empirico-logical thought of the Upanishads and of the earliest Buddhism.[18]

VI

In this paper we are not so much interested in sporadic evidences of pantheism or of monotheism in the ancient Near East as we are in the nature of the organized polytheism of the Assyro-Babylonians, Canaanites, Hurrians, Hittites, Achaeans, Egyptians, in the second millennium B.C. All of these peoples possessed a definite pantheon, which naturally varied from district to district and from period to period, but which was surprisingly stable. In the time of the First Dynasty of Babylon, before 1600 B.C.[19] the Babylonian pantheon was organized on the basis which it occupied for a millennium and a half, with little further change. Head of the pantheon was Marduk of Babylon, henceforth identified with the chief god of the Sumerian pantheon, Enlil or Ellil, "lord of the storm." As head of the pantheon Marduk was commonly called *bêlu*, "lord," and the appellation *Bêl* soon replaced his personal name for ordinary purposes. In Assyria Marduk's place was naturally held by Asshur, chief deity of the city Asshur, who was also identified with the old Sumerian god Ellil. Under the head of the pantheon were many hundreds of other deities, ranging from the great gods to minor divinities, often of only local significance. The boundary line between gods and demons was none too clear and fluctuated constantly. For our present purposes it is

---

18. There is no reason whatever to date the first appearance of strictly logical reasoning in India before the Greek period (third century B.C.). It must also be remembered that some comprehension of Greek ways of thinking must have percolated into Babylonia and even farther east through the intermediation of Greek traders and professional men during the fifth century B.C. It is hard to escape the conclusion that the remarkable development of systematic astronomical research in Babylonia during the late fifth and the fourth centuries was due to an intellectual impulse originating in Greece and transmitted through Asia Minor and Phoenicia. I expect to discuss this subject at more length elsewhere.

19. For this chronology see *Bull. Am. Sch. Or. Res.*, No. 77, pp. 25 ff. Very important confirmation of my new low dates is at hand from other sources.

important to stress the fact that most of the gods were cosmic in character and that the multiplication of names was due largely to the differentiation of originally identical divinities, whose appellations became attached to different local cults,[20] as well as to the introduction of many foreign deities. Only a small part of these figures may be said to have developed clear-cut personalities, as was undoubtedly true of Ea, Nabû, Shamash, Ishtar, etc. Almost any important deity was at the same time connected with numerous different localities and temples; he was charged with some cosmic function which required his presence in many different places and under many different conditions; he was considered to have his own residence in heaven or the underworld, or both. Nowhere except in astrological speculation of relatively late date is a great god assigned exclusive dominion over a given district or country. Marduk is called "king of (foreign) lands" (*lugal kurkurra*) by Kurigalzu III (fourteenth century). In the canonic list of gods, which was composed before 1600 B.C., we find numerous identifications of Sumero-Accadian deities with Hurrian and Northwest-Semitic ones; e.g., Ishtar is identified with Shaushka and Ashtartu, Adad is identified with Ba'al or Dad(d)a and with Teshub.

Nothing can be clearer than the universal cosmic significance of the great gods, especially of Marduk in the Creation Epic, which dates in its present form from the early second millennium. In the somewhat earlier Gilgamesh Epic we are told that Gilgamesh journeyed a prodigious distance westward in search of his ancestor, the Flood-hero Ut-napishtim. In order to reach the Source of the Rivers[21] he traversed the western desert; he reached the mythical mountains of Mashu; he traveled in darkness for twenty-four hours, with gigantic strides; he emerged into the beautiful garden of Siduri, the goddess of life;[22] he crossed the redoubtable waters of death, shunning no toil in order to attain his goal. But no matter how far Gilgamesh traveled he could not escape Shamash, who traveled around the earth in a single day. Even at the Source of the Rivers the gods are all-powerful, for they placed Ut-napishtim there after the Flood, following the command of Ellil.

Nothing can be clearer from Assyro-Babylonian literature of the second millennium than the total absence of any suggestion of henotheism, "the belief in one god without asserting that he is the only god,"[23] or, as commonly meant by Biblical scholars, the belief that the chief god or the patron deity of a given land was lord only of that land and people. Whenever the Mesopotamians came into sufficiently close and persistent contact with a foreign cult to become acutely conscious of the existence of its deity, they adopted him into their own pantheon, either identifying him directly with one of the native deities, or assigning him

---

20. See, e. g., Bertholet's instructive study, *Götterspaltung und Götterversinigung*.
21. See *Am. Jour. Sem. Lang.*, XXXV, 161–195.
22. See *Am. Jour. Sem. Lang.*, XXXVI, 258 ff.
23. *Concise Oxford Dictionary*, s. v.

some special place or function in their pantheon. Theological disputes must constantly have arisen over details. One school, for example, regarded Ishtar as daughter of the old god of heaven, Anu (Sumerian *An*, "Heaven"), while another considered her as daughter of the moon-god, Sîn. Similarly, one group regarded Ninurta as the greatest and most powerful of the gods, while another group insisted that this honor belonged exclusively to Marduk.

The recognition that many deities were simply manifestations of a single divinity and that the domain of a god with cosmic functions was universal, inevitably led to some form of practical monotheism or pantheism. To the second half of the second millennium belong, on clear intrinsic evidence, two illustrations, one monotheistic and the other pantheistic in tendency. The first is the well-known tablet in which Marduk is successively identified with a whole list of deities, each of whom is called by his name; e. g., Sîn is Marduk as illuminer of the night. The second is a document which lists all important deities, male and female, as parts of the cosmic body of Ninurta; e.g., Ellil and Ninlil are his two eyes, Marduk is his neck.

Among the Hurrians and Hittites the process of syncretism was carried so far that it becomes almost impossible to guess the origin of a god's name by the place of his residence, or rather, by the places where he is specially worshipped. The extraordinary fusion of Sumero-Accadian and Hurrian pantheons is illustrated by documents from Nuzu in northeastern Mesopotamia, from Mitanni proper, from Mari, and from Ugarit, but nowhere so clearly as in the rich material from the Hittite capital (Boğazköy). One Hurrian myth describes the primordial theomachy, in which the father of the gods, Kumarbi, is defeated by the storm-god, Teshub, with whom are allied an impressive list of Hurrian and Accadian deities.[24] Three Sumero-Accadian goddesses ranged particularly far to the west: Nikkal, whose cult is attested from different parts of Syria and Cappadocia in the second millennium; Kubaba, who apparently started as the Sumero-Accadian *kù-Baba* (the holy Baba)[25] and became increasingly popular, especially in Asia Minor, where she was finally borrowed by the Greeks as Cybebe, identified with Cybele; Ishtar of Nineveh, a long list of whose cult-centers in different countries is found in a Hittite document from about the thirteenth century.[26] To the Hittites all storm-gods were Teshub, all mother-goddesses Ḥebat; in Hittite literature there is no such thing as henotheism. The religious catholicity of the Hittites is

---

24. See provisionally Forrer, *Journal Asiatique*, CCXVII, 238 f.

25. I hope to discuss this figure elsewhere; see provisionally my note in *Melanges Syriens offerts à M. R. Dussaud*, I, 118, n. 2.

26. See Friedrich, *Der Alte Orient*, XXV, 2, pp. 20–22. The Ninevite goddess is summoned to come to the Hittite capital from Ugarit, Alalkha, and other places as far south as Sidon in Syria, from parts of northern Mesopotamia as far south as Asshur, from Cyprus, and from southern Asia Minor as far west as Masha and Karkaya (probably the Achaemenian Karkâ and therefore Caria).

shown not only by their wholesale adoption of Accadian and Hurrian deities, but also by their use of ritual formulae and incantations in several different tongues, including Babylonian.

It is increasingly evident that in many respects there was close similarity between the Anatolian (Horito-Hittite) religion of the late second millennium B.C. and the Aegean, both as we see it in Minoan and Mycenaean monuments and as we find it vividly portrayed in the Iliad and the Odyssey. While it is, of course, true that the Homeric epics in substantially their present form belong to the beginning of the first millennium, it is now recognized by virtually all scholars that they reflect the culture and the conceptual world of sub-Mycenaean times, i.e., of the last two centuries of the second millennium—in certain respects even of the Late Mycenaean (fourteenth-thirteenth centuries). In the Iliad and Odyssey there is no suggestion that any of the great gods were restricted by nationality in their sphere of action, though they often play favorites. Zeus, Hera, and Apollo are worshipped by both Achaeans and Anatolians; Odysseus encounters Poseidon and is aided by Athene wherever he wanders. From Zeus, who still bears the Indo-European appellation "father of men and gods,"[27] to Helius, whose favorite abode is in the land of the Ethiopians in the far south, the great gods are cosmic in function and unlimited in their power of movement.

Turning to Canaanite religion, we find ourselves in an entirely different situation from our predecessors, thanks especially to the religious literature of the fifteenth century B.C. from Ugarit, but also to archaeological discoveries at Ugarit, Byblus, Beth-shan, Megiddo, and Lachish. It is now certain that the religion of Canaan was of the same general type as that of Mesopotamia, Asia Minor, and the Aegean in the second millennium. Organized cult in temples played the chief role, and sacred rocks, trees, and springs were much less significant than has been supposed. Moreover, the religion of Canaan was true polytheism, not polydemonism, and no henotheism can be proved to exist in it. Thanks to the documents from Ugarit we now know that the account of Phoenician mythology preserved by Sanchuniathon of Berytus (about the seventh century B.C.?)[28] and condensed by Philo Byblius (first century A.D.) into the form in which we have it, reflects, with substantial accuracy, the mythology of the Canaanites in the middle of the second millennium. A mass of fragmentary data from Canaanite, Egyptian, and Greek sources helps to round out and complete the picture. The titular head of the pantheon was the high god, El, who no longer took too active a part in the affairs of men, and who lived far away, at the source of the rivers, "in

---

27. See Nilsson, *Archiv für Religionsgeschichte*, XXXV, 156 ff.

28. Cf. provisionally *Bull. Am. Sch. Or. Res.*, No. 70, p. 24. An earlier date is defended by Eissfeldt, *Ras Schamra und Sanchunjaton*, 1939, 67 ff., against all onomastic and historical probability.

the midst of the fountain of the two tehoms."[29] In order to reach the home of El it was necessary even for deities endowed with superhuman strength to journey through "a thousand plains, ten thousand fields."[30] El and his consort Asherah (who was much more than a sacred tree!) were the progenitors of gods and of men. Next to him was the head of the pantheon *de facto,* the storm-god Hadad, the lord (*Ba'lu, Ba'al*) *par excellence.* That Ba'al early became his personal name as well as his appellation, just as was later true of *Adonî* (Adonis), of Aramaean *Bêl* and *Bêltî,* etc., is certain from the fact that it was borrowed by the Egyptians in this sense as early as the fifteenth century and that it was listed as such in the still earlier Babylonian canonical list of gods. Baal was the lord of heaven, the giver of all life, the ruler of gods and of men, to whom it is said: *tíqqahu múlka 'ôlámika, dárkata dâta dardârika,* "thou shalt take thy eternal kingdom, thy dominion for ever and ever."[31] The throne of Baal is on a lofty mythical mountain in the far north, certainly to be compared with the Mesopotamian mountain of the gods, Arallu, also in the far north and also the mountain of gold.[32]

The extent to which Canaanite gods were fused with Egyptian has become very clear as a result of Montet's excavation in the ruins of Tanis, which was the capital of the Ramessides in the thirteenth century B.C. The native god of Tanis, Sûtaḫ (later Sêth), who became the patron deity of the dynasty, was identified with Baal, and his consort Nephthys became Anath. Canaanite Ḥaurôn was identified with Horus, Astarte with Isis. The Ugaritic texts show that the artificer of the gods, Kôshar (later Kûshôr), was identified with Egyptian Ptaḥ, as had long ago been correctly guessed by G. Hoffman,[33] and a hieroglyphic inscription from Megiddo now proves that there was a temple of Ptaḥ at Ascalon. Much older, of course, is the identification of the West-Semitic Ba'latu, "the Lady," with Egyptian Ḥathor, both at Byblus and in Sinai and Egypt itself. To the Canaanites there was no limit to the power of their deities; of Kôshar- Ptaḥ it is said, "for his is

---

29. Cf. *Jour. Pal. Or. Soc.,* XIV, 121 and notes 93–94. The text reads as follows (repeated so often that form and meaning are quite clear):

'*ima 'Éli mabbîki naharîma*	*qîrba 'ap(i)qê tihâm(a)têma*
"to El who causes the rivers to flow	in the midst of the fountains of the two deeps."

30. For this rendering, which imposes itself as soon as pointed out, see de Vaux, *Revue Biblique,* 1939, 597.

31. Ras Shamra III AB, A, line 10 (Virolleaud, *Syria,* XVI, 30).

32. Ibid., V AB, D, lines 44 f. (Virolleaud, *La déesse 'Anat,* 51 ff.). For the imagery and the cosmological ideas involved see especially Delitzsch, *Wo lag das Paradies?,* 117 ff.; Jensen, *Die Kosmologie der Babylonier,* 203 ff. (to be rectified in the direction of Delitzsch's position); Jeremias, *Das Alte Testament im Lichte des alten Orients*[2], 568; Albright, *Jour. Bib. Lit.,* XXXIX, 137 ff.

33. *Zeits. f. Assyriologie,* XI, 254, independently discovered by H. L. Ginsberg through his study of the Ugaritic material (*Orientalia,* IX, 39–44). Very important additional evidence for Ginsberg's position has since come to light and will be treated soon by the present writer.

Crete, the throne on which he sits, Egypt, the land of his inheritance."³⁴ Similarly, Canaanite, Amorite, and Accadian deities were exchanged and identified to a disconcerting degree. Gods like Hadad and Dagan, Ashirat (Asherah) and Astarte (Ishtar) were worshipped in the second millennium from the Delta of Egypt to the mountains of Iran. In the cuneiform tablets found in Syria from the period 1500–1300 B.C., we find Sumero-Accadian names and ideograms used so widely for native deities that we are often quite unable to say what their native names may have been. Such cases as Bêlit-ekalli of Qaṭna, Damu of Byblus, Ninurta of a town in the territory of Jerusalem are the rule, not the exception. Some of these deities became permanently domiciled in the West.

In Egypt also we find a similar situation, though its advanced civilization and its natural conservatism combined to produce a remarkable polarity, in which the most pantheistic and rarified monotheistic conceptions are found side by side with extremely primitive myths and beliefs. The god Amûn-Rê', who was not only the sun-god but was also creator and lord of the universe, is praised in the following terms in the great hymn to Amûn (from the fifteenth century B.C., but unquestionably older in conception):

> Thou far traveller, thou prince of Upper Egypt, lord of the land of the Matoi (Eastern Desert of Nubia) and ruler of Punt (East Africa),
> Thou greatest of heaven, thou oldest of the earth, lord of what exists ...
> Whose sweet odor the gods love, as he comes from Punt, rich in fragrance as he comes from the land of the Matoi, with fair countenance as he comes from "God's Land" (Asia) ...
> "Hail to thee!" says every foreign land, as high as heaven is and as wide as earth is and as deep as the sea is....³⁵

The archaism of the language and of the geographical terminology should not prevent us from recognizing the fact that this text forms a perfect conceptual bridge between the ideas of the third millennium, as illustrated by the hymns to Rê' in the Pyramid Texts, and the great Hymn to the Aten, which dates from the fourteenth century. Even after the reaction had set in strongly against monotheism in the late fourteenth century we find that Wen-Amûn can say to the prince of Byblus in the early eleventh century: "There is no ship on the waters that does not belong to Amûn, for his is the sea and his is Lebanon, of which thou sayest, 'It is mine.'" It is interesting to note that the Canaanite prince is represented as

---

34. See Ginsberg, *loc. cit*. My translation differs slightly from Ginsberg's, since I translate the word *klh* (left untranslated by the latter) as *ki-lahu*, "for to him (is)." The second passage, which threw Ginsberg off the track, is characteristically abbreviated and should be read: *b'l ḥkpt 'el . klh (Kptr ks'u . ṯbth . Ḥkpt 'arṣ . nḥlth)*, "lord of Egypt-of-God, for to him (i.e., to Kôshar) belongs (Crete, the throne on which he sits, etc.)."

35. For good recent translations see Scharff, *Aegyptische Sonnenlieder*, 1921, 47 ff., and Erman, *Die Literatur der Aegypter*, 1923, 350 ff.

admitting freely that Amûn is supreme and as adding that Amûn taught and equipped Egypt first, so that Egypt was able to instruct the Canaanites in the art of civilization. It may be observed that this idea agrees with the conceptions of the Ugaritic texts of the fifteenth century regarding Ptaḥ-Kôshar, as well as with the Biblical view that Canaan was son of Ham and brother of Mizraim; so there is no reason whatever for suspecting its essential authenticity.

The general character of the Aten religion is so well known that there is no occasion for us to dwell on it here at length. In spite of occasional denials by scholars, there can be no doubt that it was a true monotheism, though specifically solar in type and consequently far below the lofty spiritual monotheism of a Second Isaiah. This is proved not only by many statements in the Hymn to the Aten which sound monotheistic but also by the wave of erasing names of other gods from public monuments which then swept over the country. It is also confirmed by other points, such as the absence of shrines of other gods or of their representations in contemporary remains at Tell el-'Amârnah. The solar disk is addressed as "the only god, beside whom there is no other," as creator and sustainer of Syria and Nubia as well as of Egypt, as creator and lord of all, including the most distant lands.

After the Aten cult had been, at least officially, stamped out, the priests of Amûn had a brief period of glory. Not, however, for long. The north reacted a second time against the religious tyranny of the south, and Sûtaḫ of Tanis was made patron of the Ramesside kings of the Nineteenth Dynasty. Above we have sketched the remarkable fusion of Egyptian and Canaanite pantheons which took place at Tanis. So complete was the fusion that it is difficult to determine the origin of any given image of Sûtaḫ-Baal from iconography alone without clear stylistic indices; from Nubia to Ugarit we find substantially the same iconographic type. The extent of this amalgamation of cults may be illustrated in many ways. The phenomena are absolutely certain and it is, therefore, quite clear that nothing remotely like the "henotheism" of Biblical scholars is reflected by our Egyptian sources during the period from 1500 to 1000 B.C. In spite of the inadequacy of our treatment, which could easily be extended and amplified in many directions, the picture of ancient Near-Eastern polytheism in the second half of the second millennium is entirely clear. It was this world into which Israel was born and in which it took up its inheritance. It is hardly necessary to observe that this is not the world pictured by Wellhausen and his followers.

VII

It is quite impossible to develop my conception of early Israelite religious history here in detail. Though accepting the assured results of modern Biblical criticism, I fail absolutely to see that they carry the implications for the religious evolution of Israel with which they are generally credited. The very fact that J, E, D, and P reflect different streams of tradition gives us reasonable confidence that the outstanding facts and circumstances on which they agree are historical. It is true that J and E may have separated into two streams of tradition in the eleventh century, but this would carry us back so close to the age of Moses and Joshua that only hypercriticism could doubt the substantial historicity of the common source. Moreover, thanks to recent archaeological discoveries and to the research of such scholars as Nyberg, we are coming to have a much higher respect for the historical value of oral tradition than we had a few decades ago. If we eliminate the Book of Genesis because it reflects many pre-Israelite traditions, whose originally polytheistic character is sometimes transparent, and if we eliminate all the rhapsodist prophets of the eighth century and later, together with the Hagiographa as a whole, D and P, the latter part of the Book of Kings, and clear Deuteronomic and Priestly elements in the earlier books, we still have a very considerable body of material to illuminate the period from 1200 to 800 B.C. Only the most extreme criticism can see any appreciable difference between the God of Moses in JE and the God of Jeremiah, or between the God of Elijah and the God of Deutero-Isaiah. The rebellion against historicism of which I spoke above is justified, yet it should not be a revolt against sound historical method but rather against the unilateral theory of historical evolution, which makes such an unjustified cleft between the official religion of earlier and of later Israel. A balanced organismic position may consistently hold that the religion of Moses and of Elijah, of David and of the Psalmists was the same in all essentials, just as the religion of Jesus was substantially identical with that of St. Francis and the faith of Paul was also the faith of Augustine. In other words it is not really historicism that is at fault, but rather the philosophy of history which is too often associated with it.

I am, of course, fully aware of all the conventional arguments brought by scholars against early Israelite monotheism, but I consider virtually all of them as invalid and some of them as quite absurd. This is, however, not the place to refute them in detail. I wish only to point out that the literature of early Israel all comes from the empirico-logical age, in which there were no such concepts as philosophical interpretation or logical definition. Wisdom was gnomic or graphic; long inherited expressions were used without thought of their being treated as material for logico-analytical hermeneutics or for philosophical deductions. The sixth century B.C., with Thales and Pythagoras, with Deutero-Isaiah and Job, had not yet come. No one could have predicted that the First Commandment would have been explained in the Nineteenth Century as henotheistic; no one could have imagined that the words of Jephthah or of Elijah, written down in their present form about the seventh century, but presumably following old tradition, would have been interpreted otherwise than as simple statements of what everybody knew to be the Ammonite or Tyrian point of view. As a matter of fact there is nothing in the earlier sources which sounds any more polytheistic than the words attributed to Solomon by the Chronicler in the fourth century B.C.—"for great is our God above all gods" (1 Chr 2:5). Nor is any allusion to the "sons of God," to the angels, or to the possible existence of other deities in some form or other (invariably very vague) any more henotheistic than the views of Philo, of Justin Martyr, or of the Talmud with regard to pagan deities. As should be clear without explanation, much of the onslaught on early Israelite monotheism comes from scholars who represent certain theological points of view with reference to monotheism, i.e., who deny that orthodox trinitarian Christianity, whether Protestant or Catholic, is monotheistic and that orthodox Judaism and orthodox Islam are monotheistic. I do not need to stress the fact that neither of the last two religions can be called "monotheistic" by a theologian who insists that this term applies only to unitarian Christianity or liberal Judaism. No standard "dictionary" definition of monotheism was ever intended to exclude orthodox Christianity.

If monotheism connotes the existence of one God only, the creator of everything, the source of justice and mercy, who can travel at will to any part of his universe, who is without sexual relations and consequently without mythology, who is human in form but cannot be seen by human eye nor represented in any form—then the official religion of early Israel was certainly monotheistic. The henotheistic form constructed by scholars sinks below the level attained in the surrounding ancient Orient, where the only alternatives were polytheism or practical monotheism, henotheism being apparently unknown. There is nothing to show that the early Israelites were either ethically or religiously below their contemporaries. The highest manifestations of spiritual life among surrounding peoples cannot be raised to the level of corresponding forms among the precursors of Amos, Hosea, and Isaiah. Moses and Elijah still stand high above the religious leaders of neighboring peoples and the God of Israel remains alone on Sinai.

Who is like unto Thee, O Lord, among the gods?

The Society of Biblical Literature and Exegesis*

Julian Morgenstern
The Hebrew Union College

It is a sore temptation upon this occasion to discuss a theme of scientific import. Many such themes suggest themselves. But I must, instead, perform what I cannot but regard as a pressing duty. It is to review the present status and the apparent future of biblical studies in general and in America in particular, and the task of SBLE in relation thereto.

It is almost platitudinous to say that we stand today upon the threshold of a new epoch in biblical science; but platitudes are usually true and occasionally worth uttering. This new epoch is unfolding in two directions, and that too with unparalleled speed and urgency. The one direction is forward and, although not entirely free from traps and pitfalls, is bright with hope and promise. The other is completely negative and retrogressive and fraught with abundant danger and ever-increasing insecurity.

The first direction is that of the content and techniques of biblical science. My remarks must necessarily bear primarily upon the interpretation of the OT, for only in this field do I have a measure of competence. But I suspect that a like situation may exist in NT research also, even though perhaps to a somewhat less extent.

The techniques of documentary analysis of the OT are being increasingly outmoded. Correspondingly, many of the conclusions of the so-called Documentary Hypothesis, even some of major character, based primarily upon considerations of stylistic variation, are becoming more and more subject to question. Likewise we are learning to put only a reasonable faith in the procedures and conclusions of form-analysis. The conviction forces itself upon us that the time has come to revalue the old techniques and to bring conclusions within the bounds of more exact and reliable scientific processes.

The realization is dawning upon us, I believe, that much surer evidence of the sources, the literary history and the meaning and cultural significance of distinct

---

* The Presidential address delivered at the meeting of the Society of Biblical Literature and Exegesis, December 29, 1941, at Union Theological Seminary, New York City.

biblical documents may be found in the ideas, institutions and movements which they mirror, especially when coordinated with the unfolding historical picture. We are coming to see, with ever increasing clarity, that the writings of the OT, and of the NT as well, were not at all the offspring of timeless, impersonal, divine revelation, speaking in the vacuum of eternity, as it were, but were always firmly set in time and history. They voiced the soul of the little, God-conscious people of Israel, eternally seeking the solution of the mystery of life, eagerly aspiring to determine the divine purpose, to define the divine way, to come closer and ever closer to the divinely appointed goal, of existence. This it sought not only for itself, but also for the nations with whom it lived in intimate contact and with interacting relations and exchange of cultural possessions, and even for all mankind, whom it came, in time, to envisage as the ultimate unit in the divine scheme of things and the supreme object of divine solicitude. Accordingly the Bible, in all its parts, has its setting in time and history and can find its truest and most inspiring interpretation only in relation to history, to thoughts, doctrines, institutions, movements, events, aspirations, as these gradually unfolded in the history of Israel and its neighbors. Surely there are enough fixed and certain points in the history of Israel and its neighbors to justify this procedure and to establish it upon a firm, scientific foundation.

A wealth of new source material is being disclosed by archaeological discovery and folkloristic research; and, I may remark in passing, I like to think of folklore as archaeology too, and in a very realistic sense, the archaeology of ideas, beliefs, institutions, and rituals, of all the intangible elements of culture, which persist, even though usually in shattered and distorted form, beneath the surface of present-day cultural life. From Palestine and all lands encompassing it this wealth of new knowledge is streaming in and establishes the role of Palestine and its people in the cultural life of the Near East.

The situation today is altogether comparable to that of forty years ago, when the young science of Assyriology was in its ascendency. Just as then, so also today, we must be on guard against extravagance of claim on the part of the new science, and even more against potential rivalry and hostile competition between biblical science and the archaeology of the Near East.

As has been said, the long established postulates of biblical science must now be evaluated more searchingly and responsibly than ever before. But they may not be discredited too easily in favor of the rather apodictical claims of zealous archaeologists. The fruits of one hundred years of scientific investigation of the literary stratification of biblical writings are not to be completely overthrown in a brief moment by the results of twenty years of scientific investigation of archaeological stratification. There must be a friendly and constructive synthesis of biblical science and archaeology. And such a synthesis will come surely and in the not too distant future, when the present quite natural ardor of archaeologists of the Near East will have cooled somewhat. Then biblical science will enter upon a new era of larger research, surer conclusion and more constructive application.

It will no longer be looked upon askance by timid and reactionary religionists. Instead, it will be regarded, as it should be, as a true science, and will exert positive and progressive influence in religious and cultural thinking.

But here a warning! Biblical research is not merely one small province of a vast, all-inclusive world-empire of archaeology. It is and must remain an end in itself. Neither is the primary aim and measure of value of archaeology, even specifically the archaeology of the Near East, merely the interpretation of the Bible or the reconstruction of what is popularly called biblical history. Archaeology has a much larger sphere of investigation than this, the precise limits of which are still to be clearly defined, while biblical science, in turn, has realms of research which reach out far beyond the uttermost range of archaeology. Biblical science and archaeology are sister sciences, whose provinces overlap to no small degree. Between them a close kinship and community of purpose exist. But we must beware of sacrificing the independence and dignity of biblical science and allowing its approved techniques and well established conclusions to be undermined too readily by the impetuous extravagance of a still youthful and somewhat too assertive kindred science. Synthesis and cooperation, in mutual understanding and goodwill, must be our goal. This synthesis will come. But mutual understanding and goodwill can remove many obstacles, warn of pitfalls and speed the attainment of the goal.

With the present unparalleled expansion and progress of archaeology, and especially archaeology of the Near East, and with the impending reformulation of its conclusions and techniques it is reasonable to believe that a new day is about to dawn for biblical science, a day of sure advance and abundant achievement. But the realization of this potentially bright future makes all the more tragic the immediate prospect.

Germany was, of course, the cradle of biblical science. There it was born and tenderly nourished for over one hundred years. With few exceptions its great figures were German scholars. Not a few of us here got our stimulus, and even our technical training, in Germany under German masters. The last generation of German biblical scholars, under whom we studied, were giants in their day. The present generation have upheld the tradition valiantly. Today, however, they face overwhelming odds. The Bible, both the OT and the NT, is in Germany a discredited and spiritually proscribed book. Though the majority of biblical scholars there still carry on eagerly, and despite the oft heard but almost incredible claim of expanding interest in Bible study and of increasing enrollment in university classes, we know that in Germany biblical science is doomed. In the present atmosphere of hostility toward the Bible and toward the religions founded thereon, and under the influence of all-encompassing totalitarian pragmatism, with the consequent disorganization of academic life, biblical science must soon be stifled and must inevitably succumb. Our friends and fellow-workers, not only in Germany but also in the occupied countries, will be, of this we may be sadly certain, for the present stage of biblical science at least, the last generation of Bible scholars.

In Great Britain too the progress of biblical science cannot but be affected directly and unhappily by war conditions. Whatever the cause, the number of outstanding British biblical scholars has always been relatively small, though, it must be said in justice, their contributions have been of unusual significance. Today the unavoidable shifting of interest from what, for the moment, must necessarily be regarded as somewhat remote and purely academic research to more immediate, realistic considerations of military and economic necessity, and the inescapable loss, through the fortunes of war, of not a few potential biblical scholars, must mean inevitably that in Britain too, again at least for the next generation, Bible studies will decline in extent and ultimately in authority as well.

Sweden and Switzerland are carrying on responsibly. But their distinguished biblical scholars are necessarily few. Nor can they escape completely the effects of a torn and disorganized world and the circle of totalitarian influence which hems them in, not only materially, but also spiritually and intellectually.

It follows from all this that, for the present and the immediate future, America, i.e. the United States and Canada, must become the major center of biblical research, and that here Bible studies must be fostered wisely and devotedly, if biblical science is to endure and progress despite the present world-cataclysm. How prepared are we for this responsibility?

Let us realize at the outset that it is a responsibility which we assume of necessity, rather than of right. For we must face the bald fact that, despite a few scholars of very first rank, America's contribution to biblical research has scarcely been commensurate with the role which it has played in other fields of science. Until quite recently our nation has, not at all unnaturally, cherished a youthfully naive national philosophy, has been animated on the whole by a spirit of religious individualism and fundamentalism, and has directed its attention mainly to the content and techniques of simple, elementary Sunday School teaching of the Bible rather than to true research and productive scholarship. American intellectual interests have turned more and more in the direction of the physical and social sciences and their pragmatic applications, rather than to the humanities. Much of our college training has been superficial, especially in the humanities, and our college students have been impatient of the exacting discipline indispensable to a firm foundation for constructive biblical scholarship. For these and other causes no doubt America's standards and achievements thus far in the field of biblical science have been comparatively modest.

In the crisis which now confronts our science, for we may truthfully call it a crisis, how prepared are we in America at this moment to assume the responsibility facing us? We have in our ranks a small handful of able and honored scholars, our links with a distinguished generation, whose scientific achievements, however, in the main now lie in the past rather than in the future, but who are still a source of guidance and inspiration to the rank and file of their colleagues. We have unquestionably a fair number of younger scholars of some achievement and of larger promise. But they work, for the most part, individually, without organization, unified purpose or cooperative endeavor, and with little more external stimulus than our annual sessions can offer. Opportunities for scientific publication are woefully few. Our intellectual clergy, who should provide an understanding and supporting public for biblical and theological studies, are today far more interested in sociological activities and the related scholarship. Our present American environment can scarcely be regarded as favorable to an adequate discharge of this new responsibility.

Is our Society any better prepared than its environment? Frankly, I doubt it. Now, in its sixty-second year and with more than six hundred members, we, its constituency, may, even with the best will in the world, hardly regard it as an altogether efficient organization. The Constitution provides that "the object of the Society shall be to stimulate critical study of the Scriptures by presenting, discussing and publishing original papers on biblical subjects." This was undoubtedly an adequate program for the Society in 1881 and even for a considerable period thereafter. Today it is altogether too modest and narrow a goal.

Furthermore, the degree to which the Society is carrying out even this limited program and is promoting biblical science in America is open to serious inquiry and difference of opinion. Apparently the Society has but two major functions, viz. the holding of an annual meeting and the publication of a JOURNAL, both worthy projects indeed. But are they sufficient for a body of the age, size and dignity of the Society of Biblical Literature and Exegesis, especially when, as now, it is suddenly confronted with a responsibility grave and urgent?

And is the machinery of the Society adequate for its task? Recently Midwest and Canadian Branches of the Society have been formed, and only today we have learned of the organization of a Pacific Coast Branch. But these are, I believe, almost the only significant innovation in organization or procedure over a very long period. Despite the earnest labors of its patient and indefatigable Secretary and of its able and devoted Editor, its only officers who function with reasonable continuance, the Society seems to have mired itself in a steadily deepening rut, from which, but a little longer, it may never extricate itself.

It is surprising indeed that the Constitution makes no provision whatever for, and the Society therefore has no, standing committees, and especially no Committee on Research and Publication, which might function as its medium of contact with other learned bodies, no Committee on Membership and Resources and no Committee on Program.

The Secretary is expected to fashion an interesting and stimulating program for the annual meetings as best he may out of a conglomerate of papers, haphazardly offered by individual members of the Society, with almost no foreknowledge of the character and quality of that which is being offered, and with little discretionary authority to accept or reject. The programs of the various sessions of the annual meetings have but a minimum of unity, and the opportunity for discussion of important papers and themes is scanty indeed.

The meetings of the Society have been held, almost from time immemorial, here in New York City and in this one place, the hospitality of which, while invariably sincere and generous, has naturally, through long and unbroken usage, lost something of its pristine spontaneity and become conventional and routine in character. The Society imparts, by its meetings, but little, if any, stimulus to the biblical scholarship of its environment; still less does it receive stimulus therefrom. Meeting in the same location year after year, with much the same membership in regular attendance, with the uniform routine of a hurried business session, in which practically no consideration can be given to the progress of the Society, and with an almost unchanging program of innumerable, loosely related papers, with virtually no discussion, with no planned opportunity for social contact and becoming better and more sympathetically acquainted with fellow-members and for exchange of information and ideas, small wonder that our annual meetings fail to stimulate as they should and to not a few of our members seem even empty and boring. I do not imply that these annual meetings are futile. I do say that they fall short of being all that they might and of achieving all that they should. A change of procedure, both with regard to selection of location of annual meetings and to more constructive preparation of programs seems greatly, even urgently, needed. We may envisage a few of the specific services which the Society should inaugurate:

1. The launching of an agency and machinery for the publication of scientific studies, particularly monographs of size and compass too large for inclusion in the JOURNAL but too small to constitute each a complete volume.

2. Closer and more systematic cooperation with related institutions, such as, for example, the American Schools of Oriental Research and the American Council of Learned Societies.

3. The inauguration and coordination of important research projects, especially such as are of too large scope for individual effort, but which require the joint labors of a body of scholars in the administration of an approved, unified and supervised program.

4. The planning and preparation of authoritative, popular biblical studies, so that lay interest in the scientific investigation of the Bible may be stimulated.

5. The establishment at selected universities and seminaries, and especially at the American School for Oriental Research in Jerusalem, of fellowships for graduate study in the various provinces of biblical research, designed to promote the development of young scholars as teachers of authority.

We cannot and need not attempt, here and now, to foresee all possible services which SBLE might perform. These are merely suggestions. Other ideas, perhaps more practicable, valuable, and urgent, may well present themselves to other members of the Society. The all-important consideration is that we realize clearly and immediately the responsibility and the privilege which now fall to the lot of the Society, that it may arouse itself from its long lethargy and become once again alert and progressive.

From all this it is plain, I hope, that reorganization of the Society is advisable, even imperative. This reorganization should not be incidental and haphazard, but thoroughgoing. It should be based upon a searching study by a properly constituted commission of the Society's membership. It should not shrink from revision of the Constitution and from any and all steps, no matter how drastic, which this investigation may reveal to be necessary.

I have offered this paper somewhat reluctantly and with no negative purpose of mere expression of dissatisfaction or criticism. Rather, I have offered it out of a sense of duty and in a spirit of loyalty and affection, because I am jealous, intensely jealous, for the reputation of our Society and for the reputation of American scholarship and for the future of biblical science. My hope is that the entire membership of this Society may join with me in this jealousy. My thesis is that our science today faces a crisis, and that in this crisis a grave responsibility confronts our Society. It is my firm belief that, more than ever before in its entire history, SBLE has a task to perform of gravest import, that it is at present inadequately organized to perform this task efficiently, and that there is therefore an urgent need for reorganization. This reorganization must, however, represent the conviction and the will of the entire membership of the Society. I shall feel that this paper will not have been in vain, that it will have achieved its full purpose, if there be sufficient approval of its general thesis to warrant a motion from the floor that a commission be appointed to consider the matter carefully and in all its implications and to present at a subsequent, preferably the next, annual meeting, a plan for an effective reorganization of the Society, in order to enable it to render a maximum service and to discharge, in a manner creditable in every way to American scholarship, its full responsibility to biblical science.

The Future of Biblical Studies*

Morton S. Enslin
Crozer Theological Seminary

Like many of my recent predecessors in this office I am in a strait betwixt two. Shall I discuss some phase of a technical biblical problem in which I am greatly interested and for which I may perhaps have some competence? I confess that the temptation is great, for the presidential address provides a threefold advantage over the ordinary paper presented at our sessions: one can speak as long as his conscience allows, the number of listeners is usually larger, and there is no opportunity for debate and rebuttal. What an ideal situation to develop such a thesis as: (a) The proclamation which now stands in the gospel pages as the word of John the Baptist, *viz.*, the advent of his greater successor, is really the word of Jesus the prophet, heralding the approach of his greater successor, the supernatural son of man, destined speedily to appear to set up the final judgment; or (b) The writings traditionally ascribed to Luke are clearly dependent not only upon the Gospel of Mark but upon the Gospel of Matthew; and thus one of the greatest services to gospel analysis would be the immediate interment of the will-o'-the-wisp Q, during which commitment service a few brief words might be said as to the utter unreliability of one who through the centuries has been a heavy liability to historical research, the loquacious and irresponsible Papias of Hierapolis.

I repeat, the temptation so to use this hour is great, even though it would probably prompt some modern "most excellent Festi" to scandalized retort (at some more convenient season). Though confident that either thesis could be set forth in words of truth and soberness, I forbear, for I am convinced that at this time there are other matters which should be frankly faced. I turn to this other subject with some trepidation, for I fear that I shall seem to be assuming an unpleasantly critical, perhaps even scolding, rôle, in which I seek to weigh my colleagues in the balances and find them wanting. That is not my purpose. For nearly twenty-five years I have been devoted to this Society and to the tasks to

---

1.*The Presidential Address delivered at the annual meeting of the Society of Biblical Literature and Exegesis on December 27, 1945, at the General Theological Seminary in New York City.

which it is committed. I hope that I can assume that my colleagues will believe that though my judgment may be sadly in error, my devotion to our common task is genuine.

I have announced as the title of this address: "The Future of Biblical Studies." It might better have been stated as a question: "Is There a Future for Biblical Studies?" Frankly, to me this is far from being a rhetorical question conveniently so phrased in order the more effectively to answer confidently, "Of course there is." To me this is a very real question, and I confess that I do not know the answer. I see perils all along the line, and I am increasingly pessimistic as to the outcome.

To many this confession of pessimistic concern will probably seem particularly strange. Frequently it has been stressed in recent months that this is a time of great promise; that due to the convulsions through which we have been passing the road is clear for great advance on this side of the Atlantic. Biblical scholarship has collapsed, we are being told, in Europe. It will be decades, if ever, before German scholarship, which for long blazed the trails, will again be in the picture; and England too will find the hands of her clock so turned back that it will be many years before she will again play the part she long essayed. For the Americas—the United States and Canada—although we must feel saddened at these misfortunes which our colleagues across the seas have suffered, it is a time of promise, the sound of marching is clearly to be discerned in the branches of the balsam trees. We must be up and doing: upon our shoulders rests the problem of carrying on. It is a time of challenge, but it is a time of promise.

There is truth in all this; of course there is. German scholarship—and I am heartsick to say it, for there has been none more appreciative and devoted to it than I—has suffered a dreadful setback. Many are reviving the old charge which years ago was so popular: it is God's judgment upon the vicious higher criticism and religious infidelity. The temple has finally been destroyed. A.D. 1945 is but another anniversary of A.D. 70. Burned temples and battered cities, be they at the hands of Roman legions or due to the bombs of the holy Allies, are an unanswerable proof of the verdict of heaven and its celestial population. Once more the pure gospel is being preserved. I need not say that that sort of pious smugness appears to me both absurd and disgusting. I mention it simply to exclude it from the sphere of intelligent thought. It would be hard to believe that any member of this Society, which owes its existence to that at which the ignorant and the fanatics delight to tilt, would see this as the cause, direct or indirect, of the terrible collapse across the seas.

Nor is it, as I see it, the destruction of universities and libraries. A scholar cannot be bankrupt by the loss of his chair, his books, or—God save the mark—his notes. Their loss may cause him pain and temporary inconvenience. It is never fatal. The catastrophe is far more terrible. It is because so many have sold out to the demands of the hour, to the necessity of having their findings congenial to the outlook of those in political supremacy. That sort of prostitution ends scholarship. Undoubtedly many have refused so to sell out, have kept their torches aglow, even if temporarily under pitchers; but for these older men there can be but little future. By the time that they can get back to work, the scythe of Father Time will have reaped too many. It is the crop of new students, those who must in every age carry on when we older ones step aside, that marks the certain doom. The vicious indoctrination, the training which they have received, can scarcely fail to make it utterly impossible for the majority, in our portion of the field of scholarship at least, to learn to approach their task in the only way that can spell advance.

Nor is this the only indication, as I see it, of the decline across the Atlantic. There is another element, and it involves England as well—it is with reluctance that I mention it—the provincial ignorance of and contempt for the work of scholars in other lands, notably America. As a boy, I remember the oft-repeated remark of a relative of mine, an intimate friend of Sir Oliver Lodge. Said my relative, "Sir Oliver has often said that the only American he would really care to know and talk with is Henry Cabot Lodge." Sir Oliver was a distinguished mathematician and physicist; yet he was apparently utterly contemptuous or indifferent to the work of men eminent in his field in the land to the west. Whether the principal of Birmingham College was quoted correctly or not, of course I do not know; but from my own reading I am inclined to believe that this attitude has still persisted. In the writings of English biblical scholars, as I have come to know them—and my reading has been intensive, for in addition to the necessity of keeping myself reasonably at home in my own field, I have read many manuscripts and books from England, submitted to America for possible so-called "American editions"—I am continually amazed and pained at the almost entire neglect of American work, unless the American authors had chanced to have emigrated from the more privileged soil of England. America is a good land to come to, in which to pick up generous honoraria for casual and condescending lectures, occasionally even to settle in, and in recent years to send refugees to; but apparently that is all. I do not think that I am exaggerating. There is nothing anti-British in me. Only recently I had lunch with an Oxford professor, now a major in the British army. We chanced to mention this subject, and he entirely (and apparently regretfully) agreed. He felt that it was definitely true and that it was fatal. He inclined to explain it as the carryover from the days when English scholarship was so regarded by Germans. And I was interested to hear him refer to a German professor who had uttered almost precisely the same word which I had heard from Sir Oliver: "I should like to see Professor So and So; there is no one else in England worth seeing."

To the extent that this is a true diagnosis it is a clear-cut indication that America has one great advantage. We have not been indifferent to German and British scholarship. However this may be explained—as due to sheer necessity, to docile imitation, as an affectation of wide learning, or on more commendable grounds—the fact stands. And to that extent we have a tremendously valuable tool if we are to bear the brunt in the next decade or two of scholarly advance, for this snobbish and absurd blindness to the labors of others is fatal to true scholarship.

The pessimism which I feel is distinctly not due to any feeling that we will be forced to compete with more competent antagonists. To me such a feeling is doubly false. First, because, as I have suggested, I see little prospect of what might be styled "more competent competitors" abroad. But far more important than that, there can be no such thing as "competition" in a field such as ours. To think in such terms is basically vicious. It is only as we join hands with all other competent laborers, and with no thought of personal rewards essay the common task, that progress can be made. Nor does it appear to me that the work is over, that the mine has been emptied of its ore. On the contrary, to change the figure and to make it more appropriate to this audience, never has the field been whiter to the harvest. So much to do, so many problems to be grappled with. Much has been done, but in comparison with what has yet to be done we have scarcely started. No, there is no problem of lack of work, no need to slow down production, no need to demand a closed shop to keep out other workers whose skill might embarrass; in short, no necessity for our SOCIETY to apply for membership in the C.I.O. But there is no less a grave danger, and it may be phrased in terms of the same metaphor which I have been using: a lack of skilled workmen and the even more desperate indication that the lack will grow more and more evident. To put it brutally: as I have suggested, there is a deal of talk that biblical scholarship has collapsed in Europe, that it is up to America to carry on. To this I agree, but my alarm lies in the fact that I am far from sure that we can do it.

"It can happen here" is no longer—if it ever was—a ridiculous and unwarranted bid for cheap notoriety. It is happening here. Precisely the same virus which has poisoned German scholarship in the last few years is in our blood, though perhaps in a somewhat different form: the incentive to make our findings practical and acceptable to the self-constituted leaders. It is easy to damn the perversion of German scholarship to the so-called Nazi ideology and point of view. I see a similar peril here, and it is even more forbidding and ominous because it appears so innocent and virtuous. It is the demand that our researches strengthen faith and provide blueprints for modern conduct.

I am not thinking for the moment of the set-back to scholarship which has resulted from the onslaughts of the whorish slut Bellona; the ruthless sidetracking and derailing of everything that does not materially advance the war effort. Every civilized man deplores that and hopes that it is only a temporary nightmare which may eventually pass; that once again there may result a bit more equitable adjustment; and that campuses may once more do something else than turn out cannons and cannon fodder. (Parenthetically remarked, I am far from being a pacifist, was in the past war, and would gladly have been in this one had I been free to follow my own inclination. I am no radical, but a very conservative American, dreadfully proud of my country and flag.) There is a real peril, of course, that we shall not swing back after the apparent need is over. Habits do tend to remain seated—especially bad habits. Precisely the same evil that became an actuality in the German way of life exists as a potentiality here. But I am not thinking of that at the moment. The danger which I see is more deep-rooted and was in evidence long before this cosmic delirium under which we are now suffering set in.

The peril of the demand for the practical in biblical research is of long standing. At first it was so obvious as to constitute no especial danger. It has long been a good homiletic approach to a sermon to outline the background of a biblical narrative or to expound a custom or slant on life which existed—or at least the preacher thought it did—in biblical days. Then he was ready for the really important part of his program: its application to present-day life. That occasionally pretty weird bits of information were forthcoming in these presentations—not to mention the essentially similar, if even less guarded, attempts of the Sunday-school teacher—is not likely to be denied. This is not the time or place to criticize or even to discuss them. But when essentially the same procedure is practiced by the biblical scholar; when he becomes more concerned in the practical availability and moralistic application of his findings than he is in discovering facts, it is time to sound the tocsin. And this situation seems to me to have been reached today and to be tincturing our whole discipline. Again and again in these sessions papers have been read (and later printed) in which the tone was distinctly critical of the critical and dispassionate approach to biblical problems. Repeatedly we have been told that we owe it to our students to aid them to a warm religious attitude to life, to a deeper and more satisfying faith; that we lay too great emphasis on the critical and analytical—I have heard it styled, the minutiae—that we need a new and more positive technique; that we should realize that scholarly reserve and dispassionate appraisal are out of place in our field. We are dealing with "words of life," with materials of divine revelation, with materials vastly different from those in other disciplines. Above all we are ministers before we are scholars.

To me this emphasis is utterly false and vicious. That many theological and biblical students might profitably be encouraged to be better men with more vital religious inclinations and less cant, I do not question. I have taught them too many years to labor under any illusions in that respect. As a historian of the New Testament, however, I do not consider it a whit more my task to temper the wind to shorn and mangy lambs or to distort my findings for fear of undermining stubborn credulity masquerading as simple babelike faith than it is the task of my colleagues in the chairs of mathematics or comparative anatomy in the near-by university.

By indirection, yes; by encouraging them by precept and example—with the emphasis a hundred times stronger on the latter—to be dissatisfied with anything save the most honest and unbiased work they are capable of, to refuse to take the short cuts, to assume the answers, to discover what they want to discover, to prefer the neat and brisk encyclopaedia articles to the labor of discovering the facts themselves; above all, to rid their minds utterly of the notion that the literature which they are examining is of a different sort from that under scrutiny by their brothers, the classical students and Assyriologists; in short, to encourage them to let their findings determine their feelings, not their feelings their findings; to keep their hands off the scales when weighing evidence, even if it concerns the validity of the faith of their fathers (or pastors); to make them realize that it is the one unforgivable sin against the deities of learning to make the one pan of the balance go down because they want it to go down, even if they are convinced that their own soul's salvation is hanging in the balance.

Many of us labor under the distinct liability of being members of faculties of theological seminaries. Most of our students are destined for the parish ministry. Ideally that should be no handicap; practically, in many cases it is. Tremendous pressure is exerted, directly and indirectly, to serve out the pabulum which the professors of religious education, of parish duties, of pastoral psychiatry—and, above all, the students themselves—feel essential in the training of a jovial and not too conspicuously educated pastor. Or to put it briefly, what is being demanded today is that we provide a warm religious approach. (Again let me interject a personal remark. I am all in favor of genuine religion. To me it is one of the great essentials of life, but I do wholeheartedly detest the synthetic and add-hot-water-and-serve variety. Furthermore let me add, I teach in a seminary where I am blessed with complete academic freedom. I record this fact with gratitude.) It is common knowledge that in recent years in several of our prominent theological schools, when it became necessary to make new faculty appointments, the deciding factor was that the newcomer should be such as to cause the administration no problems in that respect. In that connection I remember the word of an old theological principal—conservative in many ways, but a genuine scholar. Said he, in answer to the query as to how he selected his faculty: "I get the most radical man I can find."

But today we are hearing windy gusts from tired pseudo-liberals about the necessity of going beyond liberalism, of the need of a new orthodoxy. Apparently they have emerged from the foliage of the tree which they thought they had been climbing, only to discover that they have been climbing out the branch instead of up the trunk. Now at the end of the branch—and a very unsteady branch it is—exposed to the rocks of the small boys on the ground beneath (but not too far beneath!) these poor tired liberals are making a great to-do with their warm religious accents, their frequent retreats, their slightly self-conscious confessions that climbing is not all that it is cracked up to be. This, it might be remarked, is simply one more case where climbing has been confused with crawling. Insofar as this sort of blight is allowed to creep into biblical scholarship—and the evidence is that it is creeping in at an alarming rate—we are destroying our future through showing ourselves unworthy of having one.

Practical values, like Maeterlinck's bluebird, if my experience is worth anything, are never discovered as the result of conscious search. They come as the by-products of honest search. As we quarry where the rock is hard, with no other purpose than to trace the illusive lode, again and again we make discoveries, find values which we never dreamed existed. But we should not have found them had we gone after them. That to me is one of the great rewards of scholarship: it teaches a man that if he is honest in his quest his dividends will be large.

But they are not dividends honored on life's Wall Streets, nor are they choired by ecclesiastical angels. The scholar must expect to be lonely. Doubts and uncertainties, receding rainbows, vanishing horizons, eternal questions which flicker before his tired eyes—these are his priceless reward. Not for him peace and certainty and the so nice absolutes; never can he be sure that he can find a solution; rarely can he be sure that there even is a solution. All he can do is toil on patiently, honestly, contemptuous of the short cuts, the easy guesses, the heart-warming certainties.

It is the growing disinclination to these rigors, to this loneliness and contempt for the neat, practical results, that make me so frankly skeptical and pessimistic of the future of American biblical scholarship.

Another source of concern is our growing ignorance of history. I do not mean primarily the history of the particular period with which we are engaged, but the history of research and criticism. To what extent are Reimarus, Herder, Strauss, Wilke, F. C. Baur, Bruno Bauer, Wrede more than names on which to hang a few label-like sentences of patronizing dismissal? This is tragic in the extreme. The most practical thing that members of this society—at least those in the New Testament section; and my guess is that my Old Testament colleagues would find it not unrewarding—could do would be to spend a year in simply reading and pondering these men. The brilliant insights they achieved, most of which have been lost sight of—in part, because of what were regarded the "extremes" they reached; in part, because some of their tools were faulty—would be of inestimable value today in the hands of men competent to use them. What folly it is that with a task so immense as ours we fail to use our resources. Each time I reread these men—and I do it not infrequently—I am reminded of that monolith lying to the south of Baalbek. Apparently it was too big for the original mechanics to use; and so not only did they not finish it, but it has lain there useless, save as a possible aid to superstitious women, ever since. So with the insights of Reimarus, of Strauss, of Bruno Bauer. We dismiss them easily, when we could learn and profit from them so much.

And one final word. What about our students? Are we training men to be ready for these tasks awaiting American scholarship of which we so glibly speak? Frankly, I doubt it. The majority of my students are unable even to make effective use of Hebrew and Greek, know little German and less Latin. It is easy to treat this with complaisance. Since intelligent men no longer believe that the divine revelation was made in these biblical tongues or can be interpreted solely in them, it may seem less important that they are being fast pushed, not from the centre of the student's stage—that happened long ago—but over the footlights. I am not so complaisant. I have no desire to have to teach compulsory Greek to most of the crop of my students—and I fancy that mine would compare very favorably with those in most schools. I shiver at the type of student we seem to be attracting. Granted that many of them will make faithful and not ineffective pastors; but where are the men to come from to do the work which is singularly elusive to the man whose professional equipment does not extend beyond a round full voice, the ability to provide an hour's retreat from reality once a week, and a perspiring readiness to apply his monkey wrench to all the sexual maladjustments in his larger parish? In a word, are we training scholars to take our places and continue our work with greater effectiveness when, to quote the ancient word, we lie prone in the dust? The way that question is answered, the question I propounded at the start of this address must be answered.

And I cannot help feeling that we in the biblical chairs in the universities and seminaries are in no small part to blame. We are not attracting the type of student we must have. Young men are as honest and ready to devote themselves today to the laborious and the painful as they ever were. But our field has received an evil name when it comes to the matter of standards and scholarly ideals. Too generally we are regarded as defenders, not as eager, restless seekers. I flinch everytime I remember the word of an eminent dean of law to his entering class: "Gentlemen, please realize that you have to work here; this is not a theological seminary." And only recently I was speaking to a colleague in the university where I also teach about one of our better-grade theological students who was taking work with him. In answer to my query as to his progress, my colleague's word was prompt: "He is doing very good work—for a theological student." Gentlemen, that was an ominous word.

I do not know the answers. I still am hoping that things are not so bad as to me they appear. I am hoping that in the coming days we shall see a new temper in biblical research, a greater integrity and dispassionate industry, the recognition that truth does not need to be apologized for or compromised even if we are desirous of gaining funds for a new expedition or a scholarly investigation, a keener cutting edge to our critical tools, a refusal to tone down and distort facts to make them less disquieting, an ability to attract students of the highest ability and most thorough training because they sense that they will not be hamstrung or fettered but that in this field, as in every other worthy of its name, they will have the opportunity to pursue truth unhampered, unafraid—and under the direction of men whom they can trust and revere.

Scholars, Theologians, and Ancient Rhetoric*

Amos N. Wilder
Harvard Divinity School

A proper interpretation of ancient texts requires a prior recognition of the kind of literature we are dealing with. It has long been agreed that account must be taken of the literary form or *genre* of the passage in question: whether it is prose or poetry, whether it is law or chronicle, whether it is liturgy or parenesis. A more general problem arises when we confront ancient texts of a mytho-poetic character, whether prose or poetry, whether liturgy or prophecy or apocalypse. Here we are often dealing with poetry in the wider sense, rather than with poetry in the strict sense. The interpretation of material of this kind is a complex matter. The extended discussion of biblical mythology has furthered our awareness of such issues. Much, however, remains to be done. Proposals for demythologizing the Scriptures have been more concerned with modern apologetics than with the basic question of the nature of religious symbol and of symbolic discourse.

Misunderstanding of the character of the biblical imagery can lead the interpreter far astray in his exegesis of particular passages or in his wider conclusions as to the religion of the OT or NT. A modern analogy will illustrate: when the Negro spirituals speak of "crossing over Jordan" we give the phrase a spiritualizing or an eschatological interpretation. We suppose it to refer to entrance into heaven. But Dr. Miles Mark Fisher, Professor of Church History at Shaw University, in his volume entitled *Negro Slave Songs in the United States*,[1] has made a very good case for the view that the Negro slaves, in their clandestine way, were alluding to crossing the Atlantic to Liberia or to crossing into free territory or to Canada, depending upon the decade in which the slave songs were sung.

---

* The Presidential Address delivered at the annual meeting of the Society of Biblical Literature and Exegesis on December 29, 1955, at the Union Theological Seminary, New York.

1. Ithaca, N.Y.: Cornell University Press, 1953. "One constantly recurring theme in all slave songs was the longing for escape. Past students have pictured this as an unworldly desire; the horrors of slavery, they said, made death welcome. This view Dr. Fisher shows to be false. The desire to escape was there, of course, but the 'heab'n' of the slave lay in Africa not on some celestial shore." From the Foreword by Ray Allen Billington, p. viii.

Religious symbol is open to various forms of misinterpretation. It is generally recognized that the interpreter can err through literalism. He can also err by too prosaic an approach. A third form of faulty exegesis is that of the rationalist who insists on seeking what he calls a clear idea in imaginative discourse.

Our understanding of the outlook of the early Christians depends not only on our knowledge of what they believed but on how they believed it. It is a question not only of the furniture of their minds but of their mentality. Here we are brought sharply up against the whole problem of religious psychology. We find ourselves dealing with the question of the religious imagination, indeed with the imagination in general. The fact is that we are handicapped in dealing with the whole topic of religious symbol and religious rhetoric because of our modern categories. We make a sharp distinction between reason and emotion, between reason and imagination. It necessarily follows that we tend to judge biblical symbol as essentially emotional and irrational or non-rational.

The most promising aspect, therefore, of the continuing discussion of NT mythology is what we may call the basic semantic question, rather than its theological corollaries. What is the nature of imaginative symbol? Any contribution I can presume to bring to this problem rises out of my special interests in modern literary criticism, a discipline which has been much concerned with imaginative and symbolic statement and with the function of myth.

This whole question of the mythology of the NT has disturbed us as historians for several reasons. We do not deny the large and even decisive place that such symbolic elements have, but we recognize the difficulties of handling such material systematically, and we have been disturbed by the seemingly arbitrary procedures that have been adopted in connection with it.

Biblical scholars have been first of all, and rightly, philologians and historians. No doubt there have been some outstanding workers, both in the classical and in the biblical fields, men like Eduard Norden, who have been both philologians and humanists. But this combination is rare. We can recall the time all too easily when the Psalms, for example, were treated without adequate recognition of their rhetorical and liturgical character by a too pedestrian or rational approach. My own original interest in NT eschatology was motivated by the conviction that the plastic character of this material had been slighted by interpreters who were primarily philologians or literary historians. Here was a tremendous expression of the religious imagination, an extraordinary rhetoric of faith; and I could not feel that justice was done to it by either critics or theologians.[2] In what concerns biblical symbolism, we seem today to be at a point where a new cross-fertilization can be helpful from the side of wider humanistic and rhetorical study.

---

2. Albert Schweitzer's greatness in this area lay in the fact that he could combine powers of imagination with his scientific attainments. Only a scholar who possessed a certain esthetic and even visionary capacity could have made the kind of cogent intuitive observations, often in dramatic image, which we find scattered through his works.

A good illustration of our dilemma is afforded by the study of ancient liturgy. We can deal with the festivals of Israel in a phenomenological way: describe the calendars, the priesthood, the sacrifices, the hymns involved. But we recognize that much has slipped through the mesh, and such protests as those of Professor Gaster in his volume *Thespis* become understandable.

> Thus far—perhaps by necessity—the material has been studied primarily (and sometimes exclusively) by philologians. Wider interpretations have therefore perforce been neglected; and a tradition has even arisen that the meaning of a text can be regarded as determined when it has been correctly translated. But this ignores the fact that words are, at best, the mere shorthand of thought, and that folk tales originate in the mind rather than in the mouth or from the pen. Our task must be to get behind the words to what semanticists call their "referents"; and this is the domain of Cultural Anthropology and Folklore rather than of Philology.[3]

Will we not all admit that in dealing with biblical symbol our usual tools come short? Yet when students of this material seek other tools we are often rightly disturbed by the results. I would like to illustrate this dissatisfaction in connection first with the work of the "myth and ritual" school, and secondly in connection with the work of some of our biblical theologians.

I

The labors of the "myth and ritual" school have certainly made a first-rate contribution to our understanding of biblical symbol. The light cast on such matters as eschatology by recognition of its cultic background is highly significant. The comparative method of these scholars, of course, begins with the philological study of the texts in question. They also recognize, however, the social and cultural factors behind the myths and sagas of the ancient Near East, and behind many elements in the traditions, oracles, and Psalms of the OT. They are surely right to identify specific ritual patterns behind much of the material.

The bearing of this approach upon NT study may be illustrated by Professor Riesenfeld's exploration of the background of the episode of the Transfiguration in the Gospels. This work, *Jésus Transfiguré*,[4] illustrates both the value and dangers of the method. Riesenfeld connects the Transfiguration narrative and its various details or motifs with the Feast of Tabernacles and the associated eschatological and messianic conceptions. In so doing, he corrects our tendency to treat NT theology as an abstraction. As he says, the connection of the national hope with the official festivals of the people "always prevented the eschatologi-

---

3. Theodor H. Gaster, *Thespis: Ritual, Myth and Drama in the Ancient Near East* (New York: Henry Schuman, 1950), p. 112.
4. København: Ejnar Munksgaard, 1947.

cal ideas from taking on a completely abstract character and passing over into a merely individual plane."[5] Riesenfeld's concrete study of the social and cultural backgrounds of such mythological symbols as those of the glory, the divine cloud, the tabernacle, the white garment, represents a right semantic approach. We may associate with it Paul Minear's similar motif study in his *Christian Hope and the Second Coming*,[6] of the trumpet, the clouds of heaven, the earthquake, etc. Riesenfeld also recognizes the important differences between living cultic symbol, the spiritualization of symbol when separated from the rite, conventional formulas, and mere poetic terminology or stage properties.[7]

Yet how great is the temptation of those using the "myth and ritual" approach to cast everything into one pattern! How easy it is to overlook the idiosyncrasy of particular texts, related as they are to different backgrounds and periods. The differentia of OT materials over against those of Canaan and Babylonia have been insisted upon by Henri Frankfort, H. J. Kraus,[8] and others. And, quite outside the OT itself, full justice must be done to the differences in the patterns of myth and ritual in the ancient Near East. Frankfort has well stated this matter in his Frazer Lecture (1950) on "The Problem of Similarity in Ancient Near Eastern Religions."[9] These observations bear also upon NT backgrounds. The danger always is that of a too facile *Gleichschaltung* of the apparently similar texts and ritual patterns.

This suggests a more fundamental criticism of the "myth and ritual" approach to the interpretation of biblical mythology. This school commonly sees the basic motivation of the pattern as utilitarian. It is a question of theurgy and dramatic magic. Now no doubt the seasonal fertility rites often had this aspect, or degenerated into it, but primal rite and myth had a much more profound significance. We have much to learn here from what is now known of the "mythic mentality" or "mythic ideation" as explored by the anthropologists and by students of the origins of language and myth. Early ritual had the aspect of enactment or mimesis, indeed, and its outcome was felt as salutary, but the emphasis lay on participation

---

5. P. 53. Note also Riesenfeld's citation of Küppers: "Herein we grasp the stature and distinctiveness of the conception of redemption which animates apocalyptic thought: for here, in fundamental contrast with surrounding Hellenism, redemption can never be thought of as *jenseitig* and individualistic."

6. Philadelphia: The Westminster Press, 1954, Part II.

7. Unconvincing aspects of Riesenfeld's study arise especially in connection with his messianic (as contrasted with eschatological) interpretation of the motifs. That enthronement motifs with an eschatological connotation were carried down through the centuries in association with the Feast of Tabernacles is most probable. What is not so clear is the central place of specific royal and messianic ideas in the Feast in the time of Jesus. Even more problematic is the association of the suffering of the Messiah with these ceremonies at this time, or the contemporary significance of such ancient motifs as those of the ritual battle (with the "rest" that followed) and the "sacred marriage" (with the nuptial pavilion).

8. *Die Königsherrschaft Gottes* (Tübingen, 1951); *Gottesdienst in Israel* (München, 1954).

9. Oxford: The Clarendon Press, 1951.

with the divine powers and their manifestation, not on an end to be sought. The ceremony and story arose as responses to, as dramatization of, the divine epiphany in the life of the group. This positive, non-utilitarian aspect of myth and cult recurs even though the pragmatic function often prevailed in particular periods and settings.[10]

Now these considerations have perhaps brought us a long way from NT symbols. We do not often find NT scholars today connecting the early Eucharist or the early confessional formulas with theurgy, but we do find a failure to perceive the distinctiveness of the Christian salvation-cult and its cult theology. We fail to recognize adequately the dynamic-mimetic character of early Christian worship and symbol. The error lies again in our understanding of symbol. It is not merely "poetry." To proclaim in worship that Christ is at the right hand of God is neither a crass statement of fact nor a literary figure of speech but a precise mytho-poetic affirmation."[11] This is part of what Paul means when he says that no one can call Christ "Lord" except by the Holy Spirit. Paul is speaking in the context of ritual procedure.

We are speaking of the problem of what tools we can use in dealing with the symbolic material in the Bible. I have referred to the difficulties that inhere in comparative mythology. We might add here that some scholars have sought to go beyond comparative mythology by the use of modern psychological insights. One of the most interesting aspects of Professor Goodenough's fourth volume in his study of Jewish symbols is just such an explanation. Frankfort does the same thing at the close of the paper to which we have referred. This approach to mythology at least has one value: it recognizes the dynamic depth of the texts. The chief handicap of the procedure lies in the competing claims made by the diverse schools of psychology, and who can arbitrate among them?

II

We turn now to several of the most-discussed attempts in contemporary NT theology to deal with this material. Brief characterization of proposals of Rudolf Bultmann, C. H. Dodd, and Oscar Cullmann should be illuminating here. We may preface our findings by saying that the biblical theologians appear too often to impoverish the vital symbols so as to obscure their concrete diversity. This makes it possible, then, to discover a dominant theme to which these diversities may all be said to witness. We can recognize the value of generalization and of schematic simplification, and we can acknowledge how much we owe to such

---

10. Cf. W. F. Otto, *Dionysos: Mythus und Kultus* (Frankfurt-am-Main: Klostermann, 1933). "What makes ritual so strange to the modern world is its non-utilitarian character" (p. 34).

11. Cf. E. G. Selwyn, "Image, Fact and Faith," *New Testament Studies*, I, 4 (May, 1955), 237–39.

scholars as those named. But we believe that one or another misunderstanding of imaginative symbol has handicapped their contribution.

Bultmann has long recognized the need of correcting and supplementing the older tools used in the study of the history of religion. In the first volume of his *Glauben und Verstehen* (1933), he calls our attention to the inward meaning of terms which the historian of religion uses in an external way. He was already concerned with that existential dimension in religion which plays so large a part in his more recent work. In his proposal with regard to demythologizing the NT and in the discussion which has ensued, he has defined the problem with which we are here concerned in such a way that scholars and theologians everywhere have had to face it. I am not interested here in the question of how he interprets the symbols of the NT but rather in the question of how he understands metaphorical language.

Most of us who are trained in history and in the history of ideas tend to read poetry for its didactic content. This is not precisely the error, if error there be, in Bultmann's method. He finds in mythology not ideas or doctrine but rather this or that "sense of existence." But this seems to me only another abstracting procedure. Take as an analogy the interpretation of a poem: we miss the meaning of a poem if we reduce it to a prose equivalent. But we also miss the meaning of a poem if we deduce from it a testimony to the poet's attitude toward life. A poem is a concrete creation which offers "news of reality," and our interest is in the experience or revelation it affords rather than in the subjectivity of the poet. So, in dealing with the symbolism of the NT, it seems to me we should take seriously the imagery we find, and not either rationalize it or existentialize it. Bultmann is, of course, alert to the diverse provenance and particularity of the mythological material which we find in the NT. This can be illustrated in the discussion in his *Johannesevangelium* of such syncretistic imagery as is found in the episode of the marriage feast at Cana, as well as in passages dealing with the Vine, the Good Shepherd, etc. Our point is, however, that in his interpretative procedure he tends to translate the plastic imagery into a uniform kerygmatic statement. Indeed, this same existential thesis is found by him consistently not only in John but in the message of Jesus and in the gospel of Paul. Where Paul uses apocalyptic or Gnostic symbol, Bultmann does not appear to be inclined to give it its rights as a genuine part of what Paul means.

It is in connection with Bultmann's interpretation of the futurist eschatological symbol that the most insistent questions have been raised. In their various forms, whether in Jesus' announcement of the Kingdom, with its vivid social imagery, or Paul's portrayal of cosmic redemption, Bultmann feels that he can discount the inherited dramatizations of the future: hence, his emphasis on the purely otherworldly and existential character of the crisis. Future is seen as wholly unpicturable possibility rather than as concrete corporate destiny. But this conclusion is based upon a semantic decision with regard to the pictorial imagery of the early Christians, a decision which may be questioned.

In the case of Dodd, the chief question to be raised has to do with his realized eschatology. We are not concerned here with his disputed rendition of several crucial passages in the Synoptic Gospels, but with his wider view of the kerygma. Dodd recognizes that after the early days the Church, by and large, came to think in futurist terms about the consummation. This futurist emphasis, however, he tends to disallow in favor of a realized eschatology in Platonic terms.

One aspect of the Platonizing tendency appears in connection with Dodd's book, *The Interpretation of the Fourth Gospel*. Bultmann's remarks upon Dodd's understanding of the symbolism of this Gospel are of special interest at this point. The symbols in question are those of the true Light, the true Bread, the true Vine, etc. Bultmann would seem to be justified in questioning Dodd's use of Platonic categories here, as though it were a matter of the contrast between appearance and reality. To quote Bultmann:

> It is not a matter here of the contrast of prototype and antitype in the Platonic sense, such that the problem of μέθεξις (participation) could arise. What is involved is rather the opposition of reality and illusion; and so far as one can speak of antitype what is involved is demonic imitation. The Johannine ἀληθινά are not transcendental ideas, but those things which are actually sought after in the demands men make upon life. Thus the Greek (Platonic) contrast of the ever-abiding over against that which becomes and which passes away is remote from the Johannine dualism.[12]

On this point, the rights of the matter would seem to be with Bultmann. Platonism here acts as an ideological thesis to do violence to the symbolic concreteness of the imagery. In his work *Ego Eimi*, Eduard Schweizer has vividly presented the widespread cultural concreteness of such images as those of the Vine, the Shepherd, and the Tree of Life.[13] The author of the Fourth Gospel is saying that all the life satisfactions of nourishment, security, and joy, so vividly appropriated in these current symbols, are to be found in their fullest reality in Christ. Bultmann himself appears to us to short-change the full value of the symbols by invoking a dialectic of the divine and the demonic here, in line with his thesis of radical choice.[14]

Thus we may claim that our biblical theological treatment of the myth and symbol of the NT suffers from an inadequate understanding of mytho-poetic language. In the case of Cullmann, we have a scholar whose interpretation submits

---

12. "The Interpretation of the Fourth Gospel," *New Testament Studies*, I, 2 (November, 1954), 80–81.

13. See also the cultural-historical interpretation of the terms, "bread of life" and "water of life" in J. Jeremias, *The Eucharistic Words of Jesus* (New York: Macmillan, 1955), pp. 155–57.

14. The contrast of the good shepherd and the false shepherds of John 10 represents a secondary theme based on Ezekiel which crosses that of the contrast of the "true" shepherd and the Hellenistic shepherd-figures.

itself more readily to the real import of the ancient vehicles of thought. Many feel, however, that in his case a selected body of material is allowed to furnish the larger pattern, while disparate expressions in the biblical text are conformed to it. Bultmann's review of *Christus und die Zeit* made the point effectively. Where in the case of Bultmann and Dodd a quasi-philosophical thesis (Existentialism or Platonism) operates to the disadvantage of the texts, in Cullmann's case, a theological pattern has the same disadvantage. It is perhaps unfair to reproach these masters in our field for seeking a unifying thesis in terms of which so rich a documentation can be given structure. We all do the same thing. Our only purpose is to expose better the basic problems of religious discourse with which we are concerned.

III

I have stated earlier that, as historians, we find that our tools for dealing with the symbolic elements in our texts are not altogether adequate. Neither are we satisfied with some of the attempts that have been made to provide such tools or to invoke new methods. I have given some examples of such proposals. Their defect lies, it seems to me, in an inadequate understanding of symbolic discourse. For light on the matter, I suggest that we turn to contemporary work on this problem, especially to literary criticism and esthetics. The question of myth and symbol is very much to the fore in these circles. One can say that both literary criticism and theology have one dominant theme today: that of the nature of symbolic statement. Bultmann is concerned finally with the same basic issue in theology which interests critics like T. S. Eliot, I. A. Richards, Jacques Maritain, and others. The attention given to writers like William Blake, Herman Melville, Dostoyevsky, Kafka, etc., revolves about basic matters of myth and symbol and their interpretation.

In many ways, the workers in esthetics have explored these matters more profitably than the theologians. This may be partly because they have learned much from anthropology and psychology. In any case, the theologian has been handicapped in this field. We see three special factors which tend to obscure the real nature of imaginative symbolism for the theologian: 1) a dogmatic prejudgment may impose the view that the biblical imagery is literally true, thus obscuring its real significance and forfeiting the kind of truth it does convey; 2) a sentimental prejudgment, associated with religious idealism, may jumble all such imagery together as "mere poetry" and so obscure its rich and specific import; 3) a rationalistic prejudgment may operate in a reductive way to extract this or that idea or doctrine. There is a cognitive element in myth, but it is not of this order. Now when we turn to the work of the literary critics and others today who have been interested in the character of symbolic discourse, we find pointers to our own task as follows:

1. Our critics tell us, for one thing, that mytho-poetic statements have a dynamic dramatic character resting on deep cultural associations. They represent the "available past" in potent form. When we are dealing with such social myth and symbol, we are dealing with the dynamics of group life. We have here the images which are used recurrently like signals to renew group loyalties and to arouse action. This whole aspect of mythology is, of course, well understood by the "myth and ritual" school. The main point for the exegete to understand here is that the symbol in question draws its meaning from its concrete social context. Evidently literalism in interpretation is ruled out, but also any colorless theological interpretation. Take, for instance, such an image as that of the New Jerusalem. This is not to be understood as gratuitous, as a merely idealistic symbol, easily exchangeable for some other token of frustrated aspiration. The particular figures are intended and specific and should be taken in all their concreteness as suggested by their social antecedents.

2. Our modern students of symbol tell us, in the second place, that myth and mytho-poetic statement cannot be paraphrased; they cannot be translated into a discursive equivalent. This means that they cannot be demythologized. They cannot properly even be remythologized. Such concrete, plastic representation of reality or process cannot be reduced to a philosophical or theological equivalent. A poem cannot be summarized in an outline or paraphrase. "Poetic truth is inseparable from poetic form." For example here, take the eschatological mythology which we find in the Gospels. The pictorial, somatic language must be accorded its right if we are to put ourselves in the place of Jesus or the Evangelists. It was not meant prosaically and literally. It was not meant allegorically. It was not meant "poetically" in the sense, that is, of gratuitous embellishment. It is not to be taken as a form of crude science or as an expression of the boundary situation at which man stands over against the future. —In the discussion between Karl Jaspers and Bultmann over the question of mythology,[15] we are afforded two examples of what seem to me to be misunderstandings of the pictorial language of the Scriptures. Jaspers characterizes the mythological expressions of the NT as "Cyphers," that is, as code terms or symbols. On this view, the mythological discourse is cypher-speech, indicative of Transcendence. "Myth," says Jaspers, "is speech concerning a reality which is not empirical reality, that reality with which we live existentially." Bultmann rejects the implication here that all mythologies can be lumped together as mere pointers to the dimension of Transcendence. Bultmann rightly insists on the variety of ancient mythologies and argues that each one, biblical, Greek, Indic, discloses a different sense of existence.[16] He thus rightly recognizes the idiosyncrasy of each mythology. But,

---

15. Bultmann, "Zur Frage der Entmythologisierung: Antwort an Karl Jaspers," *Theologische Zeitschrift*, X, 2 (März-April, 1954), 81–95.

16. *Ibid.*, pp. 85–86.

nevertheless, he reduces the meaning of NT eschatology, as of the others, to the "sense of existence" implied in it. This would seem to be an undue abstraction of the full-bodied symbolic discourse.

3. A final emphasis in the modern discussion of symbol, and one particularly important for us, runs as follows. Following on Coleridge, modern literary critics have pointed out that a poem or unit of mythopoetic discourse represents a fusion in one act of the imagination of many contributory and often apparently contradictory aspects of experience. The poet interprets the heterogeneity and disorder of common experience by a synthetic act of vision, often by the use of a mythological pattern. So far as any particular writing is concerned, this means the use of various older strata of imagery adapted to new uses. Thus, such heavily symbolic passages as Mark 13, Philippians 2, or the Book of Revelation as a whole, are "synthetic and palimpsestic," as is the wisdom which they incorporate.

The imaginative act is such that the most subtle and profound aspects of experience can be included. The medium is therefore adequate to the totality of awareness in a way not at all possible to discursive statement. Moreover, the distinction between emotional and intellectual activity is transcended. Mythological statement represents knowledge of a kind. It has a cognitive aspect. It represents not merely an emotional reaction to reality but a judgment about reality, an account of reality, and an account based upon this kind of concrete and subtle experience. Of course, there are differences in the degree of truth of such accounts. But the pictorial affirmations are to be taken seriously in their particularity. The corollaries for us of this view of symbolic statement are that we shall expect to find wisdom in NT myth, but not a wisdom that can be identified with some prose statement or some theological formula. The images or the fable must be assigned their rights in terms of all their connotations.

This paper has been concerned with method and with presuppositions. We do not have space here to apply our theses to various NT passages or conceptions. Some of these have already been suggested. We are dealing with a mythopoetic mentality and not with a prosaic or discursive one. We cannot apply to the imaginative representations in question our modern alternatives of literal versus symbolic. They were meant neither literally nor symbolically, but naively. The meaning of the imagery is to be found in the associations and connotations it possessed, discoverable for us in their traditions. These meanings and associations had a very concrete social-cultural reference, something quite different from what we mean by a philological or theological context. Just as the imagery has concrete social reference backwards, so it has reference at the time of writing to actual historical realities in the environment of the Church.

Thus, what we call the theologumena of "the principalities and powers" is not to be understood in an abstracting theological way but in a quasi-sociological way. The early Church interpreted political and social and cultural forces mythologically—in the attempt to speak most significantly about them—but we should not be misled into thinking that the Church was only concerned here with otherworldly realities. I began by saying that, as historians, we have been troubled by the problem of how to find tools and methods to deal with the mytho-poetic element in the Bible. And we have been troubled by some of the proposals that have been made, whether of the "cult and ritual" school or of one or other biblical-theological kind. I do not pretend to have solved the problem, but I believe that the results of contemporary discussion of symbolism, as I have outlined them, at least serve to correct prevailing misunderstandings in our field and open the way to more satisfactory interpretation.

The Dead Sea Discoveries:
Retrospect and Challenge*

J. Philip Hyatt
Vanderbilt University

When an Arab named Muhammed ed-Dib in the spring of 1947 stumbled upon the first of the manuscripts which have come to be known as the Dead Sea scrolls, he set in motion a series of events the consequences of which he could not possibly have foreseen. If he could have looked into the future, he would have seen sensational statements made by scholars and non-scholars, a great flood of learned books and articles, popular articles in magazines such as *The Reader's Digest, Life, The New Yorker,* and many others, four paper-backed books, and even a choral work by an American composer based on one of the Thanksgiving Psalms. Muhammed ed-Dib could hardly have predicted that the discoveries he started would some day be used as a basis for questioning the uniqueness and truth of Christianity and even the divinity of Jesus Christ.

As we approach the tenth anniversary of these initial discoveries, this is a good time to look backward and ask, Where do we stand now? and to look forward and ask, What are these discoveries likely to mean for biblical scholarship? I have used in the title of this paper "The Dead Sea Discoveries" and not simply "The Dead Sea Scrolls," because the proper assessment of the scrolls requires that they be studied in the total context of all the discoveries made in and near the original cave—all of the Qumran caves, Khirbet Qumran, the cemetery, the caves of Wadi Murabbaat, and some as yet unidentified sites. (The MSS of Kh. Mird apparently are from a different age and setting.)

I

Looking back, we can see a number of unfortunate circumstances and events. It is regrettable that the initial discoveries were made by accident rather than by

---

* The Presidential Address delivered at the annual meeting of the Society of Biblical Literature and Exegesis on December 27, 1956, at the Union Theological Seminary, New York.

trained archeologists, and that many of the subsequent discoveries have been at the hands of natives. This has led to varying accounts of the initial discovery; we shall probably never know all of the details with accuracy. We may never know precisely where some of the documents were found. All of this, however, is not really important. Biblical scholars should gratefully accept archeological discoveries however they are made. In point of fact, many of the most important discoveries in archeology have been made by accident.

We may regret the failure on the part of some competent scholars to recognize the value of the Qumran scrolls. This must be attributed to the native caution and conservatism of responsible scholars, which has been offset by a few premature statements made by both experts and non-experts. It is unfortunate that some scholars have been led prematurely into taking positions, which they have felt constrained to maintain even when later evidence should have led to their abandonment. Far-reaching theories have been advanced by some scholars who have seemed to claim the possession of "inside information" concerning the contents of some of the MSS, when in reality they have not had such information.

From one point of view, this group of discoveries has had too "good" a press. When a writer of the stature of Edmund Wilson writes a popular article and book on the Dead Sea scrolls, he is bound to attract much attention. The widespread popular interest in the scrolls must be attributed partly to the revival of interest in our time in the Bible and in all things religious.

If there have been unfortunate elements connected with these discoveries, there have been on the other hand fortunate circumstances for which we are thankful. One of these is the courage of two young scholars, John Trever and William H. Brownlee, in carefully examining the scrolls when other scholars had turned away from them. We should be particularly grateful to Trever for his care and competence in making photographs of the scrolls under very trying conditions.

We should be grateful too for the prompt and efficient publication of materials by Millar Burrows, the late E. L. Sukenik, and others; and for the activities of responsible officials and scholars in Palestine who have sought to appraise all materials brought to them and purchase those that are authentic.

II

After looking backward in this way we may go on to describe the present status of the discoveries.

First, there should be no question now as to the genuineness of these MSS. At the outset some doubts were cast upon the authenticity of the scrolls (and even the word "hoax" was used), but such doubts should be completely dissipated by the great scope of the discoveries as we now see them, by the large number of different handwritings that appear on the MSS, and by the fact that responsible scholars have found MSS under controlled scientific conditions. The Dead Sea scrolls will not suffer the fate of Piltdown Man! On the contrary, it has been claimed that these discoveries may lead to the authentication of the scroll of Deuteronomy offered for sale by Shapira seventy years ago, and declared at the time to be a forgery.[1]

The question of the general date of the principal Dead Sea MSS and related materials should no longer be a matter for serious debate. They date from some time in the second century B.C. to approximately A.D. 70 for Qumran (with a few materials probably from the late third century B.C., and a few later than A.D. 70), and down to A.D. 135 for Murabbaat. This date is supported by converging lines of evidence: archeological context, paleography, the nature of the language (the Hebrew is like that of the latest books in the OT and Mishnaic Hebrew), radiocarbon dating, historical allusions (though these are mostly vague and imprecise), and textual studies, especially comparison with the LXX. We should stress the primary importance of the archeological materials found in connection with the MSS, especially the 750 coins found at Khirbet Qumran. Ceramic materials of similar or identical nature bind together chronologically the caves, the community center, and the cemetery. There is nothing in any of the evidence which contradicts the dating by archeological context. Of course the exact dating of the composition or inscribing of particular documents is a problem for continuing debate.

The organization which built the community center at Khirbet Qumran and preserved the MSS was a Jewish community which was ascetic, eschatological, and bound together by common ownership of property. There is some kind of close relationship between this group and the Essenes.[2] We may call it "Essene" if we employ that term in a broad sense, and understand that some variations must have taken place in Essene practice and belief in the course of history; some of the variations arose from differences in time and some from differences in place. The Qumran documents span a period of at least two centuries, and these were crucial centuries in which many changes occurred. The evidence does not support the view that the Qumran sectaries were Jewish Christians or Ebionites.

III

What of the future of studies in the Dead Sea materials? In speaking to a body such as the Society of Biblical Literature one naturally emphasizes the importance

---

1. This celebrated case is being re-studied by Prof. Menahem Mansoor of the University of Wisconsin, who will publish the results of his investigations soon. See provisionally Geoffrey Wigoder, "The 'Shapira Scroll' Mystery," *The Jewish News,* August 17, 1956, p. 8 (reprinted from the *Jerusalem Post*).

2. This is treated in most of the books on the Qumran discoveries; see most recently B. J. Roberts, "The Qumran Scrolls and the Essenes," *New Testament Studies,* III (1955), 58–65. On the other hand, cf. M. H. Gottstein, "Anti-Essene Traits in the Dead Sea Scrolls," *Vetus Testamentum,* IV (1954), 141–47.

of patient, careful, and cooperative study by scholars in all the fields of learning which impinge upon these discoveries. Some of the problems can best be solved by OT critics, some by NT scholars, and still others by those who are versed in rabbinic learning. In the interest of objectivity, in an area in which objectivity may be especially difficult, studies must be carried on by both Protestants and Catholics, and by Jews as well as Christians. No single scholar is learned enough to pass judgment on all the problems involved. It is absurd to suggest—as has been done in popular books[3]—that scholars are "afraid" to study the Dead Sea materials and face the problems they raise. That is not true, as anyone can attest who has seen even a small proportion of the articles and books that have been written. We ought to take special note of the large number of important contributions at various levels which have been made by Roman Catholic scholars, both in America and abroad.[4]

With some trepidation I want now to express my opinion as to the present status and the challenge of the Dead Sea discoveries in several specific areas. I do this with trepidation partly because of the remarks I have just made, and partly because my field of specialization is only the OT. These opinions are presented not in a spirit of partisanship or dogmatism, but largely as suggestions concerning the direction future research may take.

A. *Higher Criticism of the Old Testament.* The discoveries have contributed little of a direct nature in this area, but in the course of time they may contribute much indirectly.

At the time of this writing the only book which is not represented at all is Esther. This may support the view that the book is extremely late, perhaps as late as the second century B.C.[5] Of course, its absence may indicate only that it was not recognized at Qumran. Further, the fact that Daniel is represented in what appears to be non-canonical physical form seems to support the widely held view that it was composed in the second century B.C., or partly in the third and partly in the second. (Canonical books are usually written on leather, in the Jewish bookhand or in the paleo-Hebrew script, and the columns tend to be in length double their width.)[6]

---

3. Edmund Wilson, *The Scrolls from the Dead Sea* (New York, 1955), pp. 98–100; A. Powell Davies, *The Meaning of the Dead Sea Scrolls* (New York, 1956), pp. 23–25.

4. See, e. g., the large number of articles in *Revue biblique* and *Catholic Biblical Quarterly,* and the popular volume, Roland E. Murphy, O. Carm., *The Dead Sea Scrolls and the Bible* (Westminster, Md., 1956).

5. R. H. Pfeiffer, *Introduction to the Old Testament* (New York, 1941), p. 742, dates it about 125 B.C., under John Hyrcanus.

6. Frank M. Cross, Jr., *JBL,* LXXV (1956), 122–23. A possible source of Daniel 4 is the "Prayer of Nabonidus" found in Cave IV, in Aramaic in fragmentary form; see J. T. Milik, *RB,* LXIII (July 1956), 407–15.

Some scholars have maintained that the Dead Sea discoveries tend to disprove the Maccabean dating of any of the Psalms, and the late dating of materials in the prophetic books.[7] As for the Psalms, if the fragments of MSS of the Psalter are from the second century B.C., a Maccabean dating of individual psalms is probably to be ruled out. As for the prophetic books, the dating of materials in them as late as the first century B.C., and probably the second century, must be excluded, but there is no evidence yet to rule out the dating of individual oracles in the Hellenistic age before the Maccabean revolt. In these matters we must await the further publication of materials, and more detailed studies.

B. *Textual Criticism of the Old Testament.* This is an area in which the discoveries are proving to be of tremendous value.

Because of the surprising degree of correspondence between the two Isaiah scrolls and the MT, we have overemphasized the value of the scrolls in supporting that text. The nature of the LXX version of Isaiah should warn us to go slowly, for it is one of the poorest translations in the OT. More complete study of the Isaiah scrolls, and of many fragments which have been published or studied in unpublished form, suggest that we may soon be able to set up several families of MSS, or text-types.[8] Thus the OT textual critic may find himself in a position similar to that of the NT textual critic, yet without the abundance of riches possessed by the latter.

At present we can distinguish at least three pre-Masoretic recensions or text-types: 1) One is a proto-Masoretic type represented particularly in the Isaiah scrolls.[9] 2) Another may be described as corresponding to the *Vorlage* of LXX; it is represented particularly by the fragments of Samuel and other historical books.[10] 3) The third is like the Samaritan recension of the Pentateuch.[11] In time other text-types may be identified, and by careful and complicated comparisons we may be able to get back to a Hebrew text that is prior to all of these. At Qumran there was considerable freedom, and some books appear in more than one form.[12] We cannot be sure that Jerusalem was as free in such matters as was Qumran.

---

7. See, e. g., Charles T. Fritsch, *The Qumran Community, Its History and Scrolls* (New York, 1956), p. 47.

8. W. F. Albright, "New Light on Early Recensions of the Hebrew Bible," *BASOR*, No. 140 (Dec. 1955), pp. 27–33; C. Rabin, "The Dead Sea Scrolls and the History of the OT Text," *Journal of Theological Studies*, VI N.S. (1955), 174–82; Moshe Greenberg, "The Stabilization of the Text of the Hebrew Bible, Reviewed in the Light of the Biblical Materials from the Judean Desert," *JAOS*, LXXVI (1955), 157–67.

9. Patrick W. Skehan, "The Text of Isaias at Qumran," *CBQ*, XVII (1955), 158–63.

10. Cross, "A New Qumran Biblical Fragment Related to the Original Hebrew Underlying the Septuagint," *BASOR*, No. 132 (Dec. 1953), pp. 15–26, and *JBL*, LXXIV (1955), 165–72.

11. Skehan, "Exodus in the Samaritan Recension from Qumran," *JBL*, LXXIV(1955), 182–87.

12. For example, Jeremiah is represented in two forms, one corresponding to the LXX, and one to the MT. See in general, "Le travail d'édition des fragments manuscrits de Qumrân," *RB*, LXIII (1956), 49–67.

This study will necessitate the extensive revision of all our editions of the OT, and will raise many problems. The most difficult question will be: When we have studied and defined the various text-types, which should we consider as "original"? Further, the question of the relationship of an "original" text to the ultimately canonical text will pose serious questions. The whole question of canonicity, and the date of the fixing of the canon, will have to be re-studied. Tentatively I suggest that there was a difference between the general acceptance of a book as canonical or authoritative on the one hand, and on the other hand the fixing of the text of that book so that it was considered sacrosanct. We shall probably find that the Academy of Jamnia had much more to do than we have usually thought, both in fixing the canon and in establishing the authoritative text. Before that time there was a great amount of freedom, among both Jews and Christians.

C. *The Nature of Early Judaism.* The Dead Sea discoveries have helped to reveal the fluidity, variety, and great vitality of Judaism in the period of the first two centuries B.C. and the first century of the Christian era. Previously it has been difficult for scholars to study Judaism before the year A.D. 70, partly because of the nature of the rabbinic sources. Now we have available materials which are clearly pre-70; they must be carefully compared with the apocryphal and pseudepigraphic materials, Josephus, Philo, tannaitic literature, etc. The Dead Sea discoveries have shown the importance in this period of the apocalyptic-messianic element in Judaism, which was to a large extent suppressed or obscured after A.D. 70, subsequent to the rise of Christianity.[13]

We should be careful in referring to the Judean Covenanters or Essenes as a "sect," if by that term we imply that they were heretical. This would be mistaken, because there was no generally recognized "orthodoxy," and because the Covenanters clearly lived by the Torah, as they interpreted it, and considered themselves the true Israel. There have been discussions as to whether they were Pharisaic or Sadducean in tendency. Paradoxical as it may seem, they were probably at the outset hyper-Pharisaical in many respects in their observance of the Law,[14] but at the same time they were anti-Hasmonean Sadducees.[15] They arose in a time before the differences between the Pharisees and Sadducees had crystallized.

D. *Christian Origins.* The significance of these discoveries for Christian scholars is greatest at this point. Yet it must be said, in all candor, that NT scholars and

---

13. Cf. Louis Ginzberg, "Some Observations on the Attitude of the Synagogue Towards the Apocalyptic-Eschatological Writings," *JBL*, XLI (1922), 115-36.

14. Cf. Louis Ginzberg, *Eine unbekannte jüdische Sekte*, Erster Teil (New York, 1922), pp. 177-85, 228-32; and Saul Lieberman, "The Discipline in the So-Called Dead Sea Manual of Discipline," *JBL*, LXXI (1952), 199-206.

15. Cf. Robert North, "The Qumran 'Sadducees,'" *CBQ*, XVII (1955), 164-88; and A. M. Haberman, "The Dead Sea Scrolls—A Survey and a New Interpretation," *Judaism: A Quarterly Journal of Jewish Life and Thought*, V (Fall 1956), 306-15.

specialists in early Christian history—especially in America—have not made the most of the opportunities presented by the Dead Sea discoveries.[16] Many of the books and articles dealing with them, and perhaps the most widely publicized opinions regarding their significance, have come from specialists in the OT field rather than from those who are most at home in NT study. This is unfortunate. The simplest explanation for this situation is the fact that these MSS are for the most part in Hebrew, and in "unpointed" Hebrew at that; many NT specialists are not able to study them at first hand. It has sometimes seemed to me that we are faced with a situation similar to that which prevailed a decade or two ago with respect to the problem of the Aramaic origin of certain NT books. Most of the scholars who held to the Aramaic origin of these books were Semitists and specialists in OT, who did not know as much as they should about the NT. Yet many of the NT scholars who criticized them were not able to control the primary sources.

In the course of time we should have editions of the Dead Sea MSS—those which are not altogether fragmentary—in vocalized Hebrew, even if we cannot be certain that the vocalization is wholly accurate. A. M. Haberman has made an excellent beginning in his book *'Edah we-'Eduth*.[17] When this is done, NT scholars will be in better position to read the documents themselves.

In the area of Christian origins, some scholars have been altogether too imaginative in seeing parallels to or foreshadowings of Christianity; on the other hand, some have painfully denied the obvious. Historical objectivity in this area is not easy!

At the risk of departing from my own field, let me express a few opinions and raise some questions regarding the importance of the Dead Sea discoveries for Christian origins.

1. These discoveries reveal a Jewish sect whose beliefs and practices were seriously influenced by non-Hebraic sources, either Iranian or Hellenistic or both. The most obvious influence was on the dualism of the sect, presented clearly in 1QS 3.17–4.26. The sect may be described as syncretistic in very much the same sense that early Christianity was syncretistic.[18] The Judean Covenanters held ideas deviating from OT beliefs, but on Judean soil and not far from Jerusalem. The significance of this for the origin of the Fourth Gospel[19] and for Paul's theol-

---

16. Albright, commenting briefly on the volume of studies in honor of C. H. Dodd (see note 19 below), says: "Even the Dead Sea Scrolls are noticed in a few papers, though the volume as a whole reflects the prevailing unwillingness of Anglo-American New Testament scholars to admit that such disconcerting documents exist." (*BASOR*, No. 142 [April 1956], p. 36).

17. Jerusalem, 1952 (Hebrew).

18. Cf. Rudolf Bultmann, *Primitive Christianity in its Contemporary Setting* (New York, 1956), pp. 175–79, 213–14.

19. See especially Raymond E. Brown, "The Qumran Scrolls and the Johannine Gospel and Epistles," *CBQ*, XVII (1955), 403–19, 559–74; and Albright, "Recent Discoveries in Pales-

ogy[20] has been pointed out. The net effect of the Dead Sea discoveries will be to make it possible to place more books of the NT, and thus more of the basic Christian ideas, upon Palestinian soil rather than the soil of Diaspora Judaism.

2. The sect which preserved the documents was a "literal" apocalyptic sect. The members believed they were living in the end of time, and were expecting the day of judgment and the culmination of "this age." The very existence of such a sect in Judea tends to support the interpretation of the Schweitzer school which saw early Christianity as an apocalyptic community in a very literal sense. Yet this group did not have what would now be termed an *Interimsethik,* inasmuch as the Manual of Discipline (1QS) lays down specific and precise rules for the ongoing life of the community. This has considerable bearing on the nature of early Christian ethics, and the interpretation of a document such as the Sermon on the Mount. At the same time, an element of "realized eschatology" can be seen in the directions for the "messianic banquet" given in 1QSa. This was (in my opinion) a real meal, but it anticipated the messianic banquet of the future age.

3. Does not the existence of the Essene communities make it more probable that Jesus consciously sought to organize a community of his disciples and followers? Many NT scholars believe that Jesus did not intend to establish a "church" but consider its establishment as a development that followed the death of Jesus. Yet the early Christian community reminds one in a number of respects of the Essene community—not so much of the tight-knit monastic community of Qumran as the "third order" type which must have existed in many towns and villages of Judea, if Philo and Josephus are correct. The group surrounding Jesus had a body of twelve apostles, an inner circle of three most-favored disciples, and a large group of followers. Is it not even possible that the community of possessions described in Acts (2:44–45; 4:32–37), similar to that practiced at Qumran, goes back to the lifetime of Jesus? It has always been difficult to explain how Jesus and his immediate disciples made a living. Possibly they practiced community ownership of goods and wages. Passages such as Luke 12:33 and John 12:6 could be adduced in support of this view.

A study should be made comparing the names used by the Qumran sect for itself and its individual members, and the corresponding early Christian terms. One of the commonest words used at Qumran for the community as a whole was עדה; this is the proper word in the OT for the true community of Israel. The LXX usually translates it as συναγωγη, a word used once in the NT for a Christian church (Jas 2:2). This corresponds to the Aramaic כנישתא, which in the view of some scholars was the earliest word for "church." The Qumran sect apparently did

---

tine and the Gospel of John," in *The Background of the New Testament and Eschatology,* ed. W. D. Davies and D. Daube (Cambridge, 1956), pp. 153–71.

20. Cf. S. E. Johnson, "Paul and the Manual of Discipline," *Harvard Theological Review,* XLVIII (1955), 157–65.

not often employ קהל, which is the word usually rendered in LXX by εκκλησια (which is not used to render עדה).[21]

One of the commonest words used in the NT for an individual member of the early Christian community or church was "saint" (αγιος). This corresponds to three words in the OT: חסיד, frequently used in Psalms of pious, godly men; קדוש, used of men at least in Pss 16:3; 34:9; 106:16 (but employed for divine beings in passages such as Job 5:1; 15:15; Ps 89:5, 7); and the Aram. קדיש in Dan 7:18ff. The latter two are rendered in LXX by αγιος, חסיד usually by οσιος. In one passage of the Qumran *Hodayot* (1QH 4.24–25) סוד קדושים refers to human beings;[22] in some other passages it signifies angels or divine beings. The clue is provided by the mystical idea expressed in 1QH 11.9–14, that God reveals to chosen men his mysteries, cleanses them of transgressions, and enables them to "share the lot of thy holy ones" (בגורל עם קדושיכה). The OT background for this is the belief that the true prophet was permitted to stand in the "council (סוד) of Yahweh," as expressed most clearly in Jer 23:18–22.[23]

It has been pointed out that the organization of the early Christian churches may have been seriously influenced by that of the Essenes. Here we may note that the word פקיד, which is used at least once of an Essene overseer (1QS 6.14), is translated in the LXX by επισκοπος (Judg 9:28; Neh 11:9, 14, 22).

4. It is now generally believed that the vernacular language of Palestine in the first century was Aramaic. It may therefore seem surprising that most of the documents found at Qumran are in Hebrew. Even the letters of Bar Kochba are in Hebrew, not Aramaic. There must have been a revival of the use of Hebrew in Maccabean times, which continued for the following two or three centuries. A number of competent scholars have raised the question whether Hebrew may not have been the vernacular (or a vernacular) of first-century Palestine.[24] It

---

21. See J. Y. Campbell, "The Origin and Meaning of the Christian Use of the Word ΕΚΚΛΗΣΙΑ," *JTS*, XLIX (1948), 130–42. He disputes the commonly accepted view that the early Christians, in using εκκλησια, were borrowing an OT term (equivalent to קהל) to express their claim to be the true people of God. He says that εκκλησια was simply an obvious name for those simple "meetings" which the Christians held, with some precedent in Psalms and Ecclesiastes, and in Hellenistic usage. In the course of time it came to mean the body of people who habitually met together. Qumran usage should be studied carefully to see whether it supports this view.

22. "They that walk in the way of thy heart have hearkened unto me, and rallied to thee in the council of the holy ones." T. H. Gaster translates "in the legion of the saints." Cf. the same expression in Ps 89:7, used of heavenly beings. 1QH 3.21 speaks of men who are fashioned from dust "for the eternal council" (לסוד עולם).

23. See H. Wheeler Robinson, "The Council of Yahweh," *JTS*, XLV (1944), 151–57, and Cross, "The Council of Yahweh in Second Isaiah," *JNES*, XII (1953), 274–77. Cf. Phil 3:20 "our commonwealth (πολιτευμα) is in heaven."

24. The question has been recently opened by Harris Birkeland, *The Language of Jesus* (Oslo, 1954), who believes that "the language of the common people in the time of Jesus was

may have been a Hebrew greatly influenced by Aramaic. At any rate, it would appear that many of the documents composed in the period of the first century B.C. and first century A.D. were in Hebrew, and that such writing was much more common than is often supposed. Is it not likely that τα λογια of Matthew "in the Hebrew language" (Εβραιδι διαλεκτω) of which Papias spoke were really written in Hebrew, and that Hebrew documents lie back of passages such as the first two chapters of Luke?[25]

5. The פשרים and the lists of prophetic *testimonia* which have been found among the Dead Sea discoveries give us excellent background for study of the early Christian use and interpretation of the OT. The פשרים were not commentaries in the modern sense, nor do they correspond closely to the early rabbinic commentaries. In Daniel, the word פשר means "solution of a mystery." The פשרים are apocalyptic works in which the reader is given a key by which to solve the mysteries of prophetic books or other OT passages, and understand how veiled predictions made in them were being fulfilled in his own time. The early Christians made similar use of the OT, for they viewed it in much the same way. A great amount of freedom characterizes the early Christian as well as the Essene interpretation of the OT.

6. Many studies have been made suggesting influences of Essene ideas and beliefs upon early Christianity. In the future the documents must be very carefully combed so that these ideas may be fully studied and put in their proper setting. It should not be surprising that early Christianity was in one manner or another influenced by these ideas. It is not necessary to suppose that John the Baptist, Jesus, or any of his closest disciples had been Essenes or Judean Covenanters. In all likelihood, however, some of the early Christians had been connected in one way or another with Essene communities. However, the theory of "diffusion of ideas" is sufficient to account for the influence, since the communities apparently existed in many villages and towns of Judea; Qumran may have been the "headquarters," but not the only community.

IV

Finally, a few words may be said about the question of the originality or "truth" of early Christianity, and the bearing of the Dead Sea discoveries upon the question of the divinity of Jesus Christ. These matters have loomed large in many of the popular discussions of the scrolls. Two remarks are in place here.

Hebrew." He thinks that Jesus "really used Hebrew"; however, he understood both Biblical Hebrew and Aramaic, could read the OT in Hebrew, and probably knew some Greek. Cf. M. H. Segal, *A Grammar of Mishnaic Hebrew* (Oxford, 1927), p. 6.

25. Is it not possible now to believe that τη Εβραιδι διαλεκτω in Acts 21:40; 22:2; 26:14 really means Hebrew?

First, it must be emphasized that the "truth" of the Christian faith does not rest upon the originality or uniqueness of the teachings of Jesus or of any NT writer. Scholars have long known that there is little in them that is truly original, and that in itself should not be surprising. The Christian faith rests not upon the uniqueness of Jesus' teaching, but upon belief in the incarnation, the belief that "the Word became flesh" in Jesus Christ. For the Christian the incarnation is a unique and unrepeatable event. It is a question of faith, not subject to historical verification. Genuine faith cannot be upset by anything which enriches historical understanding.

Second, I believe that all of us—whether Jew or Christian—should be proud to claim as a part of our heritage those people whom we now know as Judean Covenanters or Essenes. Nearly everything that we know about them shows that they were a people with high ideals, and genuine religious experience. In order to join the Qumran community, a person had to undergo rigorous examination and lengthy probation, make public commitment of himself to the order, renew his covenant annually, and be a constant student of the Scriptures and a faithful member of the order. The qualities emphasized were total commitment to the life and beliefs of the community, obedience to the Torah, respect for one's superiors, love of the brotherhood, justice, humility, simplicity of living, and hatred of all evil. The Christian scholar cannot afford to praise such qualities when he finds them in a Christian group, and condemn the Essenes as narrow and legalistic. The three ancient writers who describe the Essenes praise them in extravagant terms. Philo describes them as "athletes of virtue," and says that many rulers had been "unable to resist the high excellence of these people."[26] Josephus says that "they exceed all other men that addict themselves to virtue, and this in righteousness."[27] Even Pliny speaks of them as "the solitary tribe of the Essenes, which is remarkable beyond all the other tribes in the whole world."[28]

In spite of all we have said about similarities and influences, there were many significant differences between the Essenes and Christianity. It is not correct to say with Renan that "Christianity is an Essenism which has largely succeeded";[29] or with Dupont-Sommer that Christianity was "a quasi-Essene neo-formation."[30] The historian should be thankful for all the new light that has been shed on the history of religion by the Dead Sea discoveries, and the professing Jew or Christian should be proud to claim among his spiritual ancestors the devoted people who produced and preserved the Dead Sea documents.

---

26. *Quod omnis probus liber sit* XIII (Loeb ed., IX, 61–63).
27. *Ant.* XVIII. i. 5.
28. *Natural History* V. xv (Loeb ed., II, 277).
29. "Le christianisme est un essénisme qui a largement réussi," quoted by A. Dupont-Sommer, *Aperçus préliminaires sur les manuscrits de la Mer Morte* (Paris, 1950), p. 121 (English trans., p. 99).
30. *The Jewish Sect of Qumran and the Essenes* (New York, 1955), p. 150.

Parallelomania*

Samuel Sandmel
Hebrew Union College-Jewish Institute of Religion

I encountered the term parallelomania, as I recall, in a French book of about 1830, whose title and author I have forgotten,[1] in a context in which there were being examined certain passages in the Pauline epistles and in the Book of Wisdom that seem to have some resemblance, and a consequent view that when Paul wrote the Epistle to the Romans, a copy of the Book of Wisdom lay open before him, and that Paul in Romans copied generously from it. Three items are to be noted. One, that some passages are allegedly parallel; two, that a direct organic literary connection is assumed to have provided the parallels; and three, that the conclusion is drawn that the flow is in a particular direction, namely, from Wisdom to Paul, and not from Paul to Wisdom. Our French author disputes all three points: he denies that the passages cited are true parallels; he denies that a direct literary connection exists; he denies that Paul copied directly from Wisdom, and he calls the citations and the inferences parallelomania. We might for our purposes define parallelomania as that extravagance among scholars which first overdoes the supposed similarity in passages and then proceeds to describe source and derivation as if implying literary connection flowing in an inevitable or predetermined direction.

The key word in my essay is extravagance. I am not denying that literary parallels and literary influence, in the form of source and derivation, exist. I am not seeking to discourage the study of these parallels, but, especially in the case of the Qumran documents, to encourage them. However, I am speaking words of caution about exaggerations about the parallels and about source and derivation. I shall not exhaust what might be said in all the areas which members of this Soci-

---

* The Presidential Address delivered at the annual meeting of the Society of Biblical Literature and Exegesis on December 27, 1961, at Concordia Theological Seminary, St. Louis, Missouri.

1. A. T. S. Goodrick, *The Book of Wisdom*, New York, 1913, p. 405, apparently attributes the phrase to Menzel, *De Graecis in libris Koheleth et Sophiae vestigiis*, p. 40. Goodrick gives neither the place nor the date of publication. Perhaps it is P. Menzel; cf. Charles, *Apocrypha and Pseudepigrapha of the O.T.*, I, p. 533.

ety might be interested in, but confine myself to the areas of rabbinic literature and the gospels, Philo and Paul, and the Dead Sea Scrolls and the NT. That is to say, my paper is a series of comments primarily in the general area of the literatures relevant to early rabbinic Judaism and early Christianity.

An important consideration is the difference between an abstract position on the one hand and the specific application on the other. Thus, in the case of passages in Samuel-Kings and Chronicles, the concession that parallel passages do exist falls short of determining whether the Chronicler borrowed from the author of Samuel-Kings, or vice versa. That determination rests on inherent probabilities which emerge from close study. Similarly, Matthew may have borrowed from Mark, or Mark from Matthew; and still similarly, John may be later than and a borrower of the Synoptic tradition, or earlier and in some way a source for, or completely different from, the Synoptics. Hence, it is in the detailed study rather than in the abstract statement that there can emerge persuasive bases for judgment. Most of us would, I think, come to the view that the Chronicler borrowed from Samuel-Kings, and not vice versa, this because of clear phenomena in the texts. But elsewhere the phenomena may not be quite so clear. Thus, in the question of the chronological relation of John to the Synoptics, Erwin Goodenough[2] and William F. Albright[3] have adduced two different bases for dating John early instead of late. I would term these bases as abstract rather than applied. Goodenough restricts his argument to the Christology, arguing that the high Christology of John is not only no proof of John's lateness, but conceivably an indication of its earliness, for in Paul too there is an advanced Christology. Albright, in the quest of some relationship between Jesus and the Qumran community, argues that there is no reason to suppose that the Jesus who spoke one way in the Synoptics could not have spoken another way in John. Abstractly, both views are right. Yet when all the factors in the gospel problems are weighed, the decision would seem to be that although John abstractly could have been the earliest, detailed study would incline to the conclusion that it is the last of the gospels.

Abstractly, Qumran might have influenced the NT, or abstractly, it might not have, or Talmud the NT, or the Midrash Philo, or Philo Paul. The issue for the student is not the abstraction but the specific. Detailed study is the criterion, and the detailed study ought to respect the context and not be limited to juxtaposing mere excerpts. Two passages may sound the same in splendid isolation from their context, but when seen in context reflect difference rather than similarity. The neophytes and the unwary often rush in, for example, to suppose that Philo's *nomos agraphos* and the rabbinic *torah she-be'al* pe are one and the same thing,

---

2. "John a Primitive Gospel," in *JBL*, 64 (1945), pp. 145–85.

3. In his essay in William David Davies and David Daube (eds.), *The Background of the New Testament and Its Eschatology*, pp. 153–71.

for unwritten law and oral torah do sound alike.[4] But Philo is dealing with a concept of the relationship of enacted statutes to what the Greek philosophers call pure law, the law of nature, while the rabbis are dealing with the authoritative character of explanations to, and expansions of, the Pentateuch. It turns out from detailed study that the two similar terms have no relationship whatsoever. In this case we have not a true parallel, but only an alleged one.

Moreover, when we deal with rabbinic literature, the gospels, the epistles, the pseudepigrapha, and Philo we are in an area which we can momentarily describe as post-Tanach Judaism. This is the case even if the final canonization of the hagiographa is later than Paul's epistles, and is the case if one will rise above nomenclature and be willing for purposes of discussion to regard Paul's writings as an expression of a Judaism. If, accordingly, all these writings are post-Tanach Judaism, then obviously the Tanach has some status and influence in all of them. What could conceivably surprise us would be the absence of tanach influence from this literature, not its presence. Furthermore, since all this literature is Jewish, it should reasonably reflect Judaism. Paul and the rabbis should overlap, and Paul and Philo and the Qumran writings and the rabbis should overlap. Accordingly, even true parallels may be of no great significance in themselves.

In the variety of the Judaisms, as represented by terms such as Pharisees, Sadducees, Qumran, Therapeutae, it is a restricted area which makes each of these groups distinctive within the totality of Judaisms; it is the distinctive which is significant for identifying the particular, and not the broad areas in common with other Judaisms.

There is nothing to be excited by in the circumstance that the rabbis and Jesus agree that the healing of the sick is permitted on the Sabbath. It would be exciting, though, if rabbinic literature contained a parallel to the "Son of man is lord of the Sabbath." The mote and the beam do not surprise us in appearing in both; certain criticisms of the Pharisees should reasonably appear in both.

For the rabbis and Philo to agree that Noah's righteousness is relative and lower than that of an Abraham or a Moses reflects simply the close study of the Tanach and hence the ascription of some pregnant meaning to a pleonastic work or syllable. Since Genesis describes Noah as righteous "in his generations" we should not be overwhelmed at discovering that the rabbis and Philo unite in inferring from these words a reduced admiration for Noah's righteousness. That Scripture is as a source common to Philo and the rabbis is quite as reasonable a conclusion as that Philo drew the item from the rabbis, or the rabbis from Philo.

These varieties of Judaism, then, are bound to harbor true parallels which are of no consequence. The connections between two or more of these Judaisms is not determined by inconsequential parallels.

---

4. See Isaac Heinemann, "Die Lehre vom Ungeschriebenen Gesetz in Jüdischen Schrifttum," *Hebrew Union College Annual*, 4 (1927), pp. 149–72.

Furthermore, each of us operates within certain biases, and since I have one about Christianity, I must expose it here. It is that I regard early Christianity as a Jewish movement which was in particular ways distinctive from other Judaisms. This distinctiveness is an intertwining of events in, and of theology about, the career of Jesus, whether we can recover that career or not, and the histories of his direct disciples and of later apostles, and what they believed and thought. Only by such a supposition of such distinctiveness can I account to myself for the origin and growth of Christianity and its ultimate separation from Judaism. If, on the other hand, the particular content of early Christianity is contained in and anticipated chronologically by the Dead Sea Scrolls and anachronistically by the rabbinic literature, then I am at a loss to understand the movement. While I hold that Mark was a source utilized by both Matthew and Luke, I am not prepared to believe that the writers of Christian literature only copied sources and never did anything original and creative.

In the case of Paul and the rabbis, let us assume that at no less than 259 places, Paul's epistles contain acknowledged parallels to passages in the rabbis. Would this hypothetical situation imply that Paul and the rabbis are in thorough agreement? No. Is it conceivable that despite the parallels, Paul and the rabbis present attitudes and conclusions about the Torah that are diametrically opposed? Yes. Then what in context would be the significance of the hypothetical parallels? Surely it would be small. I doubt that as many as 59, let alone 259 parallels could be adduced. It was right for the scholarship of two hundred and a hundred years ago to have gathered the true and the alleged parallels. Today, however, it is a fruitless quest to continue to try to find elusive rabbinic sources for everything which Paul wrote. His first and second Adam are not found in the rabbis, the mediation of the angels at Sinai is not found in the rabbis, and his view that the *nomos* is superseded by the advent of the Messiah is not found there. To allude, as some have done, to Paul's use of Scripture as rabbinic exegesis is to forget that Philo and the Qumranites were also exegetes; it is to overlook some elementary issues in chronology. I don't believe that Paul bore the title Rabbi or that there is any genetic connection between the specific content of his epistles, or the theology in them, and that of rabbinic literature. Abstractly, it is conceivable that Paul had nothing of his own to say, and that his achievement was that he was only an eclectic. But this seems to me to break down at two points. First, no rabbinic parallels have been found to that which in Paul is Pauline; and secondly, it took Dupont-Sommer's emendations[5] of the Qumran Scrolls to have them contain pre-Pauline Paulinism. I for one am prepared to believe that Paul was a person of an originality which went beyond the mere echoing of his predecessors or contemporaries. I am prepared to believe that Paul represents more than a hodge-

---

5. See *The Dead Sea Scrolls*, tr. by E. Margaret Rowley, London, 1952, and the various critical assessments.

podge of sources. I find in his epistles a consistency and a cohesiveness of thought that make me suppose that he had some genuine individuality. I admit that I am not a partisan of his views, any more than I am of those of Philo. But I hold that he had a mind of high caliber, and an inventiveness of high order. And even were the 259 hypothetical parallels present, I should want to inquire whether they are significant or merely routine.

Indeed, I should insist on proceeding to the next question, namely, what is the significance in the context of Paul's epistles of these parallels. To distort just a little, I would ask this question, what is the use that Paul makes of those parallels which he allegedly has borrowed?

Paul's context is of infinitely more significance than the question of the alleged parallels. Indeed, to make Paul's context conform to the content of the alleged parallels is to distort Paul. The knowledge on our part of the parallels may assist us in understanding Paul; but if we make him mean only what the parallels mean, we are using the parallels in a way that can lead us to misunderstand Paul.

I am not prepared to suppose that Philo of Alexandria had to go to his mailbox at regular intervals, learn by letter what the rabbis in Palestine were saying, and then be in a position to transmute the newly received data into philosophical ideas. Again, I am not prepared to believe that there was a bridge for one-way traffic that stretched directly from the caves on the west bank of the Dead Sea to Galilee, or even further into Tarsus, Ephesus, Galatia, and Mars Hill. While I am prepared to join in speculations that John the Baptist had some connection with Qumran, I will not accept it as proved without seeing some evidence for it; and I have been considerably surprised at an essay given before this society that speculated on why John had disaffiliated from Qumran.

The various Jewish movements, whether we are satisfied to call them groups or sects or sectarians, make sense to me only if I conceive of them as simultaneously reflecting broad areas of overlapping and restricted areas of distinctiveness. The phrase "restricted areas" is a surface measurement, for its extent could well have been small, but its depth tremendous. Where the literatures present us with acknowledged parallels, I am often more inclined to ascribe these to the common Jewish content of all these Jewish movements than to believe in advance that some item common to the scrolls and the gospels or to Paul implies that the gospels or Paul got that item specifically from the scrolls.

In dealing with Qumran and Ephesians K. G. Kuhn, in "Der Epheser-brief im Lichte der Qumrantexte,"[6] after noting certain parallels which cannot come from a common biblical source, points to what he terms *Traditionszusammenhang*. The existence of a community of postbiblical tradition reflected now in Qumran, now in Philo, now in rabbinic literature, now in the NT, seems most reasonable, especially if one will emend the word into the plural, *Traditionenzusammenhang*,

---

6. *NTSt*, 7 (1960), pp. 334–46.

so as to allow for diversities among the aspects of tradition, as exemplified, for example, by the distinctions between rabbinic midrash and Philo's.

If we are, as I believe, justified in speaking of traditions in plural, then we may call to mind a distinction made a century ago between the so-called hellenistic midrash and the rabbinic. The former term has been used to describe materials found in Philo, Josephus, various apocrypha and pseudepigrapha, and the fragments preserved in Josephus and Eusebius. On the one hand, it is true that the Greek civilization represents a cultural and religious complex different from the Hebraic and Jewish; on the other hand, when Greek civilization penetrated Palestine and when Jews moved into the Greek dispersion, the Greek civilization began to penetrate the Jewish, evoking both a conscious rejection and also an acceptance and adaptation, whether conscious or unconscious. The term "hellenistic Jewish" is often better to describe certain doctrines or ideas than the bare term "hellenistic." But here exists one confusion that I doubt will ever be cleared up. It is this: when we describe something as hellenistic, are we speaking about the language in which an idea is expressed, or are we alluding to some demonstrable difference between a Jewish and a Greek idea? It seems to me that a Greek idea could receive expression in mishnaic or Qumran Hebrew, and a Jewish idea in koine Greek. Or does the term hellenistic Jewish merely describe the geography of a writing? It seems to me that a work written in Greek could have been composed on Palestinian soil, or one written in Hebrew or Aramaic in the Greek dispersion. Granted that language and ideational content can point to a great probability as to the place of origin, we go too far when we move from the probability to a predetermined inference. Therefore, at one and the same time I could assert that plural aspects of post-Tanach traditions marked the various Judaisms and also that these plural traditions do not always lend themselves to ready separation into neat categories. Hence, Qumran can in principle share traditions with the rabbis, with Philo, and with the NT, and on the one hand, Qumran can share certain traditions with the rabbis but not with Philo, certain traditions with Philo and not the rabbis, and certain traditions with NT but not with the rabbis and Philo. And Qumran can be alone in certain traditions.

In the matter of parallels, we could conceivably be justified in speaking of rabbinic versus hellenistic midrash, if we abstain from assuming that no communication took place, and providing we remain prudent in isolating in some given literature that individuality which is the hallmark of it. For Ephesians and Qumran to echo each other has a definite significance; that Ephesians has a Christology lacking in Qumran is even more significant, for it gives us the hallmark of the Christian character of Ephesians. Kuhn is quite right in telling us that "überhaupt gibt es zur Christologie ... von Qumran keinerlei Parallelen."

It would seem to me to follow that, in dealing with similarities we can sometimes discover exact parallels, some with and some devoid of significance; seeming parallels which are so only imperfectly; and statements which can be called parallels only by taking them out of context. I must go on to allege that I encounter from time to time scholarly writings which go astray in this last regard. It is the question of excerpt versus context, which I have touched on and now return to.

Let me lead into this by a related matter, for thereafter the danger in studying parallels only in excerpts can become clearer. Over a century ago the Jewish historian Graetz identified Jesus as an Essene, and in the subsequent decades there was almost as much written on the Essenes as there has been in the last decade. The earliest literary source on the Essenes is Philo's treatise entitled "That Every Good Man is Free," wherein Philo illustrates a theme by his description of the Essenes. That theme is that the life of *askesis* is both commendable and viable for attaining perfection. A second essay by Philo, "On the Contemplative Life," argues that still another way to perfection, that of contemplation, is commendable and viable, and is illustrated by the Therapeutae. Indeed, at the beginning of the essay on the Therapeutae Philo hearkens back to his "That Every Good Man is Free."

One cannot understand Philo's intent fully without some recourse to Philo's other writings. It is not methodologically sound, in view of the preservation of so much of Philo's writing, to study the material in isolation on the Essenes in "That Every Good Man is Free." The person who immerses himself in Philo necessarily goes on to note that *askesis* is symbolized recurrently by Jacob and contemplation by Abraham; a third way to perfection is intuition, symbolized by Isaac.

I have to state that my studies in Philo lead me to regard him as an apologist, and a preacher, and to have no great confidence in the reliability of his reports on either the Therapeutae or the Essenes. In the case of the latter, I suspect we deal with Philo's third-hand knowledge and not his direct contact on any intensive basis, for Philo was an Alexandrian whose known visits to Palestine turn out to number exactly one. A study of Philo discloses, for example, that he can say of Abraham's father Terah that the name means to spy out odor, and that Terah only asked questions but never got to knowledge, and that Terah is the character whom the Greeks called Socrates. Hence, I find myself somewhat disinclined to take Philo's historical statements too seriously. Moreover, he tells us that the meaning of Abraham's marriage to Hagar is that Abraham went to college, and then he proceeds to deny that Hagar and Sarah are historical characters. Accordingly my skepticism increases about his reliability. Indeed, when I consider the apologetic tendencies, and concomitant distortions, in both Philo and Josephus, I find myself taking what they say with elaborate grains of salt. Josephus tells us that the Essenes were Neo-Pythagoreans. Indeed, he makes philosophers out of all Jews, equating the movements with Greek philosophical schools. To my mind, we encounter in Josephus not precision but pretension.

I do not trust what Philo and Josephus tell about the Essenes. About six years ago I wrote that to identify the Qumran community with the Essenes is to explain one unknown by another. I should phrase it a little differently today. I would never try to identify the Qumran community by the Essenes, but I incline to some willingness to identify the Essenes by the Qumran community.

If it is foolhardy to take without sifting a long parallel from Philo's "That Every Good Man is Free," how much more foolhardy is it to take out of context a sentence from one of his laborious allegories and use it for comparison. Wilfred Knox's cautious listing of passages in Philo which have some echoes in Paul seems sounder to me than Gerald Friedlander's view that Paul had necessarily read Philo.

Harry Wolfson and Louis Ginzberg have recorded many passages which presumably reflect parallels between the rabbis and Philo. Inasmuch as the overlappings in the varieties of Judaisms would reasonably suggest that parallels would appear, it is striking that most of the paired passages which these two cite are actually not parallels, but are instead statements of considerable difference. I have discussed this at length in my book, *Philo's Place in Judaism,* and I need not here repeat myself. There I contend that Wolfson and Ginzberg suppose that parallels, both the true and the alleged, mean that Philo drew on the rabbis, as though there was no creativity in the Alexandrian Jewish community. I would only suggest that if a Wolfson, who wrote a magnificent two-volume book on Philo, could be mistaken so often about parallels, it is not prudent for the mere amateur to rush into excerpts from Philo.

What shall we make of the five immense books which constitute the Strack and Billerbeck *Kommentar zum Neuen Testament aus Talmud und Midrasch*? Let us grant that it is a useful tool. So is a hammer, if one needs to drive nails. But if one needs to bisect a board, then a hammer is scarcely the useful tool. Four major errors in the use of Strack and Billerbeck, caused by its construction, mar its usefulness. The first is to be stated as follows. When Luke, presumably of Roman origin, appends editorializing comments to Mark, then it is scarcely likely that rabbinic passages can serve as persuasive parallels or, more importantly, as the direct sources for such editorializing. Strack-Billerbeck list such rabbinic parallels, and indeed, do so for Paul, James, the Johannine literature, the Pastorals, and so on. The impression thereupon exists that the unfolding Christian literature, even after Christendom became gentile in the dispersion in the second century, still owes some immediate debt to the rabbinic literature, even in passages emerging from Babylonia in the fifth century. If it is retorted that I am addressing myself not to the value of Strack-Billerbeck but to its misuse, then I must reply that the manufacturer who shapes a hammer to resemble a saw bears some responsibility for the misuse of the tool. I would charge therefore that Strack-Billerbeck is shaped as though its compilers were out of touch with NT scholarship.

Secondly, Strack-Billerbeck misleads many into confusing a scrutiny of excerpts with a genuine comprehension of the tone, texture, and import of a literature. One recalls the proposal that in the verse, "Let the dead bury the dead," we should understand that mistranslation has occurred, and that the first "dead" really was the "place," מתא for מתיא; so that the verse should read, "Let the place bury the dead." One can go on thereafter to cite biblical and rabbinic requirements about the burial of unclaimed bodies, and thereby miss the intent, and the deliberate bite, in the gospel passage. Rabbinists have sometimes assumed that a gospel pericope was lifted bodily from the Gemara. Elsewhere I have expressed the opinion that rabbinic scholars have assumed that a mastery of the Talmud confers automatic mastery of the gospels.

I would state here that NT scholars devoid of rabbinic learning have been misled by Strack-Billerbeck into arrogating to themselves a competency they do not possess. Strack-Billerbeck confers upon a student untrained and inexperienced in rabbinic literature not competency but confusion. The list of indiscretions by NT scholars in rabbinics, or by rabbinic scholars in NT, would be a long one. I allude here to errors in scholarship and not to pseudo scholarship. By this latter I have in mind the distorted evaluation of rabbinic Judaism as merely dry and arid legalism—it is never dry *or* arid, but always dry *and* arid; or a judgment such as Friedlander's that what is good in the Sermon on the Mount is borrowed from Jewish sources,[7] and what isn't, isn't very good. I am not implying that scholars are without the right to make value judgments. I am only suggesting the lack of value in many value judgments, when these emerge from an acquaintence merely with excerpt instead of with the intent, and the nuances, of a literature.

Third, in the major sins of Strack-Billerbeck is the excessive piling up of rabbinic passages. Nowhere else in scholarly literature is quantity so confused for quality as in Strack-Billerbeck. The mere abundance of so-called parallels is its own distortion, for the height of the pile misleads him who reads as he runs to suppose that he is dealing with sifted material. The distortion lies also in the circumstance that quantity lends a tone of authority all too often submitted to. The counterbalance is notably absent, the qualifying is withheld, and the pile acts as an obstruction to seeing what really should be seen. If Philo can undergo mayhem by study in excerpt, then this is mild compared to what rabbinic literature studied only in Strack-Billerbeck undergoes. And lest my statement here seem to be some Jewish provincialism, I must hasten to say that I am paraphrasing what was said about the competency of Weber's *Theologie der alten Synagoge* and Bousset's *Religion* by a Presbyterian named George Foot Moore.[8]

The fourth and crowning sin of Strack-Billerbeck involves a paradox. On the one hand, they quote the rabbinic literature endlessly to clarify the NT. Yet even where Jesus and the rabbis seem to say identically the same thing, Strack-Billerbeck manage to demonstrate that what Jesus said was finer and better. I am a religious liberal and to the best of my knowledge a student free of conscious partisanship in dealing with the ancient past. Somewhat like Claude Montefiore,[9] I am impelled to admire some statements attributed to Jesus more than similar statements of certain rabbis, and at other places the statements of certain rabbis more than those attributed to Jesus. Scholarly impartiality, achieved by many Christian

---

7. See Gerald Friedlander, *The Jewish Sources of the Sermon on the Mount.*
8. "Christian Writers on Judaism," in *HTR*, 14 (1921), pp. 197–254.
9. See, especially, *Rabbinic Literature and Gospel Teachings.*

scholars in this Society, is not a characteristic or a goal of Strack-Billerbeck. Why, I must ask, pile up the alleged parallels, if the end result is to show a forced, artificial, and untenable distinction even within the admitted parallels?

It is scarcely cricket to pile up Strack-Billerbeck sheer irrelevances, as they do, in connection with the admirable injunction in Matt 5:43–48, not to hate one's enemies. Strack-Billerbeck concede that parallels are here lacking, yet they manage to conclude that Judaism actually teaches the hatred of enemies, almost as a central doctrine. Strack-Billerbeck carefully omit such gospel passages as Matt 23, which to any fair-minded reader, such as a man from Mars, would prevent the characterization of the gospels as expressive of love and only love. Christianity shared with other versions of Judaism both the ideal of the love of one's fellowmen and also a hostility to the out group. What else should one reasonably expect? If love was distinctively a Christian virtue, absent from Judaism, what happened to it when the church fathers dealt with fellow Christians who disagreed with them? I think, for example, of Tertullian's dealing with Marcion. Unparallel parallels which feed a partisan ego scarcely represent good scholarship, whether the dabblers are Christians or Jews. How should a serious student assess the statement of a modern writer that "in many ways the New Testament is the reassertion of the authentic Old Testament tradition over against the rabbinic distortion of it"?[10] Sober scholarship and partisan apologetics are too quite different matters.

The various literatures relevant to Judaism and Christianity are so bulky and so diverse and so complex that no one person can master them all and the secondary scholarship in full thoroughness. This has been the case for at least a century and a half or ever since modern scientific scholarship arose. The discovery of the Dead Sea Scrolls has provided an addition to the relevant literature, this in the last twelve or thirteen years. Since the scrolls are in Hebrew, the first people who worked in them were, naturally, Hebraists, not NT scholars whose milieu has been Greek. Sometimes the Hebraists have been masters of biblical Hebrew, and not of the mishnaic; and sometimes the Hebraists have failed to display a deep comprehension of the problems inherent in NT scholarship. Sometimes NT scholars have made forays into the scrolls as if they are listed in the Muratorian fragment.

If ever there was a time when interdisciplinary partnerships were called for, this should have been the case when the scrolls emerged to notice. Instead, the scrolls have been at the mercy of extreme individualists, especially on the part of those who have ascribed to them some special, indeed, unique relationship to early Christianity. When the scrolls first came to light, there were flamboyant statements made about them. Let me paraphrase four of them: one, the greatest discovery in the history of archeology; two, all the mysteries about the origins of

---

10. Fuller, in G. Ernest Wright and Reginald Fuller, *The Book of the Acts of God,* p. 209.

Christianity are now solved; three, everything that has ever been written about Judaism and Christianity must now be rewritten; and four, the scrolls, sight unseen, are a hoax.

The individualism has prompted a good many theories, most of them competently assembled in Rowley's very able article in the last issue[11] of the *Bulletin of the John Rylands Library*. There can be no doubt that the scrolls captured the imagination of the general public. They also spawned some of the most spectacular exhibitions which I have ever encountered. If I pick out one to mention, it is only because it is typical of a certain lack of restraint. I allude to the work of a British scholar, the author of many works on Jewish history, who began his essay on the scrolls by saying that the difficulty in the problem of the scrolls stemmed from the fact that up to the time of his writing, no historian had approached the scrolls. Quite modestly, this British scholar offered himself for the task. His theory wins by a length in my opinion the race for the most preposterous of the theories about the scrolls.

Edmund Wilson was the first popularizer to titillate the general public about the scrolls. Mr. Wilson has written both literary criticism and fiction—and one can be uncertain as to just where to classify his book, *The Scrolls from the Dead Sea*. He makes the contention that NT scholarship, even the liberal scholarship, has shied away from the scrolls, out of fear of theological positions being upset. This was in May, 1955. In 1954 I was invited to be part of a panel at the December meeting of the Society on the scrolls and the NT. I was not able to accept the invitation, but I still keep Franklin Young's telegram inviting me because it predates Mr. Wilson's libel on NT scholars. Since I am a NT specialist, and Jewish, I hope you can take it at face value that no theory about the scrolls, moderate or extreme, will step on my theological toes. It was not my theology which Mr. Wilson offended, but whatever learning I had acquired. NT scholars, far from shying away from the scrolls, have possibly been guilty of going overboard about them.

The vaunted novelties which the scrolls were alleged to contain did excite me at one time, but always in prospect. When I acquired my copies, this excitement receded, for I learned that those things which might have made the scrolls exciting weren't and aren't there. As the scrolls relate to early Christianity, they are notable for the absence of concrete, recognizable history, and this may possibly be pointed up in the following way. In my judgment, the Scriptural books and fragments are of infinitely greater value than the sectarian documents and the Hodayoth, and I for one would willingly trade in the sectarian documents and the Hodayoth for just one tiny Qumran fragment that would mention Jesus, or Cephas, or Paul. Until such a fragment appears, I shall continue to believe, respecting the scrolls and early Christianity, that they contribute a few more drops to a bucket that was already half-full.

---

11. Vol. 44 (1961), pp. 119–56.

With the passing of months and of years, we have come to a better perspective on the scrolls. In the light of that perspective perhaps many here will agree with me that the scrolls reflect the greatest exaggeration in the history of biblical scholarship. To speak of exaggeration is to imply that there is a basic substance. I am not denying utility and worth to the scrolls. But I do not hesitate to express the judgment that they are not nearly so useful and worthy as was initially claimed.

Further, respecting interdisciplinary partnership, virtually all of us have loyalties which we neither can nor should deny. I for one have no scruples at stating that I am Jewish and a rabbi. There is an affirmative sense in which in context one can speak of Jewish scholarship or of Christian scholarship. At the same time, there are other contexts in which scholarship needs other descriptive adjectives. Where we deal with documents from long ago, it seems to me that the ideal is sound scholarship, rather than unsound, accurate rather than inaccurate, objective rather than partisan.

Someday some cultural historian might want to study a phenomenon in our Society of Biblical Literature. Two hundred years ago Christians and Jews and Roman Catholics and Protestants seldom read each other's books, and almost never met together to exchange views and opinions on academic matters related to religious documents. Even a hundred years ago such cross-fertilization or meeting was rare. In our ninety-seventh meeting we take it as a norm for us to read each other's writings and to meet together, debate with each other, and agree or disagree with each other in small or large matters of scholarship. The legacy from past centuries, of misunderstanding and even of animosity, has all but been dissolved in the framework of our organization. Would that humanity at large could achieve what has been achieved in our Society.

It is proper that our Society should be host to differences of opinion, and even acute ones. We do not want to arrive at some pallid unanimity, but rather to be the market place in which vigorously held viewpoints, freely expressed, vie with each other for acceptance. When one recalls the occasional fervid debate in this Society, it is notable that the issues have been primarily scholarly, and never to my recollection denominational. This is as it should be.

In scholarship full accuracy and full depth are an ideal occasionally approached but never quite realized, certainly not by any one person. The realization comes the nearest to the ideal not in an individual, but in our corporate strivings, as together we seek always to know more, and always to know better.

It seems to me that we are at a junction when biblical scholarship should recognize parallelomania for the disease that it is. It is time to draw away from the extravagance which has always been a latent danger and which the scrolls have made an imminent and omnipresent one.

It would be a real achievement if biblical scholarship in the 1960s were to be characterized as the decade in which perspective and direction were restored, the older theories reassessed, and our collective learning broadened and deepened.

FORM CRITICISM AND BEYOND*

James Muilenburg
San Francisco Theological Seminary

The impact of form criticism upon biblical studies has been profound, comparable only to the subsequent influence of historical criticism as it was classically formulated by Julius Wellhausen about a century ago. Its pioneer and spiritual progenitor was Hermann Gunkel, for many years professor of Old Testament at the University of Halle. The magnitude of his contribution to biblical scholarship is to be explained in part by the fact that historical criticism had come to an impasse, chiefly because of the excesses of source analysis; in part, too, by Gunkel's extraordinary literary insight and sensitivity, and, not least of all, by the influence which diverse academic disciplines exerted upon him.[1] At an early age he had read Johann Gottfried Herder's work, *Vom Geist der Ebräschen Poesie* (1782–83), with ever-growing excitement, and it kindled within him an appreciation not only of the quality of the ancient Oriental mentality, so characteristic of Herder's work, but also and more particularly of the manifold and varying ways in which it came to expression throughout the sacred records of the Old and New Testaments. Then there were his great contemporaries: Eduard Meyer and Leopold von Ranke, the historians; Heinrich Zimmern, the Assyriologist; Adolf Erman, the Egyptologist; and perhaps most important of all Eduard Norden, whose *Antike Kunstprosa* (1898) and *Agnostos Theos* (1913) anticipated Gunkel's own work in its recognition of the categories of style and their application to the NT records. Mention must also be made of his intimate friend and associate, Hugo Gressmann, who in his detailed studies of the Mosaic traditions pursued much the same methods as Gunkel,[2] and, more significantly, produced two monumental volumes on *Altorientalische Texte und Bilder* (1909¹, 1927²), surpassed today only by the companion volumes of James B. Pritchard (1950; 1954). Gunkel possessed for his time

---

* The Presidential Address delivered at the annual meeting of the Society of Biblical Literature on December 18, 1968, at the University of California, Berkeley, California.

1. W. Baumgartner, "Zum 100 Geburtstag von Hermann Gunkel," *Supplements to VetT,* 1962, pp. 1–18.

2. *Mose und seine Zeit* (1913).

an extraordinary knowledge of the other literatures of the ancient Near East, and availed himself of their forms and types, their modes of discourse, and their rhetorical features in his delineation and elucidation of the biblical texts. What is more—and this is a matter of some consequence—he had profound psychological insight, influenced to a considerable degree by W. Wundt's *Völkerpsychologie,* which stood him in good stead as he sought to portray the cast and temper of the minds of the biblical narrators and poets, but also of the ordinary Israelite to whom their words were addressed. It is not too much to say that Gunkel has never been excelled in his ability to portray the spirit which animated the biblical writers, and he did not hesitate either in his lectures or in his seminars to draw upon the events of contemporary history or the experiences of the common man to explicate the interior meaning of a pericope.

One need not labor the benefits and merits of form-critical methodology. It is well to be reminded, however, not only of its distinctive features, but also of the many important contributions in monograph, commentary, and theology, in order that we may the better assess its role in contemporary biblical research. Professor Albright, writing in 1940, remarked that "the student of the ancient Near East finds that the methods of Norden and Gunkel are not only applicable, but are the only ones that can be applied."[3] The first and most obvious achievement of *Gattungsforschung* is that it supplied a much-needed corrective to literary and historical criticism. In the light of recent developments, it is important to recall that Gunkel never repudiated this method, as his commentary on the Book of Genesis demonstrates, but rather averred that it was insufficient for answering the most pressing and natural queries of the reader. It was unable, for one thing, to compose a literary history of Israel because the data requisite for such a task were either wanting or, at best, meager. Again, it isolated Israel too sharply from its ethnic and cultural environment as it was reflected in the literary monuments of the peoples of the Near East. Further, the delineation of Israel's faith which emerged from the regnant historico-critical methodology was too simply construed and too unilinearly conceived. Not least of all, its exegesis and hermeneutics failed to penetrate deeply into the relevant texts. The second advantage of the form-critical methodology was that it addressed itself to the question of the literary genre represented by a pericope. In his programmatic essay on the literature of Israel in the second volume of Paul Hinneberg's *Die Kultur der Gegenwart* Gunkel provided an admirable sketch of the numerous literary types represented in the OT, and many of the contributions to the first and second editions of *Die Religion in die Geschichte und Gegenwart* bore the stamp and impress of his critical methodology. It is here where his influence has been greatest and most salutary because the student must know what kind of literature it is that he is reading, to what literary category it belongs, and what its characteristic features

---

3. *From the Stone Age to Christianity,* p. 44.

are. The third merit of the method is its concern to discover the function that the literary genre was designed to serve in the life of the community or of the individual, to learn how it was employed and on what occasions, and to implement it, so far as possible, into its precise social or cultural milieu. Of special importance, especially in the light of later developments in OT scholarship, was its stress upon the oral provenance of the original genres in Israel, and beyond Israel, among the other peoples of the Near East. Finally, related to our foregoing discussion, is the comparison of the literary types with other exemplars within the OT and then, significantly, with representatives of the same type in the cognate literatures. Such an enterprise in comparison releases the Scriptures from the bondage to parochialism.

The reflections of form-critical methodology are to be discerned all along the horizons of OT studies since the turn of the century, although it must be added that it has also been consistently ignored by substantial segments of OT scholarship. Thus R. H. Pfeiffer in his *magnum opus* on the *Introduction to the Old Testament* (1941) scarcely gives it a passing nod, in sharp contrast to the introductions of Otto Eissfeldt (1934[1]; Engl. transl. 1965), George Fohrer (1965; Engl. transl. 1968), Aage Bentzen (1948), and Artur Weiser (1948; Engl. transl. 1961), all of whom devote a large part of their works to the subject. In many commentaries, too, the literary types and forms are seldom mentioned. On the other hand, there have been many commentaries, such as those in the *Biblischer Kommentar* series, where they are discussed at some length. Equally significant is the important rôle that form criticism has played in hermeneutics. In theology, too, it has influenced not only the form and structure of the exposition, but also the understanding of the nature of biblical theology, as in the work of Gerhard von Rad, which is based upon form-critical presuppositions. Many works have been devoted to detailed studies of the particular literary genres, such as Israelite law,[4] the lament and dirge,[5] historical narrative,[6] the various types of Hebrew prophecy,[7] and wisdom.[8] In quite a different fashion, the method is reflected in recent

---

4. G. von Rad, *Deuteronomium-Studien* (1948; Engl. transl. 1953); A. Alt, *Die Ursprünge des israelitischen Rechts* in *Kleine Schriften zur Geschichte des Volkes Israel*, I (1959), pp. 278–332; Engl. transl. in *Essays on Old Testament History and Religion* (1966), pp. 79–132; Karlheinz Rabast, *Das apodiktische Recht im Deuteronomium und im Heiligkeitsgesetz* (1949).

5. Hedwig Jahnow, *Das hebräische Leichenlied im Rahmen der Volkerdichtung*, BZAW, 36 (1923).

6. R. A. Carlson, *David, the Chosen King* (1964).

7. J. Lindblom, *Die literarische Gattung der prophetischen Literatur* (1924); and *Prophecy in Ancient Israel* (1962); C. Westermann, *Grundformen prophetischer Rede* (1960), Engl. transl., *Basic Forms of Prophetic Speech* (1967).

8. W. Baumgartner, *Israelitische und altorientalische Weisheit* (1933); J. Fichtner, "Die altorientalische Weisheit in ihrer israelitisch-jüdischen Ausprägung," *BZAW*, 62 (1933); J. Hempel, *Die althebräische Literatur und ihr hellenistisch-jüdisches Nachleben* (1930).

studies of the covenant formulations,[9] the covenantal lawsuits,[10] and the covenant curses.[11] Now, having attempted to do justice to the substantial gains made by the study of literary types, I should like to point to what seem to me to be some of its inadequacies, its occasional exaggerations, and especially its tendency to be too exclusive in its application of the method. In these reservations I do not stand alone, for signs are not wanting, both here and abroad, of discontent with the prevailing state of affairs, of a sense that the method has outrun its course. Thus its most thoroughgoing exponent, H. G. Reventlow, in a recent study of Psalm 8, comments: "One gets the impression that a definite method, precisely because it has demonstrated itself to be so uncommonly fruitful, has arrived at its limits."[12] It would be unfortunate if this were taken to mean that we have done with form criticism or that we should forfeit its manifest contributions to an understanding of the Scriptures. To be sure there are clamant voices being raised today against the methodology, and we are told that it is founded on an illusion, that it is too much influenced by classical and Germanic philology and therefore alien to the Semitic literary consciousness, and that it must be regarded as an aberration in the history of biblical scholarship.[13] If we are faced with such a stark either-or, my allegiance is completely on the side of the form critics, among whom, in any case, I should wish to be counted. Such criticisms as I now propose to make do not imply a rejection so much as an appeal to venture beyond the confines of form criticism into an inquiry into other literary features which are all too frequently ignored today. The first of these is the one that is most frequently launched against the method. The basic contention of Gunkel is that the ancient men of Israel, like their Near Eastern neighbors, were influenced in their speech and their literary compositions by convention and custom. We therefore encounter in a particular genre or *Gattung* the same structural forms, the same terminology and style, and the same *Sitz im Leben*.

---

9. V. Kurošec, *Hethitische Staatsverträge in Leipziger rechtswissenschaftliche Studien* (1931); G. E. Mendenhall, *Law and Covenant in Israel and the Ancient Near East* (1955); K. Baltzer, *Das Bundesformular. Wissenschaftliche Monographien zum alten Testament* (1960); Dennis J. McCarthy, *Treaty and Covenant, Analecta Biblica*, 21 (1963).

10. H. B. Huffmon, "The Covenant Lawsuit in the Prophets," *JBL*, 78 (1959), pp. 285–95; G. E. Wright, "The Lawsuit of God: a Form-Critical Study of Deuteronomy 32," in *Israel's Prophetic Heritage* (1962), pp. 26–67; Julien Harvey, S.J., "Le 'Ribpattern,' requisitoire prophetique sur le rupture de l'alliance," *Biblica*, 45 (1962), pp. 172–96.

11. Delbert R. Hillers, *Treaty Curses and the Old Testament Prophets,* in *Biblica et Orientalia,* 16 (1964); H. J. Franken, "The vassal-treaties of Esarhaddon and the dating of Deuteronomy," *Oudtestamentische Studien,* 14 (1965), pp. 122–54.

12. H. G. Reventlow, "Der Psalm 8," in *Poetica: Zeitschrift für Sprach- und Literatur-Wissenschaft,* I, 1967, pp. 304–32.

13. Meir Weiss, "Wege der neuen Dichtungswissenschaft in ihrer Anwendung auf die Psalmenforschung," *Biblica,* 42 (1961), pp. 255–302.

Surely this cannot be gainsaid. But there has been a proclivity among scholars in recent years to lay such stress upon the typical and representative that the individual, personal, and unique features of the particular pericope are all but lost to view. It is true, as Klaus Koch says in his book, *Was ist Formgeschichte?* (1964), that the criticism has force more for the prophetic books than for the laws and wisdom utterances; and I should add for the hymns and laments of the Psalter too, as a study of *Die Einleitung in die Psalmen* by Gunkel-Begrich will plainly show, although the formulations exhibit diversity and versatility here too. Let me attempt to illustrate my point. In the first major section of the Book of Jeremiah (2:1–4:4*) we have an impressive sequence of literary units of essentially the same *Gattung*, i.e., the *rib* or lawsuit or legal proceeding, and the *Sitz im Leben* is the court of law. Yet the literary formulation of these pericopes shows great variety, and very few of them are in any way a complete reproduction of the lawsuit as it was actually carried on at the gate of the city.[14] What we have here, for the most part, are excerpts or extracts, each complete in itself, to be sure, but refashioned into the conventional structures of metrical verse and animated by profuse images. Only the first (2:1–13) and final pericopes (3:1–4:4*) are preserved with any degree of completeness. But what is more, precisely because the forms and styles are so diverse and are composed with such consummate skill, it is clear that we are dealing with imitations of a *Gattung*. Even when we compare such well-known exemplars of the type as Deut 32 and Mic 6:1–8, the stylistic and rhetorical differences outweigh the similarities. The conventional elements of the lawsuit genre are certainly present, and their recognition is basic to an understanding of the passage; but this is only the beginning of the story. To state our criticism in another way, form criticism by its very nature is bound to generalize because it is concerned with what is common to all the representatives of a genre, and therefore applies an external measure to the individual pericopes.[15] It does not focus sufficient attention upon what is unique and unrepeatable, upon the particularity of the formulation. Moreover, form and content are inextricably related. They form an integral whole. The two are one. Exclusive attention to the *Gattung* may actually obscure the thought and intention of the writer or speaker. The passage must be read and heard precisely as it is spoken. It is the creative synthesis of the particular formulation of the pericope with the content that makes it the distinctive composition that it is.

Another objection that has often been made of the criticism of literary types is its aversion to biographical or psychological interpretations and its resistance to historical commentary. This is to be explained only in part as a natural, even inevitable, consequence of its disregard of literary criticism. One has only to recall the rather extreme stress upon the nature of the prophetic experience of former

---

14. Ludwig Köhler, "Justice in the Gate," in *Hebrew Man* (1956), pp. 148–75.
15. H. G. Reventlow, *op. cit.*, p. 304.

times. The question is whether the specific text or passage gives any warrant for such ventures. There are cases, to be sure, as with Jeremiah and Ezekiel, where it is difficult to see how one can cavalierly omit psychological commentary of some kind. The call of Jeremiah, for example, is something more than the recitation of a conventional and inherited liturgy within the precincts of the temple,[16] and the so-called confessions of the prophet are more than the repetition and reproduction of fixed stereotypes, despite all the parallels that one may adduce from the OT and the Near Eastern texts for such a position. Perhaps more serious is the skepticism of all attempts to read a pericope in its historical context. The truth is that in a vast number of instances we are indeed left completely in the dark as to the occasion in which the words were spoken, and it is reasonable to assume that it was not of primary interest to the compilers of the traditions. This is notably the case with numerous passages in the prophetic writings. In Jeremiah, for example, more often than not, we are simply left to conjecture. Nevertheless, we have every reason to assume that there were situations which elicited particular utterances, and we are sufficiently informed about the history of the times to make conjecture perfectly legitimate. The prophets do not speak *in abstracto,* but concretely. Their formulations may reflect a cultic provenance as on the occasion of celebration of a national festival, although one must be on his guard against exaggeration here, especially against subsuming too many texts under the rubric of the covenant renewal festival, as in the case of Artur Weiser in his commentaries on Jeremiah and the Book of Psalms, or of the festival of the New Year, as in the case of Sigmund Mowinckel in his *Psalmenstudien.*

The foregoing observations have been designed to call attention to the perils involved in a too exclusive employment of form-critical methods, to warn against extremes in their application, and particularly to stress that there are other features in the literary compositions which lie beyond the province of the *Gattungsforscher.* It is important to emphasize that many scholars have used the method with great skill, sound judgment and proper restraint, and, what is more, have taken account of literary features other than those revealed by the *Gattung,* such as H. W. Wolff's commentary on Hosea in the *Biblischer Kommentar* series. Further, we should recognize that there are numerous texts where the literary genre appears in pure form, and here the exclusive application of form-critical techniques has its justification, although one must be quick to add that even here there are differences in formulation. But there are many other passages where the literary genres are being imitated, not only among the prophets, but among the historians and lawgivers. Witness, for example, the radical transformation of the early Elohistic laws by the deuteronomists, or, perhaps equally impressively, the appropriation by the prophets of the curse formulae, not only within the OT, but

---

16. H. G. Reventlow, *Liturgie und prophetisches Ich bei Jeremia* (1963), pp. 24–77.

also in the vassal treaties of the Near Eastern peoples.[17] Let me repeat: in numerous contexts old literary types and forms are imitated, and, precisely because they are imitated, they are employed with considerable fluidity, versatility, and, if one may venture the term, artistry. The upshot of this circumstance is that the circumspect scholar will not fail to supplement his form-critical analysis with a careful inspection of the literary unit in its precise and unique formulation. He will not be completely bound by the traditional elements and motifs of the literary genre; his task will not be completed until he has taken full account of the features which lie beyond the spectrum of the genre. If the exemplars of the *Gattung* were all identical in their formulations, the OT would be quite a different corpus from what it actually is.

It is often said that the Hebrew writers were not motivated by distinctively literary considerations, that aesthetics lay beyond the domain of their interests, and that a preoccupation with what has come to be described as stylistics only turns the exegete along bypaths unrelated to his central task. It may well be true that aesthetic concerns were never primary with them and that the conception of *belles lettres,* current in ancient Hellas, was alien to the men of Israel. But surely this must not be taken to mean that the OT does not offer us literature of a very high quality. For the more deeply one penetrates the formulations as they have been transmitted to us, the more sensitive he is to the roles which words and motifs play in a composition; the more he concentrates on the ways in which thought has been woven into linguistic patterns, the better able he is to think the thoughts of the biblical writer after him. And this leads me to formulate a canon which should be obvious to us all: a responsible and proper articulation of the words in their linguistic patterns and in their precise formulations will reveal to us the texture and fabric of the writer's thought, not only what it is that he thinks, but as he thinks it.

The field of stylistics or aesthetic criticism is flourishing today, and the literature that has gathered about it is impressive. Perhaps its foremost representative is Alonso Schökel, whose work, *Estudios de Poetica Hebraea* (1963), offers us not only an ample bibliography of the important works in the field, but also a detailed discussion of the stylistic phenomenology of the literature of the OT. In this respect it is a better work than Ed. König's *Stilistik, Rhetorik, und Poetik* (1900), an encyclopedic compendium of linguistic and rhetorical phenomena, which nevertheless has the merit of providing many illuminating parallels drawn from classical literature and of availing itself of the many stylistic studies from the earliest times and throughout the nineteenth century. It would be an error, therefore, to regard the modern school in isolation from the history of OT scholarship because from the time of Jerome and before and continuing on with the rabbis and until modern times there have been those who

---

17. See n. 11.

have occupied themselves with matters of style. One thinks of Bishop Lowth's influential work, *De sacra poesi Hebraeorum praelectiones academicae* (1753), and of Herder's work on Hebrew poetry (1772–83), but also of the many metrical studies, most notably Ed. Sievers' *Metrische Studien* (I, 1901; II, 1904–05; III, 1907).[18] Noteworthy, too, are the contributions of Heinrich Ewald, Karl Budde, and Bernhard Duhm, and more recently and above all of Umberto Cassuto. W. F. Albright has devoted himself to subjects which are to all intents and purposes stylistic, as *inter alia* his studies on the Song of Deborah and his most recent work on *Yahweh and the Gods of Canaan* (1968). His students too have occupied themselves with stylistic matters, notably Frank M. Cross and D. N. Freedman in their doctoral dissertation on *Studies in Yahwistic Poetry* (1950) and in their studies of biblical poems.[19] Among the many others who have applied stylistic criteria to their examination of OT passages are Gerlis Gerleman in his study on the Song of Deborah,[20] L. Krinetski in his work on the Song of Songs,[21] Edwin Good in his analysis of the composition of the Book of Hosea,[22] R. A. Carlson in his scrutiny of the historical narratives of II Samuel in *David, the Chosen King* (1964), and William L. Holladay in his studies on Jeremiah.[23] The aspect of all these works which seems to me most fruitful and rewarding I should prefer to designate by a term other than stylistics. What I am interested in, above all, is in understanding the nature of Hebrew literary composition, in exhibiting the structural patterns that are employed for the fashioning of a literary unit, whether in poetry or in prose, and in discerning the many and various devices by which the predications are formulated and ordered into a unified whole. Such an enterprise I should describe as rhetoric and the methodology as rhetorical criticism.

The first concern of the rhetorical critic, it goes without saying, is to define the limits or scope of the literary unit, to recognize precisely where and how it begins and where and how it ends. He will be quick to observe the formal rhetorical devices that are employed, but more important, the substance or content of these most strategic loci. An examination of the commentaries will reveal that there is great disagreement on this matter, and, what is more, more often than not,

---

18. For literature on the subject see Otto Eissfeldt, *The Old Testament: an Introduction* (1967), p. 57.

19. "A Royal Song of Thanksgiving—II Samuel 22 = Psalm 18," *JBL*, 62 (1953), pp. 15–34; "The Song of Miriam," *JNES*, 14 (1955), pp. 237–50; "The Blessing of Moses," *JBL*, 67 (1948), pp. 191–210. See also Freedman's "Archaic Forms in Early Hebrew Poetry," *ZAW*, 72 (1960), pp. 101–07.

20. "The Song of Deborah in the Light of Stylistics," *VetT*, I (1951), pp. 168–80.

21. *Das Hohelied* (1964).

22. "The Composition of Hosea," *Svensk Exegetist Årsbok*, 31 (1966), pp. 211–63.

23. "Prototype and Copies, a New Approach to the Poetry-Prose Problem in the Book of Jeremiah," *JBL*, 79 (1960), 351–67; "The Recovery of Poetic Passages of Jeremiah," *JBL*, 85 (1966), pp. 401–35.

no defense is offered for the isolation of the pericope. It has even been averred that it does not really matter. On the contrary, it seems to me to be of considerable consequence, not only for an understanding of how the *Gattung* is being fashioned and designed, but also and more especially for a grasp of the writer's intent and meaning. The literary unit is in any event an indissoluble whole, an artistic and creative unity, a unique formulation. The delimitation of the passage is essential if we are to learn how its major motif, usually stated at the beginning, is resolved. The latter point is of special importance because no rhetorical feature is more conspicuous and frequent among the poets and narrators of ancient Israel than the proclivity to bring the successive predications to their culmination. One must admit that the problem is not always simple because within a single literary unit we may have and often do have several points of climax. But to construe each of these as a conclusion to the poem is to disregard its structure, to resolve it into fragments, and to obscure the relation of the successive strophes to each other. This mistaken procedure has been followed by many scholars, and with unfortunate consequences.

Now the objection that has been most frequently raised to our contention is that too much subjectivity is involved in determining where the accents of the composition really lie. The objection has some force, to be sure, but in matters of this sort there is no substitute for literary sensitivity. Moreover, we need constantly to be reminded that we are dealing with an ancient Semitic literature and that we have at our disposal today abundant parallel materials from the peoples of the ancient Near East for comparison. But we need not dispose of our problem so, for there are many marks of composition which indicate where the finale has been reached. To the first of these I have already alluded, the presence of climactic or ballast lines, which may indeed appear at several junctures within a pericope, but at the close have an emphasis which bears the burden of the entire unit. A second clue for determining the scope of a pericope is to discern the relation of beginning and end, where the opening words are repeated or paraphrased at the close, what is known as ring composition, or, to employ the term already used by Ed. König many years ago and frequently employed by Dahood in his commentary on the Psalter, the *inclusio*. There are scores of illustrations of this phenomenon in all parts of the OT, beginning with the opening literary unit of the Book of Genesis. An impressive illustration is the literary complex of Jer 3:1–4:4, with deletion of the generally recognized prose insertions. While most scholars see more than one unit here, what we actually have before us is a superbly composed and beautifully ordered poem of three series of strophes of three strophes each. The major motif of turning or repentance is sounded in the opening casuistic legal formulation and is followed at once by the indictment:

> If a man sends his wife away,
>   and she goes from him,
> and becomes another man's wife,

> will she return to him [with the corrected text]?
> Would not that land
> be utterly polluted?
> But you have played the harlot with many lovers,
> and would you return to me? (Jer 3:1).

The word שׁוּב appears in diverse syntactical constructions and in diverse stylistic contexts, and always in strategic collocations.[24] The poem has of course been influenced by the lawsuit, but it also contains a confessional lament and comes to a dramatic climax in the final strophe and in the form of the covenant conditional:

> If you do return, O Israel, Yahweh's Word!
> to me you should return (Jer 4:1 a).

The whole poem is an Exhibit A of ancient Hebrew rhetoric, but it could easily be paralleled by numerous other exemplars quite as impressive.

The second major concern of the rhetorical critic is to recognize the structure of a composition and to discern the configuration of its component parts, to delineate the warp and woof out of which the literary fabric is woven, and to note the various rhetorical devices that are employed for marking, on the one hand, the sequence and movement of the pericope, and on the other, the shifts or breaks in the development of the writer's thought. It is our contention that the narrators and poets of ancient Israel and her Near Eastern neighbors were dominated not only by the formal and traditional modes of speech of the literary genres or types, but also by the techniques of narrative and poetic composition. Now the basic and most elemental of the structural features of the poetry of Israel, as of that of the other peoples of the ancient Near East, is the parallelism of its successive cola or stichoi. Our concern here is not with the different types of parallelism—synonymous, complementary, antithetic, or stairlike, etc.—but rather with the diversities of sequence of the several units within the successive cola, or within the successive and related bicola or tricola. It is precisely these diversities which give the poetry its distinctive and artistic character. It is always tantalizing to the translator that so often they cannot be reproduced into English or, for that matter, into the other Western tongues. In recent years much attention has been given to the repetitive tricola, which is amply illustrated in Ugaritic poetry.[25] But

---

24. William L. Holladay, *The Root ŠÛBH in the Old Testament* (1958).

25. H. L. Ginsberg, "The Rebellion and Death of Baʻlu," *Orientalia*, 5 (1936), pp. 161–98; W. F. Albright, "The Psalm of Habakkuk," *Studies in Old Testament Prophecy*, ed. by H. H. Rowley (1950), pp. 1–18; idem, *Yahweh and the God of Canaan* (1968), pp. 4–27; J. H. Patton, *Canaanite Parallels in the Book of Psalms* (1944), pp. 5–11.

this repetitive style appears in numerous other types of formulation, and, what is more, is profusely illustrated in our earliest poetic precipitates:

> The kings came, they fought;
>   then fought the kings of Canaan,
> at Taanach, by the waters of Megiddo;
>   they got no spoils of silver.
> From heaven fought the stars,
>   from their courses they fought against Sisera.
> The torrent Kishon swept them away,
>   the onrushing torrent, the torrent Kishon.
> March on, my soul with might (Judg 5:19–21).

Within so small a compass we have two instances of chiasmus, the fourfold repetition of the verb נִלְחָמוּ, the threefold repetition of נַחַל, and a concluding climactic shout. There are numerous cases of anaphora, the repetition of key words or lines at the beginning of successive predications, as in the series of curses in Deut 27:15–26 or of blessings in the following chapter (Deut 28:3–6), or the prophetic oracles of woe (Isa 5:8–22), or the repeated summons to praise (Ps 150), or the lamenting "How long" of Psalm 3. Jeremiah's vision of the return to primeval chaos is a classic instance of anaphora (Jer 4:23–26). In the oracle on the sword against Babylon as Yahweh's hammer and weapon, the line "with you I shatter in pieces" is repeated nine times (Jer 50:35–38). Examples of a different kind are Job's oaths of clearance (Job 31) and Wisdom's autobiography (Prov 8:22–31). These iterative features are much more profuse and elaborate in the ancient Near Eastern texts, but also more stereotyped.[26]

The second structural feature of Israel's poetic compositions is closely related to our foregoing observations concerning parallel structures and is particularly germane to responsible hermeneutical inquiry and exegetical exposition. The bicola or tricola appear in well-defined clusters or groups, which possess their own identity, integrity, and structure. They are most easily recognized in those instances where they close with a refrain, as in the prophetic castigations of Amos 4:6–11 or in Isaiah's stirring poem on the divine fury (9:7–20, 5:25–30) or the personal lament of Pss 42–43 or the song of trust of Psalm 46 in its original form, or, most impressively in the liturgy of thanksgiving of Psalm 107. They are readily identified, too, in the alphabetic acrostics of Psalms 9–10, 25, and 119 and in the first three chapters of Lamentations. But, as we shall have occasion to observe, there are many other ways to define their limits. In the literatures of

---

26. S. N. Kramer, *The Sumerians* (1963), pp. 174 ff., 254, 256, 263; A. Falkenstein and W. von Soden, *Sumerische und Akkadische Hymnen und Gebete,* pp. 59 f., 67 f.; J. B. Pritchard, *ANET,* pp. 385b–86a, 390, 391b–92.

the other peoples of the ancient Near East the same structural phenomena are present.[27] But how shall we name such clusters? The most common designation is the *strophe*, but some scholars have raised objections to it because they aver that it is drawn from the models of Greek lyrical verse and that they cannot apply to Semitic poetic forms. It is true that in an earlier period of rhetorical study scholars were too much dominated by Greek prototypes and sought to relate the strophes to each other in a fashion for which there was little warrant in the biblical text. If we must confine our understanding to the Greek conception of a strophe, then it is better not to employ it, and to use the word *stanza* instead. The second objection to the term is that a strophe is to be understood as a metrical unit, i.e., by a consistent metrical scheme. There is also some force in this objection. Many poems do indeed have metrical uniformity, but often this is not the case. Indeed, I should contend that the Hebrew poet frequently avoids metrical consistency. It is precisely the break in the meter that gives the colon or bicolon its designed stress and importance. But we can say with some confidence that strophes have prevailingly consistent meters. My chief defense for employing the word *strophe* is that it has become acclimated to current terminology, not only by biblical scholars, but also by those whose province is Near Eastern literature. By a strophe we mean a series of bicola or tricola with a beginning and ending, possessing unity of thought and structure. The prosody group must coincide with the sense. But there is still another observation to be made which is of the first importance for our understanding of Hebrew poetry. While very many poems have the same number of lines in each strophe, it is by no means necessary that they be of the same length, although in the majority of cases they are indeed so. Where we have variety in the number of lines in successive strophes, a pattern is usually discernible. In any event, the time has not yet passed when scholars resort to the precarious practice of emendation in order to produce regularity. Just as we have outlived the practice of deleting words *metri causa* for the sake of consistency, so it is to be hoped that we refuse to produce strophic uniformity by excision of lines unless there is textual support for the alteration.

Perhaps there is no enterprise more revealing for our understanding of the nature of biblical rhetoric than an intensive scrutiny of the composition of the strophes, the manifold technical devices employed for their construction, and the stylistic phenomena which give them their unity. Such a study is obviously beyond the province of our present investigation. We may call attention, however, to a number of features which occur with such frequency and in such widely diverse contexts that they may be said to characterize Hebrew and to a considerable extent ancient Near Eastern modes of literary composition. We have already mentioned the refrains which appear at the close of the strophes.

---

27. See A. Falkenstein and W. von Soden, *op. cit.*, for full discussion, especially pp. 37 ff.

There are not a few examples of where they open in the same fashion. Thus the succession of oracles against the nations in Amos 1:3–2:16 are all wrought in essentially the same mold, and the stylistically related sequence of oracles in Ezek 25:3–17 follows precisely the same pattern. Psalm 29 is, of course, a familiar example with its iteration of קוֹל יהוה in five of the seven strophes. In the opening poem of Second Isaiah (40:1–11) the proem comes to a climax in the cry, קִרְאוּ אֵלֶיהָ. This now serves as a key to the structure of the lines that follow: קוֹל קוֹרֵא (3a), קוֹל אֹמֵר קְרָא (6a), and הָרִימִי בַכֹּחַ קוֹלֵךְ (9b). The poem which follows is a superb specimen of Hebrew literary craft and exhibits the same sense of form by the repetition of key words at the beginning of each strophe, and the succession of interrogatives couched in almost identical fashion reach their climax in the awesome וּרְאוּ מִי־בָרָא אֵלֶּה, which is answered in the final strophe by the words to which all the lines have been pointing:

> Yahweh is an everlasting God,
>   Creator of the ends of the earth (40:28 b).

Perhaps the most convincing argument for the existence of strophes in Hebrew poetry as in the poetry of the other ancient Near Eastern peoples is the presence within a composition of turning points or breaks or shifts, whether of the speaker or the one addressed or of motif and theme. While this feature is common to a number of literary genres, they are especially striking in the personal and communal laments. Psalm 22, which fairly teems with illuminating rhetorical features, will illustrate. We cite the opening lines of each strophe:

> My God, my God, why hast thou abandoned me? (1–2)
> But Thou art holy (3–5)
> But I am a worm and no man (6–8)
> Yet thou art he who took me from my mother's womb (9–11)
> I am poured out like water (14–15)
> Yea, dogs are round about me (16–18)
> But thou, O Yahweh, be not far off (19–21)
> I will tell of thy name to my brethren (22–24)
> From thee comes my praise in the great congregation (25–28)
> Yea to him shall all the proud of the earth bow down (29–31)
>   (emended text. See B. H. *ad loc.*).

Particles play a major rôle in all Hebrew poetry and reveal the rhetorical cast of Semitic literary mentality in a striking way. Chief among them is the deictic and emphatic particle כִּי, which performs a vast variety of functions and is susceptible of many different renderings, above all, perhaps, the function of motivation where it is understood causally.[28] It is not surprising, therefore, that it

---

28. James Muilenburg, "The Linguistic and Rhetorical Usages of the Particle in the Old Testament," *HUCA,* 32 (1961), pp. 135–60.

should appear in strategic collocations, such as the beginnings and endings of the strophes. For the former we may cite Isaiah 34:

> For Yahweh is enraged against all the nations (32:2 a)
> For my sword has drunk its fill in the heavens (34:5 a)
> For Yahweh has a sacrifice in Bozrah (34:6c)
> For Yahweh has a day of vengeance (34:8 a).

The particle appears frequently in the hymns of the Psalter immediately following the invocation to praise, as in Psalm 95:

> For Yahweh is a great God,
>   and a great King above all gods (95:3),

or later in the same hymn:

> For he is our God,
>   and we are the people of his pasture (95:7).

The motivations also conclude a strophe or poem:

> For Yahweh knows the way of the righteous,
>   but the way of the wicked shall perish (Ps 1:6);

or, as frequently in Jeremiah:

> For I bring evil from the north,
>   and great destruction (Jer 4:6 b);

> For the fierce anger of Yahweh
>   has not turned away from us (Jer 4:8 b);

> For their transgressions are many,
>   their apostasies great (Jer 5:6 c).

Significantly, in the closing poem of Second Isaiah's eschatological "drama" (Isa 55) the particle is employed with extraordinary force, both at the opening and closing bicola of the strophes, and goes far to explain the impact that the poem has upon the reader. As the poems open with the threefold use of the particle in the opening strophe, so they close with a fivefold repetition of the word.

A second particle, frequently associated with כִּי is הִנֵּה or הֵן, the word which calls for our attention. Characteristically it appears in striking contexts, either by introducing a poem or strophe or by bringing it to its culmination. Thus the third and climatic strophe of the long and well-structured poem of Isa 40:12–31 begins dramatically after the long series of interrogatives:

> Behold (הֵן), the nations are like a drop from a bucket,
>   and are accounted as dust on the scales;

Behold, he takes up the isles like fine dust (40:15).

The poem which follows is composed of three series of three strophes each, and the climax falls in each case upon the third strophe. The "behold" always appears in crucial or climactic contexts. The judgment of the nations appears at the close of two strophes:

Behold, you are nothing,
    and your work is nought;
    an abomination is he who chooses you (Isa 41:24);

Behold, they are all a delusion
    their works are nothing;
    their molten images are empty wind (Isa 41:29).

It is at this point that the Servant of Yahweh is now introduced:

Behold my servant, whom I uphold,
    my chosen, in whom I delight;
I have put my spirit upon him,
    he will bring forth justice to the nations (42:1).

The last of the so-called Servant poems begins in the same way:

Behold, my servant yet shall prosper,
    he shall be exalted and lifted up,
    and shall be very high (Isa 52:13).

The particle may appear in series, as in Isa 65:13–14:

Therefore thus says Yahweh God:
"Behold, my servants shall eat,
    but you shall be hungry;
behold, my servants shall drink,
    but you shall be thirsty;
behold, my servants shall rejoice,
    but you shall be put to shame;
behold, my servants shall sing for gladness of heart,
    but you shall cry out for pain of heart,
    and shall wail for anguish of spirit.

Frequently it brings the strophe or poem to a climax:

Behold your God!
Behold, the Lord Yahweh comes with might,
    and his arm rules for him;

behold, his reward is with him,
   and his recompense before him (Isa 40:9–10).

The particle appears in many other modes and guises in the OT, as, for example, in introducing oracles of judgment where הִנְנִי is followed by the active participle.²⁹

There are other particles which would reward our study, among which we may mention לָכֵן, which characteristically introduces the threat or verdict in the oracles of judgment, or לָמָה, with which the laments so frequently open, or וְעַתָּה, so central to the covenant formulations, but perpetuated in the prophets and singers of Israel.

Numerous other stylistic features delineate the form and structure of the strophes. Most frequent are the vocatives addressed to God in the invocations. Take the opening cola of the successive strophes in Psalm 7:

O Yahweh, my God, in thee do I take refuge. 7:1 a (Heb. 2 a);
O Yahweh, my God, if I have done this 7:3 a (Heb. 4 a);
Arise, O Yahweh, in thy anger 7:6a (Heb. 7a).

Or the inclusio of Psalm 8:

O Yahweh, my Lord,
   how spacious is thy name in all the earth (8:1, 9 [Heb. 2, 10]);

or the entrance liturgy:

O Yahweh, who shall sojourn in thy tent?
   Who shall dwell on thy holy hill? (15:1).³⁰

Rhetorical questions of different kinds and in different literary types appear in strategic collocations. As we should expect, they are quite characteristic in the legal encounters:

What wrong was it then that your fathers found in me
   that they went far from me? (Jer 2:5);

Why do you bring a suit against me? (Jer 2:29).³¹

---

29. Paul Humbert, *Opuscules d'un Hebräisant* (1958), pp. 54–59.

30. Cf. also Pss 3:1 (Heb. 2), 6:1 (Heb. 2), 22:1 (Heb. 2), 25:1, 26:1, 28:1, 31:1 (Heb. 2), 43:1, 51:1 (Heb. 2).

31. Cf. also Pss 2:1, 10:1, 15:1, 35:17, 49:5 (Heb. 6), 52:1 (Heb. 2), 58:1 (Heb. 2), 60:9 (Heb. 11), 62:3 (Heb. 4); Jer 5:7 a, also Isa 10:11, 14:32, 42:1-4; Jer 5:21 d, 9:9.

The questions often provide the climatic line of the strophe:

> How long must I see the standard,
>   and hear the sound of the trumpet? (Jer 4:21),

or in the moving outcry of the prophet:

> Is there no balm in Gilead?
>   Is there no physician there?
> Why then has the health of the daughter, my people, not been restored? (Jer 8:22).

Especially striking is the threefold repetition of a keyword within a single strophe. This phenomenon is so frequent and the words are so strategically placed that it cannot be said to be fortuitous. We have observed it in connection with our study of the particles. We select an example almost at random, though it is lost in translation:

> קוּמִי אוֹרִי כִּי בָא אוֹרֵךְ וּכְבוֹד יְהוָה עָלַיִךְ זָרָח׃
> כִּי־הִנֵּה הַחֹשֶׁךְ יְכַסֶּה־אֶרֶץ וַעֲרָפֶל לְאֻמִּים
> וְעָלַיִךְ יִזְרַח יְהוָה וּכְבוֹדוֹ עָלַיִךְ יֵרָאֶה׃
> וְהָלְכוּ גוֹיִם לְאוֹרֵךְ וּמְלָכִים לְנֹגַהּ זַרְחֵךְ׃ (Isa 60:1–3).

Amos' oracle on the Day of Yahweh is another good example (Amos 5:18–20). If we may accept the present masoretic text of Isa 55:1, it is not without significance that the prophet's final poem opens with the urgent invitations, which is all the more impressive because of its assonance:

> Ho, every one who thirsts,
>   come (לְכוּ) to the waters;
> and he who has no money
>   come (לְכוּ) buy and eat!
> Come (לְכוּ), buy wine and milk
>   without money and without price (Isa 55 1).[32]

Repetition serves many and diverse functions in the literary compositions of ancient Israel, whether in the construction of parallel cola or parallel bicola, or in the structure of the strophes, or in the fashioning and ordering of the complete literary units. The repeated words or lines do not appear haphazardly or fortuitously, but rather in rhetorically significant collocations. This phenomenon is to be explained perhaps in many instances by the originally spoken provenance of

---

32. Cf. Judg 5:19–21; Pss 25:1–3, 34:1–3 (Heb. 2–4), 7–10 (Heb. 8–11), 121:7–8, 139:11–12 (Heb. 12–13), 145:1–3; Isa 55:6–9; Jer 5:15 c–17.

the passage, or by its employment in cultic celebrations, or, indeed, by the speaking mentality of the ancient Israelite. It served as an effective mnemonic device. It is the key word which may often guide us in our isolation of a literary unit, which gives to it its unity and focus, which helps us to articulate the structure of the composition, and to discern the pattern or texture into which the words are woven. It is noteworthy that repetitions are most abundant in crucial contexts. Perhaps the most familiar of these is the call of Abram (Gen 12:1–3) which opens the Yahwist patriarchal narratives. As Ephraim Speiser has seen, it is a well-constructed poem of three diminutive strophes of three lines each. But what is notable here is the fivefold repetition of the word *bless* in differing syntactical forms, which underscores the power of the blessing that is to attend not only Abram, but all the nations of the earth. It is not surprising, therefore, that the motif should recur again and again and always in decisive places. An example of another kind is the much controverted verse at the beginning of the book of Hosea:

לֵךְ קַח־לְךָ אֵשֶׁת זְנוּנִים וְיַלְדֵי זְנוּנִים
כִּי־זָנֹה תִזְנֶה הָאָרֶץ מֵאַחֲרֵי יהוה (1:2).

In the following chapter the motif of the new covenant reaches its climax in another repetitive text:

> And I will betroth you to me for ever; I will betroth you to me in righteousness and in justice, in steadfast love, and in compassion. I will betroth you to me in faithfulness; and you shall know that I am Yahweh (Hos 2:19–20 [Heb 21–22]).

The structure of the first chapter of Ezekiel is determined by the recurring motif of the *demuth* at the beginning of each of its major divisions, and in the finale reaches its climax by the dramatic threefold repetition:

> And above the firmament over their heads was the likeness of a throne, in appearance like sapphire; and seated above the likeness of a throne was a likeness as it were in human form (Ezek 1:26).

Persistent and painstaking attention to the modes of Hebrew literary composition will reveal that the pericopes exhibit linguistic patterns, word formations ordered or arranged in particular ways, verbal sequences which move in fixed structures from beginning to end. It is clear that they have been skillfully wrought in many different ways, often with consummate skill and artistry. It is also apparent that they have been influenced by conventional rhetorical practices. This inevitably poses a question for which I have no answer. From whom did the poets and prophets of Israel acquire their styles and literary habits? Surely they cannot be explained by spontaneity. They must have been learned and mastered from some source, but what this source was is a perplexing problem. Are we to look to the schools of wisdom for an explanation? It is difficult to say. But there is another question into which we have not gone. How are we to explain the numerous and extraordinary literary affinities of the *Gattungen* or genres and other stylistic formulations of Israel's literature with the literatures of the other peoples of the Near East? Were the prophets and poets familiar with these records? If not, how are we to explain them? If so, in what ways? But there are other latitudes which we have not undertaken to explore. T. S. Eliot once described a poem as a raid on the inarticulate. In the Scriptures we have a literary deposit of those who were confronted by the ultimate questions of life and human destiny, of God and man, of the past out of which the historical people has come and of the future into which it is moving, a speech which seeks to be commensurate with man's ultimate concerns, a raid on the ultimate, if you will.

Finally, it has not been our intent to offer an alternative to form criticism or a substitute for it, but rather to call attention to an approach of eminent lineage which may supplement our form-critical studies. For after all has been said and done about the forms and types of biblical speech, there still remains the task of discerning the actuality of the particular text, and it is with this, we aver, that we must reckon, as best we can, for it is this concreteness which marks the material with which we are dealing. In a word, then, we affirm the necessity of form criticism, but we also lay claim to the legitimacy of what we have called rhetorical criticism. Form criticism and beyond.

Whither Biblical Research?*

Harry M. Orlinsky
Hebrew Union College-Jewish Institute of Religion

It is not always realized, or kept in mind, that biblical research, no less than any other branch of group activity, is subject to the social forces—the term "social," of course, represents the longer phrase and concept: social, economic, political, cultural, religious, and the like—at work within the community at large. Thus the kinds of interpretation of the Bible—both as a whole and even of specific passages in it that prevailed in the last couple of centuries B.C. would not have been possible in any environment but that of Hellenism as it was adopted and adapted in the Jewish communities of the Diaspora and Judea. The earliest specifically Christian exposition of what constituted the Bible differed markedly from that of the Jewish-Christian period and community that preceded it, basically because the social structure of the Roman Empire as a whole and the specific status of the Christian and the Jewish communities within it had changed significantly from those that had obtained in the first three centuries A.D., before Christianity had become in rapid succession a tolerated and then the official religion.

This principle of social forces, rather than the personal whim of a scholar here and there, being the decisive factor in the shaping of a discipline such as ours, applies of course to every epoch in history, be it the Middle Ages, the Renaissance, the Reformation, the demise of feudalism, or the birth of capitalism in Western Europe. But this point need not be belabored here, not because it has been dealt with adequately in various works on the subject—indeed, I do not think that it has been—but because it is chronologically not pertinent enough to the present discussion.[1]

---

* The Presidential Address delivered at the annual meeting of the Society of Biblical Literature on October 26, 1970, at the New Yorker Hotel, New York, N.Y.

1. The interpretation of the Bible in the light of changing historical circumstances has remained essentially virgin soil for the inquisitive and trained scholar. To *describe* Philo's or Jerome's or Rashi's or Astruc's or Wellhausen's or S. R. Driver's manner of interpreting the Bible—basic as it is—is only preliminary to the systematic attempt to *account for* their kind of biblical exegesis. It is not easy to improve upon the descriptive approach of Beryl Smalley in her fascinating treatment *of The Study of the Bible in the Middle Ages* (1941; rev. ed., 1952; reprinted

During the nineteenth century and the first quarter of our own, i.e., before the consequences of World War I took real effect, biblical research—I shall be using the terms "Bible" and "biblical" sometimes to cover both the Hebrew and the Christian Scriptures and sometimes the Hebrew alone—followed generally the pattern of research in the classical field, which was more solidly and extensively established at the time. Textual and literary criticism and comparative linguistics—in those days involving almost exclusively Hebrew, Aramaic, Arabic, Syriac, and Ethiopic, and what Babylonian-Assyrian was known—were the norm. The standard works were the grammars by König, Gesenius-Kautzsch-Cowley, and Bauer-Leander; the lexicons employed were usually those of Brown-Driver-Briggs and Gesenius-Buhl; and Brockelmann's two-volume *Grundriss* was the sole claimant to respect in comparative Semitic linguistics.[2]

This state of affairs is easy to recall, because after all the hectic years since World War I it is still these same works that are standard today—except that Bergsträsser began a notable revision of Gesenius-Kautzsch-Cowley over half a century ago, but no one has followed up his effort after his untimely death in 1933. Koehler published a lexicon (1948–1953), which even Baumgartner's considerably revised edition is hardly able to improve upon, so that it can seriously compete (in many respects) even with Brown-Driver-Briggs. (There is a good historical reason for this serious lack of progress, and I shall return to the problem below.)

Finally, the dominant philosophy of history then prevalent was Hegelianism or variations of it, so that the widely accepted reconstruction of biblical Israel's

---

in paperback, 1964 [Univ. of Notre Dame]); what remains to be done is to account for the kind of biblical exegesis practised by the Gilbert Crispins and the Peter Abailards and the Hughs and the Andrews of St. Victor in the light of the historical developments in eleventh-twelfth century England. In more recent times, an inkling of the problem may be gained from a careful reading (sometimes between the lines) of the preface (pp. III–XXI) and addenda (XXV–XXXIX) of Driver's *Introduction to the Literature of the Old Testament* (rev. ed., 1913), where the learned and careful author has to defend his philosophy of biblical interpretation. An historical analysis of the attitude of the Church of England and its supporters toward Driver's kind of exegesis would constitute a major contribution to the history of the study of the Bible (e.g., why certain theories are regarded favorably by some groups and rejected in other circles, regardless of the cogency of the argumentation).

Formal—but really really perfunctory—surveys of this aspect of biblical research may be found in such Introductions as R. H. Pfeiffer, *Introduction to the Old Testament* (New York: Harper, 1941), pp. 40–49 (Ch. 3: Historical and Critical Interest in the Old Testament); or O. Eissfeldt, *The Old Testament: An Introduction* (New York: Harper and Row, 1965), pp. 1–7 (§1: "The Nature of the Undertaking"); cf. the articles on "Biblical Criticism" (by K. Grobel, *IDB*, 1 [1962] 407–13) and "Biblical Criticism, History of" (by S. J. De Vries, *IDB*, 1 [1962] 413–18) and their bibliographies.

2. I have discussed some aspects of this in the chapter on "Old Testament Studies" (pp. 51–109) in the volume on *Religion* (ed. P. Ramsey; *Princeton Studies: Humanistic Scholarship in America*, Princeton, 1965).

history and literary creativity was largely that of Wellhausen and S. R. Driver, as found in their standard introductions and commentaries, not to mention Wellhausen's *Prolegomena* and *Geschichte,* or Eduard Meyer's several works.

World War I, among other things, opened up western Asia, northeast Africa, and the eastern Mediterranean region generally to the world at large. The Ottoman Turkish Empire gave way to British and French domination, and also to uninhibited archeological and topographical investigation. This discipline gave new direction and emphasis in biblical research to the extent that it is no exaggeration to apply the term "revolutionary" to it. But revolution can be a bad as well as a good thing; and I believe that the negative and harmful consequences of archeology can and ought no longer to be denied or brushed aside.

But good things first. By the end of World War I biblical research had become stabilized, i.e., had gotten into a rut. Excellent as they were, and in many respects still are, the dictionaries, grammars, introductions, and commentaries mentioned above were not being significantly improved upon; no really new insights or breakthroughs were apparent. A major source of new data, the Sumero-Akkadian, had become available; but progress here was only gradual and accumulative. The Documentary Theory, as refined especially by Wellhausen on the Continent and by Driver in Great Britain, reigned supreme. The Pentateuch, as everyone knew, was composite; and the composers were J, E, D, and P. For lack of other approaches and new data, scholars delved even more intensively into these four sources, decomposing the composers into J_1 and J_2, E_1 and E_2, and the like. While sensitive to the frustrations confronting our colleagues of fifty and forty years ago, we regret that so much talent and energy were spent in helping to demonstrate the law of diminishing returns.

With all their secondary disagreements about the limits of J and E, or the character, if not the very existence, of J_2 and E_2,[3] scholars generally agreed not only in the matter of the four primary documents, J, E, D, and P, but also in something that was much more important, viz., that none of the four documents was to be treated as reliable material on which to base a serious reconstruction of biblical Israel's early career. Hence not only could J, E, D, and P be separated as essentially distinct literary creations, and not only could they be dated in their preserved form with some confidence—J and E as the products of the tenth-ninth centuries, D of the seventh (pre-exilic) century, and P of the sixth-fifth (post-exilic) century—but, and this was or should have been regarded as the most

---

3. I have used the term "secondary (disagreements)" deliberately; already Driver (*Introduction,* Preface, pp. IV–VI and n. * on p. VI) had something trenchant to say about how "language is sometimes used implying that critics are in a state of internecine conflict with one another ... [so that] the results of the critical study of the Old Testament are often seriously misrepresented...." Many of us today have heard people glibly assert that archeology has "confirmed" the Bible and demolished the Documentary Theory!

important aspect of the Documentary Theory, they were considerably devoid of historical authenticity. Not one of the documents could the sober scholar use, except with the greatest reserve, for the reconstruction of the patriarchal period, or of the Mosaic, or of that of the Judges.

The great and lasting merit of archeology is that it has made it possible, and even necessary, to grant these documents considerable trustworthiness; this constituted a *revolutionary breakthrough*. Pertinent parallels and other data were brought to light so that the Dark Ages of Canaan-Israel in the second millennium (not to mention the blackout of the region during the fourth and third millennia and the prehistory before that) became the relatively well-known Middle and Late Bronze Ages. In this connection, I need only mention in passing such important excavations as that of Albright at Tell Beit Mirsim in the Twenties and such discoveries as those at Nuzu and Ugarit in the Twenties and Thirties. There is hardly an aspect of biblical research that has not benefited directly or indirectly, sometimes to a remarkable degree, from archeology, be it linguistics, lexicography, poetic structure, textual criticism, theology, history, chronology, social and legal institutions, comparative literature, mythology, and so on.

Something too should be said about the fact that the material culture of ancient Israel is now known in vastly greater detail than before. I have in mind not only the walls and houses and household articles (especially pottery) and articles in trade, and the like, but also trade and industry and the crafts in the large. And then there is archeology as a discipline in its own right, regardless of whether it sheds any light on the Bible—and far more often than not it does not. Naturally, archeology in and about the Holy Land is important to biblical scholars "not so much ... as a branch of science per se but as a handmaid, a tool for the better understanding of the Bible and the Holy Land. Unlike the Sumerologist, Akkadiologist, Hittitologist, Egyptologist, and the like, who have been laying bare the history of their area from the beginning of time to the end of the *floruit* of the civilizations that interest them, the biblical scholar has been interested in archeology mainly for its help in elucidating the Bible."[4]

This preoccupation with the biblical aspects of archeology has led to a rather unbalanced view of what archeology has meant for the Bible. Let us recall for a moment the historical background, which many, if not most of us present this evening, lived through, but sometimes tend to overlook in this connection. Ever since World War I, the depression of the early Thirties, the growth of various forms of totalitarianism in Europe and Asia, the horrors of World War II, the cold, hot, lukewarm, and warmed-over wars, domestic and international, of the past two decades, recessions and the fear of them, increasing automation and alienation, and the specter of unemployment—all this and more have convinced

---

4. Orlinsky, "Old Testament Studies," p. 66. In this connection, H. J. Cadbury's presidential address to this Society in 1936 is most germane, "Motives of Biblical Scholarship," *JBL*, 56 (1937), 1–16. [See pp. 33–43 in this volume.]

many that reason and science, the two major ingredients in the making of the Ages of Reason, Enlightenment, Ideology, Analysis, Science (in short, the Ages of Optimism)—were not able to bring our problems, international, national, group, or individual, significantly closer to solution. And so people began to come back to and seek out once again what had long been regarded as the Word of God, the Bible.

This Word, however, was no longer an isolated phenomenon in the midst of history; no longer was it a static event, independent of time and place. For archeology had changed all that.

So it was that the historical circumstances that had brought archeology into being, and had also brought the Bible once again to the fore of man's attention, led to an extraordinary increase of popular interest in the Bible in the light of archeology. Increasingly during the Forties and Fifties, and there is no sign of any appreciable let-up, people began to seek out the "truths" of the Bible as "proved" by archeology. What had been a bit of a rivulet immediately after the tomb of the late King "Tut" was cleared in 1922 became a veritable torrent of picture books on archeology, on the Bible, and on the Holy Land, a number of them good, some excellent, and many simply commercial potboilers—this apart from the daily press and literary magazines and lecture forums as a popular source of information (and misinformation and half-truths and melodramatic accounts)—of how archeology has "proved" the Bible right; as the title of a best-seller of the middle Fifties had it, *Und die Bibel hat doch Recht,* on which D. R. Ap-Thomas commented with refined British understatement (British *Book List,* 1957, p. 18), "...It will certainly have a large sale, although (perhaps in part because) the scholar would wish for a little more caution at some points...."[5]

The emphasis on archeology and the needs of the time made it all too easy for undisciplined journalists and popularizers not only to exaggerate beyond reasonableness the scope of substantiation but to take a giant, and utterly unjustified, step beyond that and assert that this substantiation demonstrated the Bible as the revealed word of God! Nothing could be more of a non-sequitur in disciplined reasoning than the juxtaposition of these two completely independent phenomena. This widespread confusion between the Bible as a religious document and the Bible as a historical document is a serious matter, and I shall touch on it below.

The rise of biblical archeology since World War I not only coincided with but has in part been responsible—to be sure, unwittingly—for the decline in biblical philology and textual criticism. In the general educational pattern of the United States and Canada, the humanities began to give way to the pure, the applied, and

---

5. Cadbury's *caveat* (p. 11 [p. 40 in this volume]), "...As experts we have some responsibility to help curb the morbid tastes of so many superficial lay book readers who prefer to hear from us some new guess than some old fact," certainly applies here.

the social sciences. The number of students studying Greek and Latin in high school and college decreased considerably in the past two or three decades, and these subjects are generally not required for ordination even in theological seminaries; so most students, by the time they have acquired the B.A. or B.D. degree and decide to specialize in Bible, must begin the study of Greek and Latin, of Hebrew, Aramaic, Canaanite, Syriac, Arabic, Akkadian, or Egyptian. And since it is much easier to do original work in connection with such expanding disciplines as archeology and Akkadian and Northwest Semitic-Canaanite, it is these areas—especially in the form of parallels between them and between passages and phrases in the Bible—that have been attracting the research efforts of so many younger scholars who otherwise would have tended toward biblical philology. As a result, in 1947, E. C. Colwell, in his presidential address to this Society, was able to begin right off with the assertion, "Biblical criticism today is not the most robust of academic disciplines … [it] is relatively sterile today.…"[6]

This widespread inadequacy in the most basic of disciplines in any field of scholarly research, that of being able to handle a text, showed up especially in the study of the biblical portions of the Dead Sea Scrolls. It is no exaggeration, as it is no pleasure, to assert that all too many of the textual studies of these biblical documents hardly rated a passing grade. The Wellhausens and the S. R. Drivers, the George Foot Moores and the Max Margolis's, and the James Alan Montgomerys would have known how to deal with biblical texts and quotations, whether copied from a *Vorlage* or written down from memory or from dictation. Instead, that gold mine of misinformation and half-truths and of errors of omission and commission, and the like, viz., the so-called critical apparatus in Kittel's *Biblia Hebraica*³, constituted the pay dirt for so many who used it when referring to or when basing arguments on the Septuagint or Targum or Syriac or Vulgate, etc., but who never saw these primary versions directly, or never realized the inner problems that not infrequently beset the primary versions. It will suffice here to reproduce the following statement from the survey article by Peter Katz(-Walters) in 1956, "Septuagintal Studies in the Mid-Century,"[7] "…Contrary to Lagarde's intentions they [Duhm and his school] confined their interest in the LXX to those passages which seemed hopeless in the Hebrew. One may say with truth: Never was the LXX more used and less studied! Unfortunately much of this misuse survives in BH³. I have long given up collecting instances. Ziegler, after ten pages of corrections from the Minor Prophets alone, rightly states that all the references to 𝔊 must be rechecked. H. M. Orlinsky who comes back to this point

---

6. "Biblical Criticism: Lower and Higher," *JBL*, 67 (1948), 1–12.

7. Subtitled "Their Links with the Past and Their Present Tendencies," *The Background of the New Testament and its Eschatology In Honour of Charles Harold Dodd* (eds. W. D. Davies and D. Daube; Cambridge: University Press), pp. 176–208.

time and again is not very far from the truth when he says that not a single line in the apparatus of BH³ is free from mistakes regarding 𝕲" (p. 198).⁸

So far as the biblical texts among the Dead Sea Scrolls are concerned, it must be said that whatever be the consensus of scholarly opinion about their value for the textual criticism of the Bible, that consensus would have very little *a priori* standing in a court of law in which competent textual critics were the judge and jury. The consensus, whatever it be, would have to undergo the most detailed and searching methodological cross examination before it could hope to be cleared by the court. The fact that the biblical scrolls have come to enjoy a fairly widespread popularity among members of our scholarly guild makes that no more authoritative and useful than the fact that for decades the critical apparatus in BH³ also enjoyed that very status; the latter is a woefully weak link in the chain of the former.⁹

Another aspect of biblical research that the fruits of archeology have unfortunately helped to bring to the fore is the current vogue to equate "parallelism" with "proof," to substitute the citation of parallels for reasoned argument. I suppose that it is inevitable in the nature of things for anyone, as well as anything, to seek the level of least resistance. When the cuneiform texts of the second and first millennia B.C. were uncovered earlier in the twentieth century, what was more natural than for scholars to jump on the Hittite and other bandwagons and find parallels in the most unlikely as well as likely places? One may readily recall the Pan-Babylonian-Hittite school, and the obsession of Hugo Winckler; or the tracing back of almost every detail in the biblical version of creation to the so-called Babylonian Genesis, Enuma Elish; or the connecting of nearly every clause in the pentateuchal laws associated with Moses to the laws of Hammurabi. It is true that, by and large, we have subsequently learned differently. We dismiss good-naturedly Winckler's Pan-Babylonianism; and probably most scholars would now agree, e.g., with T. J. Meek's statement of twenty years ago (*Hebrew Origins²*, pp. 68–69), "There is no doubt but that there is great similarity between the Hebrew

---

8. The reference is to Part I ("Kritische Bemerkungen zur Verwendung der Septuaginta im Zwölfprophetenbuch der Biblia Hebraica von Kittel," pp. 107–120) of J. Ziegler, "Studien zur Verwertung der Septuaginta im Zwölfprophetenbuch," *ZAW*, 60 (1944), 107–131. There the concluding sentence reads, "Bei einer Neuausgabe der Biblia Hebraica des Dodekapropheton muss das gesamte 𝕲—Material, wie es die eben erschienene Göttinger Septuaginta-Ausgabe vorlegt, neu bearbeitet werden" (p. 120).

For my own strictures against Kittel's *apparatus criticus,* see §§I–II (pp. 140–152) of "The Textual Criticism of the Old Testament," *The Bible and the Ancient Near East* (Fest. W. F. Albright; ed. G. E. Wright; Garden City: Doubleday, 1965; paperback reprint, 1961, pp. 113–121), with considerable bibliography. Note especially the reference to the vain attempt of E. Würthwein to suppress the sharp criticism of Kittel's BH³.

9. See §§II–III (pp. 145–157) of "The Textual Criticism of the Old Testament" (cited in n. 8).

and Babylonian codes…, but the connection is not such as to indicate direct borrowing. No one today argues that. Whatever borrowing there was came indirectly, either through common inheritance or through Canaanite influence, or much more likely through both ways."

I think, however, that we must go into the matter more deeply than that, for the problem constitutes the very heart of the question posed in our title: Whither Biblical Research? Bluntly put, it is a fact, one that is generally not recognized, that virtually none of those who are engaged in serious work in our field has been trained to do research in history, that is, to seek to account for the imporant changes, or for the serious, even unsuccessful attempts at changes, or for the failure to attempt any serious changes, in the structure of a given society. And without being able to comprehend historical forces at work, it is simply impossible to understand how a social structure functions, why it comes into being, why it is maintained, why it is changed, sometimes radically.

Let us assume that some time in the future, out of the ground and rubble of civilization, several documents, none of them intact or complete, are excavated: they are what we today recognize as the Constitution of the United States, the Charter of the League of Nations, the Yalta Agreement, and the Charter of the United Nations. And let us assume further that very little is known in any detail about the events that brought these notable documents into being, or of the social forces that brought on those events; more specifically, we know the background of these documents no better than we know, say, the two centuries preceding 586 (or is it 587?) B.C. or the two centuries following the momentous event of that date.

The scholars of that future date begin to study the numerous fragments of those four documents, trying to fit the many pieces together. They devote years to the study of the terribly fragmented texts and contexts. They recognize word formations, phrases, meanings, and the like, which have association—whether directly or indirectly, they are not always sure—with what they know of Latin and Greek, and with the languages and dialects of countries that once in the long ago had been France, Germany, Italy, the United States, Canada, England, Russia, and other such countries. The scholars have considerable difficulty in determining the precise nuance of numerous expressions; and some even suggest that it would be worthwhile compiling special glossaries of legal terms, economic terms, and political terms. Of course, a number of scholars will be busy working on the Form Criticism of these fragmented documents, for their *Sitz im Leben*. Special groups will be formed for this study, and foundations will be approached to help finance these studies. Monographs will be published on the grammatical forms employed in these documents, whether it is, say, the third or the second person that is employed, and on whether the clauses are apodictically or casuistically formulated ("you shall" as against "if one does…, then")—for then the documents may be traced back to a British, or Russian, or American, or French, or other prototype, or perhaps to a common ancestor for all four documents. In that case, it might become possible to date these four documents relatively (i.e., typologically), if not absolutely.

Naturally scholars will disagree in the matter of the relative, as well as of the absolute, dates of the documents. Old words and phrases will be found in all four documents, and so some scholars will jump to the conclusion that the older the phrase the older must be the fragment in which it was preserved. It will also become apparent that those scholars who ultimately derive from, or have an affinity to, the region or people or culture of what had once been, say, Great Britain, will tend to trace the origin and essential nature, and even the extraordinary worthwhileness of the documents—or of the Ur-Document—to that sphere, as against those who will hold out for the North American, or Central European, or Russian spheres, depending on the sphere to which they traced back their own cultural or physical ancestry.

It is obvious that one could go on in this vein, for there are many more areas and sub-areas of study in higher and lower criticism, in linguistics, in literary structure and analysis, and the like, that could be listed. But I have had something more in mind than a purely hypothetical situation in the future. What I have been leading up to is the fact that there is hardly a member of our Society who would be content with the kind of studies that I have indicated—no matter how scientifically they were done on these documents; and they would, of course, be right. After all, is the significance of these documents to be found in their linguistic history and character? Or in their literary structure? Their primary importance, when all is said and done, their major raison d'être for scholars, as well as for laymen, lies in their historical value, in the use to which they are put for the explanation of not only what happened but *why* it happened. *Why* were these documents drawn up in the first place? Who had them drawn up, not merely the names of the countries but the powerful groups within each country? What motivated each of the signatories? Why did certain major powers decline to become signatories—for surely the reason that the United States did not become a signatory of the League of Nations will not be determined through literary, or linguistic, or archeological, or theological analysis.

It is for historical matters that these documents have significance, for it is about these matters that the welfare—sometimes the very existence—of the government and people of the signatory countries, and even of a number of non-signatory countries, revolves. One can just imagine how the scholarly and lay world, where it did not simply ignore, would hoot derisively at the virtually exclusively philological, literary, linguistic, archeological, theological, and similar studies of these documents; the silence that would greet these studies would truly be golden compared to the scorn with which they would be laughed at. And the world would be right: Is that all that these documents are useful for? Is that their true significance? Yet this is precisely what we members of our biblical guild have been doing since archeology began to provide us with a breakthrough in our field half-a-century ago. Literary patterns and—what is much worse, lexical and literary *parallels*—are what have been occupying the energies of so many of us and have been filling so many of the pages of our learned journals and books. In the past decade especially, hardly an issue of our journal and of others in the field has appeared without an article or two and a book review or two, or more, that does not deal in part or in whole with a parallel, or an alleged parallel, between a biblical phrase or section on the one hand and an extrabiblical correspondent on the other. A decade ago the search for parallels in "the areas of rabbinic literature and the gospels, Philo and Paul, and [by then, especially] the Dead Sea Scrolls and the NT" had reached such proportions that the presidential address to this Society in 1962 dealt with "Parallelomania." That was actually the title of the address; and the plea was made that "biblical scholarship should recognize parallelomania for the disease that it is … and which the scrolls have made an imminent and omnipresent one."[10]

I have alluded already to the handling of the biblical texts among the Dead Sea Scrolls both per se and in relation to the received Hebrew text and the Septuagint; this is a chapter in itself, not a very happy one. But I do wish to make specific reference to the current vogue, viz., the limitless and uncritical search for extrabiblical parallels to the concept and institution of covenant in the Bible. There is hardly a treaty or contract in any part of the Near East of the second or first millennium B.C. that has not been cited as a prototype of the biblical notion of covenant. Yet I am not aware of a single study of the concept and institution of the covenant in the Bible that a historian *qua* historian could accept methodologically. True, there is the basic factor, beyond the historian's immediate control, of being unable to date most of the biblical material. Imagine working on the Constitution of the United States, the Charters of the League of Nations and the United Nations, and the Yalta Agreement, and trying to reconstruct from them the history of their signatories without being able to date these documents relatively or absolutely. Yet that is exactly what we have been doing and tolerating, even accepting, in our field. All kinds of Sumerian, Assyrian, Babylonian, Hittite, and Northwest Semitic texts of all historical climes and periods are cited indiscriminately to prove that Israel and God had agreed to a vassal treaty. I am not really being facetious when I wonder out loud where the various historians, prophets, psalmists, and chroniclers—not to mention the glossators and redactors—who composed the Bible found the time to compose what they did when they were so busy reading and keeping up with and making use of the suzerain-vassal treaties that the Hittites and Babylonians and Assyrians and Northwest Semites were signing and, so often, breaking. In point of fact, I am not sure that any scholar has ever proved—worse, I am not sure that any scholar has recently even thought of trying to prove—that the contractual relationship between Israel and God as presented in the Bible is actually one that involves an inferior and

---

10. S. Sandmel, "Parallelomania," *JBL*, 81 (1962), 1–13. [See pp. 107–18 in this volume.]

a superior in the manner of a vassal and a suzerain. My own impression is that the biblical concept of the contractual relationship between Israel and God, a relationship into which both parties entered freely and in which both are legally equals, derives ultimately—since God by the very concept of Him to begin with is the Lord, and Israel the servant—from the lord-servant (*ādôn-'ebed*) relationship that characterized Israel's (and much of Western Asia's) economy at the time. And while biblical expressions may be clarified with the aid of extrabiblical texts, I do not see how this can prove that Israel's covenant with God derived from vassal-suzerain treaties. As a matter of fact, it may well be that the more numerous the "covenant" parallels between Israel and her Asiatic neighbors during the second and first millennia B.C. become, the greater becomes the probability that the biblical concept of the Israel-God covenant developed quite independently. So that, with Gertrude Stein, a parallel is a parallel is a parallel.... The pity of it is that in pursuing and collecting parallels, scholars think that they are writing history.[11]

The net result is this: when the overwhelming majority of us are not trained textually and are unable for the most part to handle a text properly, and when even fewer of us have been trained to get at the underlying forces that shape the structure of society, to comprehend the social process, that can mean only one thing—that our work is rarely taken seriously by historians in the classical, or medieval, or modern periods of research. The most frequently used history of biblical Israel, virtually our standard textbook, is described by its author as having "been prepared with the particular needs of the undergraduate theological student in mind"; and the author of a standard textbook in biblical archeology states frankly in his preface that "only readers concerned with the religious value of the Bible will find anything of interest in these pages. The volume has been written with a frankly and definitely religious interest. It has also, of course, been written from a particular point of view, that of a liberal Protestant Christian." Whatever else it may be that we are writing, it is not *history*.

Let us understand each other correctly. I am not opposed to Form Criticism, or to linguistic study, or to excavations, or to the seeking out of similarities—as well as points of difference—between Israel and her neighbors. Quite the contrary! I am all in favor of it, and more. But these disciplines, while each of them must be studied per se and not treated as but a handmaid to something else, cannot be regarded as ends in themselves for the real comprehension of ancient Israel. A historical analysis of, say, the concept of covenant in biblical Israel's career will go quite beyond the citation and compilation of parallels between biblical and extrabiblical phrases; it will, instead, ask—and attempt to answer—such questions as, Why did the concept of covenant mean one thing to Jeremiah and something

---

11. The "covenant" parallels may turn out to be very little different from the "Hammurabi" parallels, viz., essentially parallels.

else to his opponents in the matter of pacts with Babylonia and Egypt? What did "covenant" really mean when Uriah "prophesied in the name of the Lord" against the policy of King Jehoiakim, had to flee for his life to Egypt, was brought back, executed, and denied proper burial (Jer 26:20–23)? Why did "covenant" mean one thing to King Josiah in his attempted "reformation," and the opposite to those who championed the cause of the legitimate and nonidolatrous shrines all over the country (for we fall into a trap when we follow tradition mechanically and brand the *bāmôt* as idolatrous "high places")? Was it a question of conflicting economic and political interests couched in religious terminology—a phenomenon common to historians, especially to those who study the Middle Ages. Only when all the data achieved by Form Criticism, archeology, textual criticism, the determination of parallels, and the like, are brought into proper focus and play by the trained historian do they acquire life, worthwhileness, meaning.

In fine, as a consequence of a resurgence of textual criticism and philology in the broadest sense and by the introduction of the methodology and outlook of the trained historian, we shall not have to worry about a question like "Whither Biblical Research?" and preclude the withering of meaningful biblical research.

The full title of the presidential address had been "Whither Biblical Research: The Problem of 'Sin' as a Case in Point." Since time did not permit, the latter part of the title was not discussed on the podium of the Society's banquet. Here I shall but touch on the problem of the concept "sin" in the Bible, as I see it.

Discussions of "sin" in the Bible are almost as numerous as occurrences of sin; see, e.g., the recent study by R. Knierim, *Die Hauptbegriffe für Sünde im Alten Testament* (1965; 280 pp., with bibliography). It seems to me that without significant exception, the opening paragraphs of the article on "Sin" in *The Interpreter's Dictionary of the Bible* (IV, 361a–376a) represent very well the manner in which our guild of scholars understands the concept. They read:

> The Bible takes sin in dead seriousness. Unlike many modern religionists, who seek to find excuses for sin and to explain away its seriousness, most of the writers of the Bible had a keen awareness of its heinousness, culpability, and tragedy. They looked upon it as no less than a condition of dreadful estrangement from God, the sole source of well-being. They knew that apart from God, man is a lost sinner, unable to save himself or find true happiness.
>
> It is not difficult to find biblical passages referring to sin; as a matter of fact, there are few chapters which do not contain some references to what sin is or does. It might even be said that in the Bible man has only two theological concerns involving himself: his sin and his salvation. Man finds himself in sin and suffers its painful effects; God graciously offers salvation from it. This is, in essence, what the whole Bible is about.

It is my contention that this is precisely what the Bible is not about, and that the only way that one can begin to understand what sin, as well as the Bible as a whole, is all about is to try to comprehend it naturally to the extent that our sources permit—in the light of the specific historical circumstances that prevailed at any given time. For instance, if one reads the book of Ezekiel, one gathers that the government and the people of Judah were on the greatest sinning binge in the history of Judah and Israel, if not in all of history. If only ten just men had been found living in Sodom and Gomorrah, those legendary centers of sin and all their sinful inhabitants would have been spared. But so great was the sin of Jerusalem and Judah that, even if those very models of justice, Noah, Job, and Daniel, were living there, they alone would have been spared; but all the other inhabitants would have been destroyed, along with the Temple, the great city itself, and the country as a whole.

Ezekiel, as is well known, has provided us with a most detailed description of sinful acts, some of them so perverse and striking that more than one person has been led to believe that much of the detail was due to "Ezekiel's Abnormal Personality."[12] But whether the acts of sin did or did not take place, no serious historian would permit himself to be drawn into a debate as to whether the sin of Jerusalem and Judah was greater than that of Sodom and Gomorrah, or whether such sin as Ezekiel described, regardless of its alleged quantity and quality, was responsible for King Nebuchadnezzar's decision to wage a military campaign against—*inter alia*—Judah. Rather, the modern historian would "seek—behind the religious terminology—the same kind of documented human story, with an examination of its underlying dynamics, that would be his proper objective in any other field. Otherwise he would achieve no more than a compilation of myths, chronicles, annals, oracles, autobiographies, court histories, personal apologia."[13] In dealing with the book of Ezekiel, the historian now has good reason to regard the Book as a whole as essentially reliable—unlike the situation in the late Twenties and early Thirties—thanks to the excavation of such sites as Tell Beit Mirsim, Beth Shemesh, and Lachish, and the publication in 1939 of the long-excavated and lost Babylonian texts of Nebuchadnezzar and Evil-merodach. But in his analysis of the momentous events that befell Judah at the turn of the sixth century B.C., the historian will go seeking behind such terms as "sin" and "covenant" for the fundamental economic, political, and social forces that determined the use and content—and, so frequently, the utter disregard—of these terms.[14] There is a great future for biblical research and the trained historian who devotes himself to it.

---

12. E. J. Broome, Jr., *JBL*, 65 (1940), 277–92.

13. From the writer's *Ancient Israel* (Ithaca: Cornell, 1954), p. 9 (p. 7 in the 2nd paperback edition, 1960).

14. The reader will do well to study carefully the methodology employed by M. A. Cohen in his discussion of "The Role of the Shilonite Priesthood in the United Monarchy of Ancient Israel" (*HUCA*, 36 [1965], 59–98) and in his analysis of "The Rebellions during the Reign of David: An Inquiry into the Social Dynamics of Ancient Israel," in the forthcoming volume of *Studies in Jewish Bibliography, History, and Literature in Honor of I. Edward Kiev* (ed. C. Berlin, New York: KTAV, 1971).

A Reconstruction of the Judean Restoration*

Frank Moore Cross
Harvard University

The literature dealing with the fifth and fourth centuries in Palestine appears to expand by geometric progression. I think it is fair to say, however, that little progress has been made in solving the hard problems in the history of the Restoration since the assimilation of new evidence from the Elephantine papyri published in 1911.[1] If one compares the review of literature on the date of Ezra's mission by H. H. Rowley published in 1948[2] and the review by Ulrich Kellermann in 1968,[3] one comes away disappointed; a generation of research has added at best a few plausible speculations,[4] but little, if any, hard new evidence. The scholarly procedure has been to review the same body of evidence and arguments and come boldly down on one of three dates for Ezra in relation to Nehemiah: (1) Ezra came before Nehemiah, a view we may label "the traditional view"; (2) Ezra came after Nehemiah, which for convenience we may call the "Van Hoonacker position"; (3) Ezra came during or between Nehemiah's visits to Jerusalem, the "Kosters-

---

* The Presidential Address delivered 25 October 1974, at the annual meeting of the Society of Biblical Literature, held at the Washington-Hilton, Washington, D.C.

1. I refer in particular to *AP* 21, 30, 31, 32 (*AP* = A. Cowley, *Aramaic Papyri of the Fifth Century B.C.* [Oxford: Clarendon, 1923; reprinted, Osnabrück: Zeller, 1967]).

2. "The Chronological Order of Ezra and Nehemiah," republished in *The Servant of the Lord* (2d ed.; Oxford: Blackwell, 1965) 137–68 (first published in *Ignace Goldziher Memorial Volume* [eds. S. Löwinger and J. Somogyi; Budapest: Globus, 1948], 1. 117–49); cf. "Nehemiah's Mission and Its Background," *BJRL* 37 (1955) 528–61; and "Sanballaṭ and the Samaritan Temple," *BJRL* 38 (1955) 166–98.

3. "Erwägungen zum Problem der Esradatierung," *ZAW* 80 (1968) 55–87; and "Erwägungen zum Esragesetz," *ZAW* 80 (1968) 373–85.

4. We should place J. Morgenstern's proposals ("The Dates of Ezra and Nehemiah," *JSS* 7 [1962] 1–11) and Morton Smith's assertions (*Palestinian Parties and Politics That Shaped the Old Testament* [New York: Columbia University, 1971] 99å147) in the category of the less than plausible speculations. Smith is certainly correct, however, in recognizing that "arguments from personal names (of which Rowley makes much) are generally worthless because of the frequency of papponomy at this period, and the frequency of most of the names concerned" (p. 252 n. 109).

Bertholet view." To these we should add the position of C. C. Torrey that Ezra was a fiction of the Chronicler's imagination and, consequently, had no date. Some scholars refuse to commit themselves in print, and others shift back and forth between two or more views—a decade, let us say, to Van Hoonacker, a decade to Bertholet or the traditional view.[5]

The time has come, however, for the study of the era of the Restoration to take new directions. Over the last twenty years tidbits of new evidence have accumulated and now, when brought together, give new contexts or perspectives with which to approach old problems. None of these bits of new evidence is particularly dramatic or conclusive. Taken together, however, they provide new solutions which can move the present discussion out of stalemate.

The discovery in 1962 of fourth-century legal papyri executed in Samaria is perhaps the most important source of new data.[6] From the papyri we can reconstruct the sequence of governors in Samaria by virtue of the practice of papponymy, the naming of a child after his grandfather (see the appended genealogical chart). The Samaritan genealogy overlaps with the genealogies of the Judean Restoration from the sixth to the tenth generation after the return. Sanballaṭ I, the Horonite, is the founder of the dynasty, as his gentilic suggests, the contemporary of Nehemiah and 'Elyašîb, as biblical references make clear, and the contemporary of the high priests Yōyadaʿ and Yōḥanan, as we can deduce from biblical and Elephantine references.[7] The Sanballaṭ of Josephus proves to be Sanballaṭ III, the contemporary of Darius III and Alexander, the builder of the Samaritan temple on Gerizim.[8] Equally important, the sequence of Sanballaṭids makes certain what has long been suspected, that two generations are missing in the biblical genealogy of Jewish high priests.[9] This lacuna in the fourth century is supplied by Josephus, who is correct in his record that a certain Yōḥanan killed his brother Yēšūaʿ in the temple in the time of the infamous Bagoas, the commander-in-chief of Artaxerxes III (Ochus, 358–38 B.C.) in his expeditions to Phoenicia, Palestine, and Egypt during the western insurrections,[10] and that Yōḥanan's successor was Yaddūaʿ, high priest in the days of Darius III (335–30)

---

5. This last-mentioned option, I must confess, is the one I have chosen. It at least has the advantage of giving variety.

6. See F. M. Cross, "Papyri of the Fourth Century B.C. from Dâliyeh: A Preliminary Report on Their Discovery and Significance," *New Directions in Biblical Archaeology* (eds. D. N. Freedman and J. C. Greenfield; Garden City: Doubleday, 1969) 41–62. A first volume of the final report is now in press.

7. *AP* 30:29 and *AP* 30:18.

8. *Ant* 11.7, 2 §302–3; 11.8, 2 §306å12; 11.8, 4 §325. Sanballaṭ III died in 332 B.C., of an age to have had a marriageable daughter.

9. 1 Chr 5:41; Neh 3:1, 21; 12:10, 22–23; 13:4; Ezra 10:6.

10. Most of us have assumed that Josephus confused Bagoas the general with Bagoas (*bgwhy*) of *AP* 30–32, a successor to Nehemiah, as governor of Judah; it proves to be an instance of hypercritical presumption on our part.

and Alexander.[11] In short, we can now reconstitute the end of the list of high priests as follows: Yōḥanan father of Yaddūaʿ, Yaddūaʿ father of Onias I.[12] Or in other words, in the sequence Yōḥanan, Yaddūaʿ, Yōḥanan, Yaddūaʿ there has been a simple haplography with the loss of two names, in extremely easy consequence of the device of papponymy. Whether Josephus' list of high priests was defective or he merely telescoped the genealogy in writing the history of the fifth-fourth centuries, it is clear that he confused Yaddūaʿ II and Yaddūaʿ III as well as Sanballaṭ I and Sanballaṭ III with diabolical results for the history of the Restoration. Thus the Yaddūaʿ of Neh 12:10, 22 (Yaddūaʿ II, the grandson of Yōyadaʿ, the first of the name)[13] is correctly attributed to the time of Darius II (Nothus 423–404) in the Bible, and the Yaddūaʿ of the *Antiquities* is correctly attributed by Josephus to the time of Alexander. Similarly, we can observe that Josephus is probably correct in his remark that "Israelites" (i.e., Yahwists of Samaria) frequently intermarried with the high-priestly family in Jerusalem.[14] At least two instances must be admitted, the son of Yōyadaʿ I, who married the daughter of Sanballaṭ I,[15] and Manasseh the brother of Yaddūaʿ III, who married Nikasō the daughter of Sanballaṭ III.[16] The narratives of these two marriages can no longer be regarded as the reflexes of a single instance of intermarriage. This circumstance is not unimportant in assessing the "Zadokite" character of Samaritan religion or in reconstructing the relations between Samaria and Jerusalem in the era of the Restoration. The Tobiads of Ammon appear to have enjoyed similar relations with the ruling priestly family of Jerusalem despite Nehemiah's polemics.[17]

The practice of papponymy in ruling houses of the Persian period has long been recognized. Still, new evidence for its practice has drawn our attention more sharply to its importance as a control in reconstructing genealogies. If B. Mazar's reconstruction is correct, the name Tobiah alternates over nine generations of Tobiads.[18] In a newly published Ammonite inscription the royal name

---

11. *Ant.* 11.7, 2 §302–3; 11.8, 2 §306–12; 11.8, 7 §347. Yaddūaʿ died, we are told (11.8, 7 §347), ca. 323 B.C. (the time of Alexander's death).

12. As we shall see, Onias I (ibid.) is in fact Yōḥanan IV. The name Onias is the Greek form of Hebrew Ḥōnay (byform: Ḥōni), a typical hypocoristicon of the pattern *qutay* used for so-called biconsonantal roots. Both the name Ḥōnay and the pattern *qutay* are well known at Elephantine as well as later. Cf. M. H. Silverman, *Jewish Personal Names in the Elephantine Documents* (Ann Arbor: University Microfilms, 1967) 95–96 and references. The name Ḥōnay is, in fact, merely the caritative or diminutive of Yōḥanan. Similarly, *yaddūaʿ* is the *qattil* hypocoristicon, a caritative of Yōyadaʿ.

13. See the discussion in n. 11.

14. *Ant.* 11.8, 2 §312.

15. Neh 13:28.

16. *Ant.* 11.8, 2 §306–12. See the discussion in "Papyri of the Fourth Century B.C. from Daliyeh," 54–55.

17. Neh 13:4–9.

18. B. Mazar, "The Tobiads," *IEJ* 7 (1957) 137–45, 229–38.

'Ammīnadab alternates over six generations.[19] Sanballaṭ repeats over six generations at Samaria, and if our reconstruction of the Judean family of high priests is correct, the name Yōḥanan (or the caritative Ḥōnay) occurs no fewer than seven times over twelve generations. Over against this, happily, the royal house of Judah does not practice papponymy in the first seven generations of the Restoration, giving us a measure of control over the parallel list of high priests, as we shall see.

The dating of Nehemiah's mission to 445, the twentieth year of Artaxerxes I, has not been in serious dispute since the appearance of Sanballaṭ in an Elephantine letter of 407 B.C. The new list of Sanballaṭids further confirms the fifth-century date, and finally the discovery of a silver bowl inscribed by "Qaynu son of Gašm [biblical Gešem, Gašmu],[20] king of Qedar,"[21] would appear to settle the matter finally.[22] The script of the bowl cannot be dated later than 400 B.C., placing Geshem, Qaynu's father, precisely in the second half of the fifth century B.C.

Another series of advances has been made in the developing study of the Greek versions of Ezra, notably in the recognition of the importance of the text of 1 Esdras for historical reconstruction. H. H. Howorth, C. C. Torrey, and S. Mowinckel have pioneered in these studies.[23] With the discovery of the Qumran scrolls, and their evidence for the history of Hebrew textual families, earlier views of the importance and priority of the Hebrew recension of Ezra underlying the Greek of 1 Esdras have been vindicated. The relation of the two recensions of Ezra, one preserved in the Palestinian text known from Qumran Cave 4 (4QEzra)

---

19. See F. M. Cross, "Notes on the Ammonite Inscription from Tell Sirin," *BASOR* 212 (1973) 12–15.

20. Neh 2:19; 6:1–2, 6.

21. The bowl was published with other finds in the Wādī Ṭumeilāt by Isaac Rabinowitz, "Aramaic Inscriptions of the Fifth Century B.C.E. from a North-Arab Shrine in Egypt," *JNES* 15 (1956) 1–9. He dates the script of the bowl to ca. 400 B.C., a date I should term correct but minimal. See also W. J. Dumbrell, "The Tell el-Maskhuṭa Bowls and the 'Kingdom' of Qedar in the Persian Period," *BASOR* 203 (1971) 33–44. The discovery of the bowl supports the fifth-century dating of an early Liḥyanite inscription from El-'Ulā (Dedan), which mentions Gašm bin Šahr and 'Abd, governor (*paḥat*) of Dedan, a dating held by Winnett and Albright against strong opposition. See W. F. Albright, "Dedan," *Geschichte und Altes Testament* (Beitrige zur historischen Theologie, 16; Tübingen: Mohr, 1953) 1–12, esp. p. 4 and n. 5. Albright's conjecture that the biblical formula *ṭwbyh h'bd h'mny* (Neh 2:10, 19) should be read *ṭwbyhw w'bd h'mny* (with the haplography of a single *waw*) is most tempting. It would not be strange at all if 'Abd, a Persian governor of Dedan, were an Ammonite and associated on the one side with Tobiah of Ammon, and Geshem, the Arab king of Qedar.

22. It must be observed, however, that there is evidence of papponymy in the Qedarite house. See Albright, "Dedan," 6–7.

23. See especially Torrey's *Ezra Studies* (Chicago: University of Chicago, 1910); and S. Mowinckel, *Studien zu dem Buche Ezra-Nehemiah* (3 vols.; Oslo: Universitetsforlaget, 1964–65). The citation of 1 Esdras is from the excellent new critical edition of R. Hanhart, *Esdrae Liber 1* (Septuaginta: Vetus Testamentum graecum, 8/1; Gottingen: Vandenhoeck & Ruprecht, 1974).

and from the Masoretic text, the other preserved in the Alexandrian translation of an Egyptian text type (1 Esdras), has an almost precise analogy in the two recensions of Jeremiah, the long and the short, both preserved in Hebrew manuscripts from Qumran, 4QJer^a, the Palestinian text preserved in the later Masoretic text, and 4QJer^b, the Egyptian text found also in the Old Greek translation of Jeremiah. The Egyptian textual tradition is pristine, short, and follows an earlier ordering of chapters; the Palestinian textual family is expansive and conflate, with its ordering of pericopes secondary.[24] Ralph Klein has brought together the evidence for the two recensions of Ezra.[25] The Palestinian recension is conflate, expansionistic, and follows a late, secondary ordering of pericopes. It is reflected in 4QEzra, in Esdras B, a Palestinian translation by a forerunner of the school of Theodotion,[26] and in the rabbinic recension which developed into the Masoretic text. The Egyptian textual family is reflected in 1 Esdras, translated in Egypt in the mid-second century B.C.[27] In parallel passages, 1 Esdras proves on the whole to have a shorter, better text, and, as generally recognized, its order of pericopes reflects an older, historically superior recension of the Chronicler's work (Chronicles, Ezra). Most important, 7:72b through 8:12 of Nehemiah (1 Esdr 9:37–55) is placed immediately after Ezra 10 (1 Esdr 8:88–9:36). That is to say, the entire Ezra-narrative is separated wholly from the memoirs of Nehemiah. Thus it must be said that in an earlier recension of the Chronicler's work, the missions of Ezra and Nehemiah did not overlap. Moreover, in 1 Esdr 9:49 (= Neh 8:9) the name "Nehemiah" is missing in the description of the reading of the law; there is only reference to the *Tiršātā*. That the name Nehemiah does not belong here is also evidenced by the chronological problem developed thereby: thirteen years would have passed between Ezra's return and the reading of the law that he brought with him—presuming the chronology of the final edition of the Chronicler's work. In short, we must consider it a fixed point in the discussion that the Ezra-narrative has no mention of Nehemiah in its original form and that the Nehemiah-memoirs contain no reference to Ezra.[28]

---

24. The evidence is fully presented by J. Gerald Janzen, *Studies in the Text of Jeremiah* (Harvard Semitic Monographs, 6; Cambridge: Harvard University, 1973). See also E. Tov, "L'incidence de la critique textuelle sur la critique littéraire dans le livre de Jérémie," *RB* 79 (1972) 189–99.

25. "Studies in the Greek Texts of the Chronicler" (Cambridge, MA: unpublished Ph.D. dissertation, Harvard University, 1966). A summary can be found in *HTR* 59 (1966) 449; see also his paper "Old Readings in 1 Esdras: The List of Returnees from Babylon (Ezra 2 = Nehemiah 7)," *HTR* 62 (1969) 99–107.

26. The translator of 2 Esdras is not Theodotion (*contra* Torrey), nor is he identical with the so-called καίγε recension, though he shares some of the latter's traits.

27. See the arguments of Klein in the work cited in n. 25.

28. The appearance of the name Nehemiah in Neh 10:1, of Ezra in Neh 12:36, and the mention of both in Neh 12:25 all stem from the hand of the editor of the final edition of the Chronicler's work (Chr$_3$, see below).

1 Esdras completes the Ezra-narrative (save for a fragment at its close) now found in Neh 8:13–18, the account of preparations for and the celebration of the Feast of Tabernacles. Evidently, the end of the scroll of 1 Esdras, which became the archetype of the Greek text of 1 Esdras, was defective. The reading of the Law and the celebration of the high holidays[29] were the appropriate climax and conclusion. That one recension of the Chronicler's work ended at the close of ch. 8 of Nehemiah (i.e., at the end of the original ch. 9 of 1 Esdras) is confirmed by the text of 1 Esdras used by Josephus, who carries the story of Ezra, following precisely the order of 1 Esdras through ch. 8 of Nehemiah, including the celebration of the Feast of Tabernacles.[30] As we shall see, the Chronicler's work once circulated with only the Ezra-narrative appended. The Nehemiah-memoirs were not part of the work but were circulated separately. Josephus knew a Greek translation (no doubt Alexandrian) of the Nehemiah-memoirs quite different from the received text of Nehemiah. However, the integration of the Nehemiah-memoirs into the Chronicler's history belongs to the latest stage of revisions of the Chronicler's work and did not finally oust the earlier recension until the rabbinic recension of the first century of the Christian era became authoritative following the fall of Jerusalem in A.D. 70.

1. Reconstruction of the List of High Priests in the Fifth Century b.c.

We have discussed the problems of the fourth-century sequence of high priests, restoring a haplography of Yōḥanan and Yaddūaʿ on the basis of data from the new list of Sanballaṭids and from the *Antiquities* of Josephus. The genealogy of the priests from the sixth to the fourth centuries without the addition of Yōḥanan (III) and Yaddūaʿ (III) records eight generations for a period of 275 years. This yields the figure of 34.3 years per generation, an incredibly high figure. In Near Eastern antiquity, the generation (i.e., the years between a man's birth and his begetting his first-born son) is ordinarily 25 years or less. The inclusion of the priests, Yōḥanan and Yaddūaʿ, reduces the average generation to about 27.5, still suspiciously high.

The genealogy of the Davidids gives a measure of control for the first seven generations of the Restoration and, happily, does not follow the fashion of pap-

---

29. Apropos of the high holidays, there is no reason to suppose that Ezra followed a pre-pentateuchal calendar, moving up *Sukkôt* and ignoring *Yôm Kippûr* (*pace* Morton Smith). Preparations for *Sukkôt* took more than one day.

30. There is no allusion in Josephus to the covenant-document preserved in Nehemiah 9 (historical prologue in the form of a confession) and 10 (witnesses and stipulations). The chapters belong to the latest stratum of the Chronicler's history (Chr3); it is not clear whether it is an expanded doublet of Ezra's covenant (Ezra 10:3–5) or represents a parallel covenant enacted by Nehemiah. The stipulations conform closely to Nehemiah's reforms. Greek Nehemiah (Esdras B) attributes the confession to Ezra (at 19:6 = Hebr. 9:6).

ponymy, so that the risk of names lost by haplography is slight. In any case, it appears to be complete. The list names seven Davidids, six generations of the Restoration. These occupy a period of years from before 592 (the thirteenth year of Nebuchadrezzar), to ca. 445 B.C., the birth date, roughly, of ʿAnanī, a total of 147 years. This gives the figure of 24.5 years per generation, which is close to what we should expect. Synchronisms exist for two or three of the generations of the Davidids. Zerubbabel and Yēšūaʿ, the high priest, are linked. Hóaṭṭūš returned with Ezra.[31] ʿAnanī, the last of the line recorded in 1 Chr 3:17–24, may be the ʿAnanī named in *AP* 30:19 (410 B.C.); on the other hand, his brother ʾwštn mentioned in the papyrus is not listed among his six brothers in 1 Chronicles 3 by the Persian name.

The list of high priests in the sixth-fifth century, from Yōṣadaq to Yōḥanan, extends over a period of 150 years.[32] Six priests are named in the five generations giving the figure of 30 years per generation, some five years or more per generation too high. We suspect that at least one generation, two high priests' names, has dropped out of the list through a haplography owing to the repetition produced by papponymy.

Turning to the list, we note that the first three names appear to be in order. Yōṣadaq went captive.[33] Yēšūaʿ and his son Yōyaqīm returned with Zerubbabel.[34] Similarly, the last three names—Yōyadaʿ, Yōḥanan, Yadduaʿ—seem to be correct.[35] The center of difficulties, however, is the high priest ʾElyašīb. As brother of Yōyaqīm, in the third generation of the Return, he should have been born about 545 B.C. This would make him 100 and more, when he built the wall of Jerusalem with Nehemiah,[36] and about seventy-five, when he begot Yōyadaʿ. The key to the solution, however, is in the juxtaposition of the priests Yōḥanan son of ʾElyašīb [37] and Yōyadaʿ son of ʾElyašīb.[38] We must reckon with two high priests named ʾElyašīb, and given papponymy, two priests named Yōḥanan. Thus we have the

---

31. Ezra 8:2.
32. We reckon from 595 B.C., a minimal birthdate of Yōṣadaq, who went into captivity (1 Chr 5:41; cf. *Ant.* 20.10, 2 §231, 234; and 1 Esdr 5:5), to the birth of Yōḥanan ca. 445. In Neh 12:22 Yōḥanan (along with Yadduaʿ) is said to have flourished in the reign of Darius (II, Nothus, 423–404 B.C.), and he (Yōḥanan) is high priest in 410 B.C. according to *AP* 30:18.
33. 1 Chr 5:41.
34. The key passage, to which we shall return, is 1 Esdr 5:5–6, which dates Zerubbabel's return in "the second year," i.e., the second year of Darius I, 520 B.C. The text is slightly in disorder. It should read: Yēšūaʿ the son of Yōṣadaq the son of Śarayah and Yōyaqīm his son and Zerubbabel...." Cf. *Ant.* 11.5, 1 §121; 11.5, 5 §158.
35. Neh 12:10, 22.
36. Neh 3:1, 21; cf. 13:4.
37. Ezra 10:6; Neh 12:23.
38. Neh 12:10, 22. It is possible, even likely, given the practice of papponymy, that ʾElyašīb the father of Yōyadaʿ (who succeeded him) had an older son Yōḥanan, who died young or for some other reason did not succeed to the high-priestly office. This would explain the intrusion

following sequence: (1) 'Elyašīb I,[39] father of (2) Yōḥanan I, the contemporary of Ezra, followed by (3) 'Elyašīb II, contemporary of Nehemiah and father of (4) Yōḥanan II. Evidently, one pair fell out of the list by haplography. This reconstruction solves all chronological problems. The list of high priests from Yōṣadaq to Yōḥanan II spans 150 years, a generation averaging 25 years (see chart).

More important, it places the mission of Ezra in the seventh year of Artaxerxes I, 458 B.C.,[40] and the mission of Nehemiah in 445 B.C., the twentieth year of Artaxerxes I.[41]

2. Editions of the Chroniclers Work

We have noted above the evidence from 1 Esdras and from Josephus' *Antiquities* that in an earlier edition of the Chronicler's work the narrative of Ezra and the memoirs of Nehemiah were separate and that in all likelihood Nehemiah's memoirs were only attached to the Chronicler's work in its final edition. Confirmation of this view may be found now in Neh 12:23. We read: "the sons of Levi, the heads of fathers' houses, were written in the Book of Chronicles (*sēper dibrê hay-yāmim*) even until the days of Yōḥanan the son of 'Elyašīb." In this text there is evidently a reference to an edition of the Chronicler's work which ended in the days of Yōḥanan son of 'Elyašīb, the contemporary of Ezra, in the fourth generation of the Restoration, according to my reconstruction. Thus this earlier edition reached only the era of Ezra and Yōḥanan I, and not to the era of 'Elyašīb II, the son of Yōḥanan I, who was high priest in the days of Nehemiah's governorship. Our conclusion that Nehemiah's memoirs were composed and circulated independently of the Chronicler's work also gives an explanation of the repetition of the list of those who returned with Zerubbabel in Ezra 2 (1 Esdr 5:7–47) and in Nehemiah 7. The Nehemiah-memoirs quote the Chronicler's work or draw on a common source at the time when Nehemiah was composed as an independent work.

The evidence for the two editions described above appears clear enough; however, there are also good reasons to posit three editions of the Chronicler's work. We shall label them Chr$_1$, Chr$_2$, and Chr$_3$.

Chr$_3$ is the final edition, made up of 1 Chronicles 1-9 + 1 Chr 10:1-2 Chr 36:23 + Hebrew Ezra-Nehemiah. Chr$_2$ includes 1 Chronicles 10–2 Chronicles 34 + the *Vorlage* of 1 Esdras. The two editions differ at the beginning, Chr$_3$ introducing the genealogies of 1 Chronicles 1–9. The latest member of the high priesthood

---

of the Yōyadaʿ-Yaddūaʿ sequence of names. This does not solve our problems of chronology; it still leaves a lacuna in the list.

39. Given the change of names and the requirements of chronology, it is likely that 'Elyašīb I is the brother of Yōyaqīm, or in any case belonged to the same generation.

40. The seventh year is given in Ezra 7:7 and again in 7:8.

41. Or more precisely, December, 445. Cf. Neh 1:1 and Neh 13:6 (the thirty-second year of Artaxerxes I, 433–32).

mentioned within the Esdras narrative is Yōḥanan I, son of ʾElyašīb I (1 Esdr 9:1), and the latest member of the Davidic house named is Ḥaṭṭūš (1 Esdr 8:29). On the other hand, in the introductory genealogies of 1 Chronicles 1–9, the list of Davidids continues on two generations to ʿAnanī, the contemporary of Yōḥanan II and probably also the contemporary of Yaddūaʿ II toward the end of the fifth century. Chs. 12 and 13 of Nehemiah refer to these two priests as well; moreover, Neh 12:22 names Darius II (423–404 B.C.) in its latest references to a Persian king. These dates in Chr₃ all stop at the same time, shortly before 400 B.C. These data suggest dates for Chr₂ and Chr₃, the former toward 450 B.C., the latter toward 400 B.C. or slightly later.

Other arguments can be put forth for dating Chr₃ to ca. 400 B.C. No hint of the conquest of Alexander is to be found, and perhaps more important, no reference to the suffering and chaos of the mid-fourth century B.C., when Judah joined in the Phoenician rebellion,[42] harshly put down by Artaxerxes III and his general, Bagoas.

A surprising contrast between Chr₂ and Chr₃ is in the treatment of Zerubbabel. Ezra intrudes the list of those who returned with Zerubbabel at ch. 2, making it appear that both Sin-ab-uṣur (Σαναβασσαρ)[43] and Zerubbabel returned more or less together in the reign of Cyrus. The 1 Esdras account places the list of returnees in ch. 5 after the return of Sanabassar in the days of Cyrus and after the narrative recounting Zerubbabel's return to Jerusalem in the second year of Darius.[44] This appears in a *plus*[45] in 1 Esdras and is almost surely authentic. Since we are told that Sin-ab-uṣur, the governor, returned and built the foundations of the temple, and since Zerubbabel completed the temple upon Darius' decree,[46] it is quite natural to attribute the return of Zerubbabel to the beginning of the reign of Darius. The chaos which marked the beginning of Darius' reign was the appropriate time for a return to Zion, as it was an appropriate time for prophets to arise anew and proclaim a new David and a new temple, i.e., the re-establishment of the Judean kingdom. Again, the wisdom tale of Zerubbabel's brilliance and reward in 1 Esdr 3:1–5:6 is fixed unalterably in the reign of Darius. 1 Esdr 4:56 says explicitly that the building of the temple began in the second year after he came to Jerusalem. At the same time, there is a conflict between the account of Zerubbabel's being rewarded by Darius with "letters for him and all the treasur-

---

42. For the extent of the rebellion and evidence of destroyed cities in Palestine in this period, see D. Barag, "The Effects of the Tennes Rebellion on Palestine," *BASOR* 183 (1966) 6–12.

43. As has long been argued by W. F. Albright, ššbṣr (Ezra 1:8, 11), šnṣr (1 Chr 3:17), and Σαναβασσαρ all reflect Sin-ab-uṣur, a well-known name-type; Sin-ab-uṣur, Sin-apal-uṣur, and Sin-aḫ-uṣur are all documented in cuneiform sources.

44. 1 Esdr 5:6; cf. 5:2.

45. 1 Esdr 4:58–5:7.

46. Ezra 5:16–20; 1 Esdr 6:18–20.

ers and governors and captains and satraps" and the Aramaic source in Ezra 5 where Darius, before answering Tattenay the "governor of 'Abar-nahara" and his companions, is said to search out his records for the decree of Cyrus. There can be little doubt that the wisdom-tale is secondarily attached to Zerubbabel and interpolated at some point into one recension of the Chronicler's work.[47]

David Noel Freedman has written a persuasive paper sketching the Chronicler's purpose.[48] If he is correct, we must posit a still earlier edition of the Chronicler's work, Chr_1. He contends that "the Chronicler establishes through his narrative of the reigns of David and Solomon the proper, legitimate pattern of institutions and their personnel for the people of God; and they are the monarchy represented by David and his house, the priesthood by Zadok and his descendants, the city and the temple in the promised land. City and ruler, temple and priest—these appear to be the fixed points around which the Chronicler constructs his history and his theology."[49]

The ideology of the Chronicler found in Chr_1, i.e., in 1 Chronicles 10–2 Chronicles 34 plus the *Vorlage* of 1 Esdr 1:1–5:65 (= 2 Chr 34:1 through Ezra 3:13), calls upon the old royal ideology of the Judean kings—chosen David, chosen Zion—as that ideology has been reformulated in Ezekiel 40–48, and especially in the oracles of Haggai and Zechariah. In Haggai and Zechariah, king and high priest constitute a diarchy, son of David, son of Zadok. Zerubbabel is called "my servant" by Yahweh and told, "[I] will make you as a signet; for I have chosen you."[50] In ch. 3 of Zechariah, Joshua the priest is crowned and robed for office in the prophet's vision, and the angel of Yahweh announces: "Hear now, O Joshua the high priest, you and your fellows who sit before you..., for behold I shall bring my servant, the Branch...."[51] In Chr_1 "the parallel between the first building of the temple under the direction of David (and Solomon), and the second building under Zerubbabel is too striking to be accidental, and must have formed part of the original structure of the work."[52] In short, the original Chronicler's work was designed to support the program for the restoration of the kingdom under Zerubbabel. Its extent reached only to Ezra 3:13 (1 Esdr 5:65), with the account of the celebration of the founding of the Second Temple. The future is open, and the work of restoring the ancient institutions is well begun; all is anticipation.[53] Here the program or propaganda document should end.

---

47. We are inclined to believe that this happened after Chr_1, before Chr_2, and that Chr_3 suppressed the tale in accord with his anti-monarchic, theocratic views (see below).
48. "The Chronicler's Purpose," *CBQ* 23 (1961) 436–42.
49. "The Chronicler's Purpose," 437–38.
50. Hag 2:23.
51. Zech 3:8; cf. 4:14.
52. "The Chronicler's Purpose," 439–40.
53. Here I cannot agree with Freedman that the original story of Zerubbabel is suppressed in favor of the Aramaic source (Ezra 4:6–6:18).

In order to supply the full story of the completion of the temple, the editor of Chr₂ added the Aramaic source in Ezra 5:1–6:19 as the preface to the Ezra-narrative which begins at Ezra 7:1. Chr₂ still breathes some of the monarchist fire of Chr₁. Zerubbabel is called the "servant of the Lord."[54] The story of his wisdom is preserved[55] by Chr₂, and the proper order of the Ezra-narrative is kept for the most part, found now only in 1 Esdras. The Nehemiah-memoirs were introduced only by Chr₃, who, following his belief that Ezra and Nehemiah were contemporaries, created confusion by interlarding the Nehemiah-memoirs with part of the Ezra-narrative. To Chr₃ we are indebted for the genealogies of 1 Chronicles 1–9. On the other hand, Chr₃ apparently suppressed elements exalting Zerubbabel, including his title "servant of the Lord" and the heroic tale of Zerubbabel's wisdom and piety (1 Esdr 3:1–5:2).

The primary argument which may be brought against our view of the original Chronicler's work is that the Ezra-narrative and even the Ezra-memoirs reflect the characteristic language and style of the Chronicler.[56] The argument is not compelling; a member of the school of the Chronicler (i.e., Chr₂), imitating the master's style, may easily be responsible for the similarity of style. The two editions of the deuteronomistic history provide a perfect analogy.[57] Moreover, Sara Japhet has recently attacked the thesis of the common authorship of Chronicles and the Ezra-narrative[58] with persuasive evidence of differences of style and linguistic usage. On the other hand, there seem to be distinctions to be drawn between the royal ideology of the Chronicler (Chr₁) and the final edition of his work (Chr₃). Chr₃ appears to have omitted some material which tends to exalt Zerubbabel, the anointed son of David, presumably because his movement was snuffed out and his end ignominious or pathetic.[59]

---

54. 1 Esdr 6:27; the parallel passage in Ezra 6:7 suppresses this exalted title.
55. See above, esp. n. 47.
56. The strongest statement of this view is perhaps that of C. C. Torrey, *Ezra Studies*, 238–48.
57. See F. M. Cross, *Canaanite Myth and Hebrew Epic* (Cambridge, MA: Harvard University, 1973) 274–89.
58. S. Japhet, "The Supposed Common Authorship of Chronicles and Ezra-Nehemiah Investigated Anew," *VT* 18 (1968) 330–71. Some of her arguments are based on distinctions between different orthographic practice and the use of archaic or pseudo-archaic forms; these arguments do not hold, I believe, as can be seen by an examination of the two Isaiah scrolls of Qumran Cave 1, or a comparison of 4QSam^a and 4QSam^b, where common authorship is certain.
59. In "The Purpose of the Chronicler" (p. 440), Freedman argues that in the final edition of the Chronicler's work (he reckons with only two editions), there is a positively anti-monarchical, clericalist tendency. However, none of his arguments is particularly strong.

In summary we may list three editions of the Chronicler's work, Chr₁ composed in support of Zerubbabel shortly after 520 B.C., Chr₂ written after Ezra's mission in 458 B.C., and Chr₃ edited about 400 B.C. or shortly thereafter.[60]

3. A Sketch of the Era of the Restoration

In the first year of his reign, 538 B.C., Cyrus the Great published an edict directing the temple in Jerusalem to be rebuilt, returning the sacred vessels taken as loot by Nebuchadrezzar to their place, thereby initiating the restoration of the Jewish community.[61] The leader of the first return was Sin-ab-uṣur, the heir to the house of David, son of Jehoiachin. He is given the title *nāśî'*, which Ezekiel and his circle in the Exile preferred to *melek*, "king," in designating the new David's office. Beyond the fact that Sin-ab-uṣur led a group of captive Jews to Jerusalem bearing the temple treasures, we know very little. Evidently it was a token return, for we know that a large number of Jews were flourishing in the Babylonian community under the tolerant Persian regime. Sin-ab-uṣur is credited with laying the foundations of the temple in the Aramaic source,[62] as well as being named governor.[63] Since the Persian administration frequently appointed a member of the native royal house as governor of a local state, and indeed made the governorship hereditary, there is no reason to doubt the notice. In any case, his nephew Zerubbabel succeeded to the governorship of Judah.

---

60. The fact that all genealogies in Chr₃ end shortly before 400 B.C. virtually eliminates the popular view that Ezra followed Nehemiah in the seventh year of the reign of Artaxerxes II, 398 B.C. Of the many arguments brought forward to support the position that Ezra followed Nehemiah to Jerusalem, most are without weight. The most plausible of them, perhaps, is the notice in Ezra 9:9 that God has given "to us a *gādēr* in Judah and in Jerusalem." The term *gādēr* has been taken sometimes as a reference to the city wall of Jerusalem. It must be said that there may have been attempts to build the wall of Jerusalem before Nehemiah succeeded. This would explain his surprise at his brother Ḥananī's report that "the wall of Jerusalem (*ḥwmt yrwšlm*) is shattered" (Neh 1:3). On the other hand, it is by no means clear that the term *gādēr* here refers to a city wall. Ordinarily, it refers to an "enclosure wall" (of fields or vineyards) or "fortifications." Thus it refers to the enclosure wall which fortified the temple (Ezek 42:7 and *gdrt*, Ezek 42:12). In Mic 7:11 the expression is used in the plural, *gdryk*, and evidently refers generally to the defenses or fortifications of a city. Specifically in Ezra 9:9, however, the context is quite clear. In rhetorical parallelism, Ezra speaks of "raising the house of our God," "making its ruins stand up," and "giving us a *gādēr* in Jerusalem and Judah." As Ezekiel uses *gādēr* of the temple-fortification, so does Ezra speak of the *gādēr* of the temple. Each parallel refers to Zerubbabel's temple and its enclosure wall. The temple was, of course, a bastion as well as a sanctuary.

61. The Aramaic text is found in Ezra 6:3–5; compare the ornamented version in Ezra 1:1–4.

62. Ezra 5:16.

63. Ezra 5:14.

Zerubbabel the governor and Jeshua the Zadokite high priest, according to 1 Esdras, returned at the beginning of the reign of Darius.[64] This was a time of widespread rebellion in the Persian empire, and in Judah a nationalist spirit stirred up the populace. The prophets Haggai and Zechariah arose and gave oracles reviving the old royal ideology of king and temple. Zerubbabel and Jeshua were named the new David and new Zadok, the "sons of oil," and a program was promulgated to re-establish Israel's legitimate institutions. Above all, the prophets urged the building of the temple and envisioned the return of Yahweh's "glory" to Jerusalem, there to "tabernacle" as in ancient days. Haggai prophesied the downfall of the Persian empire and blamed the little community's troubles on their failure to build the house of God.

In support of the messianic movement the Chronicler composed a history which reviewed and reshaped Israel's historical traditions to give urgency and meaning to the tasks at hand, the restoration of the Davidic rule, the building of the temple, and establishment of the divinely appointed cult with all its kindred institutions and personnel. This first edition of the Chronicler's work is to be dated to the five-year interval between the founding of the temple and the completion of the temple (520–15 B.C.).

In the face of harassment by Persian officials, including the satrap of Syria, and the jealousy and hostility of peoples who surrounded Judah, Zerubbabel and his party completed the temple on 12 March 515. The service of God "as it is written in the book of Moses" was thus restored.

We then hear no more of Zerubbabel. The prophecies of glory, wealth, and peace faded away into silence. We have no hint of Zerubbabel's fate. More than half a century passes before the story of the Restoration is taken up again. This gap in the record is significant also in reconstructing the history of the Chronicler's work. When the record resumes with the narrative of the mission of Ezra, the messianic themes of the earlier narrative are no longer to be heard. Hierocracy supplants the diarchy of king and high priest. We hear nothing of the Davidic prince either in the Ezra-narrative or in the memoirs of Nehemiah.

In 458 B.C. "Ezra the priest, the scribe of the law of the God of the heaven," set out with his company of Zionists, armed only with Artaxerxes' commission, some offerings sent to the temple in Jerusalem, and the Book of the Law. Ezra's first major effort on his arrival in Jerusalem was to undertake stern action against intermarriage with foreigners, especially marriage to foreign wives. He proposed that all enter into a covenant to put away foreign wives, and the issue of such marriages, in fulfillment of the Law. Armed with royal authority to appoint magistrates and judges, he vigorously pressed the reform against all opposition. Two months after he arrived in Jerusalem, in the seventh year of Artaxerxes, in the

---

64. The floating piece in 1 Esdr 5:63–70 (= Ezra 4:1–5) appears self-contradictory; cf. 1 Esdr 5:1–6.

seventh month, on New Year's Day, he gathered all the people in an assembly before the Water Gate, and standing on a wooden pulpit read from "the book of the Law of Moses." We judge this book to have been the Pentateuch in penultimate form.[65] On a second day, he read from the Law and then dismissed the congregation in order that they might prepare for the Festival of Succoth.[66]

Here ended the second edition of the Chronicler's work, the recension reflected in 1 Esdras, combining the Ezra-narrative with the older Book of Chronicles. The date of Chr$_2$ must fall about 450 B.C.

In 445, Nehemiah, the cupbearer to king Artaxerxes I, learned of the troubles of the restored community in Jerusalem and its defenselessness. With the king's commission as governor of Judah, he set out with a contingent of the king's cavalry for Jerusalem.[67] Spying out the city by night, he kept his own counsel as to his plans, knowing full well that his mission would be hindered by the hatred and schemes of his fellow governors round about, viz., Sanballaṭ, governor of Samaria, Ṭobiah, governor of Ammon, Gašmu, the king of the Qedarite Arabs, and perhaps 'Abd, the governor of Dedan. Upon his announcement of plans to rebuild the walls of Jerusalem, supported by 'Elyašīb II, the high priest, he was accused by the neighboring governors of rebellion against the king. When work began the governors took action and conspired to send contingents of their troops to harry them. Nehemiah countered these devices by arming his workers, so that a worker "with one of his hands worked, and with the other grasped his weapon." Ultimately, the walls were finished in fifty-two days of labor (Neh 6:15), though work must have continued longer to complete the details of the fortifications,[68] and a service of dedication was held with processions and singing to the sound of harps and cymbals. With his primary task completed, Nehemiah returned to the king in 433 B.C., leaving his brother behind to rule in his stead. On his return he appears to have carried out a number of reform measures: enforcing the payment of tithes for the benefit of Levite and singer, and preventing the violation of the Sabbath, including the hawking of merchandise by Phoenicians on the Sabbath. Like Ezra, he attempted to put an end to foreign marriage, a perennial problem, it appears. The final words of his memoirs are these: "Thus I cleansed them from all that was foreign.... Remember me, O my God, for good."[69]

---

65. The arguments of S. Mowinckel are compelling; see *Studien zu dem Buche Ezra-Nehemia*, 3. 124–41.

66. Mowinckel is surely right in assuming that the Day of Atonement was fully known and celebrated despite the omission of reference to it in Nehemiah 8.

67. Josephus (*Ant.* 11.5, 7 §168) gives 440 as the date of Nehemiah's arrival in Jerusalem. The wall was completed in December, 437 B.C., according to Josephus (*Ant.* 11.5, 8 §179), two years and four months after he began.

68. See n. 67 above and W. F. Albright, *The Biblical Period* (Pittsburgh: Private Distribution, 1950) 51–52.

69. Neh 13:30–31. It is often said that it is unlikely that great Ezra so failed in his reform that Nehemiah was required to institute a similar reform. But in the Bible the great leaders,

The memoirs of Nehemiah here briefly summarized must have been composed and circulated in the late fifth century. Toward 400 B.C. a final editor combined the Nehemiah-memoirs with the Chronicler's work (Chr₂), prefixed a collection of genealogies (1 Chronicles 1–9) and otherwise edited the whole. Again, darkness falls so far as the Bible is concerned, and the history of the fourth century remains a virtual blank until the advent of Alexander III of Macedon.

CHART OF THE HIGH PRIESTS OF THE RESTORATION AND OF THEIR CONTEMPORARIES

Generation of High Priests	Generation of Davdids	Generation of Sanballaṭids
1. Yōṣadaq before 587 father of	1. Sin-ab-uṣur b. before 592 (13th year) uncle of	
2. Yēšūaʻ b. ca. 570 father of	2. Zerubbabel b. ca. 570 father of	
3. Yōyaqīm b. ca. 545 (brother of)	3. Ḥananyah b. ca. 545 father of	
[3. 'Elyašīb I b. ca. 545] (father of)		
[4. Yōḥanan I b. ca. 520] (father of)	4. Šekanyah b. ca. 520 father of	
5. 'Elyašīb II b. ca. 495 father of	5. Ḥaṭṭūš b. ca. 495 uncle of	
6. Yōyadaʻ I b. ca. 470 father of	6. 'Ely ōʻenay b. ca. 470 father of	6. Sanballaṭ I b. ca 485 father of
7. Yōḥanan II b. ca. 445 (AP 30.18) father of	7. ʻAnanī b. ca. 445 (cf. AP 30:19)	7. Delayah b. ca. 460 father of

---

Moses and the prophets, regularly fail, or to take a closer analogy, the deuteronomistic reforms of Hezekiah and Josiah certainly were short-lived. Moreover, laws against intermarriage are notoriously difficult to enforce in any age.

8. Yaddūaʿ II b. ca. 420
   father of

[9. Yōḥanan III b. ca. 395]
   father of

[10. Yaddūaʿ III b. ca. 370]
   father of

11. Onias I b. ca. 345 (= Yohanan IV)
   father of

12. Šimʿōn I b. ca. 320

8. Sanballaṭ II b. ca. 435
   father of

9. Yēšūaʿ (?) b. ca. 410
   brother of

9. Yēšūaʿ (?) b. ca. 410
   father of

10. Sanballaṭ III b. ca. 385
    d. 332

THE WATERSHED OF THE AMERICAN BIBLICAL TRADITION: THE CHICAGO SCHOOL, FIRST PHASE, 1892–1920[*]

Robert W. Funk
University of Montana

This paper marks a voyage into waters that are, to a large extent, still uncharted.[1] Such a voyage is fraught with dangers: subsurface reefs of who knows what proportions may wreck the amateur's bark, particularly if her draft has any depth. And the compass may well prove unreliable, since the history being explored is just under our ownmost skins. Nevertheless, the premonition that the preceding period in American theological history may have been decisive for present ambivalence, particularly where Scripture and tradition in biblical scholarship are concerned, makes the risk worth taking. In any case, our history will not wait on larger knowledge, and distance sufficiently great to guarantee impartiality would mean that the reefs were no longer a threat to anything immediately significant.

1. INTRODUCTION

1.1 In the Dillenberger-Welch work, *Protestant Christianity,* there is a trio of sentences over which I have now and again paused. The authors have just spoken of the problems posed for Christian thought by the rise of biblical criticism. They continue:

> This does not mean, however, that the new conception of the Bible which came to characterize Protestant liberalism originated simply as a reaction to the discoveries of historical criticism. In fact, the situation was more nearly the reverse.

---

[*]The Presidential Address delivered 31 October 1975, at the annual meeting of the Society of Biblical Literature, held at the Palmer House, Chicago, IL.
  1. The following special abbreviations are employed in the notes:
  HS   *The Hebrew Student*
  OTS *The Old Testament Student*
  ONTS *The Old and New Testament Student*
  BW   *The Biblical World*

It was new conceptions of religious authority and of the meaning of revelation which made possible the development of biblical criticism.[2]

They then go on to describe the new conceptions of authority and revelation formulated by Hegel, Schleiermacher, and Ritschl. My pause owes not so much to the fact that the reverse interpretation has often enough been advocated, especially by biblical scholars, but to an alarm that was triggered somewhere in the recesses of the mind by the implications latent in their bold statement for the history of the biblical tradition in America. Those implications have to do with the impasse into which "biblical science," biblical scholars, theological schools, the churches, and even the "bible belters" seem to have fallen these latter days. The impasse may be characterized symptomatically as the inability of liberals and conservatives alike to determine what is to be done with and about the Bible, other than to perpetuate dispositions formed early in this century and now reified by more than a half century of repetition. The ambivalence on which the impasse rests is betrayed on every hand by the contradiction between the service of the lips and the actual relations sustained to Scripture in pulpit, theology, seminary curricula, and even the Society of Biblical Literature, so far as Protestants are concerned. (For want of time and adequate knowledge, Jewish and Roman Catholic scholarship has, unfortunately, been left out of account.)

Our present situation is extremely complex. An over-simplified analysis will not and should not satisfy. Nevertheless, I should like to return to what may prove to have been a decisive period in the shaping of the modern American biblical tradition and inquire specifically and narrowly about the destiny of Scripture in that period. In so doing, certain hunches arising out of the present situation, a study of the Chicago School, and my own history are being called into play.

1.2 Dillenberger and Welch assert that a new understanding of religious authority and revelation made possible the development of biblical criticism and not the other way around. First light on the import of this assertion comes with the recognition that both the champions of historical criticism (the liberals, so-called) and its adversaries (the conservatives), around the turn of the century, did in fact share the conviction that *the attack on biblical authority arose in some alien quarter.* It was an assault from without and had, therefore, to be resisted on correlative grounds.

This state of affairs illuminates the repeated liberal reference to what the modern consciousness will and will not tolerate, in the light of, for example, Darwinism, or the scientific method, or progressive thought. W. R. Harper, first president of the University of Chicago, though by no means an announced liberal himself, scores the point forcefully in an editorial of 1889:

---

2. John Dillenberger and Claude Welch, *Protestant Christianity Interpreted through Its Development* (New York: Scribner, 1954) 197.

> The cry of our times is for the application of scientific methods in the study of the Bible.... if the methods of the last century continue to hold exclusive sway, the time will come when intelligent men of all classes will say, "If this is your Bible we will have none of it."[3]

This reference to what the modern mind will accept, more recently associated with death-of-God theology, is thus as old as the latter part of the 19th century in the American tradition. Although the reference has still deeper roots in experiential piety, it came to the fore as a pervasive theological criterion only towards the close of the last century.

The conservatives, on the other hand, were driven to defend the authority of the text in the only way they knew, viz., by means of the conceptual theological frame in which biblical authority had been held in suspension during the preceding period in Protestant Scholasticism. The argument was not always blatant, but in retrospect it seems obvious enough. In his friendly controversies with Harper, W. H. Green of Princeton was often given to the correlation:

> No more perilous enterprise was ever attempted by men held in honor in the church than the wholesale commendation of the results of an unbelieving criticism in application both to the Pentateuch and to the rest of the Bible, as though they were the incontestable product of the highest scholarship. They who have been themselves thoroughly grounded in the Christian faith may, by a happy inconsistency, hold fast their old convictions while admitting principles, methods and conclusions which are logically at war with them.[4]

The "old convictions," of course, were those which had come to expression in orthodox Protestant dogmatics; because he felt no need for "a new theology," Green did not feel the need for "a new biblical criticism" either.

1.3 It is clear enough that the traditionalists, and later the fundamentalists, defended the integrity and authority of the biblical text on what they took to be internal grounds, but which, from our point of view, and the point of view of the earlier liberals, turns out to be the external grounds of a dogmatic theology extrinsic to the text. But the liberals, too, defended the impingement of historical criticism on biblical authority on equally external grounds, viz., the progressive, evolutionary spiral of human history linked with the emergence of the historical consciousness of modern man. *In both cases and for roughly the same reason, the biblical text was ignored precisely as biblical text.*

It may seem odd to claim that scientific historical criticism, the specific aim of which was to set the biblical text in its full historical context, actually suppressed the text. Yet for the historical critic, particularly those under the influence of Darwinism and related movements, the meaning of the text was taken up into

---

3. *ONTS* 9 (1889) 1–2.
4. *ONTS* 6 (1886–87) 318.

the larger question of the creation and conservation of human values. On the other hand, the meaning of the text did not pose a critical problem for the traditionalist because, in his case, the text was held in solution in dogmatic theology. For neither party did the text and its tradition provide *a* or *the* critical horizon of theological endeavor. In short, what in the older tradition was called the normative function of Scripture effectively disappeared; in more recent parlance: Scripture as text disappeared. Insofar as the question of Scripture was settled, it was settled on external grounds, with the result that the problem posed by the presence of the text itself in the tradition was left unresolved.

1.4 An unresolved question of such import is bound to leave its mark on all subsequent history. The unalleviated tension has been and continues to be a plague on both liberal and conservative houses, in both the church and academic biblical scholarship, precisely because it has been left, like a splinter, to fester in the tradition.

Those who give overt allegiance to the authority of Scripture from a vantage point on the theological right have continued, for more than a half century, to snipe at the indifference of liberal scholarship, but no amount of vituperation has been effective in awakening liberal intelligence to the issue. Even a sophisticated and organized assault on liberalism from the radical left, on the part of one wing of the early Chicago School between 1894 and 1920, has disappeared from the record as though it never took place. During the last quarter of the nineteenth century, the question went underground in middle-of-the-road liberalism and there it remains.

The anomaly in biblical scholarship of the liberal persuasion is that it gave and gives allegiance to descriptivism, historical relativism, and the rejection of theology while claiming the ground once held by the proponents of biblical authority. It has continued and developed specialties associated with the struggle over a sacred text, but necessarily refuses the complicity of those specialties with explicit devotion to that text. It rejects the canonical limits of its body of literature, but in fact enforces canonical boundaries. It holds questions of date, authorship, sources, authenticity, and integrity at objective range, but pursues these questions as though more than relative historical judgments were at stake. In sum, so-called scientific biblical scholarship, by and large, took up arms against traditionalism in the castle of Sacred Scripture and ended by occupying the castle itself, while denying that it had done so. These anomalies make the Society of Biblical Literature a fraternity of scientifically trained biblical scholars with the soul of a church. They also create certain incongruities for biblical studies in the humanities wing of the secular university.

1.5 These introductory remarks perhaps justify the formulation of the theme: The Watershed of the American Biblical Tradition. Watershed refers to that hypothetical point after which the lines in biblical scholarship were drawn very differently than in the preceding period. The lines in biblical study were significantly redrawn during the period, roughly 1890–1920, and our whole subsequent history has been shaped and, to a large extent, tyrannized by the fresh demarcation. It is also my opinion that the organization and development of the early biblical faculty at Chicago is paradigmatic for that remapping of the contours of biblical study which has affected the shape and course of that scholarship down to the present day.

In what follows, I shall endeavor to trace the vicissitudes of the scriptural problem through the first phase of the Chicago School. By way of conclusion, the significance of this period for the subsequent history of biblical studies in various dimensions may be indicated.

2. The Problem of Scripture:
W. R. Harper and the Chicago School, 1892–1920

2.1 The point of impact of the new science upon evangelical faith was the evangelical understanding and deployment of Scripture.[5] The questions being posed of Scripture by the emerging sciences produced a vigorous new interest in biblical study on a broad front.

W. R. Harper was keenly aware of this fresh interest and was prepared to capitalize on it as early as his appointment to the Baptist Union Theological Seminary in Morgan Park, 1 January 1879.[6] His success with the summer schools and correspondence school, both begun in 1881, was instant.[7] In 1882 he launched *The Hebrew Student* to serve the needs of the growing number of students. Between 1881 and 1885 he published the first editions of his various manuals for the study of Hebrew. He organized the American Institute of Hebrew in 1884, involving about 70 professors in the U.S. and Canada,[8] and moved his work to Yale in 1886, the same year Timothy Dwight moved from a divinity professorship to the presidency.[9] Harper held chairs in the Graduate Department and the Divinity School, and later a third one in Yale College. It is reported that the undergraduates filled the largest hall at Yale to hear him lecture on the OT.[10]

When Harper returned to the Midwest to organize the University of Chicago in 1892, the same interest in and concern for the Bible dictated the shape of the new divinity faculty. Shailer Mathews depicts the situation accurately:

> The prevailing theological interest at the time of its organization is to be seen in the size of the various departments in the Divinity School. There were as

---

5. Cf. S. Mathews, *New Faith for Old: An Autobiography* (New York: Macmillan, 1936) 60.
6. T. W. Goodspeed, *William Rainey Harper: First President of The University of Chicago* (Chicago: University of Chicago, 1928) 43.
7. Ibid., 50ff.
8. Ibid., 55.
9. Ibid., 73–74.
10. Ibid., 77–78.

many in the field of biblical and Semitic studies as in all the other departments combined. Biblical study was the representative of the new scientific interest in religion.[11]

The original divinity faculty thus mirrored the current situation and Harper's own determination to give evangelical faith the best scholarly representation he could muster. By this time, moreover, Harper was completely confident that a great biblical faculty would be matched by a corresponding widespread and deep-seated interest in the fruits of devout biblical scholarship.

2.2 Harper inaugurated *The Hebrew Student* (1882) at a time when agitation over the critical study of the OT was reaching a crescendo in the U.S. Behind and under this agitation, of course, lay the German erosion of the dogma of the verbal inerrancy of Scripture, in the form of an attack on the Mosaic authorship and integrity of the Pentateuch. The ultimate source of the attack was everywhere recognized.[12] Under the circumstances, American religious leaders found themselves largely defenseless, owing to the superiority of German arms.

With characteristic zeal and industry, Harper set to work to even up the odds. He took every opportunity to extol and encourage the study of Semitics and the establishment of Semitics departments. He held out the high standards of German scholarship[13] and enjoined Americans to emulate them,[14] while occasionally issuing a warning against "destructive criticism." The comparison of American with German scholarship is a persistent if subdued theme in Harper's journals. Harper himself went abroad for a year of study before taking up his duties as president of the new University,[15] and his example appears to have become the model for later Chicago faculty.

2.3 Upon his return to Chicago from New Haven in 1892, Harper needed a NT counterpart. He chose a man he had met in Boston during his Yale days, Ernest DeWitt Burton. Burton was NT professor at Newton and came to Chicago to head the NT department, a post he held until 1923, the year he succeeded H. J. Pratt as president of the University.

Burton's most notable works are his I.C.C. commentary on Galatians and his study of Greek moods and tenses. These books leave one with the impression that Burton was to the NT exactly what Harper was to the OT. Closer examination reveals, however, that Burton brought fresh views to Chicago, views that led him

---

11. *New Faith*, 58.

12. The German origin of critical theories is recognized in almost every issue of Harper's journals. Note especially the article by G. H. Schodde, "Old Testament Criticism and the American Church," *OTS* 3 (1883–84) 376–81, esp. pp. 377–78. Cf. S. Mathews, *New Faith*, 60.

13. *HS* 2 (1882–83) 216–17.

14. *OTS* 6 (1886–87) 225–26.

15. T. W. Goodspeed, *Harper*, 108; E. J. Goodspeed, *As I Remember* (New York: Harper & Brothers, 1953) 58.

to appoint Shailer Mathews to the department in 1894, and later to seek the services of Shirley Jackson Case (1908).

The differences between Burton and Harper can be exposed by reference to their understanding of Scripture. This criterion provides important clues to the way in which the first phase of the Chicago School developed. One might go so far as to say that Harper and Burton stand at the head of the two lines at Chicago, one of which later became marginal at Chicago but continued to predominate in American biblical scholarship, the other of which became dominant at Chicago but then effectively died in biblical scholarship.

The tradition that died a scholarly death has probably proved, over the next half century, to be a more accurate index of the emerging common consciousness than the surviving line. If so, it is ironic that one side of the Chicago School should have anticipated the common mind so accurately, while failing so dramatically to perpetuate itself among biblical scholars. It is equally ironic that the other side, which struggled so hard to capture the common mind, could only maintain its grip on the scholarly tradition. But these remarks are to anticipate.

Editorials in the Chicago journals attributable to Harper with certainty after about 1895 are scarce. However, one published in 1898, on the general theme, criticism and the authority of the Bible, is almost certainly his work.[16] In the same year, Burton published his first systematic statement on the same subject.[17] It will be illuminating to compare the two statements closely.

2.4 If Harper had any fears regarding the destructive consequences of higher criticism, they were mostly submerged in his enthusiastic estimate of its constructive possibilities. In an earlier editorial note of 1882, he quotes C. A. Briggs with hearty approval:

> We will not deny that the most who are engaged in it [higher criticism] are rationalistic and unbelieving, and that they are using it with disastrous effect upon the Scriptures and the orthodox faith. There are few believing critics, especially in this country. There is also a widespread prejudice against these studies and an apprehension as to the results. These prejudices are unreasonable. These apprehensions are to be deprecated. It is impossible to prevent discussion. The church is challenged to meet the issue. It is a call of Providence to conflict and to triumph of evangelical truth. The divine word will vindicate itself in all its parts.[18]

Harper never quite lost his naive conviction that "evangelical truth" would triumph and the divine word be vindicated.

By 1898, Harper had perhaps become more apprehensive. In his editorial of that year, he goes about as far as he was ever able to accommodate what must

---

16. *BW* 11 (1898) 225–28.
17. "The Function of Interpretation in Relation to Theology," *AJT* 2 (1898) 52–79.
18. *HS* 2 (1882–83) 218.

have struck him then as the rising tide of the new Chicago School. The fear that criticism has an adverse effect on the authority of Scripture is not groundless, he writes. Authenticity and authority are linked, but not absolutely. On the one hand, criticism has actually corroborated the authority of the Bible, i.e., it has demonstrated authenticity in certain cases, such as those of Jeremiah, Hosea, the real Isaiah, Jesus, and Paul. In these instances, "criticism has largely remade the foundations of confidence." These teachers are the more credible as the result of criticism, "and if more credible, then more authoritative."[19] On the other hand, criticism has undermined authority, if authority is taken to be wholly dependent upon authenticity. But authority may also be substantiated by experience; "some teachings are true apart from those who present them.... Truths thus established can no more be shaken by the discovery that they were not uttered by the men whose names they bear than the law of gravitation would be affected should it appear that it was discovered by some other man than Newton."[20] What can be said about those portions of Scripture whose authenticity is not confirmed by criticism and whose truth cannot be verified by experience? In such cases one may appeal to the experience of other men for whom that teaching is confirmed as true, and then draw the inference that other matters taught in the same document are also true. Very little in the Bible falls outside these three domains; what does can be considered marginal to faith. "If all this is true, it cannot be said that criticism is necessarily hostile to the authority of scripture."[21]

Harper was driven simultaneously by a variety of motives. He was deeply devoted to Scripture and the body of divine truth he never for one moment doubted that it contained. At the same time, he had a respect for scientific investigation that ranked it close to the numinous. He never came to believe that the relentless search for facts, the free exchange of ideas, the scholarly pursuit of truth wherever it might lead, would not in the end produce the desired result. He was thus committed to the authority of Scripture and to the freedom of research and expression, a double allegiance that undoubtedly caused him personal pain at Chicago before his death.

2.5 Burton's programmatic essay of 1898, viewed in retrospect, is epoch-making. While one may discern in the work of Harper, particularly after 1892, some premonitory signs of what was to come, it is to Burton that we owe the first explicit statement of the direction the Chicago School of biblical interpretation was to take.

"Theology," he writes, "by its very definition has to do with *truths*, i.e. with knowledge of things as they are."[22] Interpretation, on the other hand, has as its object the discovery of meanings, which by all means must be *true* meanings in

---

19. *BW* 11 (1898) 226.
20. Ibid., 227.
21. Ibid., 228.
22. *AJT* 2 (1898) 52 (italics mine).

the sense that they are really the meaning intended. The truth of interpretation, however, has nothing directly to do with theological truth. The interpreter does not ask whether the testimony of a witness is truth in the theological sense, but only whether his interpretation is true to the intention of the witness. If, in fact, the interpreter raises the question of ultimate truth, "he is in danger of vitiating his own work."[23]

The interpreter who seeks to determine not merely the meaning of the Bible but also the truth of the Bible, will almost inevitably test his interpretation by reference to what he, the interpreter, takes to be true, and thus finally by reference to his own opinions and convictions. By thus forcing the truth question upon the text, he is treating the Bible with "gross irreverence" by making it echo his own convictions. The only way to steer clear of this fallacy and so honor the text is to confine interpretation to its legitimate descriptive limit.

In contrast, theology has for its field and source the whole of the universe; nothing is excluded *a priori*. The demand that theology be wholly biblical therefore reflects "a semi-deistical conception of the universe,"[24] i.e., the notion that God has expressed himself solely in the Scriptures. The scope of interpretation should be as broad, therefore, as the field of theology: "The field of interpretation is as wide as the field of things that have meaning, i.e. of existences back of which there lies thought."[25] Interpretation which limits itself to the interpretation of expression is thus truncated, since the higher mode of interpretation is the interpretation of fact.[26]

If biblical interpretation is confined to the interpretation of literary documents, the outcome of the process is *thought* and nothing more.[27] It is a legitimate function of the biblical interpreter to determine the thoughts of the biblical authors—the systematic result is so-called biblical theology[28]—but in this form the interpretation has nothing whatever to do with the truth of these thoughts,[29] nor does it provide any material directly for theology.[30] Literary interpretation, then, cannot accomplish the whole task; it requires to be supplemented by the interpretation of fact,[31] and the process by which the facts are determined is called *biblical criticism*.

The end product of criticism is a *connected* narrative of biblical history, including both the history of biblical thought and the history of external events.

---

23. Ibid., 53. Cf. the discussion, 59.
24. Ibid., 55.
25. Ibid.
26. Ibid., 56; cf. 60ff.
27. Ibid., 58.
28. Ibid., 68–69.
29. Ibid., 58.
30. Ibid., 59, 66.
31. Ibid., 61ff.

It must be a connected narrative because "facts can be interpreted only in their relations."[32] When this full, sequential narrative lies before him, the biblical interpreter will then be faced with his highest task. Burton should be allowed to state his own conclusion:

> With the facts before him, dealing no longer with records, but with events, searching no longer for thoughts, but for truths, his task will be to find in this unparalleled history the great truths of divine revelation. Then will he be able, on solid and substantial ground, to construct the doctrine of Scripture, the doctrine, that is, of the nature of revelation made in the Bible, and of the character of the books that the Bible contains. On the basis of such a doctrine he will be able to read the complete and solid structure of the truth of God revealed in the Bible. And not only so, but he will also be able to verify the results thus reached by an independent process of investigation. For the same material and the same process by which he will reach *this* doctrine will enable him, in large measure at least, to reach independently the other truths which he seeks concerning God and man in their mutual relations.[33]

Biblical criticism first uses the biblical documents, together with such extra-biblical sources as are available to it, to establish the correlative history; it may then employ the correlative history to establish the biblical documents. The interpretation of facts, consequently, produced "an immense confirmation and strengthening of the argument for the divine origin of the Bible, and still more for the divine elements in the biblical history."[34] The Bible is confirmed primarily as a part of history under divine guidance.

Burton is thus not prepared to allow the orthodox understanding of the function of Scripture in theology for two reasons: (1) the orthodox view excludes the significance of the narrative portions of the Bible and thus of the facts; (2) the didactic portions of the Bible are taken as the direct, unmediated thoughts of God.[35] Burton wants to give priority to the narrative history, and to emphasize the human element in the biblical interpretation of that narrative, owing to his own predilections for scientific method. But in assigning these priorities, he in fact reverses the position of Harper and his orthodox predecessors by looking first at the history underlying the biblical documents and only then at the biblical interpretation of that history. In this he anticipates the social history of Christianity so characteristic of Mathews and Case.

The significance of the reversal might best be discerned in his own statement of how theology ought to proceed.[36] What is needed, he suggests, is a body

---

32. Ibid., 67; cf. p. 63.
33. Ibid., 69.
34. Ibid., 71.
35. Ibid., 63–64.
36. Ibid., 77–78.

of theological truths divided into three categories or three concentric circles. In the first belong those truths "which can be verified, and are verified constantly, in the experience of man."[37] In the second belong those truths which are already established on the basis of biblical criticism and interpretation, and those truths furnished by the "non-biblical sciences." And finally, in the larger, outer circle go "all merely traditional theology" and unsolved theological problems. It should be the aim of biblical criticism, science, and theology to transfer the items in the third category to the second as quickly as knowledge permits.

It is thus clear that for Burton Scripture has lost its primary function. It is to play an ancillary role at best. When he comes to additional statements regarding the place of NT study in theology in 1905 and 1912,[38] he is looking back, as it were, on the orthodox dogma of the plenary inspiration of Scripture. As he puts it in his essay of 1912:

> We shall not in the future ascribe to the affirmations of Peter and Paul the same measure of authority which the preachers of the last generation were wont to impute to them.[39]

This means that it is our duty

> to enact our part in the continuous evolution of that religion and its continuous readjustment of itself in doctrine and life to the needs of successive ages....[40]

By 1920, in an essay on "Recent Tendencies in the Northern Baptist Churches,"[41] he can even speak of the normative character of the Scriptures as a thing of the past for most Northern Baptists.[42]

On the crucial point of the authority of Scripture, Burton stands in strong contrast to Harper. His essay of 1898 contradicts an editorial of Harper in the same volume. While George Burman Foster and Shailer Mathews were already on the scene, I can find no earlier considered statement of the direction in which the Chicago School was to move decisively after Harper's death in 1906.

2.6 The mature position of Shailer Mathews on biblical authority is succinctly stated in *The Faith of Modernism,* published in 1924.[43] His position needs

---

37. Ibid., 77.
38. "The Present Problems of New Testament Study," *AJT* 9 (1905) 201–37; "The Place of the New Testament in a Theological Curriculum," *AJT* 16 (1912) 181–95.
39. *AJT* 16 (1912) 192.
40. Ibid., 191–92.
41. *AJT* 24 (1920) 321–38.
42. Ibid., esp. pp. 325–26.
43. New York: Macmillan (reprinted January, 1925; September, 1925) 37–53.

to be set in the context of his understanding of his own role in the social process, for which his autobiography, *New Faith for Old*,[44] is readily available.

Despite the fact that Mathews became the front man for the Modernist movement emanating from Chicago, he remained something of a bridge-man between Harper and the more radical elements at Chicago.[45] It is illuminating to read Mathews' memorial article on Harper, "As an Editor,"[46] where he describes how Harper had to teach him and others the wisdom of the editorial policy for *The Biblical World*. Like Harper, Mathews had piety not just in his bones but in his fingertips. Technically, he was a radical on the subject of the authority of the Bible. Humanly, he was warmly, even blatantly, evangelical. And he felt virtually no contradiction in the two.

The Modernist, he writes, studies the Bible "with full respect for its sanctity but with equal respect for the student's intellectual integrity."[47] He affirmed inspiration but denied inerrancy. Modernists believe "in the inspiration of men, not of words. Men were inspired because they inspire."[48] He thus joins Burton in shifting such authority as the text has from the text itself to the men who wrote the texts.

The Modernist, like the Fathers of the Church, insists "that revelation must conform to the realities of the universe."[49] "Reality," as established by the historian and the scientist, is thus the final test of any truth allegedly discovered in the Bible. The Modernist also affirms that the Bible is "a trustworthy record of the human experience of God."[50] The Modernist wants, as a consequence, to resist only the doctrine of the literal inerrancy of Scripture; he by no means wants to shake faith in the value of the Bible, rightly understood, for the religious life.[51]

Mathews understood himself as an evangelical in the service of a great religious movement within the church.[52] He rejected detached criticism of the churches just as he rejected detached scholarship. In view of his understanding of the social process, he had no choice but to give himself to what he termed, "the democratization of religious scholarship."[53] In this he was completely one with Harper and thus eminently qualified to assume the deanship of the Divinity School in 1908, a post he held until 1933. The organization of the Hyde Park Baptist Sunday School in Chicago is somehow paradigmatic of the whole devel-

---

44. New York: Macmillan, 1936.
45. See esp. *New Faith*, 284, where Mathews says he endeavored to be conciliatory.
46. *BW* 27 (1906) 204–8.
47. *Modernism*, 37.
48. Ibid., 52.
49. Ibid., 47.
50. Ibid.
51. Ibid., 37.
52. *New Faith*, 72.
53. Ibid., 72–89.

opment of the divinity faculty: Harper was superintendent, E. D. Burton was superintendent of instruction, and Mathews director of benevolence, in addition to which they had an examiner and a director of public worship![54]

In sum, Mathews was ideologically akin to Burton but the evangelical progeny of Harper.

2.7 The most radical of the second-generation divines at Chicago turned out to be Shirley Jackson Case. Although he had been trained at Yale by B. W. Bacon and F. C. Porter (B.D., 1904; Ph.D., 1906), he appears to have put greater stock in the historical method than either of his teachers.[55] Nor does he seem to have become blindly enamored of German scholarship during his brief period of study in Marburg, since he was subsequently severely critical of German thought. In short, Case was his own man, a rigorous, unrelenting scholar and thinker, in pursuit of a distinctive methodology and a grand overview of history.

The radical character of Case's position is confirmed by the fact that he trained his fire on German and American liberals as much as on the orthodox. The burden of his protest was that the history of Christianity was conceived too narrowly as literary history (or institutional history), and not broadly as social process. He points out that the higher critic's interest in the authorship and date of documents, the two-document solution to the synoptic problem, and even form criticism, is highly deceptive, unless this work is clearly understood to be preliminary to the real task of the historian.[56] As important as documents are to the historian, it is the social context rather than documents that is his focus.[57] Just as the mere study of documents may maim the historian, the NT itself may hamper the historian of Christianity.[58] The documentary notion of history, moreover, is closely associated with "the static conception of history."[59]

Case's phrase, "the static conception of history," recalls a battery of terms and phrases he used to characterize deficient conceptions of history. In his 1914 work, *The Evolution of Early Christianity,* he surveys the work of Hegel, F. C. Baur, Ritschl, Herder, Schleiermacher, and Troeltsch, with this conclusion:

> This survey of opinion shows how generally Christianity has been defined in static and quantitative terms.... The question of contemporary influences is

---

54. Ibid., 246.
55. Cf. F. C. Porter, "The Historical and the Spiritual Understanding of the Bible," and B. W. Bacon, "New Testament Science as a Historical Discipline," in the Yale memorial volume, *Education for Christian Service* (New Haven: Yale University, 1922).
56. *The Social Origins of Christianity* (Chicago: University of Chicago, 1923) 21–32; *Jesus: A New Biography* (Chicago: University of Chicago, 1927) 73ff., 94–95, 103–4.
57. "The Historical Study of Religion," *JR* 1 (1921) 4.
58. *Social Origins,* 1ff. At an earlier time, the notion of canonicity hindered the study of the documents: *Jesus,* 58–60.
59. *JR* 1 (1921) 4.

wholly secondary, since it relates only to the later history of this given original and never to its primary constitution.[60]

Every effort to fix an "essence" of Christianity inevitably produced distortion,[61] since an "essence" is by definition static.[62] The notion of essence is related to the belief in a divine deposit of truth, a historic revelation vouchsafed to certain persons in the past.[63] This, in turn, is linked to the view that the past has normative significance.[64] And "the normative function of history rests ultimately upon that pessimistic philosophy of life which interprets the present as a deterioration of humanity, a condition to be remedied only by the restoration of an idealized past."[65]

Case set himself against all this in the name of an evolutionary or developmental understanding of history, and hence of Christianity, with a focus on the social process.[66] When history is viewed as an evolutionary process, the past is stripped of its normative character.[67] The modern student of history puts his faith in the future; it is in the present and future that new standards and norms are to be found.[68]

The bearing of Case's systematic position on the Bible would not be difficult to infer, were that necessary. He is quite explicit. He calls into question not only the authority of the Bible as a whole, he rejects the effort to retain certain portions of Scripture and history "as an authoritative guide to the present."[69] He goes even further in rejecting the normative significance of the men and events that lie behind Scripture. In this respect he is more patently radical than Mathews. Whatever appeals to living men out of the past does so, he argues, not because of its historical attestation,[70] but because it retains a measure of functional value for moderns.[71] One does not settle the question of religious values out of Scripture,

---

60. *The Evolution of Early Christianity* (Chicago: University of Chicago, 1914) 21–22.
61. Ibid., 22–23.
62. Ibid., 24; "The Problem of Christianity's Essence," *AJT* 17 (1913) 542.
63. The connection is made in *Evolution*, 21–22. Cf. ibid., 27–28; *Social Origins*, 33–34; "The Religious Meaning of the Past," *JR* 4 (1924) 578.
64. *JR* 4 (1924) 579.
65. *JR* 1 (1921) 14; cf. ibid., 15–16.
66. E.g., *Evolution*, 1–25.
67. *JR* 1 (1921) 14.
68. Ibid., 17; *JR* 4 (1924) 589.
69. *JR* 4 (1924) 581–82.
70. Case tends to link beliefs about the origin of Scripture with inspiration and revelation, as do others in the period: demolish one and the other is also demolished. Cf. *JR* 4 (1924) 580–81.
71. *JR* 4 (1924) 581–82.

or even out of history, but by some other authority to be independently determined.[72]

As a consequence, the student of religion, in his search for facts, will strive to interpret religious movements, and "only incidentally to expound sacred literatures." The work of higher criticism is only preliminary to the work of the modern historian of early Christianity.[73] The student of the NT will abandon the techniques of traditional scholarship as exemplified, for example, by the commentary, with its meticulous, "phrase-by-phrase exposition."[74]

Case would appear to be a historical relativist pure and simple. After a careful study of the whole Case corpus, however, Paul Schubert concludes that Case never quite made up his mind on this point. Schubert is of the opinion "that Case's own relativist criteria led him to an absolutist persuasion as regards the prospects of future progress."[75] Although Case consistently affirms the neutrality of historical inquiry,[76] he does not seem to have confined himself to the role he espoused as his ideal.

At all events, Case occupied new ground at Chicago in endeavoring to shake himself entirely free of the "dead hand of the past." Together with G. B. Smith, he set the stage for the emergence of the second major phase at Chicago, and put a period to the dominance of the biblical question.

3. The Fate of a Tradition

3.1 Harper assumed that the battle with science and with religious orthodoxy would be fought on biblical ground. It was an assumption widely shared in his day. He also assumed that a victory for Scripture and for the historical method required the creation of a new high scholarship in America. This scholarship had to specialize in those areas most closely associated with a sacrosanct text, viz., biblical languages, textual criticism, grammar, lexicography, verse-by-verse interpretation, and translation. Such scholarship would be motivated by an evangelical respect for the text—or at least by the memory of it—and by a desire to control the battleground. Textual criticism became the surest means, for example, of combating the verbal inerrancy of Scripture. The victory would come in the form of a new respect for Scripture, in the spirit but not the letter of orthodoxy, and in accordance with the canons of historical science.

It was thus fully deliberate that Chicago sought the highest level of competence in the traditional biblical disciplines. But the new high scholarship also had to compete with German scholarship, and this meant mastery of "higher

---

72. Ibid., 583.
73. *JR* 1 (1921) 9–10.
74. *Evolution*, 8–9.
75. "Shirley Jackson Case, Historian of Early Christianity: An Appraisal," *JR* 29 (1949) 41.
76. E.g., *JR* 4 (1924) 585.

criticism." In this domain Chicago, like most other faculties in the U.S. of the period, represented little more than a rehearsal of German theories. Yet it was on this point that controversy with orthodoxy tended to focus, and it was the realm which offered the greatest hope for the reconciliation of science and biblical religion. But the first generation was so preoccupied with assembling primary credentials, catching up, and competing for the lay mind, that it had little time for attention to broader theological problems, including the problem of biblical authority.

The rejection of dogmatic theology and the development of ancillary disciplines went hand in hand with the emergence of a new biblical scholarship. Dogmatics had become the enemy personified since it was theology that had brought the Bible to its present state of disrepute by virtue of its tyranny over biblical scholarship. The salvage operation had to begin with the overthrow of theology. The ancillary disciplines, such as biblical archaeology, social history, comparative religions, were involved in the divestment campaign and to support the conclusions of critical scholarship arrived at largely by means of literary criticism. At the same time, these disciplines contributed enormously to the reconstruction of the "biblical world," so crucial to the later years of the first phase of the School.

3.2 It is not accidental that Harper and Burton specialized in the biblical languages, wrote grammars, and produced commentaries. One looks in vain for similar work, at least in the form of publication, among second-generation NT scholars at Chicago. E. J. Goodspeed is perhaps the exception. As E. C. Colwell observes, philological expertise died with Burton.[77] Mathews notes the passing of the commentary genre,[78] and Case rejected the older forms of scholarship, including the literary-critical work of contemporary Germans, who were quite liberal theologically. Such scholarship, on his view, paid too much attention to literary monuments and not enough to social history.[79]

As a consequence, the second generation chose to gird up its scholarly loins in a slightly different fashion from Harper and Burton. Alongside a reduced commitment to philological expertise, they prepared to meet the full thrust of the social and physical sciences. This accounts for the heavy concentration in history, sociology, and psychology. By these means they hoped to compete more fully on the secular terrain of the sciences, without sacrificing the prestige that still attached to philological competence. At the same time, they sought new ground for the faith.

With Burton leading the way, then, Mathews and Case quietly abandoned the primacy of Sacred Scripture, and with it they also gradually abandoned those disciplines that were oriented primarily to the interpretation of Scripture. They

---

77. "The Chicago School of Biblical Interpretation," typescript, 12.
78. *New Faith*, 97–98; cf. S. J. Case, Evolution, 8–9.
79. *JR* 1 (1921) 9–10.

gave up the means along with the end. In so doing, they did not think they were betraying the cause for which Christianity stood, but actually promoting it the only way it could be promoted in the modern world.

The Burton wing of the Chicago School could not perpetuate itself in its initial form, if it were to be true to itself. Once Scripture was abandoned as the anchor of the tradition, there was no longer reason to continue biblical scholarship in its traditional mold. Note that Mathews moved, formally, to theology and Case to church history. Their continuing interest in the prophets and Jesus was secondary support for their commitment to the social gospel. Above all, they looked not to the past, but to the present and future for their notions of "essential" and "normative" Christianity.

The second phase of the Chicago School stands as the legitimate successor to the first. The reason for the ascendancy of the philosophy of religion at Chicago during the 1930s, according to Bernard Meland,[80] was that "the grounds for belief in the historic truths had given way in the modern age, and a new rationale must be found." Without a biblical basis for faith, a new basis had to be found, and it was to this continuing issue that the second phase of the School devoted itself.

The line that runs from Burton through Mathews and Case to G. B. Foster, G. B. Smith, and Henry Nelson Wieman—the Burton wing—is a better index to common American consciousness, in my opinion, because it strikes me as evident that the biblical basis of faith was effectively eroded away before the era of the Scopes trial, precisely in that lay mind which Harper and his colleagues sought so desperately to reach. That may be the reason, too, that Chicago abandoned the battle for the lay mind: the issue was dead. In any case, the biblical question was not reopened; on the contrary, it was considered to be out of the running.

3.3 While Burton, Case, and Mathews may reflect the broader drift of cultural history, it is equally evident that the trajectory charted by them has not basically affected the course of biblical scholarship in America. This means, among other things, that W. R. Harper did indeed survive and, in fact, came to prevail nearly everywhere but at Chicago, simply because biblical scholarship elsewhere was largely in league with the same program.

In Harper's view, a new high biblical scholarship would control the contested terrain of Scripture by virtue of its competencies in those disciplines most closely akin to a sacrosanct text. Moreover, the critical historical method was taken to be the solution to the hermeneutical problem, and thus also to the problem of Scripture. On the other hand, the laity could be taught the fundamentals of the historical method, including the axiom that they had to rely on the scholar-specialist for judgments on larger, higher critical matters.

At the base of the historical method is philological expertise, the immediate issue of which is adequate translation into the current idiom (Harper's linguistic

---

80. *Criterion* (1962) 25.

method correlated with lay communication), and the more remote issue of which is the commentary or surrogate (technical, homiletical, popular). One can almost draw a direct line from Harper's method through Goodspeed and the *American Translation* to the *RSV,* the *Interpreter's Bible,* and the *Anchor Bible.*[81] Goodspeed himself confirms the first connection.[82] This understanding is undergirded by what might be termed a degenerate form of the Reformation doctrine of the clarity of Scripture, coupled with democratic confidence in the essential literacy of the common man. Thus, lower and higher criticism together would vanquish the orthodox enemy and enlighten the common mind.

The Harper leg of the Chicago School, like the Burton line, was never able to address the scriptural problem on internal grounds. The major reason was, of course, that the problem was taken to have been solved by method. As a corollary, this leg was also deeply anti-theological and for the same reasons. It, too, wanted to divest itself of premodern dogmatic theology and to win academic respectability. And there is another reason. For a time, the rearguard action against fundamentalism devolved upon Harper's heirs and latter day comrades, e.g., Goodspeed's defense of his *American Translation;* but when this battle died away, the liberal victors constituted themselves the new custodians of the biblical tradition in America over the firm resolve never again to allow themselves to be provoked by the question of biblical authority. They have hewed firmly to the line, even over against the minority tradition fostered by the other wing of the Chicago School. Relative to that position and with the passing of fundamentalism, they constitute the new right in American biblical scholarship.

A constellation of factors thus conspired to drive the question of Scripture underground during the critical period, 1890–1920, in the major surviving line of liberal biblical scholarship. No amount of provocation appears sufficient to bring it back to the surface. To do so now, of course, would be to call a half century of work into question and cause us to revert to the issue that prevailed at the turn of the century.

3.4 It remains to inquire whether the issue can be left buried. Or are there reasons why it should be exhumed and faced? Response to these questions must necessarily be only suggestive.

3.4.1 When last seen, the Chicago School of biblical interpretation was on its way to the open university, i.e., to a secular academic context. That it never quite arrived, or arrived and was subsequently evicted, may be regarded as an accident of history. By contrast, the Harper legacy of liberal biblical scholarship has been sheltered by and large in the theological seminary and church-related college, in more or less close proximity to the church. In this protective atmosphere, the study of the Bible has not had to compete quite as openly for sustenance with the

---

81. I owe this suggestion to Bernard Scott.
82. *As I Remember,* 117; cf. p. 302.

other humanities; furthermore, conservative theological forces have often constituted a certain drag on scholarship. A biblical scholarship, unsupported by special scriptural favors, has thus been retarded on the American scene.

There is evidence that the era of kept liberal scholarship is passing. There has been a perceptible shift in the academic base of biblical studies from the seminary to the university department of religion or Semitics; at the same time, the academic base for biblical scholarship is visibly contracting. It is probably ironic and maybe even a little prophetic that W. R. Harper's university, with a biblical faculty at its heart, may come to be the first major church-founded institution to drop biblical studies altogether. The Chicago School may have anticipated the necessity with which biblical scholarship is now faced. At all events, it appears certain that biblical scholars will increasingly have to justify their existence in the secular university without benefit of scriptural ploy. That in itself will cause the question of Scripture to surface once again but in an entirely new form.

3.4.2 The status of Scripture is closely related to the problem of the limits of Scripture. In seminaries and many church colleges it is difficult to justify courses which major in non-canonical Jewish and Christian literature. In the university, on the other hand, a canonical bias must not be too evident. This discrepancy goes together with the Harper legacy: biblical scholarship gives allegiance to the relativistic position of historical science, while maintaining a hidden deference to the Jewish and Christian canons.

To be sure, the Society of Biblical Literature has long entertained papers on Ugarit, Nag Hammadi, and the Early Bronze age at Jericho. But there has been a silent agreement to maintain connections, however remote in some instances, with the canon of Scripture in both the annual meeting and the journal. So long as arbitrary limits—arbitrary from the standpoint of historical science—are imposed upon the biblical scholars, it will be difficult to come entirely clean with colleagues and students in the secular university.

3.4.3 Finally, the continuing anti-theological bias of biblical scholarship should be noted. This bias is particularly ironic in view of the abiding subterranean deference to the status and limits of Scripture. Biblical scholarship in America has been virtually untouched by developments in Europe, principally Germany, since the First World War. Why, in strong contrast to the *post bellum* period, has this been the case?

The questions posed by Barth and Bultmann—to give a greatly abbreviated answer—were or are felt to be inadmissible on the American scene. They are inadmissible because they raise the forbidden question: The question of Scripture. Barth and Bultmann have been understood, consequently, as mounting an attack on the Bible itself (Bultmann) or on biblical scholarship (Barth). In some quarters the opposite is taken as the case, and they are relegated to the fundamentalist camp. In either case, they are put down as German theological laundry beneath the dignity of Americans to wash.

Because the question of Scripture is just below the surface in American liberal scholarship, it is systematically suppressed in discussion. It is for this reason that the hermeneutical problem cannot be pursued directly. Philological detail and certain ancillary disciplines, such as biblical archaeology, support scholarly "objectivity," while permitting one to evade the question of meaning. The scholar can present an evening of stereopticon slides on biblical sites without so much as touching on the question of religion. Yet, for those with memories of the tradition, viewing the very ground on which the prophets and Jesus walked can kindle a warm glow. It is a question of whether biblical scholarship can continue to trade on a sentiment it is not willing to recognize.

I am not suggesting that the scriptural issue should be reopened as a traditional theological problem. I am suggesting that the question of the text as text—whether the biblical text "means" significantly or at all in our tradition—is a question which should be deliberately permitted, perhaps under literary guise (the modes of prophetic speech; the parable as religious discourse) or under the banner of the history of interpretation (how was the Bible interpreted in the American tradition?). To continue to suppress this issue is to blink at the increasingly precarious academic posture of biblical scholarship and to close our eyes to a rich tradition hoary with age. The early Chicago School has taught us that the issue needs to be faced. It has also taught us how painful that facing will be. American biblical scholarship must come to the point at which it can afford full dignity to an ancient and honorable discipline without a scriptural crutch. The transition will not be easy. Yet, we must make it for the sake of ourselves and for the sake of the discipline. And once we have made it to fresh ground, the issue of Scripture as Scripture will surface naturally and without guilt.

"OTHER SHEEP NOT OF THIS FOLD":
THE JOHANNINE PERSPECTIVE ON CHRISTIAN
DIVERSITY IN THE LATE FIRST CENTURY*

Raymond E. Brown, S.S.
Union Theological Seminary

Was the Johannine community a sect? This has become a burning issue with implications both for Fourth Gospel studies and for our understanding of Christian origins.[1] To some extent the answer to the question depends on the definition of "sect." Does one define "sect" in terms of a stance over against another religious body (in this instance, either against parent Judaism or against other Christians), or of a stance over against society at large (against "the world")?[2]

Working in the context of the latter understanding of "sect," R. Scroggs[3] argues that the whole early Christian movement was sectarian, for it met the following basic characteristics of a sect: (1) it emerged out of an agrarian protest movement; (2) it rejected many of the realities claimed by the establishment

---

*The Presidential Address delivered 29 December 1977, at the annual meeting of the Society of Biblical Literature, held at the San Francisco Hilton, San Francisco, CA.

1. It would also have implications for the nature of scripture, since a sectarian understanding of the Johannine community might imply that the church canonized within the NT the writings of groups who would not have acknowledged each other as true Christians.

2. W. Meeks (*JBL* 95 [1976] 304) distinguishes between Americans who are accustomed to use "sect" as a sociological term, and many European scholars who use the term only in a theological and church-historical sense. His own solution to my opening question is clear from the title of his article: "The Man from Heaven in Johannine Sectarianism," *JBL* 91 (1972) 44–72. Caution is inculcated by D. M. Smith, Jr. ("Johannine Christianity: Some Reflections on Its Character and Delineation," *NTS* 21 [1974–75] 224): "If this [Johannine] sectarian or quasi-sectarian self-consciousness is not a matter of dispute, its roots, causes and social matrix nevertheless are. What thereby comes to expression? A Christian sense of alienation or separation from the world generally? From the Synagogue? From developing ecclesiastical orthodoxy?"

3. "The Earliest Christian Communities as Sectarian Movement," in *Christianity, Judaism and Other Greco-Roman Cults-Studies for Morton Smith at Sixty* (ed. J. Neusner; 4 vols.; Leiden: Brill, 1975) 2. 1–23. He gives a bibliography on the sociology of "sect," as does R. A. Culpepper, *The Johannine School* (SBLDS 26; Missoula: Scholars Press, 1975), 259, n. 10.

(claims of family, of religious institution, of wealth, of theological intellectuals); (3) it was egalitarian; (4) it offered special love and acceptance within; (5) it was a voluntary organization; (6) it demanded a total commitment of its members; and (7) it was apocalyptic. Obviously, in such an understanding of "sect," the Christian community known to us through the Fourth Gospel and the Johannine Epistles was a sect, as part of the larger Christian sectarian movement.[4]

Even if one takes "sect" in a purely religious framework, the whole early Christian movement may have been considered a sect, or at least the Jewish Christian branch of it. In Acts 24:5, 14, Jews who do not believe in Jesus describe other Jews who do believe in him as constituting a *hairesis*—the same word used by Josephus (*Life* 10) when he speaks of the three "sects" of the Jews: Pharisees, Sadducees, and Essenes. But my interest here is the applicability of the religious term "sect" to the Johannine community in its relationship to other Christian communities at the end of the first century. Was this community an accepted church among churches or an alienated and exclusive conventicle? In this dialectic, the Johannine community would *de facto* be a sect, as I understand the term, if explicitly or implicitly it had broken *koinōnia* with most other Christians,[5] or if because of its theological or ecclesiological tendencies, most other Christians had broken *koinōnia* with the Johannine community.

Some have argued for Johannine sectarianism on the basis of the relatively quick acceptance of the Gospel by second-century Gnostics.[6] The logic is that these "heretics" had correctly recognized the innate tendencies of Johannine thought. D. M. Smith, however, correctly observes that Irenaeus was able to accept the gospel as orthodox, so that second-century usage is not a clear criterion of the sectarian status of Johannine thought in the first century: "If there was a Johannine line of development [trajectory], it has not yet proved possible to identify it clearly in the second century and thus to follow it back into the first."[7]

Still another argument for Johannine sectarianism has come from radical interpretations of the theology and ecclesiology of the Fourth Gospel.[8] The

---

4. The Johannine community may fit certain of these characteristics better than do other Christian groups, e.g., No. 4; yet (at least as seen through the Fourth Gospel) it would fit poorly other characteristics, e.g., No. 7.

5. See S. Brown, "Koinonia as the Basis of New Testament Ecclesiology?" *One in Christ* 12 (1976) 157-67.

6. That the Fourth Gospel was first accepted by groups who could be classified as heterodox has been proposed by J. N. Sanders and by M. R. Hillmer; the opposite thesis has been defended by F.-M. Braun. See my AB commentary, 1. *lxxxi, lxxxvi*; also E. H. Pagels, *The Johannine Gospel in Gnostic Exegesis* (SBLMS 17; Nashville: Abingdon, 1973).

7. "Johannine Christianity," 225.

8. I shall confine myself in this paper to the Fourth Gospel, with occasional references to the Johannine Epistles. More could be determined about Johannine ecclesiology through recourse to Revelation with its seven letters to the churches. E. S. Fiorenza, "The Quest for the Johannine School: the Apocalypse and the Fourth Gospel," *NTS* 23 [1976-77] 402-27) argues

likelihood that the Johannine community was a sect sharply different from most other Christians would be increased if the Fourth Gospel is antisacramental or decidedly nonsacramental (so Bultmann who attributes the clearly sacramental passages to an ecclesiastical redactor of the gospel), or if the gospel is anti-Petrine (with the understanding that Peter is symbolic of the larger church's interest in apostolic foundation);[9] or if the gospel is anti-institutional, rejecting the presbyter/bishop structure that was emerging at the end of the century;[10] or if its christology is a naive docetism, so that the church committed an error when it ultimately declared the gospel to be orthodox (Kasemann). However, since such radical interpretations of the Fourth Gospel have often been challenged (and in my judgment, refuted), I prefer here another approach to the problem of the relation of the Johannine community to other Christian communities.

This approach is based on the supposition that from the story of Jesus' ministry in the Fourth Gospel we can deduce much information about the Johannine community. J. L. Martyn[11] brought such a method of investigation into prominence by using the dialogues between Jesus and "the Jews" to determine the relationship between the Johannine community and the synagogue. Recently Martyn, G. Richter, and I have all attempted to reconstruct the pre-gospel history of the Johannine community from hints in the gospel.[12] The three of us agree that the Johannine community originated among Jews who believed that Jesus had fulfilled well-known Jewish expectations, e.g., of a messiah or of a prophet-like-Moses. (The best indicator of this is John 1:35–50 where the first disciples are Jews who accept Jesus under titles known to us from OT and intertestamental

---

that the author of Revelation "appears to have been more familiar with Pauline than with Johannine school traditions." I am willing to accept the thesis that the author of Revelation is an unknown Christian prophet named John (not the son of Zebedee); but I find Fiorenza's hypothesis exaggerated both as regards Pauline similarities and Johannine dissimilarities. Nevertheless, I shall not use Revelation in this paper.

9. See G. F. Snyder, "John 13:16 and the Anti-Petrinism of the Johannine Tradition," *BR* 16 (1971) 5–15.

10. E. Schweizer (*Church Order in the New Testament* [SBT 32; London: SCM, 1961] 127): "Here [in the Johannine Epistles in continuity with the Gospel] there is no longer any kind of special ministry, but only the direct union with God through the Spirit who comes to every individual; here there are neither offices nor even different charismata."

11. *History and Theology in the Fourth Gospel* (New York: Harper & Row, 1968). This will soon be published in a new edition by Abingdon.

12. J. L. Martyn, "Glimpses into the History of the Johannine Community," in *L'Evangile de Jean: Sources, rédaction, théologie* (ed. M. de Jonge; BETL 44; Gembloux: Duculot, 1977) 149–75. This paper was given at the 1975 Colloquium Biblicum Lovaniense (Journées Bibliques) and will be republished in a collection of Martyn's Johannine essays (New York: Paulist Press, 1978). G. Richter, "Präsentische und futurische Eschatologie im 4. Evangelium," in *Gegenwart und kommendes Reich: Schülergabe Anton Vögtle* (ed. P. Fiedler and D. Zeller; Stuttgart: Katholisches Bibelwerk, 1975) 117–52. An English digest by A. J. Mattill appears in *TS* 38 (1977) 294–315. R. E. Brown, "Johannine Ecclesiology—the Community's Origins," *Int* 31 (1977) 379–93.

literature.) At a later stage there developed within the Johannine community a higher christology that went beyond Jewish expectations by describing Jesus as a pre-existent divine savior who had lived with God in heaven before he became man. (As an indicator of this, in John 4 there is a description of new converts in Samaria who recognize Jesus as the savior of the world; and in 5:18 and 8:48 there are accusations that Jesus is making himself equal to God and is a Samaritan.) This high christology led to friction between the Johannine community and the synagogue and ultimately to its expulsion (9:22; 10:31–33; 16:2). And so we find a community increasingly conformed to its own image of Jesus, for he too had been rejected by "his own" (1:11). This estranged community, like Jesus, found itself in the world but not of it (17:16).

At the end of his study of pre-gospel history, Martyn[13] concluded that when the gospel was written there were at least four groups in the Johannine religious purview:

(1) The synagogue of "the Jews."
(2) Crypto-Christians (Christian Jews) within the synagogue.
(3) Various communities of Jewish Christians who had been expelled from the synagogue.
(4) The Johannine community of Jewish Christians, in particular.

I am now going to suggest that the situation was more complicated, and that at the end of the century, if we include the witness of the Johannine Epistles, we can detect no less than six groups. (See the accompanying chart on pp. 194–95.)

More important, I think that an analysis of these groups throws considerable light on the question of whether the Johannine community was a sect within Christianity. Let us discuss the groups one by one.

I. "The Jews" or the Synagogue

In the pre-gospel history of the Johannine community there was a severe struggle with Jews who did not believe in Jesus and who reacted hostilely to those who did believe in him—a struggle fought in part with the weapon of scriptural exegesis (5:39, 46–47). This struggle led to banning from the synagogues Jews who believed in Jesus (9:22; 16:2). By the time that the Fourth Gospel was written,[14]

---

13. "Glimpses," 174.

14. There is reasonably wide consensus that the Fourth Gospel was written after the destruction of the temple when the teaching center of Judaism had moved to Jamnia (Jabneh)—now largely a pharisaic Judaism, and thus no longer so pluralistic as before 70. The hostility between the Johannine community and the synagogues may well have developed over several decades after the mid-60s; but Martyn (*History and Theology*) has argued well for dating the written gospel after A.D. 85, the approximate date for the introduction into the synagogues of the reworded Twelfth Benediction (of the *Shemoneh Esreh*) called the *Birkat ha-Minim*, involving a curse on heretical deviators, including those who confessed Jesus to be the messiah.

the polemics between the Johannine community and the synagogues included topics known to us from other NT or early Christian writings, e.g., that Christians violate the sabbath and thus violate the law given by God to Moses (5:16; 7:19, 22-24); that there was no resurrection of Jesus (2:18-22); that the eucharist is incredible (6:52); that Jesus was no great teacher (7:15); and that he could deceive only the uneducated (7:49). Nevertheless, these are only secondary issues; the primary object of contention is the Johannine Christian proclamation of the divinity of Jesus. As S. Pancaro[15] has shown, even the battles over the law and the sabbath have become christological battles, for the sovereign attitude of the Johannine Jesus flows from his being above and beyond the law. There is a uniqueness to the Jesus of the Fourth Gospel:[16] he is the Word who was in God's presence from the beginning (1:1), the only one who has heard God's voice and seen his face (5:37); and now that he has descended from heaven, he is the exclusive means of knowing the Father (3:13; 8:19); indeed, he is one with the Father (10:30). In response to such claims "the Jews" charge that Jesus is being made a god; but John answers subtly that such claims do not *make* anything of Jesus; rather Jesus is entirely dependent upon the Father for all that he is and does (5:19-47).

That the issue of ditheism is the primary bone of contention has been recognized by many scholars, and most clearly by Martyn. But I think there is a second major point of contention, namely, the Jewish cult. Derivatively from his high christology, John contends that the most sacred cultic institutions of Judaism have lost their significance for those who believe in Jesus. Jesus is now the place of divine tabernacling (1:14: *skēnoun*); his body is the temple (2:21); and what Jesus says on the occasion of prominent Jewish feasts (Sabbath, Passover, Tabernacles, Dedication) systematically replaces the significance of those feasts.[17] If the Jewish synagogues have expelled Christians, John's Christianity has negated and replaced Judaism. The believer in Jesus is a true Israelite (1:47); "the Jews" are the children of the devil (8:44).

In my analysis of pre-gospel Johannine history,[18] I suggested that it was the entrance into the community of a second group of believers which explained the high christology that surpassed Jewish expectations. This second group of believers I saw reflected in John 4, and speculated that it consisted of Jews with anti-temple views (4:21) and their Samaritan converts (4:35-38). That the existence of such a group is not pure imagination may be seen from the description

---

15. *The Law in the Fourth Gospel* (NovTSup 42; Leiden: Brill, 1975).

16. Although I stress the uniquely high christology of John, this gospel is still a long way from the theology of Nicaea: "true God of true God ... consubstantial with the Father." See C. K. Barrett, "'The Father is greater than I' (Jo 14, 28): Subordinationist Christology in the New Testament," in *Neues Testament und Kirche* (Festschrift für R. Schnackenburg; ed. J. Gnilka; Freiburg: Herder, 1974) 144-59.

17. See my *AB* commentary, 1. cxliv, 201-4, for the outline of chaps 5-10.

18. "Johannine Ecclesiology," 388-90.

DIFFERENT RELIGIOUS GROUPINGS IN THE JOHANNINE PURVIEW OF THE LATE FIRST CENTURY*

VI. Secessionist Johannine Christians	V. The Johannine Christians	IV. Christians of Apostolic Churches
Following the high christology of the Fourth Gospel to what they considered its logical conclusion, they thought that the One who had come down from heaven and did not belong to this world was not fully human. It was of no salvific import that he had truly "come in the flesh" and had really died. In turn they relativized the importance of earthly life for Christians and the decisiveness of moral behavior. They interpreted the freedom brought by Jesus as a freedom from the guilt of sin. In a dispute with members of Group V, they had withdrawn and broken *koinōnia*, leaving themselves open to the charge of not loving the brethren. They defended their views as the work of the Spirit.	Although now of mixed Jewish and Gentile stock, in earlier history they originated among various types of Jewish converts (perhaps followers of John the Baptist mixed with antitemple Jewish Christians who had evangelized Samaria). In conflict with "the Jews" (I), they had developed a very high christology. Not only had they been separated from the synagogues over the charge that they were ditheists, but also they had no *koinōnia* with Jewish Christians of a low christology (II and III). They retained *koinōnia* with Christians who confessed Jesus as Son of God (IV), although for them true unity could be based only on a christology of the preexistence of Jesus and his oneness with the Father. The priority they placed on unity with Jesus relativized for them the importance of church office and structure; and sacraments were seen as continuations of the actions of Jesus.	Quite separate from the synagogues, mixed communities of Jews and Gentiles regarded themselves as heirs of the Christianity of Peter and the twelve. Theirs was a moderately high christology, confessing Jesus as the messiah born at Bethlehem of Davidic descent and thus Son of God from conception, but without a clear insight into his coming from above in terms of preexistence before creation. In their ecclesiology Jesus may have been seen as the founding father and institutor of the sacraments; but the church now had a life of its own with pastors who carried on apostolic teaching and care.

*The columns are meant to be read in order from right to left.

DIFFERENT RELIGIOUS GROUPINGS IN THE JOHANNINE PURVIEW OF THE LATE FIRST CENTURY (continued)

III. The Jewish Christians	II. The Crypto-Christians	I. "The Jews"
Christians who had left the synagogues but whose faith in Jesus was inadequate by Johannine standards. They may have regarded themselves as heirs to a Christianity which had existed at Jerusalem under James the brother of the Lord. Presumably their low christology based on miraculous signs was partway between that of Groups II and IV. They did not accept Jesus' divinity. They did not understand the eucharist as the true flesh and blood of Jesus.	Christian Jews who had remained within the synagogues by refusing to admit publicly that they believed in Jesus. "They preferred by far the praise of men to the glory of God." Presumably they thought they could retain their private faith in Jesus without breaking from their Jewish heritage. But in the eyes of the Johannine Christians (V), they thus preferred to be known as disciples of Moses rather than disciples of Jesus. For practical purposes they could be thought of along with "the Jews" (I).	Those within the synagogues who did not believe in Jesus and had decided that anybody who acknowledged Jesus as Messiah would be put out of the synagogue. The main points in their dispute with the Johannine Christians (V) involved: (a) claims about the oneness of Jesus with the Father—the Johannine Jesus "was speaking of God as his own Father, thus making himself God's equal"; (b) claims that understanding Jesus as God's presence on earth deprived the temple and the Jewish feasts of their significance. They exposed the Johannine Christians to death by persecution and thought that thus they were serving God.

of Hellenist theology in Acts 7:47–49 and of the Hellenist mission in Samaria in Acts 8:4–8.[19] Added support for associating Johannine high christology and the Johannine attitude of replacing the Jewish cult is supplied by Hebrews, a work with Johannine affinities.[20] High christology appears in the use of "God" for Jesus in the psalm exegesis of Heb 1:8, and this is followed by a lengthy argument that Jesus has made otiose an earthly cult centered on tabernacle, priesthood, and sacrifice. In both John and Hebrews the ramifications of a belief in the divinity of Jesus involve a reinterpretation of new covenant to mean that the old covenant has been replaced.

II. The Crypto-Christians or Christian Jews within the Synagogues

John 12:42–43 is our clearest reference to a group of Jews who were attracted to Jesus and could be said to have believed in him, but were afraid to confess their faith publicly lest they be expelled from the synagogues. John has contempt for them and holds up the blind man as an example of the kind of courage such people should have—courage to leave the synagogue and come to Jesus (9:22–23, 34–35). Undoubtedly, much of the Johannine polemic against "the Jews" who did not believe in Jesus would touch these Christian Jews as well; for in John's judgment, by not publicly confessing Jesus, they were showing that they did not really believe in him. Like "the Jews" the Crypto-Christians had chosen to be known as disciples of Moses rather than as disciples of "that fellow" (9:28). Yet John's very attention to them implies that he still hopes to sway them, while he has no hope of swaying "the Jews."

From this mirror view of the Crypto-Christians it is difficult to reconstruct the details of their christology and ecclesiology. We may suspect that in their view the Johannine Christians had unnecessarily and tragically brought about a division. The blind man, whom John presents as a hero, may have seemed to them an uncompromising and rigid fanatic determined on eyeball-to-eyeball confrontation, a figure whose rudeness to the synagogue authorities made expulsion a virtual necessity. Perhaps the Crypto-Christians recalled that Jesus was a Jew who had functioned *within* the synagogue, as had James, and Peter and other

---

19. O. Cullmann has rendered service in seeking to relate Johannine Christianity to the Hellenists of Acts (as did B. W. Bacon before him), even if Cullmann's position may need more nuance. See the reviews of his *The Johannine Circle* (Philadelphia: Westminster, 1976) in *JBL* 95 (1976) 304–5 and *TS* 38 (1977) 157–59. C. H. H. Scobie, in a paper delivered at the 1976 SBL St. Louis meeting ("The Origin and Development of the Johannine Community") stressed the role of the Hellenists in a modified form of the Cullmann hypothesis.

20. C. Spicq (*L'Epître aux Hebreux* [2 vols.; Paris: Gabalda, 1952] 1. 109–38) treats sixteen parallels between John and Hebrews. I am attracted to the possibility that, if we use the language of Acts 6–7, Hebrews is a Hellenist Christian tract addressed to Hebrew Christians, trying to convince them that in the last third of the century it was no longer possible for them to remain within Judaism as it had been during the middle third of the century.

Christian leaders. Like the recipients of the Epistle to the Hebrews, they may have felt no necessity to have Jesus exalted over Moses and to have their whole cultic heritage negated. One's judgment on their presumed preference for compromise rather than confrontation will depend on the extent to which one thinks it really was possible to put new wine into old wineskins.

III. The Jewish Christians of Inadequate Faith

In isolating the first two groups within the Johannine purview I have been in harmony with Martyn and others, but now I would seriously modify that aspect of Martyn's treatment which applies to the Crypto-Christians all the unfavorable Johannine references to Jews who believe in Jesus. I think there were also Jewish Christians who had left the synagogues (or been expelled) but toward whom John had a hostile attitude. For instance, to whom does John refer in 2:23–25 when he speaks of the many in Jerusalem who believe in Jesus' name on the basis of his signs, but to whom Jesus refuses to entrust himself? These are quite distinct from "the Jews" of the preceding episode who deny the resurrection (2:18–22), and I see no reason to think that they represent Crypto-Christians within the synagogues.[21] We are more plausibly dealing with a Jewish Christian community, associated in some way with Jerusalem, in whom John has no trust.

I find even more difficult to interpret as Crypto-Christians the disciples of 6:60–66 who are clearly distinct from "the Jews" of the synagogue debate which ends in 6:59. Nor do they seem to be Crypto-Christians since they have gone about with Jesus publicly (6:66) in a manner not hitherto distinct from that of the twelve (6:67). Since this scene takes place in Galilee rather than in Jerusalem, the object of the author's ire may be Jewish Christians in Palestine.

The picture may be filled out by the Johannine hostility toward the brothers of Jesus recorded shortly afterwards: his brothers, who have urged him to show off his miracles in Judaea, "did not really believe in him" (7:3–5).[22] In 2:12, John had distinguished between the family of Jesus ("his mother and his brothers") and "his disciples,[23] even though both groups went with Jesus to Capernaum. In the gospel, John refers once more respectively to Jesus' mother and to Jesus' brothers. The reference to the brothers is in terms of unbelief, as just mentioned. The mother appears at the foot of the cross (19:25–27) as part of a faithful community

---

21. If the Jerusalemites of 2:23–25 are represented by Nicodemus who makes his appearance immediately afterwards (3:1–2), it becomes clear in 19:39 that Nicodemus ultimately became a public follower of Jesus.

22. Their lack of faith in 7:5 continues a sequence of reactions to Jesus begun in 6:66: some disciples would no longer accompany Jesus (6:66); Simon Peter as a spokesman for the twelve continues to believe in Jesus (6:68–69); Judas, one of the twelve, will betray him (6:71); and his brothers do not believe in him (7:5).

23. For the textual problems and critical suggestions, see my *AB* commentary, 1. 112.

who will remain on after Jesus' death. Indeed, she is associated with the Johannine hero *par excellence,* the beloved disciple, who becomes her son—perhaps an attempt to redefine the family of Jesus so that the beloved disciple replaces the unbelieving brothers.[24] In any case, the hostile portrait of the brothers of Jesus, without any hint of their conversion, is startling when we reflect that the Fourth Gospel was written after James, the brother of the Lord, had led the Jerusalem church for almost thirty years and had died a martyr's death. Since his name was revered as a teaching authority by Jewish Christians (James 1:1; Jude 1), are we having reflected in John a polemic against Jewish Christians, particularly in Palestine, who regarded themselves as the heirs of the Jerusalem church of James?[25] Are their church leaders the hirelings of 10:12 who do not protect the sheep against the wolves, perhaps because they have not sufficiently distanced their flocks from "the Jews"?[26]

In John 8:31 there begins a difficult section addressed to Jerusalem Jews who believe in Jesus.[27] This probably refers to Crypto-Christians still within the synagogue since the author soon calls them simply "the Jews" (8:48) and describes them as seeking to stone Jesus (8:59). John might think that some Jewish Christian churches outside the synagogue no longer truly follow Jesus, but he would scarcely accuse them of seeking to kill Jesus. Nevertheless, some of what John ascribes to "Jews who had believed in him" in 8:31–59 may pertain to Jewish Christians as well as to Crypto-Christians, namely, that although they remain proud that they are Abraham's children (8:39), they firmly reject the thought that before Abraham even came into existence, Jesus is (8:58–59). John would then be seeing a double-defect in the faith-commitment of the Jewish Christians. Although they could accept Jesus as a wonder-worker, they refused to identify him as the divine "I AM." Secondly, they did not believe that in the eucharist Jesus had really given his flesh to eat and his blood to drink (6:60–64). The existence of such Jewish Christians just after A.D. 100 is attested in the letters of Ignatius of Antioch. Recently the Jewish Christian opponents of Ignatius were

---

24. For a development of this idea see R. E. Brown, "The 'Mother of Jesus' in the Fourth Gospel," in *L'Evangile de Jean* (see n. 12 above) 307–10. Note too that in 20:17–18 the disciples of Jesus are actually called his brothers.

25. According to church tradition James was succeeded as head of the Jerusalem church by other brothers or relatives of the Lord (Eusebius, *Hist. eccl.* 3.11.20, 32).

26. Martyn ("Glimpses," 171) sees these as leaders among the Crypto-Christians. The figurative language would seem to portray them, however, as openly acknowledged shepherds of Christian groups. Even though outside the synagogue, presumably they were not so persecuted as the Johannine community whose divine claims for Jesus they did not share.

27. See B. E. Schein, "'The Seed of Abraham'—John 8:31–59," Abstracts of SBL Meeting, Atlanta, 1971, S159, pp. 83–84: "The opponents of the Johannine circle called 'Jews who had believed' are the circle of tradition-minded, pharisaic-oriented Christians from Jerusalem."

described thus:[28] "They reverenced Jesus as a teacher, but perhaps were not prepared to allow his person to upset the unity of the Godhead.... They adopted the sacred meal ... and thought of it in terms of fellowship rather than as a sacrament on Ignatian lines." John may be giving us a picture of similar Jewish Christians twenty years earlier.

IV. Christians of Apostolic Churches

There are two groups of Jesus' disciples sharply contrasted in John 6:60–69. The first group who left the synagogue with him but subsequently drew back has been discussed above. Over against their inadequate faith stands the confession of the twelve who through Peter acknowledge that Jesus has the words of eternal life. Here we have the traces of those who in Martyn's quadrilateral church situation are characterized as: various communities of Jewish Christians who had been expelled from the synagogue but with whom there is hope of unification. I wish to change the description somewhat. If we speak of a group of late first-century Christians represented in the Fourth Gospel by Peter and other members of the twelve (Andrew, Philip, Thomas, Judas-not-Iscariot, Nathanael[29]), the very choice of symbolic representatives suggests that they were Jewish Christian in origin. Everything said about Peter and the twelve would lead us to think that such Christians were no longer in the synagogue (see 16:2 addressed to a group which includes members of the twelve). But I see no reason to assume that there were not many Gentiles among these Christians. Philip and Andrew are involved in the scene where the Greeks come to Jesus at the end of the ministry (12:20–26); and elsewhere I have argued (against Martyn) that this scene, taken with 7:35, points to the presence of Gentiles in the Johannine community as well.[30] Moreover, any attempt to restrict the Christians represented by Peter to Jewish Christians would run against solid NT evidence that Peter was a Jewish Christian leader open to the admission of the Gentiles (Acts 10:1–11:18; Gal 2:9). Therefore, I prefer to designate the Christians under discussion with a term that is more neutral, "Christians of Apostolic Churches,"[31] and to hold open the possibility that there is no ethnic

---

28. C. K. Barrett, "Jews and Judaizers in the Epistles of Ignatius," in *Jews, Greeks and Christians* (W. D. Davies Festschrift; ed. R. Hamerton-Kelly and R. Scroggs; Leiden: Brill, 1976) 220–44, esp. 242.

29. I am not suggesting that Nathanael is to be identified with anyone listed in the synoptic lists of the twelve, e.g., with Barnabas. But since the three synoptic gospels show disagreement on who should be named among the twelve (see *JBC* 78:171), Nathanael may have been counted in the never-given listing of the twelve by the Johannine community.

30. Brown, "Johannine Ecclesiology," 391–93.

31. I use the term "apostolic," not necessarily because John would have used it, but because most of the symbolic representatives are called apostles in other NT works; and so the term may represent the self-understanding of this group.

difference between them and the Johannine Christians—both groups consisted of Jews and Gentiles.

If we call upon Peter and the other named disciples as clues to John's attitude toward these Apostolic Christians, his attitude is fundamentally favorable. They are clearly distinct from Jewish Christians who no longer follow Jesus, and their presence at the last supper means that they are included in Jesus' "own" whom he loves to the very end (13:1). They are among those who have kept Jesus' word (17:6); and he prays for them (17:9), since they are hated by the world (17:14). They see the Risen Lord (20:24); and their most prominent spokesman, Simon Peter, glorifies God by his death in the following of Jesus (21:19).[32]

Nevertheless, these named disciples do not seem to embody the fullness of Christian perception. We see this when we compare them in general, and Simon Peter in particular, to the beloved disciple, the symbolic representative of the Johannine community.[33] The others are scattered at the time of Jesus' passion leaving him alone (16:32), while the beloved disciple remains with Jesus even to the foot of the cross (19:26–27). Simon Peter denies that he is a disciple of Jesus (18:17, 25), a particularly serious denial granted the Johannine emphasis on discipleship as the primary Christian category; and so he needs to be rehabilitated by Jesus who three times asks whether Peter loves him (21:15–17). No such rehabilitation is necessary and no such questioning is even conceivable in the case of the disciple *par excellence,* the disciple whom Jesus loved. Closer to Jesus both in life (13:23) and in death (19:26–27), the beloved disciple sees the significance of the garments left behind in the empty tomb when Peter does not (20:8–10); he also recognizes the risen Jesus when Peter does not (21:7). The Johannine Christians, represented by the beloved disciple, clearly regard themselves as closer to Jesus and more perceptive than the Christians of the Apostolic Churches.[34]

---

32. I think that John 21 is the work of a redactor, but a redactor whose theology has considerable continuity with that of the evangelist; see my *AB* commentary, 1. *xxxvi–xxxviii.*

33. Though of symbolic value in the Fourth Gospel (even as is Simon Peter), the beloved disciple is no less historical than Simon Peter. I agree with Culpepper (*Johannine School,* 265): "The actual founder of the Johannine community is more likely to be found in the figure of the Beloved Disciple ... [who] probably represents the idealization of a historical person.... the role of the BD is the key to the character of the community." I think that his background was similar to that of the prominent members of the twelve, but he underwent a christological development that placed a distance between him and them. He achieved his identity as the beloved disciple in a christological context, and that is why he is not mentioned by title in the gospel until "the hour" has come (13:1): see my "Johannine Ecclesiology," 386–88.

34. O. Cullmann (*The Johannine Circle,* 55) notes: "Its members were probably aware of the difference which separated them from the church going back to the Twelve and also saw that their particular characteristics laid upon them the obligation of a special mission, namely to preserve, defend and hand on the distinctive tradition which they were sure had come down from Jesus himself."

The one-upmanship of the Johannine Christians is centered on christology; for while the named disciples, representing the Apostolic Christians, have a reasonably high christology, they do not reach the heights of the Johannine understanding of Jesus. Andrew, Peter, Philip, and Nathanael know that Jesus is the messiah, the fulfiller of the law, the Holy One of God, and the Son of God (1:41, 45, 49; 6:69);[35] but they are told that they are yet to see greater things (1:50). As Jesus says to Philip at the last supper, "Here I am with you all this time and you still do not know me?" (14:9)—a rebuke precisely because Philip does not understand the oneness of Jesus with the Father.[36] When later on the disciples make the claim, "We believe that you came forth from God," Jesus' skepticism is obvious: "So now you believe? Why, an hour is coming, and indeed already has come, for you to be scattered, each on his own, leaving me all alone" (16:29–32). Even after the resurrection, the scene with Thomas indicates that the faith of the twelve can stand improvement (20:24–29). In fact, Thomas' reluctant confession of Jesus as "My Lord and my God" may be paradigmatic of the fuller understanding of Jesus' divinity to which, John hopes, the Apostolic Christians may ultimately be brought. We may make an informed guess that the precise aspect of christology missing in the faith of the Apostolic Christians is the perception of the pre-existence of Jesus and of his origins from above.[37] Both Apostolic and Johannine Christians say that Jesus is God's Son, but Johannine Christians have come to understand that this means that he is ever at the Father's side (1:18), not belonging to this world (17:14), but to a heavenly world above (3:13, 31). Once again the christology I attribute to the Apostolic Christians is not a pure hypothesis based on an interpretative reading of the Fourth Gospel. From the gospels of Matthew and Luke we know of late first-century Christians who revered the memory of Peter and the twelve and who acknowledged Jesus as the Son of God through conception without a human father; but in whose christology there is no hint of pre-existence. They know a Jesus who is king, lord, and savior from the

---

35. Since I think it possible that the figure who *became* the beloved disciple is the unnamed disciple of 1:35–50, I find no difficulty in using 1:35–50 to detect the christology both of the Apostolic Christians and of Johannine *origins*. However, the Johannine community and the beloved disciple moved beyond this christology by accepting into their midst another group of Jewish and Samaritan Christians who introduced new categories, such as preexistence. See my "Johannine Ecclesiology," 388–91.

36. M. de Jonge ("Jesus as Prophet and King in the Fourth Gospel," *ETL* 49 [1973] 162) writes: "Jesus' kingship and his prophetic mission are both redefined in terms of the unique relationship between Son and Father, as portrayed in the Fourth Gospel." This redefinition constitutes the difference between Apostolic and Johannine Christians.

37. In the NT, preexistence christology is not peculiar to John; but only John has this christology in a nonpoetic narrative context (indeed on Jesus' lips) and only John makes it clear that the preexistence was before creation. It would seem logical that the gospel format, rooted in the historical memory of Jesus, would be more resistant to preexistence speculation than would the theology of hymns.

moment of his birth at Bethlehem, but not a Jesus who says, "Before Abraham was, I AM."[38]

A difference in ecclesiology may also have separated Johannine Christians from Apostolic Christians. Other NT works of the late first-century, especially Luke/Acts, show that continuity with the "apostles" was becoming an important factor in church identity and self-security. The Fourth Gospel, however, gives virtually no attention to the category of "apostle"[39] and makes "disciple" the primary Christian category, so that continuity with Jesus comes through the witness of the beloved *disciple* (19:35; 21:24).[40] Furthermore, Matthew, Luke/Acts, and the Pastorals all testify to the increasing institutionalization of churches toward the end of the century, with a developing interest in ecclesiastical offices. On the one hand, I have repeatedly opposed the assumption by E. Schweizer and others that the Johannine community had no ecclesiastical offices—we simply do not know that, and there are contrary indications in the Johannine Epistles, especially 3 John. On the other hand, there is much in Johannine theology that would relativize the importance of institution and office at the very time when that importance was being accentuated in other Christian communities (including those who spoke of apostolic foundation). Unlike Paul's image of the body and its members which is invoked in 1 Corinthians 12 to accommodate the multitude of charisms, the Johannine image of the vine and branches places emphasis on only one issue: dwelling on the vine or inherence in Jesus.[41] (If John was interested in diversity of charism, he could have written of branches, twigs, leaves, and fruit, even as Paul wrote symbolically of foot, hand, ear, and eye.) The category of discipleship based on love makes any other distinction in the community rela-

---

38. John's lack of interest in Jesus' Davidic origins and birth at Bethlehem, as reflected in the debates with "the Jews" (7:41–42), *may* constitute a correction of the kind of christology we find in Matthew and Luke, a christology which (in John's eyes) puts too much emphasis on a matter of Jewish concern. Similarly John's exaltation of Jesus on the cross relativizes the importance of resurrection appearances and so implicitly corrects a christology which associates divine sonship with the resurrection (Acts 2:32, 36; 5:31; 13:33; Rom 1:4). As M. de Jonge points out ("Jewish Expectations about the 'Messiah' according to the Fourth Gospel," NTS 19 [1972–73] 264), in the debates described in the Fourth Gospel, "Johannine christology is developed not only in contrast with Jewish thinking but also with other christological views."

39. *Apostolos* appears only in the nontechnical sense of messenger (13:16). The verb *apostellein* appears, sometimes interchangeably with *pempein,* but the sending is scarcely confined to those who are considered "apostles" in other NT documents.

40. C. K. Barrett (*The Gospel of John and Judaism* [Philadelphia: Fortress, 1975] 75), following Hoskyns, catches the paradoxical Johannine attitude well: "John intended to bind the church to the apostolic witness; but in other respects he meant to leave it free." For the prominence that John gives to women disciples, to the point that they seem to be on the same level as members of the twelve, see R. E. Brown, "Roles of Women in the Fourth Gospel," TS 36 (1975) 688–99.

41. See J. O'Grady, "Individualism and Johannine Ecclesiology," BTB 5 (1975) 227–61, esp. 243: "As with the flock, the point of interest [in the vine and the branches] is the relationship between Jesus and the individual believer."

tively unimportant, so that even the well-known Petrine and presbyteral image of the shepherd[42] is not introduced without the conditioning question, "Do you love me?" (21:15–17). The greatest of the named apostles in the NT, Peter, Paul, and James of Jerusalem, all died in the 60s; and in the subsequent decades the churches which invoked their names solved the teaching gap that resulted from these deaths by stressing that the officials who succeeded the apostles should hold on to what they were taught without change (Acts 20:28–30; Titus 1:9; 2 Pet 1:12–21). But the Fourth Gospel, which knows of the problem of the death of the beloved disciple (21:20–23), stresses that the teacher is the Paraclete who remains forever within everyone who loves Jesus and keeps his commandments (14:15–17); he is the guide to all truth (16:13).[43] Finally, unlike Matt 28:19 and Luke 22:19, John has no words of Jesus commanding or instituting baptism and the eucharist just before he left this earth. The image of Jesus instituting sacraments as a final action tends to identify them with the sphere of church life, while for John the sacraments are continuations of the power that Jesus manifested during his ministry when he opened the eyes of the blind (baptism as enlightenment) and fed the hungry (eucharist as food).[44] In summary, let me stress that I do not interpret these Johannine ecclesiological attitudes as aggressively polemic, for there is no clear evidence that the Johannine community was condemning apostolic foundation and succession, church offices, or church sacramental practices. The Fourth Gospel is best interpreted as voicing a warning against the dangers inherent in such developments by stressing what (for John) is truly essential,[45] namely, the living presence of Jesus in the Christian through the Paraclete. No institution or structure can substitute for that. This outlook and emphasis would give Johannine ecclesiology a different tone from that of the Apostolic Christians

---

42. The shepherd image is found in Acts 20:28; 1 Pet 5:1–5; Matt 18:12–14.

43. For the Paraclete as the Johannine answer to the problems raised by the death of the first generation of Jesus' followers who had been community founders, see my *AB* commentary, 2. 1142. D. M. Smith ("Johannine Christianity," 232–33, 244) thinks there was a strong component of spirit-inspired prophets in the Johannine community to whom some of the "words of Jesus" in the Fourth Gospel may be attributed.

44. For this approach to Johannine sacramentalism, see my *AB* commentary, 1. cxiv. O. Cullmann (*Johannine Circle*, 14): "In each individual event of the life of the *incarnate* Jesus the Evangelist seeks to show that *at the same time* the *Christ present in his Church* is already at work."

45. Barrett (*Gospel of John and Judaism*, 74) writes: "John combines a deep interest in the apostolic foundation of the church with an indifference toward it as an institution dispensing salvation." O'Grady ("Individualism," 254) notes: "It may very well be true that the Johannine community and its spokesman saw its contribution to early Christianity mainly as emphasizing purpose and meaning as the Church found itself in need of structure, organization and ritual expression." See also the balanced treatment by O'Grady, "Johannine Ecclesiology: A Critical Evaluation," *BTB* 7 (1977) 36–44.

known to us from other late first-century NT writings—a Johannine ecclesiology the peculiarity of which reflects the peculiarity of Johannine christology.

V. The Johannine Christians

In the four preceding sections I have already delineated much of what was unique about the Johannine Christians. But there remains the question with which I began: Were the Johannine Christians a sect, which had broken *koinōnia* with most other Christians? In answering this, let us recall the Johannine relationships with each of the four groups already discussed. The Johannine Christians were not the only Christians hostile to the synagogue and its leaders (Group I: "The Jews"),[46] even though the bitterness attested in John may be more acute than in other NT works. The sectarian element in the Johannine picture would be the peculiar sense of estrangement from one's own people (1:11). As for the attitude of the Johannine Christians toward the Crypto-Christians (Group II) and the Jewish Christians (Group III), once more they were not the only NT Christians to condemn other Christians as false.[47] But, more than others, John's community may have moved toward clearly excluding their opponents from Christian fellowship, e.g., by counting the Crypto-Christians as aligned with "the Jews" (12:42–43) and by charging that the Jewish Christians who were associated with the brothers of the Lord followed Jesus no longer and did not really believe in him (6:66; 7:5).

Besides these specific rejections of Groups I, II, and III there is much that is sectarian in John's sense of alienation and superiority. The Johannine Jesus is a stranger who is not understood by his own people and is not even of this world. The beloved disciple, the hero of the community, is singled out as the peculiar object of Jesus' love and is the only male disciple never to have abandoned Jesus. Implicitly then, the Johannine Christians are those who understand Jesus best, for like him they are rejected, persecuted, and not of this world. Their christology is more profound, and they can be sure that they have the truth because they are guided by the Paraclete. To some extent even the literary style of the Fourth Gospel reflects Johannine peculiarity, with its abstract symbolism (life, light, truth) and its technique of misunderstanding.[48]

---

46. Hostility dates from Paul's passing reference to "the Jews" in the first preserved Christian writing (1 Thess 2:14–15). The saying "No one puts new wine into old wineskins" (Mark 2:22 and par.) lays the groundwork for a replacement attitude toward the institutions of Judaism.

47. The fear in Acts 20:30 is almost typical: "There will arise from among yourselves men who speak perversity to mislead disciples after them."

48. Yet I find exaggerated the thesis of H. Leroy (*Rätsel und Missverständnis* [BBB 30; Bonn: Hanstein, 1968])—see my review in *Bib* 51 (1970) 152–54—that the language of the Johannine community, as attested in the Fourth Gospel, is a special form of speech, a type of riddle-language, unintelligible to outsiders. Meeks ("Man from Heaven," 57) makes the same point: "Only a reader who is thoroughly familiar with the whole Fourth Gospel or else acquainted by some

Nevertheless, despite all these tendencies toward sectarianism, I would contend that the Johannine attitude toward the Apostolic Christians (Group IV—probably the "larger church") proves that the Johannine community, as reflected in the Fourth Gospel, had not really become a sect. They had not followed their exclusivistic tendencies to the point of breaking *koinōnia* with these Christians whose characteristics are found in many NT works of the late first-century. If we can judge from the presence of Simon Peter and the other named disciples at the last supper, the Johannine Christians looked on the Apostolic Christians as belonging to Jesus' own (13:1) to whom they were bound by the commandment: "As I have loved you, so must you love one another" (13:34). Their hopes for the future may be expressed by 10:16, if that verse is a reference to the Apostolic Christians, as Martyn[49] has argued: "I have other sheep, too, that do not belong to this fold. These also must I lead, and they will listen to my voice. Then there will be one sheep herd, one shepherd." Even more probable is the suggestion that at the last supper (where Simon Peter and the beloved disciple are both present), when Jesus prays for those who believe in him through the word of his disciples, "That they all may be one" (17:20–21), he is praying for the oneness of the Apostolic and the Johannine Christians. Here the Johannine attitude is just the opposite of the outlook of a sect.

Ah, one may object, the Johannine prayer for unity with the Apostolic Christians carried a price tag—those other Christians would have to accept the exalted Johannine christology of pre-existence if there was to be one sheep herd, one flock. If this did not happen, one may argue, the Johannine Christians would reject the Apostolic Christians from *koinōnia* even as they had previously rejected the Jewish Christians. Yet we are spared discussing that theoretical possibility, for in fact the larger church did adopt Johannine pre-existence christology. Already in Ignatius of Antioch we hear of Jesus both as the Word coming forth from the silence of God (*Magn.* 8:2) and as born of the virgin Mary (*Eph.* 19:1)—almost a combination of Johannine and Matthean/Lucan christologies.[50] Some scholars may ponder on the luck of the beloved disciple that his community's gospel was not recognized for the sectarian tractate that it really was. But other scholars will see this as a recognition by Apostolic Christians that the Johannine language was

---

non-literary means with its symbolism and developing themes ... can possibly understand its double entendre and its abrupt transitions. For the outsider—even for an interested inquirer (like Nicodemus)—the dialogue is opaque." To the contrary, I would maintain that this gospel is a literary work where the reader is expected to be more intelligent than those dramatis personae who serve as foils of the dialogue of Jesus; it is an ancient example of the Conan Doyle technique where the reader is expected to be more intelligent than Dr. Watson but still amazed at Sherlock Holmes' profundity. The christology of the Fourth Gospel is partially unintelligible and quite unacceptable to Groups I, II, and III, but is not meant to be unintelligible to Christians of Group IV whom it hopes to persuade.

49. "Glimpses," 171–72.
50. See also Aristides, *Apology* 15.1 and Justin, *Apology* 1.21 and 33.

not really a riddle and the Johannine voice was not alien—a recognition facilitated by strains of preexistence christology among non-Johannine communities.[51] What the Johannine theologians claimed to have had from the beginning seems to have been accepted by many other Christians as a recognizable and embraceable variant of what they also had from the beginning.

However, if Ignatius and other early church writers bear witness to a wide second-century acceptance of a christology similar to John's, the same documents betray an ecclesiology quite unlike John's—specifically Ignatius stresses ecclesiastical offices and church control over baptism and the eucharist. To explain the success of a christology like John's in the larger church and the simultaneous failure of Johannine ecclesiology, let me discuss briefly the last group in the Johannine purview of Christianity.

VI. Secessionist Johannine Christians

I emphasize that my treatment will be brief because the main evidence for this group is within the Johannine Epistles; and elsewhere I shall discuss more fully the church situation in those Epistles.[52] The First Epistle (2:19) speaks of a group that had withdrawn from the community: "It was from our ranks that they went out." The christology of these Secessionists seems to have been so high that it did not matter for them that Jesus was the Christ come in the flesh (1 John 4:2). A plausible case can be made that these Secessionists were not formal docetists but adherents of Johannine theology who had carried out some aspects of the high christology of the Fourth Gospel to the nth degree.[53] If Jesus was not of this world (John 17:16), they might argue, what significance did his earthly actions, including his death,[54] really have? The only important reality would be that the pre-existent Word of God had come into the world to enlighten his own who were not of the flesh but begotten from above (John 3:3–7); like Jesus they were not of this world (17:16) but were destined to join him in the otherworldly mansions he was preparing for them (14:2–3).[55] Presumably they emphasized that

---

51. Possible instances are Phil 2:7; 1 Cor 8:6; Col 1:15; Heb 1:2; but see note 37 above.

52. At the Shaffer Lectures at Yale in February, 1978, and in my *AB* commentary on the Johannine Epistles, projected for 1980.

53. R. E. Brown, "The Relationship to the Fourth Gospel Shared by the Author of I John and by His Opponents," *Matthew Black Festschrift*, to be published in 1978.

54. T. Forestell (*The Word of the Cross: Salvation as Revelation in the Fourth Gospel* [AnBib 57; Rome: Biblical Institute, 1974] 191) writes: "The cross of Christ in Jn is evaluated precisely in terms of revelation in harmony with the theology of the entire gospel, rather than in terms of a vicarious and expiatory sacrifice for sin."

55. E. Käsemann (*The Testament of Jesus* [Philadelphia: Fortress, 1968] 26) speaks of John's christology of glory as "naïve, unreflected" docetism. (If one must be anachronistic, I would prefer "monophysitism.") I doubt that such was the christology of the evangelist, but his gospel left itself open to this reading; and it was thus interpreted by the Johannine Secessionists. See

eternal life consisted in knowing the one whom God had sent (17:3), but not in being cleansed by his blood (1 John 1:7). The indifference to sin ascribed to the Secessionists (1 John 1:8, 10) is explicable as a derivative from their high christology: if Jesus' actions on earth were not of intrinsic salvific value, what import for salvation could be attributed to the actions of his followers? After all, had not the truth set them free (John 8:32)?

In short, through the First Epistle one can detect the existence of two groups of Johannine Christians, each drawing on the kind of Johannine theology known to us in the Fourth Gospel, but interpreting it very differently. Opposed as he is to the Secessionist christology and ethics, the author of 1 John still cannot silence or demolish his opponents by appealing to the authority of a church teaching office,[56] as would have been the case in the Pastorals. True to Johannine tradition, he makes appeal to a teaching Spirit abiding in the Christian through anointing by Christ, a principle that relativizes any human teachers (1 John 2:20, 27). If the Secessionists reply that what they teach flows from an anointing with the Spirit,[57] the author of the epistle is not free to reject that idea in principle but must demand a testing of the spirits (4:2). In other words, Johannine ecclesiology did not supply an authoritarian solution to such a division within the community. The later church, through canonization of the First Epistle, showed which side of the dispute it thought to be right and true to the gospel, but the author of 1 John hints (4:5) that his opponents were winning over the majority to their cause.

I would judge that these two groups of Johannine Christians continued into the second century. It was in the Secessionists, perhaps the larger group, that the sectarian tendencies of the Johannine tradition came to fruition. Ultimately they became a Gnostic sect, breaking *koinōnia* with the Apostolic Churches (or having it broken); for it was probably their extremely high christology and Spirit-dominated ecclesiology, presented as an interpretation of the Fourth Gospel, which made that gospel so readily acceptable to second-century Gnostics.[58] A smaller group of Johannine Christians, represented by the author of the First Epistle, seems to have kept *koinōnia* with the Christians of the Apostolic Churches by sufficiently correcting Secessionist (mis)interpretations of the gospel, so that other Christians saw no contradiction between its pre-existence christology and a soteriology based on Jesus' ministry and death. (The work of the redactor of the

---

also J. L. Martyn, "Source Criticism and *Redactionsgeschichte* in the Fourth Gospel," *Perspective*, 11 (1970) 259.

56. The "we" of the prologue of 1 John does not refer to a lineage of church officers, but is the author's attempt to show that his interpretation of Johannine tradition is the ancient one implied from the beginning and in harmony with that of previous Johannists, such as the evangelist.

57. D. M. Smith ("Johannine Christology") thinks that the spirit-inspired prophets had now become a problem. See footnote 43 above.

58. See note 6 above.

gospel may have facilitated this "orthodox" reading of the work.) I would conjecture that it was through this branch of Johannine Christians that the gospel found acceptance among second-century traditionalists such as Irenaeus. The very experience of the secession and the alienation of a large (if not the larger) group of their confreres may well have made these Johannine Christians more amenable to the authoritative structures of the Apostolic Christians—they had found to their bitter experience that to preserve their christology from "left-wing" extremism they needed to make a compromise with "right-wing" ecclesiology. (The turmoils of the emergence of authority structures within the Johannine tradition may be echoed in 3 John.)

If this reconstruction of the unity and diversity of Johannine Christianity in the first century has even partial validity, such history represents in microcosm problems which have tortured Christianity ever since.

THE BIBLE AS A CLASSIC
AND THE BIBLE AS HOLY SCRIPTURE*

Krister Stendahl
Harvard Divinity School

Thirty years ago there was hardly any attention to an alternative like the Bible as a classic and the Bible as Holy Scripture. Then the proper discussion was about the Bible as history and the Bible as Holy Scripture. And the battle was about *geschichtlich und historisch,* historic and historical, about historicity and myth, the historical Jesus and the kerygmatic Christ, history of salvation and just plain history.

Now there has been a shift from history to story: the Bible as story, theology as story.[1] For both philosophical and literary reasons the focus on language and on forms of literary criticism demand the center stage. The odd idea of a "language event" strikes me as a hybrid in the transition from the one perspective to the other.

It is tempting to speculate about deeper cultural forces at work in this shift. Could it be that preoccupation with history comes natural when one is part of a culture which feels happy and hopeful about the historical process? Hegel's pan-historic philosophy belongs, after all, to the ascendancy of western imperial-

---

*The Presidential Address delivered 18 December 1983 at the annual meeting of the Society of Biblical Literature held at the Loews Anatole Hotel, Dallas, TX.

1. This shift has many facets. There is the literary dimension as found in Northrop Frye, *The Great Code: The Bible and Literature* (New York/London: Harcourt, Brace, Jovanovich, 1982). There is the movement represented by the Society of Biblical Literature journal *Semeia* (1974–), edited by J. Dominic Crossan and foreshadowed by the pioneering work of Amos N. Wilder (see *Semeia* 12–13, 1978). The depth of the philosophical and theological shifts are perhaps best expressed in David Tracy, *The Analogical Imagination: Christian Theology and the Culture of Pluralism* (New York: Crossroad, 1981). Tracy significantly uses as one of his main categories "The Classic." For a theological critique see the review by Peter Manchester, *Cross Currents* 31 (1981/82) 480–84. See also Patrick A. Kiefert, "Mind Reader and Maestro: Models for Understanding Biblical Interpreters," *Word and World* 1 (1980/81) 153–68; and in the same issue (entitled "The Bible as Scripture") Karlfried Froehlich, "Biblical Hermeneutics on the Move," 140–52.

ism—it was even said that other parts of the world were lifted "into history" when conquered, colonized, or converted by the West. Now the western world is not so sure or so optimistic about where history—that is, "our" history—is going. So the glamour, the glory, the Shekinah has moved away from history.

There is a striking analogy to such a move from history to story and wisdom. I think of the major move of rabbinic Judaism after the fall of Jerusalem and the Bar Kokhba catastrophe. Rabbinic Judaism—a child of the very tradition which is often credited with having given "the idea of history" to the world—cut loose from the frantic attempts at finding meaning in and through history. At Jamnia and through the Mishnah the center of religious existence was placed in Halakah, i.e., in the lifestyle and wisdom of Torah. To be sure, the historical consciousness remained strong in Judaism, but not any more as the center of attention. It becomes exactly "story," Haggadah, with far less binding authority. To be sure, the Mishnah and the Talmud are not the sum total of Judaism. There are the prayers and the memories, but the center, the equivalent to what Christians came to call theology, is in Torah as Halakah. Those Jewish writings that struggled with meaning in and through history, writings like 4 Ezra and 2 Baruch, have survived through Christian transmission.[2] They were not part of the living tradition of Judaism. It was the Christians, new on the block, who inherited and renewed the historical mode. To them history was not mute, for now "in these last days God has spoken to us by a Son" (Heb 1:2). With continuity and with fulfillment, history worked well—or what turned out to be a very long time—a time which now may come to an end in western theology.

Whatever the value and truth of such rather wild speculations, the shift in contemporary biblical and theological work from history to story is obvious and well substantiated by a perusal of the program for the annual meeting of our Society of Biblical Literature and of our sister, the American Academy of Religion.

Thus it has become natural to think in the pattern of the Bible as a classic and the Bible as Holy Scripture. The shift is appealing for a very simple additional reason. It expresses so much better the way in which the Bible actually exists within our western culture, and sometimes even beyond its confines: as a classic with often undefined distinctions on a sliding scale of holiness and respect.

By "classic" I mean any work that is considered worth attention beyond its time, and sometimes also beyond its space—although I doubt there is any truly global classic—across all cultures. It would be western myopia to claim such recognition for Homer or for Shakespeare, or even for the Bible. For it is its recognition that makes a classic a classic, not its inner qualities. Hence I try to avoid the more romantic terminology in which modern studies abound, such as "excess of meaning" or "the power of disclosure." Such terminology tends to obscure the

---

2. See now Jacob Neusner, *Ancient Israel after Catastrophe: The Religious World View of the Mishnah* (Charlottesville, VA: University Press of Virginia, 1983). Note also Neusner's observation about the revelatory style of 4 Ezra and Baruch in contrast to the Mishnah (p. 26).

societal dimension of a classic. It is common recognition by a wide constituency of a society that makes a certain work into a classic. No inner quality suffices unless widely so recognized.

Thus I limit myself to western culture and its classics. There is the Bible, Dante, Milton, Cervantes' Don Quixote, and Shaw's Pygmalion—becoming even more of a classic by dropping the Greek name for the English title, "My Fair Lady." And there are the classics of philosophy and science: Plato, Aristotle, Kant's Critiques, and Darwin's Species. There are classics of law and classics of medicine. There is even Kierkegaard, who wrote a novel with the title *Fear and Trembling*—he did call it a novel.

Furthermore, as the West broadens its perspective there are ways in which the Quran and the Gita become classics in our eyes. We read the holy texts of other communities as classics, mostly without consciousness of their being "only" classics. Readers find that such classics speak to them, often in undefined ways.

So there are many types of classics, and they come in many shapes and forms, in various styles and genres. And awareness of the genre is part of their being a classic for the reader. To speak of the Bible as a classic is therefore not the same as speaking of it as a literary classic. The issue is rather how to assess what kind of a classic we are dealing with. Scholars are of course free to pronounce it—or its various parts—a literary classic, or a classic of language, or a classic of history, or a classic of philosophy, or whatever. But as a living classic in western culture the perceptions of common discourse on a more democratic basis are decisive. And it is my contention that such perceptions include an irreducible awareness of the Bible as Holy Writ in church and/or synagogue.

What then about Holy Scripture? That designation is not innocent of culture and theology. It is our language. After all, Quran means "recitation," not "scripture," and the Hebrew Bible knows not only the kĕtîb but also the qĕrê—Jesus presumably never used the kĕtîb Yahweh.

It is as Holy Scripture, Holy Writ, that the Bible has become a classic in the West. Personally, I prefer the plural form, Holy Scriptures. I do so not primarily in recognition of the fascinating and often elusive ways in which the Hebrew Bible is common to Jews and Christians—the same text word for word, and yet so different when it becomes the Old Testament of the Christian Bible. I speak rather of "Holy Scriptures," plural, in order to highlight the diversity of style and genre within the scriptures. In various ways such diversity becomes important for those to whom the scriptures function as the bearer of revelation.[3] When the

---

3. See Paul Ricoeur's Dudleian Lecture at Harvard Divinity School, "Toward a Hermeneutic of the Idea of Revelation," *HTR* 70 (1977) 1–37. Here Ricoeur differentiates Prophetic Discourse, Narrative Discourse, Prescriptive Discourse, Wisdom Discourse. The first constitutes to him the "basic axis of inquiry" concerning revelation. Indeed, this is the discourse which declares itself to be "pronounced in the name of [God]," p. 3. Cf. the Book of Revelation—the only NT book which claims such authority.

Bible functions as a classic in culture, such distinctions play no significant role, but for theological and philosophical reflection it is crucial. In the scriptures we have the oracles, the laws, the prophets, the dreams, the interpreters of dreams, the wisdom, the history, the stories, the psalms, the letters, and so on. To be sure, it is a whole library. Bible means, after all, "the little books."

Nevertheless, what makes the Bible the Bible is the canon. Here is where the Bible as a classic and as Holy Scripture meet: the canonical books, bound together by those complex historical acts of recognition in the communities of faith which we can trace as the history of canonization. For it is as Bible that the biblical material has become a classic of the western world, and whatever part of the Bible is in focus—be it Job or Leviticus, the Christmas story or the Sermon on the Mount—it functions as a classic by being part of the Bible. It is perceived and received as a classic by being part of the Bible.

The Bible as a classic exists in western culture with an often undefined but never absent recognition of its being the Holy Scriptures of the church and/or the synagogue. I have my doubts that it—or substantial parts of it, at least—would have ever become a classic were it not for its status as Holy Scripture. Perhaps not even Job, the literary favorite; certainly not Leviticus, except as a legal classic. And Arthur Darby Nock used to say that the Gospel of John did not become beautiful as literature until 1611, when the King James Version gave it a beauty far beyond what the Greeks perceived.[4]

It is as Holy Scripture that the Bible is a classic in our culture. Therefore there is something artificial in the idea of "the Bible as literature." Or rather, it can be artificial and contrary to the perception of both most believers and most unbelievers, as artificial as "the Bible as history" or "the Bible as a textbook in geology or biology" or—the Bible as anything but Bible.

Most readers know, in often undefined ways, that the Bible is Holy Scripture, and it is a classic exactly as that special kind of classic. I wonder if some of our attempts at literary analysis—be it structuralism or not so new "new criticism"— are not, when all is said and done, a form of apologetics, sophisticated to a degree which obfuscates the apologetic intention even to its practitioners.

I do not consider apologetics to be a sin, provided that the apologetic intention is conscious and not obscured by having it masquerade as something else or offered as an alternative to a traditional apologetic of theological and doctrinal special pleadings. About such apologetics Northrop Frye says: "Such systems of faith, however impressive and useful still, can hardly be definitive for us now, because they are so heavily conditioned by the phases of language ascendant in their time, whether metonymic or descriptive." Then he continues:

---

4. For a penetrating understanding of the glories of the King James Version see J. L. Lowes, "The Noblest Monument of English Prose," *Essays in Appreciation* (1936), 3–31.

A reconsideration of the Bible can take place only along with, and as part of, a reconsideration of language, and of all structures, including the literary ones, that language produces. One would hope that in this context the aim of such a reconsideration would be a more tentative one, directed not to a terminus of belief but to the open community of vision, and to the charity that is the informing principle of a still greater community than faith (*The Great Code*, p. 227).

It seems rather obvious to me that Frye's program of reconsideration in all its humble tentativeness is an apologetic attempt with its own theology, appealing to charity over against the outdated "systems of faith," and addressing "a still greater community than faith." In short, here is an attempt at cutting loose from the moorings of Holy Writ. It is an attempt at allowing the text to speak as literature freed from the very claims which made the Bible a classic in the first place.

That can be done, and with great effect, not least in the hands of masters of exposition like the Auerbachs and the Fryes of literary criticism. In Frye's case the very fact that the Bible is already in itself a continuum of interpretation and reinterpretation, then becomes a glorified manifestation of a "capacity of self-recreation," and that "to an extent to which I can think of no parallel elsewhere" (p. 225). Such an approach yields significant insights and opens the senses that have been numbed by overly familiar ways of reading, greedily hunting proof texts for cherished doctrines. Titles like *Mimesis* and *The Great Code* help our mental liberation.

Or to shift to Ricoeur's proposal of a "non-heteronomous dependence of conscious reflection on external testimonies," a literary approach allows new space for the imagination. He suggests that we "too often and too quickly think of a will that submits and not enough of an imagination that opens itself.... For what are the poem of the Exodus and the poem of the resurrection addressed to if not our imagination rather than our obedience?" Thus there is the non-heteronomous possibility of encountering revelation "no longer as an unacceptable pretension, but a nonviolent appeal."[5] Frye and Ricoeur both address the imagination, but while Frye looks away apologetically from the revelatory dimension of Scripture, Ricoeur defines a way in which revelation can be revelation in a "nonviolent" manner. But Ricoeur is driven toward a dichotomy between imagination and will or obedience. Yet in speaking of an appeal, be it nonviolent, it seems that the issue for him is not will versus imagination, but rather *how* the scriptures affect the readers, in their full persons, imagination as well as will and action.

This attention to revelation, will, obedience, and action is important for our discussion, and it would seem that any culture-apologetics that circumvents those dimensions of scripture misjudge the ways in which the Bible is actually perceived as a classic by the common reader in western culture. For such readers do recognize the Bible as a classic just in its belonging to the genre of Holy Scripture.

---

5. *HTR* 70 (1977) 37.

Thereby there is a recognition of the normative nature of the Bible. That is an irreducible component in the kind of classic that the Bible is. In this it is different from Shakespeare or from the way one now reads Homer.[6]

How one relates to that normativeness is a very different question. The spectrum here is wide indeed, both within and outside the communities of faith, all the way from rejection of that claim to the most minute literal obedience. But that does not change the fact that the normative claim is recognized as intrinsic to the Bible.

In may be worth noting that the more recent preoccupation with "story" tends to obscure exactly the normative dimension. Following upon the history-kerygma preoccupation—via the "language event"—we come to story. It should be remembered, however, that even much of biblical story was preserved and shaped by the halakic needs of the communities of faith, rather than by the kerygmatic urge of communication. What was told or remembered was shaped by the need for guidance in the life of the communities; hence the normative nature of the texts as they are given to us.

It is this element of the normative which makes the Bible into a peculiar kind of classic. This is of course true in an intensive sense within the Christian community (and what a sliding scale of intensity there is). But I find it important to remember that the normative character is present also in the minds of most people who read the Bible "only as a classic."

When biblical scholarship has become greatly enriched by learning methods of literary criticism, it seems that this sense of the "normative expectation" has been lost or overlooked, for the literary models have been non-normative genres. To ask poets (or artists) what they actually meant or intended with a piece of art is often an insult, and they are apt to answer: "It is for you to answer what it means to you." That is fair enough. The more meanings the merrier.

The normative nature of the Bible requires, however, a serious attention to original intentions of texts. The intention of the original sayings, or stories, or commandments can hardly be irrelevant, as they might well be in other genres of literature. Let me give only one example, the "lex talionis" (Exod 21:22–25; Lev 24:20): "... eye for eye, tooth for tooth, hand for hand...," words that must strike most contemporary readers as ferocious. Self-serving Christians even quote it as an example of that spirit of vengeance which is supposed to characterize Judaism

---

6. There was, of course, a time when Homer served as a "sacred" text which became the object for religious and philosophical interpretation. The Stoics are famous for this approach, and such commentaries on Homer came to serve as prototypes for both Jewish and Christian commentators on the Bible in the Hellenistic and Graeco-Roman world. See Rudolf Pfeiffer, *History of Classical Scholarship: From the Beginnings to the End of the Hellenistic Age* (Oxford: Clarendon, 1968) 237ff.

as compared with Christianity, the religion of love and forgiveness.[7] But attention to "what it meant," to the intention of the legislation, to descriptive historical exegesis, all make it abundantly clear that the point made was the quantum jump from "a *life* for a tooth." Thus it was a critique of vengeance, not a sanction for vengeance. Such examples could be multiplied seventy times seven—and more.

All of this leads me to the conclusion that it is exactly the Bible as a classic and as Holy Scripture which requires the services of the descriptive biblical scholars and their simple reminder "that from the beginning it was not so," as Jesus said. That is as true about the commandments as it is about the theological constructs or the human self-understandings of the Bible.

Actually, the more intensive the expectation of normative guidance and the more exacting the claims for the holiness of the Scriptures, the more obvious should be the need for full attention to what it meant in the time of its conception and what the intention of the authors might have been.[8] But also where the Bible is enjoyed in a far more relaxed mood as a classic, people do like to find its support or sanction for their thoughts and actions. The low intensity of the normativeness often makes such use of Scripture less careful. Many even think they give honor to God and Christianity by such use of the Bible. Not least in such situations, the call to historical honesty by access to what it meant is necessary and salutary, lest vague biblical authority become self-serving, trivializing or even harmful.

In conclusion: we are a Society of Biblical Literature. The word "biblical" includes both the Bible as a classic and the Bible as Holy Scripture, and I have tried to argue that in both respects the normative dimension is an irreducible part of biblical literature. Hence our responsibilities include the task of giving the readers of our time free and clear access to the original intentions which constitute the baseline of any interpretation. This task is both one of critique and of making available those options which got lost in the process. For true criticism is also the starting point for new possibilities, hidden by the glories and by the shame of a long history under the sway of the Bible.

---

7. On the Jewish interpretation of the lex talionis, see W. Gunther Plaut, et al., *The Torah: A Modern Commentary* (New York: Union of American Hebrew Congregations, 1981) 568, 571-75; and Jakob J. Petuchowski, *Wie unsere Meister die Schrift erkliren* (Freiburg: Herder, 1982) 58-64.

8. Since I have placed so much emphasis on the Bible as canon, it is important to stress this point. Contemporary stress on the Bible in its canonical wholeness is often coupled with disregard for the intention of the various strata and theologies within the Bible. I would argue rather that exactly the normative quality of scripture necessitates the attention to original intentions; see my discussion with Brevard Childs in the introductory essay in my forthcoming book Meanings (Philadelphia: Fortress, 1984) and also the essay on "One Canon is Enough" in that volume.

The Ethics of Biblical Interpretation: Decentering Biblical Scholarship*

Elisabeth Schüssler Fiorenza
Episcopal Divinity School

It is a commonplace that presidential addresses have primarily rhetorical functions. They are a ceremonial form of speech that does not invite responsive questions nor questioning responses. Such presidential rhetoric is generally of two sorts: either it addresses a particular exegetical, archaeological, or historical problem, or it seeks to reflect on the status of the field by raising organizational, hermeneutical, or methodological questions. The latter type sometimes attempts to chart the paradigm shifts or decentering processes in biblical scholarship which displace the dominant ethos of research but do not completely replace it or make it obsolete.

Almost eighty years ago, in his presidential address entitled "The Bearing of Historical Studies on the Religious Use of the Bible," Frank Porter of Yale University charted three such shifts: (1) The first stage, out of which biblical scholarship had just emerged, was the stage in which the book's records are imposed upon the present as an external authority. (2) The second stage, through which biblical scholarship was passing in 1908, was that of historical science, which brings deliverance from dogmatic bondage and teaches us to view the past as past, biblical history like other histories, and the Bible like other books. (3) Porter envisioned a third stage "at which, while the rights and achievements of historical criticism are freely accepted, the power that lives in the book is once more felt."[1] He likens this third stage to the reading of great books, whose greatness does not consist in their accuracy as records of facts, but depends chiefly on their symbolic power to transfigure the facts of human experience and reality. In the past fifteen years or so, biblical studies has followed Parker's lead and adopted insights and methods

---

* The Presidential Address delivered 5 December 1987 at the annual meeting of the Society of Biblical Literature held at the Copley Marriott Hotel, Boston, MA.

1. Frank C. Porter, "The Bearing of Historical Studies on the Religious Use of the Bible," *HTR* 2 (1909) 276.

derived from literary studies[2] and philosophical hermeneutics; but it has, to a great extent, refused to relinquish its rhetorical stance of value-free objectivism and scientific methodism.

This third literary-hermeneutical paradigm seems presently in the process of decentering into a fourth paradigm that inaugurates a rhetorical ethical turn. This fourth paradigm relies on the analytical and practical tradition of rhetoric in order to insist on the public-political reponsibility of biblical scholarship. It seeks to utilize both theories of rhetoric and the rhetoric of theories in order to display how biblical texts and their contemporary interpretations involve authorial aims and strategies, as well as audience perceptions and constructions, as political and religious discursive practices. This fourth paradigm seeks to engender a self-understanding of biblical scholarship as communicative praxis. It rejects the misunderstanding of rhetoric as stylistic ornament, technical skills or linguistic manipulation, and maintains not only "that rhetoric is epistemic but also that epistemology and ontology are themselves rhetorical."[3] Biblical interpretation, like all scholarly inquiry, is a communicative practice that involves interests, values, and visions.

Since the sociohistorical location of rhetoric is the public of the *polis*, the rhetorical paradigm shift situates biblical scholarship in such a way that its public character and political responsibility become an integral part of our literary readings and historical reconstructions of the biblical world. "The turn to rhetoric" that has engendered critical theory in literary, historical, political and social studies fashions a theoretical context for such a paradigm shift in biblical studies[4] Critical theory, reader response criticism, and poststructuralist analysis,[5] as well

---

2. Amos N. Wilder articulated this literary-aesthetic paradigm as rhetorical. See his SBL presidential address, "Scholars, Theologians, and Ancient Rhetoric," 75 (1956) 1–11 [pp. 83–93 in this volume] and his book *Early Christian Rhetoric: The Language of the Gospel* (Cambridge, MA: Harvard University Press, 1971).

3. Richard Harvey Brown, *Society as Text: Essays on Rhetoric, Reason, and Reality* (Chicago: University of Chicago Press, 1987) 85. See also, e.g., J. Nelson, A. Megills, D. McCloskey, eds., *The Rhetoric of the Human Sciences: Language and Argument in Scholarship and Public Affairs* (Madison: University of Wisconsin Press, 1987); Hayden White, *Tropics of Discourse: Essays in Cultural Criticism* (Baltimore, MD: Johns Hopkins University Press, 1978); Ricca Edmondsen, *Rhetoric in Sociology* (New York: Cambridge University Press, 1985); John S. Nelson, "Political Theory as Political Rhetoric," in *What Should Political Theory Be Now?* (ed. J. S. Nelson; Albany: State University of New York Press, 1983) 169–240.

4. See my article "Rhetorical Situation and Historical Reconstruction in I Corinthians," *NTS* 33 (1987) 386–403 and Wilhelm Wuellner, "Where is Rhetorical Criticism Taking Us?" *CBQ* 49 (1987) 448–63 for further literature.

5. For bringing together the insights of this paper I have found especially helpful the works of feminist literary and cultural criticism. See, e.g., S. Benhabib and D. Cornell, eds., *Feminism as Critique* (Minneapolis: University of Minnesota Press, 1987); Gayatri Chakravorty Spivak, *In Other Worlds: Essays in Cultural Politics* (New York: Methuen, 1987); Teresa de Lauretis, ed., *Feminist Studies/Critical Studies* (Bloomington: University of Indiana Press, 1986); E. A. Flynn

as the insight into the rhetorical character and linguisticality of all historiography, represent the contemporary revival of ancient rhetoric.

The ethics of reading which respects the rights of the text and assumes that the text being interpreted "may say something different from what one wants or expects it to say,"[6] is highly developed in biblical studies. Therefore, I will focus here on the ethics of biblical scholarship as an institutionalized academic practice. I will approach the topic by marking my present rhetorical situation as a "connected critic"[7] who speaks from a marginal location and that of an engaged position. Then I will explore the rhetoric of SBL presidential addresses with respect to the shift from a scientific antiquarian to a critical-political ethos of biblical scholarship. Finally, I will indicate what kind of communicative practice such a shift implies.

I. SOCIAL LOCATION AND BIBLICAL CRITICISM

In distinction to formalist literary criticism, a critical theory of rhetoric insists that context is as important as text. What we see depends on where we stand. One's social location or rhetorical context is decisive of how one sees the world, constructs reality, or interprets biblical texts. My own rhetorical situation is marked by what Virginia Woolf, in her book *Three Guineas*, has characterized as the "outsider's view":

> It is a solemn sight always—a procession like a caravanserai crossing a desert. Great-grandfather, grandfathers, fathers, uncles—they all went that way wearing their gowns, wearing their wigs, some with ribbons across their breasts, others without. One was a bishop. Another a judge. One was an admiral. Another a general. One was a professor. Another a doctor.... But now for the past twenty years or so, it is no longer a sight merely, a photograph ... at which we can look

---

and P. P. Schweickart, eds., *Gender and Reading: Essays on Reader, Texts, and Contexts* (Baltimore, MD: Johns Hopkins University Press, 1986); G. Greene and C. Kaplan, eds., *Making a Difference: Feminist Literary Criticism* (New York: Methuen, 1983); Elizabeth A. Meese, *Crossing the Double Cross: The Practice of Feminist Criticism* (Chapel Hill: University of North Carolina Press, 1986); J. Newton and D. Rosenfelt, eds., *Feminist Criticism and Social Change* (New York: Methuen, 1985); M. Pryse and Hortense J. Spillers, eds., *Conjuring: Black Women, Fiction and Literary Tradition* (Bloomington: University of Indiana Press, 1985); Chris Weedon, *Feminist Practice and Poststructuralist Theory* (London: Blackwell, 1987).

6. J. Hillis Miller, "Presidential Address 1986. The Triumph of Theory, the Resistance to Reading, and the Question of the Material Base," *PMLA* 102 (1987) 284.

7. Michael Walzer characterizes the "connected critic" as follows: "Amos prophecy is social criticism because it challenges the leaders, the conventions, the ritual practices of a particular society and because it does so in the name of values shared and recognized in that same society" (*Interpretation and Social Criticism* [Cambridge, MA: Harvard University Press, 1987] 89).

with merely an esthetic appreciation. For there, trapesing along at the tail end of the procession, we go ourselves. And that makes a difference.[8]

Almost from its beginning women scholars have joined the procession of American biblical scholars.[9] In 1889, not quite one hundred years ago, Anna Rhoads Ladd became the first female member of this Society. Ten years later, in 1899, Mary Emma Woolley, since 1895 chair of the Department of Biblical History, Literature and Exegesis at Wellesley College, and from 1900 to 1937 President of Mount Holyoke College, is listed in attendance at the annual meeting. In 1913 Professor Elleanor D. Wood presented a paper on biblical archaeology, and in 1917 Professor Louise Pettibone Smith, who also served later in 1950–51 as secretary of the Society, was the first woman to publish an article in the *Journal of Biblical Literature*. Mary J. Hussy of Mount Holyoke College had held the post of treasurer already in 1924–1926. At the crest of the first wave of American feminism, women's membership in 1920 was around 10 percent. Afterwards it steadily declined until it achieved a low of 3.5 percent in 1970. Presently the Society does not have a data base sufficient to compute the percentage of its white women and minority members.

The second wave of the women's movement made itself felt at the annual meeting in 1971, when the Women's Caucus in Religious Studies was organized, whose first co-chairs were Professor Carol Christ of AAR and myself of SBL. A year later, at the International Congress of Learned Societies in Los Angeles, the Caucus called for representation of women on the various boards and committees of the Society, the anonymous submission and evaluation of manuscripts for *JBL*, and the establishment of a job registry through CSR. At the business meeting two women were elected to the council and one to the executive board. Fifteen years later, I am privileged to inaugurate what will, it is hoped, be a long line of women presidents, consisting not only of white women but also of women of color,[10] who are woefully underrepresented in the discipline. The historic character of this moment is cast into relief when one considers that in Germany not a single woman has achieved the rank of ordinary professor in one of the established Roman Catholic theological faculties.

However, the mere admission of women into the ranks of scholarship and the various endeavors of the Society does not necessarily assure that biblical scholar-

---

8. Virginia Woolf, *Three Guineas* (New York: Harcourt, Brace, Jovanovich, 1966) 61.

9. For the following information, see Dorothy C. Bass, "Women's Studies and Biblical Studies: An Historical Perspective," *JSOT* 22 (1982) 6–12; Ernest W Saunders, *Searching the Scriptures: A History of the Society of Biblical Literature, 1880–1980* (Chico, CA: Scholars Press, 1982) 70, 83f.; and Carolyn De Swarte Gifford, "American Women and the Bible: The Nature of Woman as A Hermeneutical Issue," in *Feminist Perspectives on Biblical Scholarship* (ed. A. Yarbro Collins; Chico, CA: Scholars Press, 1985) 11–33.

10. To my knowledge only one Afro-American and one Asian-American woman have yet received a doctorate in biblical studies.

ship is done in the interest and from the perspective of women or others marginal to the academic enterprise. Historian Dorothy Bass, to whom we owe most of our information about women's historical participation in the SBL, has pointed to a critical difference between the women of the last century who, as scholars, joined the Society and those women who sought for a scientific investigation of the Bible in the interest of women.[11] Feminist biblical scholarship has its roots not in the academy but in the social movements for the emancipation of slaves and of freeborn women. Against the assertion that God has sanctioned the system of slavery and intended the subordination of women,[12] the Grimke sisters, Sojourner Truth, Jarena Lee, and others distinguished between the oppressive anti-Christian traditions of men and the life-giving intentions of God. Many reformers of the nineteenth century shared the conviction that women must learn the original languages of Greek and Hebrew in order to produce unbiased translations and interpretations faithful to the original divine intentions of the Bible. Nineteenth-century feminists were well aware that higher biblical criticism provided a scholarly grounding of their arguments. Women's rights leaders such as Frances Willard and Elizabeth Cady Stanton were the most explicit in calling on women to learn the methods of higher biblical criticism in order to critique patriarchal religion.

Although Elizabeth Cady Stanton and the editorial committee of the *Woman's Bible* sought to utilize the insights and methods of "higher criticism" for interpreting the biblical texts on women, no alliance between feminist biblical interpretation and historical-critical scholarship was forged in the nineteenth century. Cady Stanton had invited distinguished women scholars "versed in biblical criticism" to contribute to the *Woman's Bible* project. But her invitation was declined because—as she states—"they were afraid that their high reputation and scholarly attainments might be compromised"[13] This situation continued well into the first half of the twentieth century. In the 1920s Rev. Lee Anna Starr and Dr. Katherine Bushnell, both outside the profession, used their knowledge of biblical languages and higher criticism to analyze the status of women in the Bible and the theological bases for women's role in scripture.[14]

---

11. Bass, "Women's Studies," 10–11.
12. Barbara Brown Zikmund, "Biblical Arguments and Women's Place in the Church," in *The Bible And Social Reform* (ed. E. R. Sandeen; Philadelphia: Fortress, 1982) 85–104; For Jarena Lee, see William L. Andrews, ed., *Sisters of the Spirit: Three Black Women's Autobiographies of the Nineteenth Century* (Bloomington: Indiana University Press, 1986).
13. Elizabeth Cady Stanton, ed., *The Original Feminist Attack on the Bible: The Woman's Bible* (1895, 1898; facsimile ed. New York: Arno, 1974) 1. 9; see also Elaine C. Huber, "They Weren't Prepared to Hear: A Closer Look at the Woman's Bible," *ANQ* 16 (1976) 271–76 and Anne McGrew Bennett et al., "The Woman's Bible: Review and Perspectives," in *Women and Religion: 1973 Proceedings* (Tallahassee: AAR, 1973) 39–78.
14. Lee Anna Starr, *The Bible Status of Women* (New York: Fleming Revell, 1926); Katherine C. Bushnell, *God's Word to Women: One Hundred Bible Studies on Woman's Place in the Divine Economy* (1923; reissued by Ray Munson, North Collins, NY).

The androcentric character of biblical texts and interpretations was not addressed by a woman scholar until 1964 when Margaret Brackenbury Crook, a longstanding member of the SBL and professor of Biblical Literature at Smith College, published *Women and Religion*.[15] Although Brackenbury Crook repeatedly claimed that she did not advocate feminism or animosity toward men but that as a scholar she was simply stating the facts on the basis of evidence, she did so in order to insist that the masculine monopoly in biblical religions must be broken and that women must participate in shaping religious thought, symbols, and traditions.

In the context of the women's movements in the seventies and eighties, women scholars have not only joined the procession of educated men but have also sought to do so in the interest of women. We no longer deny our feminist engagement for the sake of scholarly acceptance. Rather we celebrate tonight the numerous feminist publications, papers, and monographs of SBL members that have not only enhanced our knowledge about women in the biblical worlds but have also sought to change our methods of reading and rconstruction, as well as our hermeneutical perspectives and scholarly assumptions. The Women in the Biblical World Section has since 1981 consistently raised issues of method and hermeneutics that are of utmost importance for the wider Society.

And yet, whether and how much our work has made serious inroads in biblical scholarship remain to be seen. The following anecdote can highlight what I mean. I am told that after I had been elected president of the Society a journalist asked one of the leading officers of the organization whether I had been nominated because the Society wanted to acknowledge not only my active participation in its ongoing work but also my theoretical contributions both to the reconstruction of Christian origins and to the exploration of a critical biblical hermeneutic and rhetoric.[16] He reacted with surprise at such a suggestion and assured her that I was elected because my work on the book of Revelation proved me to be a solid and serious scholar.

Interpretive communities such as the SBL are not just scholarly investigative communities, but also authoritative communities. They possess the power to ostracize or to embrace, to foster or to restrict membership, to recognize and to define what "true scholarship" entails. The question today is no longer whether women should join the procession of educated men, but under what conditions we can do so. What kind of ethos, ethics, and politics of the community of biblical scholars would allow us to move our work done in "the interest of women" from the margins to the center of biblical studies?

---

15. Margaret Brackenbury Crook, *Women and Religion* (Boston: Beacon, 1964); see also Elsie Thomas Culver, *Women in the World of Religion* (Garden City, NY: Doubleday, 1967).

16. Schüssler Fiorenza, *In Memory of Her: A Feminist Theological Reconstruction of Christian Origins* (New York: Crossroad, 1983); idem, *Bread Not Stone: The Challenge of Feminist Biblical Interpretation* (Boston: Beacon, 1985).

I hasten to say that I do not want to be misunderstood as advocating a return to a precritical reading and facile application of biblical texts on and about *Woman*. Rather I am interested in decentering the dominant scientist ethos of biblical scholarship by recentering it in a critical interpretive praxis for liberation. Ethos is the shared intellectual space of freely accepted obligations and traditions as well as the praxial space of discourse and action.[17] Since ethos shapes our scholarly behavior and attitudes, it needs to be explored more explicitly in terms of its rhetorical aims, which seek to affect a common orientation among its practitioners. The rhetoric of previous addresses of SBL presidents can serve as a text for engaging us in a critical reflection on the ethos as well as the rhetorical aims of biblical studies.

II. The Rhetoric of Biblical Scholarship

Only a few presidential addresses have reflected on their own political contexts and rhetorical strategies. If my research assistant is correct,[18] in the past forty years, no president of SBL has used the opportunity of the presidential address for asking the membership to consider the political context of their scholarship and to reflect on its public accountability. Since 1947 no presidential address has explicitly reflected on world politics, global crises, human sufferings, or movements for change. Neither the civil rights movement nor the various liberation struggles of the so-called Third World, neither the assassination of Martin Luther King nor the Holocaust has become the rhetorical context for biblical studies. Biblical studies appears to have progressed in a political vacuum, and scholars seem to have understood themselves as accountable solely—as Robert Funk puts it—to the vested interests of the "fraternity of scientifically trained ... scholars with the soul of a church."[19] This ethos of American biblical scholarship after 1947 is anticipated in the following letter of R. Bultmann written in 1926:

> Of course the impact of the war has led many people to revise their concepts of human existence; but I must confess that that has not been so in my case.... So I do not believe that the war has influenced my theology. My view is that if anyone is looking for the genesis of our theology he [sic] will find, that internal

---

17. See Calvin O. Schrag, *Communicative Praxis and the Space of Subjectivity* (Bloomington: Indiana University Press, 1986) 179–214.

18. I want to thank Ann Millin, Episcopal Divinity School, for checking SBL presidential addresses for references to and reflections of their political contexts as well as Margret Hutaff, Harvard Divinity School, for proofreading the manuscript. I am also indebted to Francis Schüssler Fiorenza for his critical reading of several drafts of this paper.

19. Robert Funk, "The Watershed of the American Biblical Tradition: The Chicago School, First Phase, 1892–1920," *JBL* 95 (1976) 7 [p. 172 in this volume].

discussion with the theology of our teachers plays an incomparably greater role than the impact of the war or reading Dostoievsky [sic].[20]

My point here is not an indictment of Bultmann, who more than many others was aware that presupposition-less exegesis is not possible nor desirable. Rather, it allows me to raise the question: Does the immanent discourse between teachers and students, between academic fathers and sons—or daughters for that matter—between different schools of interpretation jeopardize the intellectual rigor of the discipline? Do we ask and teach our students to ask in a disciplined way how our scholarship is conditioned by its social location and how it serves political functions?

In his 1945 address, President Enslin of Crozer Theological Seminary ironizes the British snobbishness of Sir Oliver Lodge, who thought that the only American worth speaking to was Henry Cabot Lodge.[21] He nevertheless unwittingly supports such a scholarly in-house discourse by advocating an immersion in the works of the great scholars of the past while at the same time excoriating the "demand for the practical in biblical research." He rejects the requirement that biblical research "strengthen faith and provide blueprints for modern conduct" as one and the same virus which has poisoned German scholarship and made it liable to Nazi ideology. He therefore argues that biblical critics must be emotionally detached, intellectually dispassionate, and rationally value-neutral. Critical detachment is an achievement that turns the critic into a lonely hero who has to pay a price in comfort and solidarity. However, Enslin does not consider that this scholarly ethos of dispassionate industry, eternal questioning, utter loneliness, detached inquiry, patient toil without practical results, and the unhampered pursuit of truth "under the direction of men [sic] whom students can trust and revere" could be the more dangerous part of the same political forgetfulness that in his view has poisoned German biblical scholarship.

This scientist ethos of value-free detached inquiry insists that the biblical critic needs to stand outside the common circumstances of collective life and stresses the alien character of biblical materials. What makes biblical inter-

---

20. Letter to Erich Forster, pastor and professor in Frankfurt, as quoted by Walter Schmithals, *An Introduction to the Theology of Rudolf Bultmann* (Minneapolis: Augsburg, 1968) 9–10; See also Dorothe Soelle, "Rudolf Bultmann und die Politische Theologie," in *Rudolf Bultmann: 100 Jahre* (ed. H Thyen; Oldenburger Vorträge; Oldenburg: H. Holzberg, 1985) 69ff.; and Dieter Georgi, "Rudolf Bultmann's Theology of the New Testament Revisited," in *Bultmann Retrospect and Prospect: The Centenary Symposium at Wellesley* (ed. E. C. Hobbs; HTS 35; Philadelphia: Fortress, 1985) 82ff.

21. Morton S. Enslin, "The Future of Biblical Studies," *JBL* 65 (1946) 1–12 [see pp. 75–82 in this volume]. Already Julian Morgenstern had argued "that in Germany biblical science is doomed." Since in Europe Biblical Studies are in decline, North America, i.e., the U.S. and Canada "must become the major center of biblical research" ("The Society of Biblical Literature and Exegesis," *JBL* 61 [1942] 4–5 [pp. 69–70 in this volume]).

pretation possible is radical detachment, emotional, intellectual, and political distanciation. Disinterested and dispassionate scholarship enables biblical critics to enter the minds and world of historical people, to step out of their own time and to study history on its own terms, unencumbered by contemporary questions, values, and interests. A-political detachment, objective literalism, and scientific value-neutrality are the rhetorical postures that seem to be dominant in the positivistic paradigm of biblical scholarship. The decentering of this rhetoric of disinterestedness and presupposition-free exegesis seeks to recover the political context of biblical scholarship and its public responsibility.

The "scientist" ethos of biblical studies was shaped by the struggle of biblical scholarship to free itself from dogmatic and ecclesiastical controls. It corresponded to the professionalization of academic life and the rise of the university. Just as history as an academic discipline sought in the last quarter of the nineteenth century to prove itself as an objective science in analogy to the natural sciences, so also did biblical studies. Scientific history sought to establish facts objectively free from philosophical considerations. It was determined to hold strictly to facts and evidence, not to sermonize or moralize but to tell the simple historic truth—in short, to narrate things as they actually happened.[22] Historical science was a technique that applied critical methods to the evaluation of sources, which in turn are understood as data and evidence. The mandate to avoid theoretical considerations and normative concepts in the immediate encounter with the text is to assure that the resulting historical accounts would be free of ideology.

In this country, Ranke was identified as the father of "the true historical method," which eschewed all theoretical reflection. Ranke became for many American scholars the prototype of the nontheoretical and the politically neutral historian, although Ranke himself sought to combine theoretically his historical method with his conservative political views.[23] This positivist nineteenth-century understanding of historiography as a science was the theoretical context for the development of biblical scholarship in the academy. Since the ethos of objective scientism and theoretical value-neutrality was articulated in the political context of several heresy trials at the turn of the twentieth century, its rhetoric continues to reject all overt theological and religious institutional engagement as unscientific, while at the same time claiming a name and space marked by the traditional biblical canon. Such a scientist posture of historical research is, however, not displaced when it is decentered by an objectivist stance that arrogates the methodological formalism of literary or sociological science. The pretension

---

22. George G. Iggers, *The German Conception of History: The National Tradition of Historical Thought from Herder to the Present* (rev. ed.; Middletown, CT: Wesleyan University Press, 1983) 64.

23. Robert A. Oden, Jr., "Hermeneutics and Historiography: Germany and America," in *SBL 1980 Seminar Papers* (ed. P. J. Achtemeier; Chico, CA: Scholars Press, 1980) 135–57.

of biblical studies to "scientific" modes of inquiry that deny their herme neutical and theoretical character and mask their historical-social location prohibits a critical reflection on their rhetorical theological practices in their sociopolitical contexts.

Although the dominant ethos of biblical studies in this century seems to have been that which is paradigmatically expressed in Bultmann's letter and Enslin's address, there have nevertheless also been presidential voices that have challenged this self-understanding of biblical scholarship. Already in 1919, James Montgomery of the University of Pennsylvania had launched a scathing attack on the professed detachment of biblical scholars when addressing the Society:

> We academics flatter ourselves on what we call our pure science and think we are the heirs of an eternal possession abstracted from the vicissitudes of time. We recall Archimedes working out his mathematical problems under the dagger of the assassin, or Goethe studying Chinese during the battle of Jena. But we dare not in this day take comfort in those academic anecdotes nor desire to liken ourselves to the monastic scholars who pursued their studies and meditations in their cells undisturbed by the wars raging without....[24]

Almost twenty years later, at the eve of World War II, Henry Cadbury of Harvard University discussed in his presidential address the motives for the changes in biblical scholarship. He observed that most members of the Society are horrified by the perversions of learning and prostitutions of scholarship to partisan propagandistic ends in Nazi Germany. He noted, however, that at the same time most members are not equally aware of the public responsibility of their own scholarship and of the social consequences of their research. He therefore challenged the membership to become aware of the moral and spiritual needs in contemporary life and to take responsibility for the social and spiritual functions of biblical scholarship.[25]

At the end of World War II, Leroy Waterman of the University of Michigan also called in his address for the sociopublic responsibility of scholarship. Biblical scholarship must be understood as situated in a morally unstable world tottering on the brink of atomic annihilation. Students of the Bible should therefore take note of the deep moral confusion in their world situation and at the same time make available "any pertinent resources within their own keeping." While biblical scholars cannot forsake their research in "order to peddle their wares," they also cannot remain in the ivory tower "of privileged aloofness."

---

24. James A. Montgomery, "Present Tasks of American Biblical Scholarship," *JBL* 38 (1919) 2 [p. 18 in this volume].

25. Henry J. Cadbury, "Motives of Biblical Scholarship," *JBL* 56 (1937) 1–16 [pp. 33–43 in this volume].

Waterman argued that biblical studies and natural science have in common the "claim to seek truth in complete objectivity without regard to consequences."[26] But biblical scholarship and natural science sharply diverge with respect to their public influence. Whereas science has cultivated a public that is aware of the improvements science can effect for the increase of human welfare or its destruction, biblical scholarship has taken for granted the public influence of the Bible in Western culture. Therefore, it has cultivated as its public not society as a whole but organized religion, "whose dominant leadership has been more concerned with the defense of the status quo than with any human betterment accruing from new religious insights."[27] The task of biblical studies in this situation is therefore to make available to humanity on the brink of atomic annihilation the moral resources and ethical directives of biblical religions. At the eve of the Reagan-Gorbachev summit on nuclear arms reduction, Waterman's summons of the Society to public responsibility is still timely.

III. The Ethos of Biblical Scholarship: Critical Rhetoric and Ethics

Although I agree with his summons to public responsibility, I do not share his optimistic view of positivist science. The reluctance of the discipline to reflect on its sociopolitical location cannot simply be attributed, as Waterman does, to the repression of biblical scholarship by organized religion. It is as much due to its ethos of scientist positivism and professed value-neutrality. Scientist epistemologies covertly advocate an a-political reality without assuming responsibility for their political assumptions and interests. "Scientism has pretensions to a mode of inquiry that tries to deny its own hermeneutic character and mask its own historicity so that it might claim a historical certainty."[28]

Critical theory of rhetoric or discursive practices, as developed in literary, political, and historical studies, seeks to decenter the objectivist and depoliticized ethos of biblical studies with an ethos of rhetorical inquiry that could engage in the formation of a critical historical and religious consciousness. The reconceptualization of biblical studies in rhetorical rather than scientist terms would provide a research framework not only for integrating historical, archaeological, sociological, literary, and theological approaches as perspectival readings of texts but also for raising ethical-political and religious-theological questions as constitutive of the interpretive process. A rhetorical hermeneutic does not assume that the text is a window to historical reality, nor does it operate with a correspondence theory of truth. It does not understand historical sources as data and evidence

---

26. Leroy Waterman, "Biblical Studies in a New Setting" *JBL* 66 (1947) 5.
27. Ibid.
28. David Tracy, *Plurality and Ambiguity: Hermeneutics, Religion, and Hope* (New York: Harper & Row, 1987) 31.

but sees them as perspectival discourse constructing their worlds and symbolic universes.[29]

Since alternative symbolic universes engender competing definitions of the world, they cannot be reduced to one meaning. Therefore, competing interpretations of texts are not simply either right or wrong,[30] but they constitute different ways of reading and constructing historical meaning. Not detached value-neutrality but an explicit articulation of one's rhetorical strategies, interested perspectives, ethical criteria, theoretical frameworks, religious presuppositions, and sociopolitical locations for critical public discussion are appropriate in such a rhetorical paradigm of biblical scholarship.

The rhetorical understanding of discourse as creating a world of pluriform meanings and a pluralism of symbolic universes, raises the question of power. How is meaning constructed? Whose interests are served? What kind of worlds are envisioned? What roles, duties, and values are advocated? Which social-political practices are legitimated? Or which communities of discourse sign responsible? Such and similar questions become central to the interpretive task. Once biblical scholarship begins to talk explicitly of social interests, whether of race, gender, culture, or class, and once it begins to recognize the need for a sophisticated and pluralistic reading of texts that questions the fixity of meaning, then a *double ethics* is called for.

An *ethics of historical reading* changes the task of interpretation from finding out "what the text meant" to the question of what kind of readings can do justice to the text in its historical contexts. Although such an ethics is aware of the pluralism of historical- and literary-critical methods as well as the pluralism of interpretations appropriate to the text, it nevertheless insists that the number of interpretations that can legitimately be given to a text are limited. Such a historical reading seeks to give the text its due by asserting its original meanings over and against later dogmatic usurpations. It makes the assimilation of the text to our own experience and interests more difficult and thereby keeps alive the "irritation" of the original text by challenging our own assumptions, world views, and practices. In short, the methods of historical- and literary-critical scholarship and its diachronic reconstructions distance us in such a way from the original texts and their historical symbolic worlds that they relativize not only them but also us. By illuminating the ethical-political dimensions of the biblical text in its historical contexts, such an *ethics of historical reading* allows us not only to relativize through contextualization the values and authority claims of the biblical text but also to assess and critically evaluate them.

---

29. See the discussion of scientific theory choice by Linda Alcoff, "Justifying Feminist Social Science," *Hypatia* 2 (1987)107–27.

30. Maurice Mandelbaum, *The Anatomy of Historical Knowledge* (Baltimore, MD: Johns Hopkins University Press, 1977) 150.

The rhetorical character of biblical interpretations and historical reconstructions, moreover, requires, an *ethics of accountability* that stands responsible not only for the choice of theoretical interpretive models but also for the ethical consequences of the biblical text and its meanings. If scriptural texts have served not only noble causes but also to legitimate war, to nurture anti-Judaism and misogynism, to justify the exploitation of slavery, and to promote colonial dehumanization, then biblical scholarship must take the responsibility not only to interpret biblical texts in their historical contexts but also to evaluate the construction of their historical worlds and symbolic universes in terms of a religious scale of values. If the Bible has become a classic of Western culture because of its normativity, then the responsibility of the biblical scholar cannot be restricted to giving "the readers of our time ... clear access to the original intentions" of the biblical writers.[31] It must also include the elucidation of the ethical consequences and political functions of biblical texts in their historical as well as in their contemporary sociopolitical contexts.

Just as literary critics have called for an interpretive evaluation of classic works of art in terms of justice, so students of the Bible must learn how to examine both the rhetorical aims of biblical texts and the rhetorical interests emerging in the history of interpretation or in contemporary scholarship. This requires that we revive a responsible ethical and political criticism which recognizes the ideological distortions of great works of religion. Such discourse does not just evaluate the ideas or propositions of a work but also seeks to determine whether its very language and composition promote stereotypical images and linguistic violence. What does the language of a biblical text "do" to a reader who submits to its world of vision?[32]

In order to answer this question, the careful reading of biblical texts and the appropriate reconstruction of their historical worlds and of their symbolic universes need to be complemented by a theological discussion of the contemporary religious functions of biblical texts which claim scriptural authority today in biblical communities of faith. To open up biblical texts and the historical reconstructions of their worlds for public discussion requires that students learn to traverse not only the boundaries of theological disciplines but also those of other intellectual disciplines.[33]

To enable students to do so, biblical studies will have to overcome the institutionalized dichotomy between graduate training in the university and ministerial

---

31. Krister Stendahl, "The Bible as a Classic and the Bible as Holy Scripture," *JBL* 103 (1984) 10 [p. 215 in this volume].

32. See Wayne C. Booth, "Freedom of Interpretation: Bakhtin and the Challenge of Feminist Criticism," in *The Politics of Interpretation* (ed. J. T. Mitchell; Chicago: University of Chicago Press, 1983) 51–82.

33. See Francis Schüssler Fiorenza, "Theory and Practice: Theological Education as a Reconstructive, Hermeneutical and Practical Task," *Theological Education* 23 (1987) 113–41.

education in schools of theology. M.A. and Ph.D. students interested in teaching in seminaries and church-related schools are to become skilled in critical-theological reflection just as M.Div. and D.Min. students should be versed in the analysis of religion and culture. Moreover, in view of the insistence that all professions and research institutions should become conscious of the values they embody and the interests they serve, students in religious studies as well as in Theology must learn to engage in a disciplined reflection on the societal and public values[34] promoted by their intellectual disciplines.

Finally, the growth of right-wing political fundamentalism and of biblicist literalism in society, religious institutions, and the broader culture feeds anti-democratic authoritarianism and fosters personal prejudice. In the light of this political situation, biblical scholarship has the responsibility to make its research available to a wider public. Since literalist biblical fundamentalism asserts the public claims and values of biblical texts, biblical scholarship can no longer restrict its public to institutionalized religions and to the in-house discourse of the academy. Rather, biblical scholarship must acknowledge the continuing political influence of the Bible in Western culture and society.

If biblical studies continues to limit its educational communicative practices to students preparing for the professional pastoral ministry and for academic posts in theological schools, it forgoes the opportunity to foster a critical biblical culture and a pluralistic historical consciousness. Therefore, the Society should provide leadership as to how to make our research available to all those who are engaged in the communication of biblical knowledge, who have to confront biblical fundamentalism in their professions, and especially to those who have internalized their oppression through a literalist reading of the Bible. Such a different public location of biblical discourse requires that the Society actively scrutinize its communicative practices and initiate research programs and discussion forums that could address issues of biblical education and communication.

In conclusion: I have argued for a paradigm shift in the ethos and rhetorical practices of biblical scholarship. If religious studies becomes public deliberative disourse and rhetorical construction oriented toward the present and the future, then biblical studies becomes a critical reflection on the rhetorical practices encoded in the literatures of the biblical world and their social or ecclesial functions today. Such a critical-rhetorical paradigm requires that biblical studies continue its descriptive-analytic work utilizing all the critical methods available for illuminating our understanding of ancient texts and their historical location. At the same time, it engages biblical scholarship in a hermeneutic-evaluative discursive practice exploring the power/knowledge relations inscribed in contemporary biblical discourse and in the biblical texts themselves.

---

34. See also Ronald F Thiemann, "Toward an American Public Theology: Religion in a Pluralistic Theology," *Harvard Divinity Bulletin* 18/1 (1987) 3-6, 10.

Such an approach opens up the rhetorical practices of biblical scholarship to the critical inquiry of all the disciplines of religious studies and theology. Questions raised by feminist scholars in religion, liberation theologians, theologians of the so-called Third World, and by others traditionally absent from the exegetical enterprise would not remain peripheral or nonexistent for biblical scholarship. Rather, their insights and challenges could become central to the scholarly discourse of the discipline.

In short, if the Society were to engage in a disciplined reflection on the public dimensions and ethical implications of our scholarly work, it would constitute a responsible scholarly citizenship that could be a significant participant in the global discourse seeking justice and well-being for all. The implications of such a repositioning of the task and aim of biblical scholarship would be far-reaching and invigorating.

The Eighth, the Greatest of Centuries?*

Philip J. King
Boston College

In 1909 a book appeared with the title *The Thirteenth, the Greatest of Centuries*. The author, James Walsh, wrote in the introduction:

> It cannot but seem a paradox to say that the Thirteenth was the greatest of centuries. To most people the idea will appear at once so preposterous that they may not even care to consider it. A certain number, of course, will have their curiosity piqued by the thought that anyone should evolve so curious a notion. Either of these attitudes of mind will yield at once to a more properly receptive mood if it is recalled that the Thirteenth is the century of the Gothic cathedrals, of the foundation of the university, of the signing of Magna Charta....[1]

To suggest that the eighth century BCE was the greatest of centuries may evoke the same kind of reaction, but the "attitudes of mind" may become more receptive when it is recalled that the eighth was the century of the resurgence of Israel and Judah, the Neo-Assyrian empire, and the classical prophets. To allow for other opinions the title of this paper is punctuated deliberately with a question mark.

I. Resurgence of Israel and Judah

Several events converged at the beginning of the eighth century to catapult Israel and Judah into prominence. The defeat of Aram-Damascus by Adad-nirari III about 796 BCE liberated Israel from Aramean oppression. As Aram's power waned, Assyria, in turn, experienced a half century of decline when it had to contend with its own internal affairs as well as with threats from Urartu, its greatest rival in the eighth century. At the same time, Israel and Judah expanded their

---

* The Presidential Address delivered 19 November 1988 at the annual meeting of the Society of Biblical Literature held at the Chicago Hilton and Towers, Chicago, IL.

1. J. J. Walsh, *The Thirteenth, the Greatest of Centuries* (New York: Catholic Summer School Press, 1909) 1.

territory, and profited from their relationship with Phoenicia, which controlled trade in the Mediterranean world. All these factors created for Israel and Judah what Martin Noth called "a kind of Golden Age."[2]

The first half of the eighth century marked the final period of greatness for Israel and Judah. In power and prosperity they were comparable to the kingdom of David and Solomon. Both the northern and southern kingdoms had especially able leaders in Jeroboam II and Uzziah. Reclaiming territory, Jeroboam II extended his borders to the north and east "from the entrance of Hamath as far as the Sea of the Arabah" (2 Kgs 14:25), that is, to central Syria and to the Dead Sea. Uzziah expanded his borders south to Elath and west to Ashdod; also, he strengthened the defenses of Judah and the city walls of Jerusalem. As a result, their joint kingdoms stretched as far as the geographical limits of Solomon's realm. That Israel and Judah were at peace with each other was to their mutual advantage; for example, both profited from the fact that they controlled the major trade routes.

Jeroboam II, comparable to David and Solomon in territorial expansion and economic prosperity, was a powerful Israelite king. Indicative of Israel's affluence was the heavy tribute which Tiglath-pileser III exacted when Menahem succeeded Jeroboam II (2 Kgs 15:19–20), tribute raised by assessing the wealthy landowners of Samaria. The reluctant acknowledgment of Jeroboam II in 2 Kings (14:23–29) contrasts sharply with what archaeology has revealed about his political and military achievements.

Samaria was at the peak of its prosperity and expansion in the reign of Jeroboam II. Its strategic location near the international trade routes, as well as conquests and commerce, accounted for its great affluence. The fertile region of Samaria was ideally suited for agriculture, with the valleys producing wheat and barley, and, as the Samaria ostraca attest, the hillsides yielding grapes and olives. An impressive acropolis or citadel with strong fortifications and public buildings, modeled after those of Omri and Ahab, crowned the capital city of Samaria.

Other cities of the northern kingdom, including Hazor, Megiddo, and Dan were also prosperous and had monumental architecture. According to Yigael Yadin, the excavator of Hazor, the largest site in Upper Galilee, "Judging by the standard of its buildings, during the times of Jeroboam II the city of Hazor enjoyed an era of great prosperity.... The buildings themselves are among the finest of the entire Israelite period...."[3] The Megiddo of the Omride dynasty, with its offset-inset wall and four-chamber gate, stable complexes, and water system remained in existence through the eighth century until destroyed by Tiglath-pileser III in

---

2. M. Noth, *The History of Israel* (2d ed.; New York: Harper & Brothers, 1960) 250.

3. Y. Yadin, *Hazor: The Rediscovery of a Great Citadel of the Bible* (London: Weidenfeld & Nicolson, 1975) 151.

733 BCE. Dan may well have reached the height of its culture during the reign of Jeroboam II.

Although Israel was better situated and endowed than Judah, the southern kingdom reached the zenith of its economic and military power in the reign of Uzziah. Another distinguished Judahite king in the eighth century was Hezekiah; he, too, developed the trade routes as well as the economy. Hezekiah is best remembered for his major cultic reform which was religiously, not politically, motivated.[4] Politically astute, Hezekiah had a prominent role in forming from 705 BCE on an anti-Assyrian alliance, which included Philistia, Egypt, Tyre, and Judah. In addition, the construction in Jerusalem of the tunnel which bears his name among modern scholars and the strengthening of Jerusalem's fortifications attest to his vigor as a ruler.

Jerusalem is reputed to be the most excavated city in the world, and intensive digging since 1967 continues to illuminate Jerusalem's history. While excavating in the modern Jewish Quarter of the Old City, situated on the western hill or the Upper City, Nahman Avigad uncovered a portion of a stone wall, forty meters long and seven meters wide. This city wall, constructed in all probability by Hezekiah, may be the new wall "outside" the city which 2 Chronicles (32:5) attributes to Hezekiah. It served to protect the western perimeter of Jerusalem against Assyrian attack. The location of this wall indicates that eighth-century Jerusalem was not confined to the Temple Mount and the City of David but also included the western hill, or Mishneh.[5] After the fall of the northern kingdom large numbers of refugees from Samaria, seeking a place to live in Judah, without doubt swelled the population of Jerusalem.

In Hezekiah's reign Lachish was a city of strategic importance, second only to Jerusalem. Sennacherib certainly thought so when he presided in 701 BCE over the siege of Lachish and the deportation of its inhabitants. Both the series of bas-reliefs in Sennacherib's palace at Nineveh and the current excavation of the city attest to Lachish's strong fortifications, consisting of a revetment wall and a city wall, as well as a gate complex composed of an outer and inner gate. The six chambers of the stratum III gate, constructed possibly by Rehoboam and destroyed by Sennacherib, resemble the Solomonic gates at Hazor, Megiddo, and Gezer, although the Lachish gate is larger. Also, the excavator, David Ussishkin, discovered a defensive counter-ramp inside the city wall, opposite the Assyrian siege ramp against the southwest corner of the tell.[6]

---

4. M. Cogan and H. Tadmor, *II Kings* (AB 11; Garden City, NY: Doubleday, 1988) 218–20.
5. N. Avigad, *Discovering Jerusalem* (Nashville: Thomas Nelson, 1983) 26–49.
6. D. Ussishkin, "Excavations at Tel Lachish 1978–1983: Second Preliminary Report," *Tel Aviv* 10 (1983) 97–175; "Defensive Judean Counter-Ramp Found at Lachish in 1983 Season," *BARev* 10/2 (1984) 66–73.

II. Neighboring Countries: Phoenicia, Aram, Philistia

The central location of ancient Israel in relation to the rest of the Near East accounts for the fact that Israel and Judah were exposed to political, cultural, economic, and religious influences of neighboring countries, especially Phoenicia, Aram, and Philistia. The biblical text as well as material remains attest to such influence.

Archaeology and the Bible furnish evidence of the close relationship between Israel and the Phoenicians. Lacking political organization at the state or territorial-kingdom level, the city-states constituting Phoenicia functioned independently. Like the cities of Philistia, they opted for local autonomy over state control while retaining their individual names: Arvad (Ruad), Byblos (Gebal), Beirut (Berytus), Sidon. Zarephath (Sarafand), and Tyre. Corresponding roughly to modern Lebanon, ancient Phoenicia at its height extended along the east Mediterranean coast from Arvad in the north to Acco in the south.

The Phoenicians are not well known among the ancient peoples, and much remains to be learned about the Phoenician homeland. Among the sites excavated are the following: in the 1920s Pierre Montet began digging at Byblos, the Greek name of the ancient town of Gebal; Maurice Dunand succeeded him in 1925. Maurice Chehab excavated the Roman and later levels at Tyre; Georges Contenau dug the acropolis of Sidon, but the ancient city has not been excavated. In the 1960s Roger Saidah undertook excavations at Khalde, just south of Beirut. Two sites have been under investigation recently: James Pritchard excavated Zarephath (modern Sarafand) until interrupted by the civil war, and Patricia Bikai made soundings at Tyre.[7]

In the mid-1960s the American Schools of Oriental Research (ASOR)planned to establish a research center in Beirut to study firsthand the diverse cultural heritage of Lebanon, including Phoenician, Hittite, Egyptian, Greek, Roman, Byzantine, and Arab. Civil war intervened before ASOR was able to realize its plan. Since the mid-1970s Lebanon has been a battlefield, making it practically impossible to dig there.

In addition to Vassos Karageorghis's digs at Kition and Salamis in Cyprus, several sites along the ancient Phoenician coast, lying in modern Israel, have shed light on Phoenicia; they include Achzib, Acco, Tel Keisan, Tel Abu Hawam, and Shiqmona. Two other sites in Israel, Tel Dor and Tel Mevorakh,[8] excavated by

---

7. J. B. Pritchard, *Recovering Sarepta, A Phoenician City* (Princeton: University Press, 1978); P. M. Bikai, "The Late Phoenician Pottery Complex and Chronology," *BASOR* 229 (1978) 47–56; *The Pottery of Tyre* (Warminster: Aris & Phillips, 1978).

8. E. Stern, "The Excavations at Tel Mevorach and the Late Phoenician Elements in the Architecture of Palestine," *BASOR* 225 (1977) 17–27; E. Stern, respondent to J. D. Muhly, "Phoenicia and the Phoenicians," in *Biblical Archaeology Today: Proceedings of the International*

Ephraim Stern, came under Phoenician influence; they, too, have valuable information to contribute.

The Phoenicians enjoyed greatest independence between 1200 and 750 BCE, before the advent of Tiglath-pileser III, founder of the Neo-Assyrian empire; then the relationship between Phoenicia and Assyria changed radically.[9] In the eighth and seventh centuries the Assyrians levied heavy taxes on Phoenicia; at the same time they granted Phoenicia a good measure of autonomy. Maritime trade played the most important role in the economy of Phoenicia, and it was to Assyria's advantage to allow Phoenicia to conduct its own trade. The Phoenicians also excelled in art and architecture, as pottery, ivory, and masonry attest.

The close alliance between Phoenicia and Israel during the reigns of David and Solomon is well documented in 1 Kings. The Phoenician influence exerted on the architecture of the Jerusalem Temple is but one manifestation of this relationship. The marriage of Ethbaal's daughter, Jezebel, to Ahab solidified the two states, but also introduced religious syncretism against which Elijah railed. Jehu's purge of the Omride dynasty dampened the relationship between Phoenicia and Israel but did not extinguish it. Material remains unearthed in Israel witness to the strong influence of Phoenicia in the eighth century, especially in the time of Jeroboam II, when commerce between the two states was vigorous.

With the waning of Phoenician influence on Israel in the second half of the ninth century, there was a concomitant increase of Aramean influence. From that time on, the city-states constituting Aram were perennial political rivals of Israel. In the ninth and eighth centuries Damascus was the most important of the Aramean kingdoms. During the ninth century Aram sometimes controlled Israel; at other times Israel was independent. After Jeroboam II subdued Aram, its importance declined. When Damascus fell to Tiglath-pileser III in 732 BCE, it became the capital of an Assyrian province.[10]

The extent of Aram's influence on Israel is not well documented because epigraphic and archaeological evidence is limited. Archaeologists have done practically no excavating in Damascus itself, despite its antiquity and strategic location on the major trade routes. However, some sites in the Aramean empire have been dug, and others are under excavation. In the 1930s Harald Ingholt excavated at the citadel of Hamath (modern Hama), which has Iron II remains. Tell Qarqur, a double mound with Iron II remains on the east side of the Orontes, is under excavation. The modern name of the site is reminiscent of ancient Qarqar, where in 853 BCE Syria, Israel, and other western states fought against

---

Congress on Biblical Archaeology (ed. A. Biran et al.; Jerusalem: Israel Exploration Society, 1985) 226–27.

9. B. Oded, "The Phoenician Cities and the Assyrian Empire in the Time of Tiglath-pileser III," *ZDPV* 90 (1974) 38–49.

10. W. T. Pitard, *Ancient Damascus* (Winona Lake, IN: Eisenbrauns, 1987) 175–89.

Shalmaneser III. Between Damascus and the Jordanian frontier are many more Iron Age sites to be dug.

Among the rivals of Israel and Judah were the Philistine city-states; there was intermittent warfare beginning in the twelfth century and continuing through the period of the divided kingdom, especially in the eighth century when both Uzziah and Hezekiah conducted successful campaigns against them. The Philistine pentapolis, five independent principalities, enjoyed strategic advantages; in addition to being situated close to the overland trade routes, they had ports for maritime trade. In Neo-Assyrian times the Philistines, like the Phoenicians, were semi-independent. When Tiglath-pileser III campaigned against Philistia in 734 BCE, it was to gain control of the Mediterranean seaports for Assyrian commerce. In the eighth and seventh centuries the Philistine kings were jockeying between Assyria and Egypt, the two leading bipolar political powers, to seek advantage between them.

In an effort to increase our knowledge of the Philistines and their relationship with Judah and Israel, archaeologists have been concentrating on Philistine sites. The lack of written records leaves much to be learned about the Philistines. The 1980s have seen two long-term excavations in the field: one at Ashkelon directed by Lawrence Stager, the other at Tel Miqne directed by Seymour Gitin and Trude Dothan. Ashkelon, one of the most important seaports in the eastern Mediterranean and the major seaport of the Philistines, has a history extending from 3500 BCE to 1500 CE. Stager's dig has revealed evidence of Assyrian interests in Ashkelon in the eighth century. There has been a rich ceramic yield, consisting of fine ware imported from Phoenicia and perhaps east Greek imports.

Tel Miqne, identified with inland Ekron, covers a fifty-acre area and was justly famous for its olive oil production. The excavations are providing new insight into the period between the tenth and eighth centuries; Ekron was conquered by Sargon II in 712 BCE, and by Sennacherib in 701 BCE. Ekron remained a Philistine city until the end of the seventh century. The high-quality pottery and other artifacts found at Tel Miqne attest that the Philistines were far from uncouth; they were builders of an advanced civilization.[11]

Of the other major Philistine cities, Ashdod was partially excavated by Moshe Dothan; its harbor Ashdod-Yam has yielded nothing of early date. Gath has not been identified, although it is probably located at Tell eṣ-Ṣafi, as Frederick Bliss, its original excavator, proposed almost a century ago. The time is inauspicious to excavate Gaza, which is buried under the modern city. Other sites such as Deir el-Balaḥ, Tel Batash (Timnah), Tel Seraʻ (Tell esh-Shariʻa), Gezer, Tel Jemmeh, and Tel Qasile are also illuminating Philistine history and culture.

---

11. S. Gitin and T Dothan, "The Rise and Fall of Ekron of the Philistines: Recent Excavations at an Urban Border Site," *BA* 50 (1987) 197–222.

III. Neo-Assyrian Empire

The resources for reconstructing Assyrian history are more numerous than in the case of neighboring peoples. In addition to the Old Testament, there are the royal annals supplemented by Assyrian art. The Assyrian reliefs, for example, are notable for their detail and realism. David Ussishkin described his experience while digging at Lachish in this way:

> There is no other case in biblical archaeology in which a detailed Assyrian relief depicting a city under attack can be compared to the actual remains of that city and that battle uncovered by the archaeologist's spade, while the same events are corroborated by the Old Testament as well as the Assyrian sources.[12]

Assyria's greatest period of empire was in the Neo-Assyrian era; the classic phase of this empire began when Tiglath-pileser III usurped the throne in 745 BCE and extended to about 609 BCE. His empire incorporated almost the whole Near East under one head. Based on "expansion, domination, and exploitation," the political institution "empire" has been defined by M. Trolle Larsen as "a supernational system of political control, and such a system may have a city-state or a territorial state at its center."[13]

Several features distinguished the Neo-Assyrian empire from other kinds of states in antiquity. Jana Pečírková listed three:

> 1) consistent and deliberate expansion which resulted in territories of a varied economic, ethnic and cultural character being united under one single centre, in a united system of administration of provinces which gradually took the place of the former vassal states; 2) an army whose equipment and organization put it far above the armies of the neighbouring states; 3) an imperialist politico-religious ideology tending toward universalism, i.e. toward the loss of the cultural and ethnic differences within a community "of subjects of the Assyrian king."[14]

While commercial and trading interests were the motive for the formation of the Neo-Assyrian empire, a highly developed administrative system was responsible in large measure for the success of Assyrian imperialism. In Pečírková's words, "Assyrian imperialism did not depend solely on violence, exploitation and ruthless plunder, but primarily on a well-organized and well-functioning admin-

---

12. D. Ussishkin, *The Conquest of Lachish by Sennacherib* (Tel Aviv: Institute of Archaeology, Tel Aviv University, 1982) 11.

13. M. T. Larsen, "The Tradition of Empire in Mesopotamia," in *Mesopotamia: Power and Propaganda: A Symposium in Ancient Empire* (ed. M. T. Larsen; Copenhagen Studies in Assyriology 7; Copenhagen: Akademisk, 1979) 91.

14. J. Pečírková, "The Administrative Methods of Assyrian Imperialism," *ArOr* 55 (1987) 164.

istrative apparatus."[15] On the other hand, Assyria's formidable military machine, including composite bows, slings, war chariots, and siege machines, was quite capable of inflicting mortal blows.[16]

Lands conquered by the Assyrians were classified as vassal states or as provinces. In his administrative reorganization Tiglath-pileser III reduced the size of some provinces and converted a large number of vassal states into provinces. Economically and politically the vassal states were in a far more advantageous position than the provinces. So long as they fulfilled their economic obligations in the form of tribute and did not plot against the imperial power, they enjoyed autonomy. Otherwise, vassal states became provinces administered directly by Assyrian officials. The conversion from the status of vassal to province meant the destruction of urban centers and the deportation of the population.[17]

Israelite territory had a special attraction for imperial powers because the principal trade routes between Egypt and Mesopotamia, connecting with the Mediterranean seaports, passed through Israel and Judah. The northern kingdom revolted against imperialists Tiglath-pileser III, Shalmaneser V, and Sargon II; consequently, Israel became a province of Assyria in 720 BCE, during Sargon II's reign. Judah, on the other hand, retained its status as vassal because it remained loyal to Assyria during these rebellions. In Sennacherib's reign, however, Judah joined the revolt.

Israel lost its political and cultural identity when it became a province; Judah by retaining its vassal status kept its identity and was never annexed to the Assyrian empire. As Pečírková points out, this "is one of the reasons why even after the Exile, it was Judah that remained the centre of Judaism and the vehicle of the concept of Jewish statehood."[18]

As noted, all conquered peoples were not treated alike. The Phoenician monopoly on maritime trade made them special in the eyes of the Assyrians, who needed imports because they lacked natural resources such as metals, stone, and timber. Even when Tyre failed to meet its obligations toward the imperial power, it did not lose its vassal status. Likewise, revolt did not cause the Philistines to lose their vassal status. Maritime activity and trade are the reasons Phoenicia and Philistia remained as vassals.

The fact that Assyrian imports were less evident in vassal states than in the provinces indicates that vassals were permitted to retain their cultural identity.

---

15. Ibid., 175.
16. I. Eph'al, "The Assyrian Siege Ramp at Lachish: Military and Linguistic Aspects," *Tel Aviv* 11 (1984) 60–70.
17. Pečírková, "The Administrative Methods of Assyrian Imperialism," 164–66; J. Eph'al, "Assyrian Dominion in Palestine," in *The World History of the Jewish People* 4/1 (ed. A. Malamat; Jerusalem: Masada Press, 1979) 286; H. W. E. Saggs, *The Greatness That Was Babylon* (New York: Hawthorn, 1962) 105–39.
18. Pečírková, "The Administrative Methods of Assyrian Imperialism," 175.

They were also allowed to keep their religious identity. In a study of the political-religious relationship between the Neo-Assyrian empire and the Israelite states, Morton (Mordechai) Cogan rejects Albert Olmstead's view that "the whole [Assyrian imperial] organization centered around the worship of Ashur, the deified state and reigning king fanatically imposing active worship of Assyrian gods upon defeated populations."[19] He concludes that no cultic obligations were imposed upon vassal states, but the cult of Ashur and the great gods appears to have been incumbent upon formally annexed provinces because their residents were considered to be Assyrian citizens.

IV. Material Culture

Material culture is used here in a broad sense to denote not only the material objects or artifacts themselves but also the ideas and institutions that produced them. Inscriptions, pottery, and ivory of the eighth century are included under this heading.

Before considering individual inscriptions it is useful to deal with the more basic issue of literacy. According to Joseph Naveh, "A society may be considered 'literate' if, in addition to the professional scribes, there are people who can write, not only among the highest social class, but also among the lower middle classes."[20] Most would agree with Naveh that at least from the twelfth century there was writing in ancient Israel. It is often assumed that literacy became widespread in Israel with the introduction of the alphabet. Frank Cross observed that literacy spread rapidly after the alphabet was standardized at the beginning of the Iron Age.[21] Alan Millard and a host of scholars argue for widespread literacy in Israel, especially during the late period of the monarchy.[22]

Menahem Haran, on the other hand, questions the basis for asserting that literacy was widespread in ancient Israel.[23] Arguing against the view that the alphabet produced a widespread rate of literacy, Sean Warner insists that paleographic studies are not adequate of themselves to determine the spread of literacy

---

19. M. Cogan, *Imperialism and Religion: Assyria, Judah and Israel in the Eighth and Seventh Centuries B.C.E.* (SBLMS 19; Missoula, MT: Scholars Press, 1974) 60.

20. J. Naveh, "A Paleographic Note on the Distribution of the Hebrew Script," *HTR* 61 (1968) 68.

21. F. M. Cross, "Early Alphabetic Scripts," in *Symposia Celebrating the Seventy-Fifth Anniversary of the Founding of the American Schools of Oriental Research* (ed. F. M. Cross; Cambridge, MA: ASOR, 1975) 11.

22. A. Millard, "An Assessment of the Evidence for Writing in Ancient Israel," in *Biblical Archaeology Today: Proceedings of the International Congress on Biblical Archaeology* (n. 8 above) 301–12.

23. M. Haran, "On the Diffusion of Literacy and Schools in Ancient Israel," in *Congress Volume: Jerusalem, 1986* (ed. J. A. Emerton; VTSup 40; Leiden: Brill, 1988) 85.

and the influence of the alphabet in Israelite society, but sociological, economic, and religious factors must also be considered.[24]

Although the last word is yet to be pronounced on how widespread the use of writing was in ancient Israel, Naveh argues soundly that "the quantity of the epigraphic material from the 8th century and onwards shows a gradual increase of the distribution of the knowledge of writing among the people of Israel and Judah."[25] A majority of texts are from the late eighth to the sixth century. An early witness to Hebrew writing is the Samaria ostraca, the most significant collection of inscribed documents from Israel. Most scholars agree that these potsherds date from the time of Jeroboam II, but they continue to disagree about their purpose, whether they were invoices, labels, receipts for wine or oil shipments, or had another function.

The Siloam inscription, carved in the east wall of Hezekiah's tunnel, dates from the end of the eighth century and is the only monumental inscription in biblical Hebrew from the First Temple period. It is surprising that the inscription does not bear the name of its supposed builder, Hezekiah, unlike all other monumental inscriptions in the Near East at that time.

Kuntillet 'Ajrud, the remote wayside shrine in northeastern Sinai, has furnished the first ancient dedicatory inscriptions, dating from 800 BCE. In addition to their epigraphic value, they are shedding light on Israelite cult, especially as it relates to Asherah. The remains uncovered at Kuntillet 'Ajrud reflect the practices of popular religion in the eighth century, which the prophets condemned.[26]

Tell Deir 'Alla in the Jordan Valley, on the east side of the River, yielded fragments of wall plaster inscribed in a Northwest Semitic dialect; they refer to "Balaam, son of Beor, seer of the gods"; undoubtedly, the same Balaam described in Numbers 22–24. This mural inscription dates from the mid-eighth century.[27]

Seals have a wide cultural significance, as Nahman Avigad has indicated. Few Hebrew seals are to be dated before the eighth century; a large number date from the late eighth century and especially from the seventh century and later. Inscribed seals are valuable for the information they convey about government, administration, and religious practice. One of the best known is the "Shema" seal from Megiddo, which dates from the eighth century. Seal impressions found on jar handles bearing the inscription *lmlk* date from the reign of Hezekiah and continued in use until the destruction of Jerusalem in 586 BCE.

Culture is reflected in such objects as pottery and ivory. Besides pottery's principal use today as a chronological indicator, it may also have aesthetic or

---

24. S. Warner, "The Alphabet: An Innovation and Its Diffusion," *VT* 30 (1980) 81–90.

25. Naveh, "A Paleographic Note," 71–72.

26. Z. Meshel, "Did Yahweh Have a Consort?" *BARev* 5/2 (1979) 24–35; P. Beck, "The Drawings from Horvat Teiman (Kuntillet 'Ajrud)," *Tel Aviv* 9 (1982) 3–68.

27. J. A. Hackett, *The Balaam Text from Deir 'Alla* (HSM 31; Chico, CA: Scholars Press, 1984).

economic value, depending on what it contained. Among the most distinctive pottery in Israel was the Samaria ware. These fine egg-shell thin vessels with polished red slip were produced in Phoenicia and were part of the tableware that graced the palace banquets of Samaria. Samaria ware continued to be produced in Phoenicia after Samaria fell; it is found in late eighth-seventh century BCE contexts as an import in Ashkelon. The Samaria ivories which were used decoratively as inlays and insets were Phoenician in origin. Some were carved locally, but the majority came from Phoenicia. Samaria yielded over five hundred eighth-century ivory fragments, many adorned with Egyptian motifs, characteristic of Phoenician style. The pair of crouching lions carved in the round typifies the ivory pieces found at Samaria and are indicative of Samaria's luxury, which exasperated the prophets.

V. Urban Layout

Iron II architecture was not distinctive of the eighth century alone, but the quality of architecture in the eighth century was impressive. Large cities in Iron II were fortified with offset-inset walls and casemates, as well as with multichambered gate systems. Some of the fortified cities had water systems; the most ambitious was Hezekiah's tunnel, dug through the bedrock beneath Ophel Hill. This extraordinary engineering feat carried water from the Gihon spring to the Siloam pool.

An impressive example of architectural ornamentation in the Iron II period was the Proto-Aeolic capitals. These capitals, decorated with volutes derived from the stylized palm-tree motif, have been uncovered in the royal cities of Jerusalem, Samaria, Hazor, and Megiddo. The technique of ashlar or hewn masonry was used in the construction of buildings and walls; the best example is the inner wall of Samaria. Fine ashlar masonry was combined with Proto-Aeolic capitals in the construction of the royal cities. Many scholars accept that ashlar masonry and Proto-Aeolic capitals originated in the Phoenician culture, although Yigal Shiloh and others have questioned this assumption.[28]

VI. Economic Situation

Morris Silver has looked at biblical problems from an economist's viewpoint in his *Prophets and Markets*.[29] As he has pointed out, several factors (already mentioned) were responsible for the prosperity of Israel and Judah under Jeroboam II and Uzziah. In the eighth century, Israel was an advanced agrarian society; agriculture was the primary means of subsistence. Israel's control over the fertile

---

28. Y. Shiloh, *The Proto-Aeolic Capital and Israelite Ashlar Masonry* (Qedem 11; Jerusalem: Institute of Archaeology, Hebrew University, 1979).

29. M. Silver, *Prophets and Markets: The Political Economy of Ancient Israel* (Boston: Kluwer-Nijhoff, 1983).

plains of Bashan was a boon to agriculture. Agricultural surplus was used in payment of imported goods and for government support.

International commerce was an important source of income for Israel and Judah. Phoenicia provided Israel with luxury items such as ivory; Israel in turn traded grain, olive oil, and wine with Phoenicia. At the same time, Israel supplied Egypt with olive oil and wine.

VII. Classical Prophets

In the midst of the internationalism and prosperity of the eighth century, the classical prophets appeared in Israel and Judah. Alongside the luxury and syncretism of that period stood the orthodox Yahwism of the writing prophets. Prophetism seems to have flourished in the midst of leisure and prosperity.

The classical prophets made the eighth century great, but it is difficult to explain their appearance for the first time in the eighth century. As John Holladay observed, "The explosive emergence of the so-called 'writing prophets' in the history of Israel is one of the great historical mysteries of Old Testament scholarship."[30] Two of the most insightful, and at the same time complementary, articles on this topic are by James Ross and John Holladay.[31] In his article "The Prophet as Yahweh's Messenger" Ross analyzes the characteristics of the messenger speech, the relationship of messenger to sender, as well as the task and responsibility of the messenger. In his article "Assyrian Statecraft and the Prophets of Israel," Holladay, emphasizing the prophet's role as messenger, sees classical prophecy as a response to the international political situation, when Neo-Assyria under Tiglath-pileser III was on the rise. Noting the changing nature of the prophetic office, he states that the preclassical prophets were primarily "court" prophets, while the classical prophets were principally "popular" prophets. Originally the prophets addressed their messages exclusively to the ruling houses of Israel and Judah; beginning with the eighth century the prophets spoke to the whole people of Israel. Holladay observes striking parallels between the role of the eighth-century prophets and that of the Assyrian royal messengers, who addressed not just the king but the subject people as well. According to the policy of Assyria, the entire community bore responsibility for its actions. In the case of rebellion, not only the king but all his subjects were punished by slaughter, deportation, or national exile.

In response to the question why were the sermons of the eighth-century prophets preserved, the answer resides at least in part with the spread of writing—the prophets themselves, or their scribes, actually wrote down the oracles. This

---

30. J. S. Holladay, "Assyrian Statecraft and the Prophets of Israel," *HTR* 63 (1970) 29.

31. J. F Ross, "The Prophet as Yahweh's Messenger," in *Israel's Prophetic Heritage* (ed. B. Anderson and W. Harrelson; New York: Harper & Row, 1962) 98–107; J. S. Holladay, "Assyrian Statecraft and the Prophets of Israel."

marked the progression from oral to written compositions. Yehezkel Kaufmann answered, "The chief reason is surely the new level of thought that was reached in these writings. Unlike their predecessors, the classical prophets were important for what they said more than for what they did."[32] Their stirring oracles like the following are immortal.

Amos's uncompromising attack on the social immorality of his day is without parallel: "They sell the righteous for silver, and the needy for a pair of shoes—they that trample the head of the poor into the dust of the earth, and turn aside the way of the afflicted" (Amos 2:6–7). Hosea's portrayal of God's unmerited love and mercy is found nowhere else: "How could I give you up, O Ephraim, or deliver you up, O Israel? How could I treat you as Admah, or make you like Zeboiim? My heart is overwhelmed, my pity is stirred" (Hos 11:8). Isaiah's ideal of peace is unmatched: "They shall beat their swords into plowshares and their spears into pruning hooks; nation shall not take up sword against nation; nor shall they train for war again" (Isa 2:4). Micah's epitome of the prophetic message is one of the noblest statements in scripture: "You have been told, O man, what is good, and what the Lord requires of you: only to do justice, to love kindness, and to walk humbly with your God" (Mic 6:8).

---

32. Y. Kaufmann, *The Religion of Israel* (Chicago: University of Chicago Press, 1960) 361–62.

AT THE MERCY OF BABYLON:
A SUBVERSIVE REREADING OF THE EMPIRE*

Walter Brueggemann
Columbia Theological Seminary

Biblical theology as a study of Israel's faithful speech may be said to revolve around two organizing questions. The first question of biblical theology is, How does Israel speak about God? Israel characteristically does not speak about God unless it speaks at the same time about the world in which God is present and over which God governs. For that reason, the second question of biblical theology is, What else must Israel talk about when it talks about God? It belongs decisively to the character of this God, as artistically rendered in Israel's text, to be always engaged in ways that impinge both upon God and upon God's "other." One aspect of that God-other engagement which is typical of Israel's theological speech is God in relation to the nations. The God of Israel is a God who deals with the nations, and the nations inescapably deal with the God of Israel. Together they form a common subject in Israel's theological speech.

I

The great powers, north and south, dominate Israel's public life and policy.[1] In this paper I will pay attention to one of the great northern powers, Babylon, and the way in which Babylon enters into Israel's speech about God. Although Babylon may be regarded as simply one among several great powers that concern Israel, it is also clear that Babylon peculiarly occupies the imagination of Israel.

Babylon goads and challenges Israel's theological imagination in remarkably varied ways. As a theological metaphor, Babylon is not readily dismissed or easily categorized. Indeed, in the postexilic period, it is Babylon and not Persia

---

*The Presidential Address delivered 17 November 1990 at the annual meeting of the Society of Biblical Literature held at the New Orleans Marriott, New Orleans, Louisiana.
1. On the bipolar geopolitical situation of Israel, see A. Malamat, "The Kingdom of Judah Between Egypt and Babylon: A Small State Within a Great Power Confrontation," in *Text and Context* (ed. W. Claassen; JSOTSup 48; Sheffield: JSOT Press, 1988) 117–29.

that continues to function as a powerful theological metaphor for Israel. Babylon operates supplely in Israel's theological speech because Babylon is a partner and an antagonist in Israel's political life and is perceived as a partner and an antagonist worthy of Yahweh. As Yahweh cannot be settled or reduced in Israel's discernment, so Babylon cannot be settled or reduced, but remains as a tensive, energizing force in Israel's faith and imagination. Moreover, if the experience of exile was decisive for the canonizing process, as seems most probable, then it is equally probable that Babylon takes on imaginative power that is not simply historical and political but canonical in force, significance, and density.

By considering the theological function of Babylon, we are concerned with the question, What happens to *speech about Babylon* when it is drawn into the sphere of speech about God? In a lesser fashion, we will also ask, What happens to *speech about God* when God is drawn into the sphere of speech about the empire? In posing these questions, it is clear that we are taking up issues of artistic construal that are not fully contained in historical and political categories. As George Steiner has said of great art in general, we are dealing in the Bible not simply with a formulation but with a reformulation and a rethinking.[2] We are concerned with a canonizing process whereby Israel voices its normative, paradigmatic construal of imperial power. Israel's rhetoric at the interface of God and empire is a concrete attempt to hold together the inscrutable reality of God (which is at the center of its rethought world) and the raw power of the empire (which is a daily reality of its life). Israel's self-identity, presence in the world, and chance for free action depend upon how these two are held together.

By joining speech about God to speech about Babylon, Israel's faith radically rereads the character of the empire, consistently subverting every conventional reading of the empire in which complacent Babylon and intimidated Israel must have colluded. That is, Babylon presented itself as autonomous, invincible, and permanent. When Israel entered fully into the ideology of Babylon (and abandoned its own covenantal definitions of reality), it accepted this characterization of Babylon and, derivatively, its own fate as completely defined by Babylonian reality. This is a classic example of the phenomenon, noted by Marx, of the victim willingly participating in the ideology of the perpetrator.[3] This conventional collusion about power practiced by perpetrators and victims is controverted, however, in Israel's alternative reading, which is deeply and inherently subversive. When Israel, in a Yahwistic context, could discern that Babylon was not as it presented itself, then Israel did not need to define its own situation so hopelessly. Thus Yahwistic faith makes an alternative to imperial ideology available to those who live from this counterrhetoric.

---

2. George Steiner writes of "un-ending re-reading" and reevaluation (*Real Presences: Is There Anything in What We Say* [London: Faber & Faber, 1989]).

3. See Karl Marx and Friedrich Engels, *The German Ideology Part One* (ed. C. J. Arthur; London: Lawrence & Wishart, 1970) 64–68.

II

I have selected six texts concerning Babylon on which to focus: Jer 42:9–17; 50:41–43; Isa 47:5–7; 1 Kgs 8:46–53; 2 Chr 36:15–21; and Dan 4:19–27.[4] My thesis, which I will explicate in relation to these texts, is that when Israel's speech about Babylon is drawn into Israel's speech concerning God, the power of the empire is envisioned and reconstructed around the issue of mercy (*rḥm*)[5] The intrusion of the rhetoric of mercy into the *Realpolitik* of Babylon derives from the uncompromising character of God. It also arises from the deepest yearning of the exilic community which must have mercy to live, which expects mercy from God, and which by venturesome rhetoric dares to insist that the promised, yearned-for mercy cannot be ignored by the empire.

JEREMIAH 42:9–17

In its final form the book of Jeremiah has a decidedly pro-Babylonian slant, mediated through the Baruch document and perhaps powered by the authority and influence of the family of Shaphan.[6] The sustained urging of the text is that the people of Jerusalem must stay in the jeopardized city and submit to the occupying presence of Babylon and not flee to Egypt. This announcement reflects a political judgment and a political interest that cooperation with Babylon is a safer way to survival. This voice of advocacy also concluded that cooperation with Egypt would only cause heavier, more destructive Babylonian pressure. That political judgment, however, is given as an oracle of God. The urging therefore is not simply political strategy, but is offered as the intent of God for God's people. Thus the oracle is not simply speech concerning the empire but also speech about God.

The oracle of Jeremiah 42 is cast in two conditional clauses: one positive, "if" you remain in the city (vv. 10–12); the other negative, "if" you flee to Egypt (vv.

---

4. Texts on Babylon that I will not consider include Isaiah 13–14; materials in Isaiah 40–55; references in the Ezekiel collection of oracles against the nations; 2 Chr 30:6–9; and Dan 1:5–9.

5. In the texts I will consider, there are two exceptions to the use of the term *rḥm*. In 2 Chr 36:15–21, the term is *ḥml*. In Dan 4:24, the term used is *ḥnn*. Both these terms, however, belong in the same semantic field as *rḥm*. On the political, public dimensions of *rḥm*, see Michael Fishbane, "The Treaty Background of Amos 1:11 and Related Matters" *JBL* 89 (1970) 313–18; and Robert B. Coote, "Amos 1:11: RḤMYW," *JBL* 90 (1971) 206–8. On the intimate, interpersonal nuances of the term, see Phyllis Trible, *God and the Rhetoric of Sexuality* (OBT; Philadelphia: Fortress, 1978) 31–59.

6. Christopher R. Seitz has discerned the conflicting and competing ideologies concerning exile present in the book of Jeremiah (*Theology in Conflict: Reactions to the Exile in the Book of Jeremiah* [BZAW 176; Berlin: de Gruyter, 1989]). On the peculiar and decisive role of the family of Shaphan in the Jeremiah tradition, see J. Andrew Dearman, "My Servants the Scribes: Composition and Context in Jeremiah 36," *JBL* 109 (1990) 403–21.

13-17). The positive conditional clause is cast as a promise that God will repent of evil and issues in a salvation oracle:[7]

> Do not fear the king of Babylon
>   of whom you are afraid,
> Do not fear him, says the Lord, for I am with you
>   to deliver you from his hand. (v. 11)

The Jeremiah tradition takes a conventional speech form, the salvation oracle, and presses it into new use. The conventional form is "Do not fear," followed by an assurance; here, however, the form is daringly extended to identify the one not to be feared, the king of Babylon.[8] Moreover, the speech form is utilized exactly to juxtapose the fearsome power of Nebuchadnezzar and the resolve of the Lord: "Do not fear him … I will deliver." The oracle counters the empire with God's good resolve. The assurance of God continues:

> I will grant you mercy (*raḥămîm*)
>   that (*wĕ*) he will have mercy on you[9]
>   and let you remain in the land. (v. 12)

The connection between "I" and "he" (the king of Babylon) is elusive, bridged only by a *waw* consecutive. The oracle does, however, insist on this decisive, albeit elusive, link between Yahweh's resolve and anticipated imperial policy. The oracle asserts that Babylon can indeed be a source of mercy to Jerusalem, when the empire subscribes to God's own intention. The negative counterpart of vv. 13-17 indicates that if there is flight to Egypt and away from Babylon, the same Babylonian king who is capable of mercy will indeed be "the sword which you fear" (v. 16).

Our historical-critical propensity is to say that the oracle of Jer 42:9-17 simply reflects a wise, pragmatic political decision. Such a reading, however, ignores the casting of the speech in which the "I" of God's mercy directly shapes the "he" of Nebuchadnezzar's policy. That rhetorical linkage is crucial for the argument of the

---

7. On the theological implications of this text, see Terence E. Fretheim, *The Suffering of God* (OBT; Philadelphia: Fortress, 1984) 138-44; and Francis I. Andersen and David Noel Freedman, *Amos: A New Translation with Introduction and Commentary* (AB 24A; Garden City, NY: Doubleday, 1989) 659-63.

8. See Edgar W. Conrad, *Fear Not Warrior* (BJS 75; Chico, CA: Scholars Press, 1985) 48-51.

9. The LXX reads the second verb in the first person, "I will have mercy on you," thus removing the tension that is crucial to our argument. That rendering makes the text irrelevant to the interface we are seeking to identify. Recent major commentaries consistently prefer the MT reading. See John Bright, *Jeremiah: Introduction, Translation, and Notes* (AB 21; Garden City, NY: Doubleday, 1965) 256.

whole of the tradition. This rhetorical maneuver recasts the empire as an agent who is compelled, under the right circumstance, to show mercy. The speech practice of the Jeremiah-Baruch-Shaphan tradition includes Babylon in the sphere where mercy will be practiced as a public reality.

JEREMIAH 50:41–43

Scholars tend to read these "oracles against the nations" as a separate literary unit and in terms of historical, political developments. The MT places the oracles against the nations, and especially chaps. 50–51 against Babylon, at the end of the book; this arrangement invites us to pay attention to their canonical intention, that is, to move beyond historical, political concerns to notice the connection between these oracles and other parts of the Jeremiah tradition.[10]

In the MT ordering of materials, the midterm verdict of the book of Jeremiah is that Nebuchadnezzar will triumph and rule, even in Jerusalem (25:8–11; 27:5–7b). That midterm verdict, however, is overcome by the final verdict of the MT book of Jeremiah (see also 25:12–14; 27:7b). In the end, it will be God and not Nebuchadnezzar who prevails in the historical process. Again, we can read this assertion simply in relation to the politics of the nations, so that we anticipate (in retrospect) that the Persians will have defeated and succeeded the Babylonians.

Israel's way of speaking, however, is not rooted simply in historical analysis. The ominous verdict against Babylon in Jer 50:41–43 is rather an intentional rhetorical effort that intends to answer and resolve the so-called Scythian Song of 6:22–24. This is not simply a conventional recycling of poetic images, but this reuse of poetic material intends to counter and refute the first use. The purpose of the Scythian Song (6:22–24) is to invoke in the most threatening fashion the coming of the intruder from the north. The coming threat is portrayed in this way:

They lay hold on bow and spear,
    they are cruel and have no mercy (*rḥm*). (6:23)

In contrast to the anticipated Babylonian accommodation of chap. 42, the poetry of 6:23 knows that there will be "no mercy" from the invading army. The coming of the invader with "no mercy" in chap. 6 is God's resolve to punish recalcitrant Jerusalem.

---

10. The alternative placement of these texts by the LXX after 25:14 anticipates the debate about whether Nebuchadnezzar's massive power is temporary (MT chaps. 27–28) and whether Jerusalem will indeed be given a future (MT chap. 29). See William L. Holladay, *Jeremiah: A Commentary on the Book of the Prophet Jeremiah* (2 vols.; Hermeneia; Minneapolis: Fortress, 1986, 1989) 2. 312–14. Note the abrupt "until" in 27:2, 11. Moreover, 25:12–14 anticipates the demise of Babylon and asserts that the Babylonians will in time be reduced to a status of slavery (cf. Isa 47:1–4).

Chapter 50 uses the same rhetoric to reverse the earlier verdict of 6:23. Now the threatening intruder from the north is not Babylon, but one who comes against Babylon. This coming people, like Babylon, is savage in its invasion.

> They lay hold of bow and spear;
> they are cruel, and have no mercy ($rḥm$). (50:42)

The ones who come against Babylon have "no mercy." Thus the poem threatens and destabilizes Babylon with the same phrasing that authorized Babylon in 6:22–23.

The use of the same phrasing in 6:22–24 and 50:41–43 greatly illuminates the way in which Yahweh relates to the nations. On the one hand, Yahweh is in both situations the one who takes initiative, the one with authority. On the other hand, Yahweh's purpose is multidimensional, so that in different times and circumstances, the rule of God may be evidenced both for Babylon and against Babylon. In both postures, the way of Yahweh is the implementation of a policy of "no mercy."

The prose commentary that follows this oracle in 50:44-46 interprets the poetry. It makes a sweeping theological claim: God has a plan ($ʿṣh$) and a purpose ($mḥšb$) and can appoint and summon "whomever I choose" (v. 44). The retention and exercise of imperial power are tentative and provisional. Even the great Nebuchadnezzar, the rhetoric asserts, is subject to the rule of Yahweh which concerns the practice of "mercy" and "no mercy." Thus the oracle of Jeremiah 50–51 at the end of the canonical book asserts the rule of God over international affairs. The reuse of 6:22–23 is, for our purposes, particularly important. The double use connects the dispatch of Babylon by God with "no mercy," and then the destruction of Babylon, with "no mercy."

Two things strike us in this construal of Babylon's destiny. First, God deals directly with Babylon and Persia, without any reference to Judah or Jerusalem. God is indeed the God of the nations. Second, the exercise of God's sovereignty concerns matters of mercy and no mercy. The destiny of Babylon turns on Yahweh's various initiatives with mercy. Thus the rhetoric of Israel reconstitutes the geopolitics of the Fertile Crescent with reference to mercy.

The sequence of 6:22–24 (which anticipates Babylon) and 50:41–43 (which dismisses Babylon) stands in an odd relation to the salvation oracle of chap. 42. The editing of the book of Jeremiah is complex, so that we may indeed have different editorial hands. In the text as we have it, the Baruch document promises mercy from Babylon, though that mercy is conditional (42:9–17). The poetic units, both the "early" poem (6:22–23) and the oracle against the Babylonians (50:41–43), refute the option of mercy. Yet in all of the texts, whatever their origin, the rise and fall of empires have been drawn into the language of mercy. The tradition insists about Babylon, Persia, Jerusalem, and God's assurance, that the play of power around the city of Jerusalem raises the question and the possibility of mercy.

ISAIAH 47:5–7

Because we do not know when to date the Jeremiah materials, we do not know about the relative dating of Jeremiah 50 and Isaiah 47.[11] I take up Isaiah 47 after the Jeremiah text because conventionally Deutero-Isaiah is placed after Jeremiah, though Jeremiah 50 may indeed be later. In any case, Isaiah 47 permits a more comprehensive and reflective commentary on the mercy questions posed in the Jeremiah tradition. In brief form, Isaiah 47 offers one of the most comprehensive statements of Israel's theology of the nations. God's dealing with the empire is elaborated in four stages:

1. I was angry with my people. (v. 6a)

The tradition insists that the destruction of Jerusalem was not an accomplishment of Babylonian policy but happened at the behest of God (cf. Jer 25:8–11; 27:5–6; Isa 40:1–2). The destruction is a sovereign act of God, only implemented by Nebuchadnezzar.

2. I profaned my heritage,
    I gave them into your hand. (v. 6bc)

It is God who submits Jerusalem to the invasion of Babylon. These first two elements of the speech of God constitute a conventional prophetic lawsuit. Israel is indicted for its failure to obey God. Israel is placed under the judgment of foreign invasion. The coming of the invader is God's stance of "no mercy" toward Jerusalem.

3. The third element of this oracle is unexpected and moves well beyond the conventional lawsuit speech:

You [Babylon] showed no mercy (*rḥm*). (v. 6d)

The text offers no grammatical connection between this statement and what has just preceded. We expect "but" or "however" or "nevertheless," but we get nothing.[12]

4. This parataxis then leads to a rebuke of the empire:

---

11. The current options for dating the materials are reflected in the commentaries of William L. Holladay, (*Jeremiah*) and Robert P. Carroll (*Jeremiah: A Commentary* [OTL; Philadelphia: Westminster, 1986]). The dating of the materials is not important for our argument about rhetoric but would illuminate the sequence in which the texts might be taken up.

12. On the function of such parataxis, see G. B. Caird, *The Language and Imagery of the Bible* (Philadelphia: Westminster, 1980) 117–21.

You said, "I will be mistress forever,"
So that you did not lay these things to heart
or remember their end. (v. 7)

The first two elements in Isa 47:5–7, then, are conventional: God is angry with Israel. God punishes Israel by summoning a punishing nation, in this case Babylon. We are not prepared for the third and fourth elements, however. The speech is constructed as though Nebuchadnezzar (and Babylonian policy) was all along supposed to have known that mercy toward Jerusalem was in order and expected, appropriate even in light of God's anger. Inside the drama of the text, I imagine Nebuchadnezzar could react to these third and fourth elements in God's speech by saying in indignation, "Mercy? You never mentioned mercy." Of course, Nebuchadnezzar is not permitted to speak at all, except in the poetic self-indictment of v. 7a.

The turn in the third element of Isa 47:5–7 is precisely pertinent to our thesis. "Mercy" readily intrudes into political talk where it is not expected. Mercy impinges on the policies and destiny even of the empire. In conversation about God and empire, mercy operates as a nonnegotiable factor. Nebuchadnezzar should have known that Yahweh is that kind of God. From the beginning, Yahweh has been a God of mercy, and mercy is characteristically present where Yahweh is present. In the end, even the empire stands or falls in terms of God's resilient commitment to mercy. Ruthless power cannot circumvent that resolve of God.

It is clear that rhetorically something decisive has happened between the second and third elements of this oracle. The first two phrases look back to 587 and echo the predictable claims of lawsuit, long anticipated by the prophets. In the third and fourth phrases, however, the poet has turned away from conventional lawsuit claims, away from 587, away from destruction and judgment. Now the poet looks forward, out beyond the exile. Now God's very tool of exile has become the object of God's indignation. In this moment, God's old, old agenda of mercy reemerges (cf. Exod 34:6–7). The practice of this rhetoric, in the horizon of the poet, destabilizes the empire. Israel's speech knows that empires, in their imagined autonomy, will always have to come to terms with God's alternative governance.[13] The empire is never even close to being ultimate, but always lives under the threat of this rhetoric, which rejects every imperial complacency, every act of autonomy, every gesture of self-sufficiency. The poem of Isaiah 47 ends with an awesome verdict emerging from this exchange about arrogant autonomy and mercy: "There is no one to save you!" (v. 15).

---

13. See, e.g., Isa 37:22–29; and Donald E. Gowan, *When Man Becomes God* (PTMS 6; Pittsburgh: Pickwick, 1975) 31–35.

1 KINGS 8:46–53

This text is commonly taken to belong to the latest layer of deuteronomic interpretation.[14] It is cast as part of the prayer of Solomon. It is structured as an if-then formulation, echoed in 2 Chr 30:9. The petition anticipates a conditional exile. It contains an "if" of repentance in exile (v. 48) and a "then" followed by four imperatives addressed to God on the basis of repentance:

> hear thou in heaven ...
> maintain their cause, and
> forgive thy people ...
> grant them compassion (*rḥm*). (vv. 49–50)

A motivation is offered to God in v. 51; an additional petition is voiced in v. 52; and a final motivational clause is given in v. 53.

What interests us is the fourth imperative of petition in vv. 49–50: "Grant them compassion (*rḥm*) in the sight of those who carried them away captive, that they may have compassion (*rḥm*) on them." It is clear in the prayer that it is God and only God who gives mercy. God is the only subject of the verb *ntn*. God must grant mercy if any is to be given. The last word of the petition adds, however, "that they [the captors] may have mercy" Again the inclination of God and the disposition of Babylon are intimately related to each other. It is not doubted that the Babylonian empire could be a place of mercy. The exile can be a place of compassion, but that can only be because God hears prayers and attends to the needs of the exiles. The empire is a place where God's inclination for mercy can indeed be effected in a concrete, public way. Babylon can enact what God grants.[15] The claim of this text is close to the affirmation of Jer 42:12.

2 CHRONICLES 36:15–21

This text is the penultimate paragraph of 2 Chronicles. In these verses the Chronicler gives closure to the narrative, and engages in a sweeping retrospective. The term "mercy" (*ḥml*) occurs twice in this concluding and ominous statement. First, the God of Israel is a God of mercy who has practiced long-term, persistent mercy toward Israel: "The Lord, the God of their fathers, sent persistently to them by his messengers, because he had mercy (*ḥml*) on his people and on his

---

14. See Hans Walter Wolff, "The Kerygma of the Deuteronomic Historical Work," in *The Vitality of Old Testament Traditions* (ed. W. Brueggemann and H. W. Wolff; Atlanta: Knox, 1982) 95–97.

15. Richard Nelson suggests that the promise of mercy from "your captors" "is the thinnest possible offer of a chance at return for the exiles, one the narrator dares not even whisper" (cf. Ps. 106:46) (*First and Second Kings* [Interpretation; Atlanta: Knox, 1987] 54–55).

dwelling place" (v. 15). The whole history of prophecy is an act of mercy. In this usage, however, mercy is not rescue but warning, to deter Jerusalem from its self-destructive action. Israel, however, refused and resisted, until God's wrath arose and there was "no remedy" ('*ên marpē*', v. 16).

This passage is constructed so that Babylon does not appear in the text until God's mercy is spent. Only then does the empire enter the scene: "Therefore, he [God] brought up against them the king of the Chaldeans, who slew their young men with the sword in the house of their sanctuary, and had no mercy (*ḥml*) on young man or virgin, old man or aged; he gave them all into his hand" (v. 17). It was the designated work of Babylon to destroy, reflective of God's exhausted mercy. The statement is framed so that the active subject at the beginning and end is God; only in between these statements is the king of Babylon permitted as an active agent. Thus far the argument with the double use of "mercy" closely parallels the first two elements of the argument in Isaiah 47.

It is to be recognized that the key term in this text is *ḥml* and not *rḥm*, as elsewhere in our analysis. However, the explicit reference to Jeremiah in v. 21 suggests that this text in the Chronicler is an intentional development of the Jeremiah tradition.[16] The Chronicler reiterates the assertions of the Jeremiah tradition which justify the catastrophe of 587. Yet the Chronicler also moves beyond the reflections of the Jeremiah tradition. Thus the text of Jeremiah is cited as an anticipation which now comes to fresh fulfillment. This penultimate paragraph with the double, albeit negative, reference to "mercy" prepares the way for the final paragraph of vv. 22–23, which moves dramatically beyond judgment to God's new act of mercy among the nations: "Now in the first year of Cyrus, king of Persia, that the word of the Lord in the mouth of Jeremiah might be accomplished, the Lord stirred up the spirit of Cyrus the Persian so that he made a proclamation throughout all his kingdom and also put it in writing" (v. 22). Even this new world power is to fulfill the word of Jeremiah. Now begins the new phase of Jewish history with Cyrus. It is a new beginning to which Jeremiah 50 has made negative reference, and to which Isaiah 44–47 makes positive reference. Our pivotal point of interpretation juxtaposes *the exhausted mercy of Yahweh* and *the lacking mercy of Babylon*.

These texts from Jeremiah, Isaiah, 1 Kings, and the Chronicler seem to be intimately connected to each other in a sustained reflection on the destiny of Israel vis-à-vis Babylon and the workings of God. The salient point is that mercy from God and mercy from Babylon live in an odd and tense relation; neither will work effectively without the other. That is, when Babylon has mercy, it is derivative from the mercy of God. Conversely, when God has no mercy left, there will be none from Babylon. This straightforward connection, however, is disrupted

---

16. On this text as an example of intertextual reading, see Michael Fishbane, *Biblical Interpretation in Ancient Israel* (Oxford: Clarendon, 1985) 481–82.

by the discernment of Isa 47:6. It is this text that creates tension between the mercy of heaven and the mercy of earth. The tension occurs because the empire can indeed exercise autonomy. That autonomy characteristically is self-serving, against mercy, and sure to bring self-destruction, even upon the empire.

In all these texts, Israel is now prepared to move toward the newness embodied in Cyrus the Persian. Thanks to Deutero-Isaiah, the Persian period, in contrast to that of the Babylonians, is perceived as a new saving action of God which permits the survival and modest prosperity of Judaism. Yet Persia never takes on the imaginative power or metaphorical force of Babylon. In the OT, the theological struggle concerning public power and divine purpose remains focused on the reality, memory, experience, and symbolization of Babylon.

Daniel 4:19–27

When we come to the book of Daniel, we see that Israel's theological reflection cannot finally finish with Babylon. It is clear that by the time of the Daniel texts, we have broken free of historical reference; Nebuchadnezzar now looms on the horizon of Israel as a cipher for a power counter to the Lord.[17] It is, moreover, evident that Babylon is not a reduced or flattened metaphor, for then Nebuchadnezzar could be defeated and dismissed in the literature. Nebuchadnezzar, however, is kept very much alive and present by the rhetoric of Israel.

The narrative of Daniel 4 concerns the dream of Nebuchadnezzar that the "great tree" will be cut down. As Daniel interprets this dream, it anticipates Nebuchadnezzar's loss of power. Two assumptions operate for the narrator which make the story possible. First, it is proper, legitimate, and acceptable for Jewish lore to entertain a story about Nebuchadnezzar. As we might expect, such a story is told in order to mock and deride the great king. As we shall see, the narrative is not finally a mocking or dismissal of Nebuchadnezzar, but in fact portrays his remarkable rehabilitation. Thus the horizon of the Bible does not flatly dismiss the empire but entertains its possible transformation to an agent of obedience.

Second, the narrative assumes that the great king and his governmental apparatus are dysfunctional. In the end, the great king must step outside his own official circles of power and influence for the guidance he needs. On one level the narrative is a rather conventional contrast between the stupid wielder of power and the shrewd outsider who is able to turn the tables. As we shall see, however, the narrator moves in a different, somewhat unexpected direction. This story is not primarily about how a Jew prevails over Babylon. It is a story, in the end, about the well-being of Babylon and its power.

---

17. On the freedom of the Daniel text from historical reference, see W. S. Towner, "Were the English Puritans 'the Saints of the Most High?' Issues in the Pre-Critical Interpretation of Daniel 7," *Int* 37 (1983) 46–63; and more programmatically Brevard S. Childs, *Introduction to the Old Testament as Scripture* (Philadelphia: Fortress, 1979) 618–22.

Daniel's interpretation of the dream of the king turns on three crucial affirmations. (1) "It is you, O King" (v. 22). The interpretation by Daniel brings the dream into immediate political risk with rhetoric that recalls Nathan's indictment of David (2 Sam 12:7). (2) The purpose of the dream is "until you know that the Most High has sovereignty over the kingdom of mortals and gives it to whom he will" (v. 25). This formula dominates the narrative, occurring in vv. 14, 22, and 29, and with greater variation, v. 34. Moreover, the formulation contains an echo of Jer 50:44, to which we have already made reference (cf. 49:19): "I will appoint over him whomever I choose. For who is like me? Who will summon me? What shepherd can stand before me? Therefore, hear the plan which the Lord has made against Babylon...." In the Jeremiah usage, the transfer of power away from Babylon to "a people from the north" is sure and settled.

In the Daniel narrative, however, there is a third point which leads the narrative in a surprising direction. At the end of his interpretive account, Daniel says, "Therefore, O King, let my counsel be acceptable to you; break off your sins by practicing righteousness, and your iniquities by showing mercy ($ḥn$) to the oppressed" (v. 24).[18] Daniel's counsel to the king is unexpected in this context. We have been given no reason to anticipate this narrative development. Daniel ceases here to be an interpreter and becomes a moral instructor of and witness to the great king. For our purposes, it is important to recognize that the empire is understood by the narrative as a potential place of mercy; Nebuchadnezzar is presented as a ruler who is capable of mercy to the oppressed and would be wise to practice such mercy and righteousness.

In the unfolding of the narrative, we are never told that Nebuchadnezzar heeded Daniel and practiced righteousness and mercy. We are later told, however, that his "reason ($minda'$) returned" (v. 31). He submitted in praise to the Most High (vv. 31–32). Thus it is legitimate to imagine that the narrative understands the "return of reason," the capacity to praise, and the reception of majesty and splendor to Nebuchadnezzar (v. 36) as evidence of the practice of mercy as urged by Daniel.

We may now consider the sequence of texts we have discussed concerning the recurring interplay of God, mercy, and the destiny of the empire: (1) In Jer 6:23 and 2 Chr 36:1, there is no mercy because God intended that there should be no mercy. (2) In Isa 47:6, there is no mercy, and Nebuchadnezzar is sharply admonished for this lack, which violates God's intention. (3) In Jer 42:12 and 1 Kgs 8:50, Babylon is judged to be capable of mercy, and Jews may legitimately expect mercy. (4) In Dan 4:27, which is a late, perhaps climactic word on Babylon in the OT, the hope of Daniel again counts on the mercy of the empire, as that mercy is anticipated in Jer 42:12 and 1 Kgs 8:50.

---

18. As indicated, the term here is not $rḥm$ but $ḥnn$. On the cruciality of the old creedal formulation in which they are closely related, see Hermann Spieckermann, "Barmherzig und gnädig ist der Herr...," ZAW 102 (1990) 1–18.

To be sure, this good word about Nebuchadnezzar and Babylon may be simply part of a Jewish strategy of political quietism and cooperation. We should not, however, neglect the theological force of Dan 4:22 and its fruition in vv. 34–37. The theological claim of the narrative, regardless of what it may mean for Jewish conduct and hope, is that the empire is transformable and can become a place of mercy and righteousness. This transformation happens when the God of Israel is accepted as the Most High, that is, when the empire is brought under the rule of the Lord. Thus the nations, given this example of Babylon, are redeemable, transformable, and capable of salvage for the humane purposes of God. Moreover, the narrative of Daniel 4 is a warning to all would-be Nebuchadnezzars that the exercise of power uninformed by righteousness and mercy will lead to insanity and loss of authority. The empire is a place that may host mercy. It is a place which, in its self-interest, must host mercy. There is no alternative strategy for royal power that can possibly succeed.[19]

III

At the outset, I offered two questions to focus the task of theological interpretation: How does Israel speak about God? And what else must Israel talk about when it talks about God? The answer to the first question, given our topic, is that Israel talks about God in terms of the reality of mercy. The answer to the second question, I have suggested, is that when Israel speaks of the mercy of God, it must speak of the nations, specifically *Babylon,* more specifically, *the mercy of Babylon.* To say that Israel's speech about God entails speech about the mercy of the Babylonian empire evidences the delicate, daring enterprise that Israel's theological speech inescapably is. In its theological speech, Israel recharacterizes God. At the same time, it recharacterizes the empire and the meaning of worldly power.

Israel's speech about God requires and permits Israel to say that the empire is not what it is usually thought to be. It is not what it is thought to be by Israelites who fear and are intimidated by the empire. Conversely, it is not what it is thought to be by the wielders of power themselves, in their presumed self-sufficiency. Negatively, this claim of mercy asserts that imperial rule is not rooted simply in raw power. Israel, when it is theologically intentional, will not entertain the notion that "might makes right." Positively, this claim asserts that political power inherently and intrinsically has in its very fabric the reality of mercy, the

---

19. In addition to the several texts that juxtapose "mercy" and "Babylon," there is a large number of texts dated in and around the exilic period that speak of God's mercy: see Isa 14:1; 49:13–15; 54:7–10; 55:7; 60:10; Mic 7:19; Jer 12:15; 30:18; 31:20; 33:26; Lam 3:22, 32; Hab 3:2; Zech 1:12, 16; 10:6. These texts suggest that "mercy" became an extremely important theological issue in a time when Israel's relation to God appeared to be in jeopardy. These texts, however, lie outside the scope of this study because they do not explicitly concern the empire, and because the mercy is promised after the exile by the empire, and not in the midst of it.

practice of humanness, or as Daniel dares to say to Nebuchadnezzar, the care of the oppressed (Dan 4:27). This daring rhetoric which follows from Israel's speech about God does not mean that the holder of power will always accept this characterization of power. Israel nonetheless refuses to allow any enterprise of power to exist and function outside the zone of its theological rhetoric.

This claim about imperial power is even more stunning when the subject of such speech is characteristically Babylon. The same playful, ambiguous, venturesome rhetoric of Israel is also employed concerning Egypt and Assyria, but perhaps not as extensively. While Babylon functions in this regard as a metaphor for all such power, no doubt Babylon, in and of itself, occupies a peculiar and distinctive role in Israel's theological horizon. In the Bible Israel would never finish with Babylon, and therefore its speech about Babylon is of peculiar importance.

We may suggest two reasons for this odd focus. First, there is good historical reason for such an insistence concerning Babylon. The deportation of the Jerusalem elite required honest and alarming theological reflection by the makers of Judaism. It was Babylon that had the capacity to create a situation in which God's mercy was experienced as null and void; Israel was left to wonder what that nullification signified (see Lam 5:20–22). Second, there is surely canonical reason for such a focus on Babylon. It is most plausible that the process of displacement in the sixth century not only was decisive for the community that experienced it but also became, through the process of canonization, a decisive paradigmatic reality for continuing generations of Jews.[20]

Thus the exile became paradigmatic for all Jews, including the God of the Jews. Jews and the God of the Jews must come to terms with the definitional role of Babylon. It was exactly the experience and metaphor of *Babylonian exile* that made the question of *mercy* so acute. It was exactly the mercy of God, remembered, experienced, and anticipated, that made a redefinition of Babylon so urgent and so problematic.

Israel's rhetoric accomplished a stunning claim. It asserted that no savage power in the world could separate Israel from God's mercy. It did more than that, however; it also asserted that no savage power, no matter its own self-discernment, can ever be cut off from the reality of God's mercy. It is for that reason that the burden of mercy is repeatedly thrust upon Nebuchadnezzar.

For that reason Daniel finally, at the end of this literature, has Nebuchadnezzar's "reason return" (Dan 4:31). Now Nebuchadnezzar "knows."[21] What he

---

20. Jacob Neusner has shown how the displacement in the sixth century became a shaping paradigm for the self-understanding of all Judaism, a paradigm only loosely connected with the historical realities (*Understanding Seeking Faith* [Atlanta: Scholars Press, 1986] 137–41).

21. The term usually rendered as "reason" is *ydʿ*. Thus the "reason" of Nebuchadnezzar is the acknowledgment that the world is indeed shaped through the intention and governance of Yahweh. Though the term *ydʿ* is here removed from the notion of "covenantal acknowledgment," it still participates in that covenantal reality whereby "knowing" consists in reckoning

knows is that power is held by the God who gives it as God wills.[22] Moreover, "God wills" always toward mercy. No amount of cunning or force can escape this intentionality of God. The rhetoric of Israel about the nations is rooted in the very character of Israel's God. The very character of God, however, lives in this rhetoric, which is not negotiable. The rhetoric assures that God is bound to Babylon even in the work of mercy. The rhetoric assures as well that Babylon is bound to mercy, because it is the purpose of this God who gives power to whom God wills. Nebuchadnezzar persistently has refused this reality of God's powerful resolve for mercy. His rule culminates in sanity, praise, majesty, splendor, and more greatness—however, only when he accepts God's rule of justice and abandons the option of autonomous pride. Nebuchadnezzar's reason is his "knowing," knowing the truth of Israel's rhetoric and knowing the one who is the primal subject of that rhetoric.

IV

I want now to situate my comments in relation to two addresses by distinguished occupants of this presidential office. I suggest that a contrast between the presidential addresses of James Muilenburg and Elisabeth Schüssler Fiorenza will illuminate the claim I am making for the theological intentionality of Israel's rhetoric.

On the one hand, my esteemed and beloved teacher James Muilenburg delivered his remarkable paper on rhetoric criticism in 1968.[23] It is among the most influential addresses—arguably the most influential—in the history of this office. It was Muilenburg who both noted and, in my view, enacted the decisive methodological turn in the guild toward literary analysis. One can hardly overstate the cruciality of what Muilenburg accomplished in his address, and more generally in his work.

Nonetheless, it is fair to say that Muilenburg's presentation of the importance of speech and of rhetoric was quite restricted. There is no hint in his presidential address of an awareness that speech is characteristically and inevitably a political act, an assertion of power that seeks to override some other rhetorical proposal of reality.[24] One can rightly say of Muilenburg's horizon either that he was not interested in such issues or that the whole critical awareness of the political

---

with in loyal obedience (cf. Jer 22:16). See H. B Huffmon, "The Treaty Background of Hebrew *Yada*'," *BASOR* 184 (1966) 31–37.

22. On this phrase, see Gowan, *When Man Becomes God*, 121–28, and its use in Jer 50:44.

23. James Muilenburg, "Form Criticism and Beyond," *JBL* 87 (1969) 1–18. [See pp. 119–37 in this volume.]

24. On the political dimension of all rhetoric, see Terry Eagleton, *Literary Theory, An Introduction* (Minneapolis: University of Minnesota Press, 1983); and Richard Harvey Brown, *Society as Text: Essays on Rhetoric, Reason, and Reality* (Chicago: Chicago University Press,

dimension of speech came much later to our discipline. In any case, it is time to move beyond such innocence in rhetorical criticism, as many in our field have done, to an awareness that the text entrusted to us is a major act of power. Our own interpretation is derivatively an act of power even as we pose, or perhaps especially as we pose, as objective in our interpretation. One can detect Muilenburg's lack of interest or attention to this issue at the end of his address, when, in juxtaposition to T. S. Eliot's phrase "raid on the inarticulate," he speaks of a "raid on the ultimate." I suggest that such a formulation bespeaks a kind of untroubled transcendentalism. Of course Muilenburg was not untroubled, and he knew the text was not untroubled. Nonetheless, he moves directly from the text to "the ultimate." Given what we know of the political power of rhetoric, we dare not speak of a "raid on the ultimate" unless we first speak of a "raid on the proximate."[25]

There are available to us a variety of theories of speech and rhetoric. The move beyond Muilenburg's innocent analysis of rhetoric can benefit from Jean-François Lyotard's presence in the conversation.[26] Lyotard suggests that speech is fundamentally agonistic, that it intends to enter into conflict with other speech claims. One figure he uses for this agonistic understanding is that speech is like the taking of tricks, the trumping of a communicational adversary, an assertively conflictual relation between tricksters.[27]

Without following Lyotard's complete postmodern program, I suggest that in the Society of Biblical Literature we shall more fully face the danger and significance of the texts entrusted to us, if we notice how these texts enter into conflict with other rhetorical options. Concerning my theme of mercy and empire, the several texts I have cited and their shared rhetorical claim do not constitute an innocent, neutral, or casual act. In each case the text is a deliberate act of combat against other views of public reality which live through other forms of rhetoric.

1987). Eagleton insists that traditional literary criticism has always refused to think of "the 'aesthetic' as separable from social determinants" (p. 206).

25. Eagleton writes: "Rhetoric, which was the received form of critical analysis all the way from ancient society to the eighteenth century, examined the way discourses are constructed in order to achieve certain effects.... Its particular interest lay in grasping such practices as forms of power and performance" (*Literary Theory*, 205). Muilenburg's focus on the "ultimate" may not give sufficient attention to "power and performance."

26. Jean-François Lyotard, *The Postmodern Condition: A Report on Knowledge* (Minneapolis: University of Minnesota Press, 1984) xi, 10, 16, and *passim*.

27. Lyotard's strictures are aimed especially against Jürgen Habermas's theory of "communicative action." On the latter, see Habermas, *Knowledge and Human Interests* (Boston: Beacon, 1968); and the utilization of Habermas by Richard J. Bernstein, *Beyond Objectivism and Relativism: Science, Hermeneutics, and Praxis* (Philadelphia: University of Pennsylvania Press, 1983). Lyotard holds that speech is much more adversarial than Habermas allows. I am suggesting that such an adversarial perspective is helpful in understanding what the rhetoric of Israel does concerning great concentrations of political power and the mandate of mercy. These texts we have considered are in no way innocent about their claims.

Thus the "trump" of this rhetoric seeks to override the assured autonomy of Babylon which dares to say, "I am and there is no other" (Isa 47:10). Conversely, this rhetoric enters into combat with Israel's rhetoric of complaint, which asserts that "there is none to comfort" (Lam 1:2, 17, 21); "the hand of the Lord is shortened" (Isa 50:2; 59:1) and "my way is hid from the Lord, and my right is disregarded by my God" (Isa 40:27). Both the arrogance of autonomous Babylon and the despair of doubting Israel generate, authorize, and commend a politics of brutality and intimidation.

The rhetorical trajectory I have traced refuses to leave either Israel or the empire at peace in its mistaken rhetoric. This counterrhetoric, this "strong poetry," which seeks to reread the empire and the faith community is a radically subversive urging.[28] Aside from the specific argument I have made about *empire and mercy*, I suggest that our scholarly work requires a theory of rhetoric that is more in keeping with the relentlessly critical, subversive, and ironic voice of the text which sets itself endlessly against more conventional and consensual speech. Thus we are at a moment not only "beyond form criticism," which Muilenburg had judged to be flat and mostly sterile, but also beyond rhetorical analysis, which is too enamored of style to notice speech as a means and source of power.[29]

On the other hand, in 1987, nineteen years after Muilenburg, Professor Elisabeth Schüssler Fiorenza delivered a major challenge to the society.[30] Alluding to the presidential addresses of James Montgomery in 1919, Henry Cadbury in 1937, and Leroy Waterman in 1947 as the only exceptions in presidential addresses, Schüssler Fiorenza protested against scholarly detachment and urged that members of the society have public responsibility in the midst of their scholarship.[31] She proposed that attention to rhetorical rather than scientific categories of scholarship would raise ethical-political issues as constitutive of the interpretive process. Moreover, she observed that no presidential address since 1947 had made any gesture in the direction of public responsibility.

---

28. My reference here of course is to Harold Bloom, *Anxiety of Influence: A Theory of Poetry* (New York: Oxford University Press, 1973). See William H. Rueckert, *Kenneth Burke and the Drama of Human Relations* (Minneapolis: University of Minnesota Press, 1963) 8–33, on Burke's early notion of rhetoric as counterstatement and counterdiscourse.

29. In reflecting on my critique of Professor Muilenburg, it occurred to me (and may to others), that my own statement appears to be an attempt to "trump" the influence of Muilenburg, thus to enact myself the force of rhetoric as Bloom and Lyotard suggest. That is, of course, far from my intention, but I am not unaware of that dynamic. Perhaps it could be suggested that the assignment of a presidential paper invites some such procedure.

30. Elisabeth Schüssler Fiorenza, "The Ethics of Interpretation: De-Centering Biblical Scholarship," *JBL* 107 (1988) 3–17. [See pp. 217–31 in this volume]

31. The addresses to which Schüssler Fiorenza alludes are James A. Montgomery, "Present Tasks of American Biblical Scholarship," *JBL* 38 (1919) 1–14 [pp. 17–26 in this volume]; Henry J. Cadbury, "Motives of Biblical Scholarship, *JBL* 56 (1937) 1–16 [pp. 33–43 in this volume]; and Leroy Waterman, "Biblical Studies in a New Setting," *JBL* 66 (1947) 1–14.

It is not my purpose to enter directly into an assessment of previous presidential addresses. It is, however, my purpose to reflect on the task and possibility of biblical theology. The dominant line of scholarly argument has insisted that biblical theology must be a descriptive and not a normative enterprise. Or to put it with Stendahl, it must be concerned with what the text "meant" and not with what the text "means."[32] In my judgment, that urging contains within it not only a considerable fear of authoritarianism but also a decision about "strict constructionism" concerning the text, a preoccupation with "authorial intent," and a positivistic notion of rhetoric, image, metaphor, and finally of text.

If we move in Muilenburg's direction of rhetoric and in Schüssler Fiorenza's direction of public rhetoric, and if we understand that the rhetoric of a classic text is always and again a political act, then it is, in my judgment, impossible to confine interpretation to a descriptive activity. The text, when we attend to it as a serious act of rhetoric, is inherently agonistic and makes its advocacy in the face of other advocacies.

The trajectory of texts I have cited may be taken as a case in point. There is no doubt that the primary references in these texts are the God of Israel and the Babylonian empire, a datable, locatable, identifiable historical entity. There is also no doubt, however, that the term "Babylon" has become a metaphor for great public power and that the term spills over endlessly into new contexts. A primary example of such spilling over is the power of the metaphor "Babylon" in the book of Revelation. The Babylon metaphor has exercised enormous influence in the church's thinking about "church and state." There is no doubt that that spilling over happens in the text itself and, as W. S. Towner has shown, that spillover has continued in any but the most flattened historical interpretation.[33] Thus we never have in the text the concrete historical reference to Babylon without at the same time the potential for spillover into other contexts. That spillover, I suggest, is not evoked simply by willful, imaginative interpreters, but is also

---

32. Krister Stendahl, "Biblical Theology, Contemporary," *IDB* 1. 418–32. See the careful and critical response to the categories of Stendahl by Ben C. Ollenburger, "Biblical Theology: Situating the Discipline," in *Understanding the Word* (ed. James T. Butler et al.; JSOTSup 37; Sheffield: JSOT Press, 1985) 37–62, and more fully in "What Krister Stendahl 'Meant'—A Normative Critique of Descriptive Biblical Theology," *HBT* 8 (1986) 61–98.

33. Towner, "Were the English Puritans 'the Saints of the Most High?'" (n. 17 above). Robert P. Carroll observes that Babylon has become "the symbol of hubristic opposition to Yahweh" (*Jeremiah*, 832). For an amazing example of such a spillover into contemporaneity, see Octavio Paz, *One Earth, Four or Five Worlds: Reflections on Contemporary History* (New York: Harcourt Brace Jovanovich, 1985) 151. In commenting on the power of the U.S. in the Latin American countries, Paz writes: "This contradiction revealed that the ambivalence of the giant was not imaginary but real: the country of Thoreau was also the country of Rossevelt-Nebuchadnezzar."

rooted in the metaphors and images themselves, which reach out in relentless sense making.[34]

Thus we have before us in these six texts concern for the God of Israel, who is the God of mercy, and the empire, which must be endlessly concerned with mercy. In attending to these texts, we seek to enter Israel's rhetoric and to notice Israel's agonistic intent in this set of metaphors. We read the text where we are. We read the text, as we are bound to read it, in the horizon of China's Tiananmen Square and Berlin's Wall, of Panama's Canal and South Africa's apartheid, of Kuwait's lure of oil. Or, among us, when we are daring, we may read the text in relation to the politics of publication, the play of power in promotion and tenure, the ambiguities of grantsmanship, and the seductions of institutional funding. We inevitably read the text where we sit. What happens in the act of theological interpretation is not an "application" of the text, nor an argument about contemporary policy, but an opened rhetorical field in which an urgent voice other than our own is set in the midst of imperial self-sufficiency and "colonial" despair.[35] We continue to listen while the voice of this text has its say against other voices which claim counterauthority.

Thus the agenda that Schüssler Fiorenza proposes is not an agenda extrinsic to the work of the Society. The spillover of the text into present social reality is not an "add-on" for relevance, but it is a scholarly responsibility that the text should have a hearing as a serious voice on its own terms. One need subscribe to no particular ideology to conclude that our public condition is one of deep crisis. Since we have invested our lives in these texts, one may ask directly how or in what way this text is an important voice in the contemporary array of competing rhetorics. Less directly, one may ask if we want to be the generation that withholds the text from its contemporary context, the generation that blocks the spillover that belongs intrinsically and inherently to the text. It is possible that we would be the generation that withholds the text from our contemporary world in the interest of objectivity and in the name of our privileged neutrality. Such an act, I should imagine, is a disservice not only to our time and place but also to our text. Such "objective" and "neutral" readings are themselves political acts in the service of entrenched and "safe" interpretation.

---

34. On the notion of spillover, I am utilizing the notion of Paul Ricoeur concerning "surplus" (*Interpretation Theory: Discourse and the Surplus of Meaning* [Fort Worth: Texas Christian University Press, 1976]). The term "surplus" as a noun is too static, however, and so I have chosen an active verb to suggest that the text actively moves beyond its intended or ostensive meaning to other meanings.

35. Mary Douglas and Aaron Wildavsky provide convenient phrasing for this context in their formulas "The Center is Complacent, The Border is Alarmed" (*Risk and Culture: An Essay on the Selection of Technical and Environmental Dangers* [Berkeley: University of California Press, 1982] 83–125).

It can, however, be otherwise. Without diminishing the importance of our critical work, it is possible that the text will be permitted freedom for its own fresh say. That, it seems to me, is a major interpretive issue among us. The possibility of a fresh reading requires attentiveness to the politics of rhetoric, to the strange, relentless power of these words to subvert and astonish.[36] When our criticism allows the rhetoric of the text to be voiced, the way mercy crowds Babylon continues to be a crucial oddity, even in our own reading. Those of us who care most about criticism may attend with greater grace to readings of the text that move even beyond our criticism.

---

36. On fresh and liberated readings, see William A. Beardslee, "Ethics anid Hermeneutics," in *Text and Logos: The Humanistic Interpretation of the New Testament* (ed. Theodore W. Jennings; Atlanta: Scholars Press, 1990) 15–32. Beardslee concludes his proposal for a reading of the text that will permit a "relational, participatory view of justice" with this comment: "This path will move away from the rigid image of hermeneutics as 'translation,' which presupposes a fixed element to be re-expressed. It will contribute to the formation of a hermeneutics that can fully recognize the strangeness of the text, which offers no 'pure' disclosure, and yet can release the ethical power that successive generations have found in an encounter with the New Testament." Beardslee's proposal is congruent with what I see happening in these "mercy/Babylon" texts.

JESUS THE VICTIM*

Helmut Koester
Harvard University

I. THE ORIGINAL QUEST OF THE HISTORICAL JESUS

In the second half of the nineteenth century, Albrecht Ritschl, the influential theologian who taught for many decades at the University of Göttingen, defined the kingdom of God as the achievement of the universal moral community. This, he proposed, is the goal of the divine action in the world and the purpose of the ministry of Jesus. As God's action is motivated by his love, Jesus incorporates this love in his teaching as well as in his suffering and death. Jesus indeed *is* God, but only insofar as he represents fully God's moral purpose for humankind. Nothing in the ministry of Jesus documents Jesus' divinity in metaphysical or supernatural terms. Rather, this divinity is revealed because Jesus as a human being remained faithful to his vocation to the very end, in spite of the resistance and hatred of the world. What Jesus demands of us is to make the kingdom of God a reality in this world; we can fulfill this demand if we live the life of love and patience that has been revealed in Jesus. The goal of the kingdom of God is the uniting of the entire world as a community, in which the love of God is realized by all as the moral purpose of God's creation and of all human life.

It was this understanding of Jesus' divinity, as wholly defined by Jesus' faithfulness to God's moral purpose, that was called into question by the rebellious young scholars of the Göttingen history-of-religions school: Johannes Weiss, William Wrede, Hermann Gunkel, Wilhelm Bousset, Ernst Troeltsch, later also Hugo Gressmann, Wilhelm Heitmüller, and Rudolf Otto. Hermann Gunkel's dissertation, "The Activities of the Holy Spirit," published in 1888,[1] ended once and for all an understanding of the Holy Spirit as the guiding principle of institutional-

---

* The presidential address delivered 23 November 1991 at the annual meeting of the Society of Biblical Literature held at the Allis Plaza Hotel, Kansas City, Missouri.

1. H. Gunkel, *Die Wirkungen des heiligen Geistes nach der populären Anschauung der apostolischen Zeit und der Lehre des Apostels Paulus* (3d ed.; Göttingen: Vandenhoeck & Ruprecht, 1909).

ized religion and secularized moral action—an understanding that dominated, as Gunkel stated, "exegetes who are influenced by unhistorical and rationalistic thinking."[2] On the contrary, he argued, the Bible understands "spirit" as the uncontrollable and supernatural power of miracle, irrational inspiration, and divine action.

Johannes Weiss's book *The Preaching of Jesus about the Kingdom of God* appeared a few years later in 1892.[3] It no longer offended his father-in-law, Albrecht Ritschl, who had died three years earlier. This book, as well as those of his other Göttingen friends, advertised the discovery that the rationalistic and moralistic categories of their time were not capable of comprehending the early Christian concept of the kingdom of God. Whereas these categories had their roots, as Johannes Weiss states, in Kant's philosophy and in the theology of enlightenment, Jesus' concept of the kingdom of God was informed by the apocalyptic mythology of ancient Judaism and was thoroughly eschatological, messianic, and supernatural.

Albert Schweitzer characterized Johannes Weiss's work as the beginning of a new area in the life-of-Jesus research. Recognizing its significance, he asks why the book did not have an immediate impact:

> Perhaps ... according to the usual canons of theological authorship, the book was much too short—only sixty-seven pages—and too simple to allow its full significance to be realized. And yet it is precisely this simplicity which makes it one of the most important works in historical theology. It seems to break a spell. It closes one epoch and begins another.[4]

What was characteristic for this new epoch of the view of Jesus? Albert Schweitzer described this well at the conclusion of his *Quest of the Historical Jesus*:

> The study of the Life of Jesus ... set out in quest of the historical Jesus, believing that when it had found Him it could bring Him straight into our own time as a Teacher and Savior.... The historical Jesus of whom the criticism of the future ... will draw the portrait, can never render modern theology the services which it claimed from its own half-historical, half-modern Jesus. He will be a Jesus who was Messiah, and lived as such, either on the ground of literary fiction of

---

2. Ibid., iii.

3. J. Weiss, *Die Predigt Jesu vom Reiche Gottes* (Göttingen: Vandenhoeck & Ruprecht, 1892; 2d ed. 1900; 3d ed. 1964).

4. Albert Schweitzer, *The Quest of the Historical Jesus: A Critical Study of Its Progress from Reimarus to Wrede* (New York: Macmillan, 1959). This work was first published in the year 1906 under the title *Von Reimarus zu Wrede: Eine Geschichte der Leben-Jesu-Forschung* (Tübingen: Mohr). The first English translation of the second edition of Schweitzer's work (now entitled *Geschichte der Leben-Jesu-Forschung*) appeared in 1910 (London: Black).

the earliest Evangelist, or on the ground of a purely eschatological Messianic conception.[5]

II. THE NEW QUEST OF THE HISTORICAL JESUS

The insights of the history-of-religions school dominated the interpretation of the preaching of Jesus and his ministry for the first half of the twentieth century in critical New Testament scholarship.[6] What has come to be known as "A New Quest of the Historical Jesus" was quite well aware of the danger of modernizing Jesus. Ernst Käsemann, who opened the "new quest" with his lecture of 1953[7] vehemently rejected the continuation of the old type of life-of-Jesus study.[8] The new quest of the historical Jesus was informed by the search for the historical foundation of the Christian kerygma.

It had no interest in bypassing the proclamation of the early Christian community in order to get uninhibited access to a real and original historical Jesus. On the contrary, James M. Robinson, who has coined the formulation "A New Quest of the Historical Jesus,"[9] had titled his original lecture "The Kerygma and the Quest of the Historical Jesus."[10] What was at stake here was the validity of the Christian kerygma. Is this kerygma bound to a myth, a mere legend? Or is it formed as a response to the life and death of a human being and to his words and actions?

Like Albert Schweitzer's "(old) quest of the historical Jesus," the "new quest" also rejected unequivocally all life-of-Jesus study. Käsemann insisted that Christian faith can never rest on such knowledge; it remains bound to the proclamation of the kerygma, in whatever form.[11] For those who are inclined to disregard the Christian kerygma and who want to go directly to the historical Jesus, the search will never produce anything but an artificial justification for their cause, however worthy.

---

5. Ibid., 398–99.
6. For a general survey of the influence of the work of Johannes Weiss, see Dieter Georgi, "Leben-Jesu Theologie/Leben-Jesu Forschung,"' *TRE* 20. 570–72 (bibliography pp. 573–75).
7. E. Käsemann, "Die Frage nach dem historischen Jesus," *ZTK* 51 (1954) 125–53; Eng. trans. "The Problem of the Historical Jesus," in Ernst Käsemann, *Essays on New Testament Themes* (SBT 41; London: SCM, 1964) 15–47.
8. See his critical discussion of Joachim Jeremias's call for a return to the Jesus of history: "The 'Jesus of History' Controversy," in Ernst Käsemann, *New Testament Questions of Today* (Philadelphia: Fortress, 1969) 24–35.
9. This is the title of James M. Robinson's book in its English edition (SBT 25; London: SCM, 1960).
10. The German edition of his book retains the original title: *Kerygma und historischer Jesus* (2d ed.; Zurich/Stuttgart: Zwingli, 1967).
11. Käsemann, "The 'Jesus of History' Controversy," 24–35.

Nevertheless, almost exactly one hundred years after the first publication of the discoveries of the history-of-religions school, the renaissance of the quest of the historical Jesus has returned full circle to a position that is not unlike that of Albrecht Ritschl and of the portraits of Jesus drawn by the nineteenth-century authors of a "life of Jesus."

In a recent article, Marcus Borg describes two fundamental features of this renaissance: (1) "The eschatological consensus that dominated much of this century's Jesus research ... had seriously eroded." (2) "We ... not only know more 'facts' about first-century Palestine, but we also understand the dynamics of that social world better."[12] To be sure, the degree to which eschatology is seen as informing Jesus' ministry is different in these portraits discussed by Marcus Borg.[13] But all more recent attempts want to reconstruct a historical Jesus while bypassing the early Christian kerygma.

Such moves are consistent with the primary methodological approaches to those materials that can be assigned to the historical Jesus. The various portraits of Jesus that have come to us in ancient Christian materials are the result of the theologizing of the early Christian churches. It seems a matter of course that one isolates those units of the tradition which are not completely altered, or even altogether created, by eschatological and other theological interpretations, which were put forward later by the early church. What must be stripped away are early attempts at gnosticizing or catholicizing Jesus' message, adherence to patriarchal, anti-feminist, and hierarchical structures of society, the desire to establish rule

---

12. M. Borg, "Portraits of Jesus in Contemporary North American Scholarship," *HTR* 84 (1991) 1–22. The recent book by Dale Allison (*The End of the Ages Has Come: An Early Interpretation of the Passion and Resurrection of Jesus* [Philadelphia: Fortress, 1985] esp. 101–14), once more arguing for the eschatological character of Jesus' preaching of the kingdom of God, seems to be incompatible with a new consensus that has emerged from the current renaissance of scholarship concerning Jesus' preaching and ministry.

13. E. P. Sanders depicts a historical Jesus who is entirely in agreement with certain eschatological and messianic concepts of the Judaism of his time (*Jesus and Judaism* [Philadelphia: Fortress, 1985]). For Richard Horsley, Jesus belongs firmly to the radical prophetic, and in this sense "eschatological," tradition of Israel; see his *Bandits, Prophets and Messiahs: Popular Movements at the Time of Jesus* (with John S. Hanson; Minneapolis: Winston-Salem, 1985); idem, *Jesus and the Spiral of Violence* (San Francisco: Harper & Row, 1987); idem, *Sociology and the Jesus Movement* (New York: Crossroad, 1989). Burton Mack denies any relationship of Jesus' ministry to Judaism and its apocalyptic mythology (*A Myth of Innocence: Mark and Christian Origins* [Philadelphia: Fortress, 1988). For Elisabeth Schüssler Fiorenza, whatever could be called eschatological in the earliest Jesus movement is integrated in Jesus understanding of himself as the prophet and messenger of Sophia *(In Memory of Her: A Feminist Theological Reconstruction of Christian Origins* [New York: Crossroad, 1983]). Marcus J. Borg, although he depicts Jesus as part of the charismatic-prophetic tradition of Israel, also denies the essential significance of eschatology in Jesus message and ministry; see his *Conflict, Holiness and Politics in the Teachings of Jesus* (New York/Toronto: Mellen, 1984); idem, *Jesus: A New Vision* (San Francisco: Harper & Row, 1987).

and order in religious communities with their worship, liturgy, creeds, and systems of subordination. What emerges in all instances is a portrait of Jesus, drawn as scientifically verifiable history, which is free of these secondary accretions and alterations. It makes little difference here, whether one ascribes the newfound insights just to Jesus himself or to Jesus *and* to the earliest group of his followers, no longer called "the early church" but "the Jesus movement."[14] The latter approach is certainly more judicious. However, in each case one is dealing with phenomena that are assigned to dates earlier than the first Christian texts, both the Pauline letters and the earliest Gospels, because it is evident that the deterioration into an ecclesiastical establishment and organized religion was a very early process. Thus the very brief period of the ministry of Jesus and an equally brief period after Jesus' death emerge as the only enlightened time, which might have been extended for a few more decades only in the isolation of the rural areas of Galilee among followers of Jesus who ultimately composed the Synoptic Sayings Source. In any case, while the "new quest," thirty years ago, was concerned with the discontinuity between Jesus the preacher and the kerygma in which Jesus had become the object of the proclamation, the more recent portraits of Jesus find a continuity between Jesus' historical sayings and the use of these sayings among his followers—and ultimately between Jesus and ourselves.

The tendency in recent scholarship toward a noneschatological Jesus is, of course, closely related to the discovery of the *Gospel of Thomas* and to the hypothesis of an earlier stage of the Synoptic Sayings Source (Q), in which the apocalyptic expectation of the coming Son of man was still absent[15]—a hypothesis that I myself have supported. It is questionable, however, whether this early stage of Q can really be defined as noneschatological,[16] even more doubtful whether one can draw from such observations the conclusion that the preaching of the historical Jesus had no relation to eschatology.[17]

Other factors that contribute to the portrait of a noneschatological preaching of the historical Jesus are the terms of our own view of the world, which leaves little room for reckoning with supernatural powers such as God and Satan, not to mention apocalyptic mythologies. We are again on the way toward a human Jesus who is just like one of us, one who holds values that are very close to our ideolog-

---

14. The word "church" seems to have very negative connotations; "movement" seems to be preferable today. I cannot help but remember that Hitler and the National Socialists called their own endeavor a "movement" (*Die national-sozialistische Bewegung*).

15. John S. Kloppenborg, *The Formation of Q: Trajectories in Ancient Wisdom Collections* (Studies in Antiquity and Ancient Christianity; Philadelphia: Fortress, 1987); see also my *Ancient Christian Gospels* (Philadelphia: Trinity Press International, 1990) 133–49.

16. The myth of Wisdom is in itself eschatological. The Wisdom of Solomon speaks of a future or transcendental vindication of the rejected righteous people.

17. Even the *Gospel of Thomas* presupposes, and criticizes, a tradition of eschatological sayings of Jesus.

ical commitments, a Jesus who is a social reformer and who attacks patriarchal orders, a Jesus who, as a real human person, can stand as an example and inspiration for worthy causes. This stands in stark contrast to such scholars as Johannes Weiss and Albert Schweitzer. Their worldview did not include an eschatological orientation either, but they acknowledged that Jesus' mythical and eschatological worldview was an utterly strange feature that left them bewildered and did not allow the development of an image of Jesus that would fit their categories.

Of the Jesus of Paul and of the Gospels, Albert Schweitzer knew that he is a life-giving power, but at the same time one who "Himself destroys again the truth and goodness which His Spirit creates in us, so that it cannot rule the world."[18] However, of the historical Jesus he remarks: "We can ... scarcely imagine the long agony in which the historical view of the life of Jesus came to birth. And even when He was once more recalled to life, He was still, like Lazarus of old, bound hand and foot with grave-clothes."[19] And Albert Schweitzer had enough courage and honesty to design his personal moral and religious commitment without the blessings of the Jesus of history.

III. THE HISTORICAL JESUS AND THE CHRISTIAN PROCLAMATION

For whatever reason, there is no question that the true historical Jesus, that extraordinary human person, remains a very intriguing and attractive topic even today. The widespread interest in the newly discovered *Gospel of Thomas* proves the point. Perhaps this gospel reveals the real and uncontaminated Jesus as well as his most original words. Be it simple curiosity, be it in the service of a serious religious search, or be it in the interest of a vital ideological commitment, to have Jesus on one's side is evidently important even in the postmodern late twentieth century. The general public's interest in, and sometimes very hostile reaction to, the findings of the "Jesus Seminar" illustrates the point. On the other hand, one might refer to the continuing claim of evangelical Christians that it is Jesus himself, and he alone, who provides the foundation for their religious commitment. Whether it is the Jesus one seeks as a personal savior, or a historical Jesus who might respond to a cherished cause—the question is still the same. The only difference is that critical scholars might claim that, as historians, they have some advantages over the more simple-minded believers in Jesus as their savior, a more accurate knowledge of the historical and social situation in first-century Palestine, a better critical ability to identify sources, a more learned approach to the reconstruction of past history. But is the fundamental question really different?

The problem of the historical Jesus has been short-circuited here, because access to the historical Jesus as a person has become the very *first* item on the

---

18. Schweitzer, *Quest of the Historical Jesus*, 2.
19. Ibid., 4.

agenda. Such an approach has its pitfalls, because it isolates persons of the past from their historical context and from the situation in which those who transmitted all available information were called into a departure for new shores. Isolation from the historical context is especially hazardous in the case of Jesus, as also in the case of Socrates or of Julius Caesar. All three, Socrates, Caesar, and Jesus were either executed or murdered. That was experienced by their followers as an event that radicalized their critical interpretation of that world. For Plato, the historical Socrates could no longer explain the world that had radically changed because of his death. For Augustus, what mattered was Caesar's testament that gave him the legitimation and the vision to create a new world. For the disciples of Jesus, his execution implied a denial of all values of a world order that had made Jesus its victim. In Plato's dialogues, Socrates speaks as one who has already experienced that the soul is immortal. In Augustus's politics, the murdered dictator became the *divus Julius,* the god Caesar. Jesus' followers endeavored to write paradoxical biographies of a Jesus whose words and works are those of a being who had already died and had risen to a new life.

While a reflection about Jesus' death plays no central role in the more recent portraits of Jesus, all early Christian traditions are acutely aware of this fact. All sources—and this includes the tradition of the wisdom sayings and its theology—agree that the tradition about Jesus must be seen in this light: his rejection, suffering, and death. Whatever the personal aspirations and hopes of Jesus of Nazareth were, his message of the coming of God's kingdom did not leave him as the victor, but as the victim. The entire tradition about the historical Jesus is bound into the testimony of his followers, who were charged to design a new order of the world in which the victim was vindicated.

To be sure, some went out to imitate the great Jesus in their own performance of miracles and religious demonstrations. Jesus as a great person became the standard for following him. This portrait of Jesus as the divine human being has haunted especially the spirit of Western culture ever since. It became important and frightening in the nineteenth-century idea of the genius, from Goethe to Nietzsche and Adolf Hitler,[20] a development that was not unrelated to the life-of-Jesus research.

In another instance, the message of Jesus the victim was spelled out in more metaphysical terms. Jesus was seen as Wisdom/Sophia, who had come into this world but was despised and rejected and so returned to her heavenly abode (John 1:5, 9–13; *Gos. Thom.* 28). The response of the believer here is the development of realized eschatology and wisdom mysticism as we find it in the *Gospel of Thomas* and among the opponents of Paul in 1 Corinthians.[21] Such belief has its social consequences; the regular bonds of patriarchal family structures and economic

---

20. See my essay "The Divine Human Being," *HTR* 78 (1985) 243–52.
21. See my *Ancient Christian Gospels: Their History and Development* (Philadelphia: Trinity Press International, 1990) 55–62, 124–28.

dependence were broken down in favor of freedom and equality. In this understanding, the followers of Jesus competed with other messages of nonpolitical and sometimes noneschatological views of salvation, for example, those propagated by Neopythagorean philosophers and Cynic preachers, or by Jewish mystics and apologists like Philo of Alexandria.

However, Jesus as a victim was also understood as a political message, in which the early Christian proclamation was confronting the political eschatology of the Roman imperial period, both in its pagan and Jewish forms. The components are explicitly eschatological and political, with all their social, communal, and revolutionary implications. It is decisive that the core of the message of these Christian missionaries was the proclamation of a ruler of the new age who was the victim of the established authoritarian political order. Since this order was in turn based on an ideology of realized eschatology, it was impossible for Jesus' followers to ignore the realized eschatology of imperial Rome.

One could discuss the confrontation of early Christian communities with several variants of ancient Jewish eschatology and apocalyptic theology; however, the confrontation with the eschatology of Rome was decisive for the formation of the message of Jesus the victim. Indeed, the dying Jesus is explicitly confronted with the Roman order of realized eschatology in the inscription on his cross: "Jesus of Nazareth, King of the Jews" (John 19:9; cf. Mark 15:26 par.). His death was a political execution by Roman authorities—it must be remembered that only at a later time did the Christians assign the responsibility for Jesus' death to the Jewish authorities. The name Pontius Pilate remained the symbol for the confrontation with Rome and its political order. The proclamation of Jesus' vindication was as eschatological as Rome's ideology. It should be considered within the general framework of the Roman imperial propaganda of a realized eschatology.

IV. THE AGE OF AUGUSTUS AS REALIZED ESCHATOLOGY

Hellenistic utopian concepts played an important role as early as the founding of Heliopolis by the slave Andronicus, when the last king of Pergamum gave his country to Rome by testament in 133 BCE. Also the slave insurrections of Eunus of Apamea (136–132 BCE) and Spartacus (73–71 BCE) seem to have been inspired by utopian revolutionary ideas. The strong influence of Hellenistic utopian concepts on the eschatology and organization of the Essenes has been demonstrated by Doron Mendels.[22] To be sure, Jewish apocalypticism had its special roots and its special features. But, in the Roman imperial period, it was nevertheless part and parcel of the general eschatological spirit of the time,[23] and it was even

---

22. D. Mendels, "Hellenistic Utopia and the Essenes," *HTR* 72 (1979) 207–22.
23. See also the *Jewish Sibylline Oracles*; see J. J. Collins, "Sibylline Oracles" in *OTP* 1. 317–417. A significant collection of relevant essays was edited by David Hellholm, *Apocalypticism in the Mediterranean World and the Near East* (Tübingen: Mohr-Siebeck, 1979).

present in the spiritualized eschatology of Jewish Gnosticism that rejected the entire this-wordly reality as bondage to evil powers. Once Augustan Rome had adopted these eschatological and utopian ideals and domesticated them for its own purposes, every movement of liberation would naturally confront the state-sponsored realized eschatology of the Caesars.

Rome's political eschatology grew out of the announcement of doom that had come over the entire political and natural world:

> Already the second generation is destroyed in the civil war,
> Rome falls into ruin through its own power.

With these words, Horace begins his *16th Epode,* written in the midst of the civil wars that ravaged Rome during the first century BCE. In the verses that follow, Horace calls for the emigration by ship over the high seas, like the boat people who fled from the horrors of Vietnam, for all those who still have a vision of a blessed future and who have the courage of hope. They will return only after a cosmic catastrophe and not until the establishment of a new paradise will signal the beginning of an eschatological restitution. The Appenine Mountains will plunge into the ocean, and then the paradise will come when the tiger mates with the deer and the falcon with the dove, when the earth grows fruit without the hurt of the plow and when honey flows from the bark of the oak.

Dieter Georgi has called attention to the prophetic eschatology of the Roman poets.[24] Indeed, from the time of Caesar to the false Neros of the time of Domitian, the Roman world was dominated by prophetic eschatology. It was an eschatology that was political, revolutionary, and saturated with the sense of doom and the expectation of paradise. The vision of paradise appears in Virgil's famous *Fourth Ecloge.*

> Of themselves, untended, will the she goats then bring home their udders swollen with milk, while flocks afield shall of the monstrous lion have no fear.... No more shall mariner sail, nor pine-tree bark ply traffic on the sea, but every land shall all things bear alike.... The sturdy ploughman shall loose yoke from steer....

Virgil adds two other elements to the eschatological vision: first, the birth of the divine child shall usher in "the last age by Cumae's Sibyl sung," "the child of gods, great progeny of Jove"; and second, the end-time will fulfill the promises and the righteousness of the primordial time—Virgil accomplished this vision in his great epic, the *Aeneid,* in which he connects the destiny of Rome to the mythic origins described in Homer's *Iliad.* Eduard Norden argued that these Roman eschato-

---

24. D. Georgi, "Who Is the True Prophet?" in *Christians among Jews and Gentiles: Essays in Honor of Krister Stendahl* (ed. George MacRae, George Nickelsberg, and Albert Sundberg; Philadelphia: Fortress, 1986) 100–26.

logical expectations had their origins in the same Egyptian prophecies that also influenced Isaiah 9–11 and, in turn, Jewish and Christian eschatology.[25]

Augustus was not only aware of these prophetic eschatological poems; he consciously announced his new order of peace as their fulfillment. Horace, two decades after the writing of his prophecies of doom, commissioned by Augustus to compose the festive ode[26] for the secular celebrations in the year 17 BCE, summarizes the themes of the prophecy in the form of a realized eschatology: the new age is beginning right now. The reference to Troy and to Aeneas indicates that the promises of the story of Rome's foundation are now fulfilled. Apollo (Phoebus) as the god of the new age is addressed in the very beginning and several times throughout the ode. Fruitfulness of the earth and fertility of the womb will characterize the new saeculum, as peace, honor, and respect have already begun to return.

The Ara Pacis, erected by Augustus in the year 9 BCE to commemorate the new age of peace, repeats in its sculpture the same eschatological topics. The most exquisitely executed relief sculptures show on the western side Aeneas sacrificing to the *penates publici*, the "Great Gods,'" whom he had brought from Samothrace to Rome; on the eastern side *Terra* is depicted, set in a paradisiac idyll.

Realized eschatology appears also in the inscriptions that record the introduction of the new Julian calendar. The following is a quotation from the inscription of Priene from the year 9 BCE:

> Because providence that has ordered our life in a divine way … and since the Caesar through his appearance (ἐπιφανείς) has exceeded the hopes of all former good messages (εὐαγγέλια), surpassing not only the benefactors who came before him, but also leaving no hope that anyone in the future would surpass him, and since for the world the birthday of the god was the beginning of his good messages (Ἦρξεν δὲ τῷ κόσμῳ τὴν δι' αὐτόν [sc. τὸν Σεβαστὸν] εὐαγγελίων ἡ γενέθλιος ἡμέρα τοῦ θεοῦ [may it therefore be decided that…].[27]

There are several characteristic features of this Roman imperial eschatology: (1) The new age is the fulfillment of prophecy, and it corresponds to the promises

---

25. E. Norden, *Die Geburt des Kindes: Die Geschichte einer religiösen Idee* (Leipzig: Teubner, 1924; reprint: Darmstadt: Wissenschaftliche Buchgesellschaft, 1958). Georgi suggests that Horace was directly influenced by Jewish missionary theology ("Who Is the True Prophet?" 110).

26. The *Carmen saeculare* (Hans Färber and Wilhelm Schöne, eds., *Horaz: Sämtliche Werke* [Darmstadt: Wissenschaftliche Buchgesellschaft, 1982]).

27. For the entire Greek text of the inscription, see Wilhelm Dittenberger, *Orientis Graeci inscriptiones selectae* (2 vols.; Hildesheim: Olms, 1960) #458, vol. 2, pp. 48–60. The text quoted above is found in lines 40–42. The Greek text of the portion of the inscription quoted above is conveniently reprinted with a brief commentary in *Griechische Inschriften als Zeugnisse des privaten und öffentlichen Lebens* (ed. Gerhard Pfohl; Tusculum; Munich: Heimeran, n.d.) 134–35.

given in the primordial age. (2) The new age includes this earth as well as the world of the heavens: Apollo as Helios is the god of the new age; the zodiac sign of the month of Augustus's birth appears on the shields of the soldiers. (3) The new age is universal; it includes all nations: the new solar calendar is introduced by the vote of the people of the cities all over the empire. (4) There is an enactment of the new age through the official celebrations of the empire, like the secular festivities of the year 17 BCE, mirrored by the subsequent introduction of Caesarean games in many places. (5) The new age has a savior figure, the greatest benefactor of all times, the *divi filius,* usually translated into Greek as υἱὸς τοῦ θεοῦ— "Son of God"—the victorious Augustus.

V. Jesus and Eschatology

After Jesus' death, his followers had to answer the question, Who was this, whose cross had borne the inscription "Jesus of Nazareth, King of the Jews"? Their answer was unanimous: he was the victim of the world and the age, whose end he had announced. That he was proclaimed now as the one who was living, who had been raised from the dead, who was present in the power of the Spirit, does not simply mean that he was victorious after all. The mythical symbolism in which such beliefs about Jesus' vindication are described is a secondary question. It does not matter whether it was the pouring out of the Spirit, or the appearances of the living Jesus, or the witness of his resurrection, or the recognition that his words remained as a life-giving power—in every instance Jesus' followers believed that the new world and the new age had arrived, or could be obtained, through the one who was rejected, who suffered, who did not find a home in this world, and who had been put to death.

Therefore, the proclamation was thoroughly eschatological. It pointed to a future that was radically different from that promised by any of the ideologies and realities of which Jesus had become a victim. As a victim of this world and of its political powers, Jesus could not be resurrected, as it were, as a great human being, an insightful preacher, and an example of moral and religious virtues. The message—though founded in an actual event within human history, a real human life, and in words spoken by this human being—could no longer rely on the memory of the life, words, and deeds of a human individual, no matter how great and powerful. On the contrary, the portrait of the great human or even superhuman personality itself belonged to the world that had killed Jesus.

This proclamation has found its most radical expression in Paul, who insists that we no longer know Christ according to the flesh,[28] and for whom "imitation of Christ" is identical with becoming nothing oneself and everything for all

---

28. For the discussion of this paradoxical statement in 2 Cor 5:16, see Dieter Georgi, *The Opponents of Paul in Second Corinthians* (Philadelphia: Fortress, 1986).

people (see 1 Cor 10:32–11:1; Phil 3:17–19). Moreover, the Gospels of the NT make clear that discipleship, following after Jesus, is identical with taking one's cross and giving away one's life (Mark 8:34–38 par.)[29] Even in the *Gospel of Thomas*, Jesus the Living One cannot be understood by his disciples as someone who is just like them. On the contrary, Jesus is always beyond their grasp, part of a new world that the disciples want to measure with the yardstick of a world that has passed: "His disciples said to him, 'Twenty-four prophets spoke in Israel, and all of them spoke in you.' He said to them, 'You have omitted the one living in your presence and have spoken (only) of the dead'" (*Gos. Thom.* 52).[30]

But were the life and words of Jesus of Nazareth indeed eschatological? Or were the eschatological schemata of his early followers subsequently assigned to a Jesus whose original ministry and message did not contain any eschatological elements? That seems very unlikely. Within a year or two of Jesus' death, Paul persecuted the followers of Jesus because of their eschatological proclamation. That leaves precious little time in which the followers of a noneschatological Jesus could have developed an entirely new eschatological perspective without a precedent in the preaching and actions of Jesus.[31] The problem is not whether Jesus of Nazareth preached an eschatological message. Rather, the difficulty arises from the fact that the shape and the details of Jesus' eschatology can be discerned only insofar as they are refracted in the eschatological imagery of Jesus' followers.[32] What one finds in the relevant sources is a bewildering variety of traditional eschatologies, used as the framework for the Christian message, ranging from the Messiah, Wisdom/Sophia, and the coming Son of man to Temple ideology and to the Pauline proclamation of Jesus' resurrection as the turning point of the ages. How can one decide which of these refractions represents most legitimately what Jesus himself had preached?

That question cannot be answered by choosing one of these eschatologies and assigning it to the historical Jesus. The church had to respond to political and metaphysical systems based on ideologies of eschatological fulfillment. This response had to be given in the terms of whatever these ideologies proclaimed and could not simply be informed by whatever Jesus had said and done. After Jesus' death, continuity was no longer possible.

---

29. The Gospel of Luke is the only exception; here Jesus indeed appears as an example of piety and, in his death, as the exemplary martyr.

30. Trans. Thomas O. Lambdin, in Ron Cameron, *The Other Gospels: Non-Canonical Gospel Texts* (Philadelphia: Westminster, 1982).

31. Paul was called within not more than five years of Jesus' death, probably within two or three years, and he was called to proclaim an eschatological message that he had previously persecuted (Gal 1:13–16), namely, that the new age had begun with the resurrection of Jesus.

32. The only eschatological term that can be assigned to Jesus with certainty is "rule of God" (βασιλεία τοῦ θεοῦ); see esp. Luke (Q) 6:20; 13:28–29. Perhaps also the term "this moment" (ὁ καιρὸς οὗτος) belongs to the eschatological terms of Jesus; see Luke (Q) 12:54–56.

The coming of the new age through "Jesus the victim" implied a complete reversal of all political, social, and religious values that were held sacred and holy in the world of ancient Judaism as well as in the Roman system of realized eschatology. How did the reversal of traditionally accepted values, which became the very basis of the founding of communities of the new age and the new world, correspond to the ministry of Jesus of Nazareth?[33] If that correspondence cannot be established, "we may be," as Käsemann warned, "superimposing the predicate 'Christian' on an understanding of existence and of the world, in which Jesus acts merely as occasioner and Christ merely as a mythological cipher."[34] Were the new eschatological values proclaimed by the Christians true to the preaching of Jesus of Nazareth?

Critical historical inquiry may be able to establish that in the earliest tradition of Jesus' sayings he himself proclaimed and lived such a reversal of values, that serving others rather than lording over them was the order of the rule of God,[35] that lending to those who cannot repay their loan was the way of the new age (Luke 6:34),[36] that loving one's enemy was the only possible response to hostility (Luke [Q] 6:27–28), that people from all the nations of the world would be invited to the feast of the kingdom (Luke [Q] 13:28–29), and that those who had nothing to lose—the poor, those who were hungry, and those who weep— would inherit it (Luke [Q] 6:20–21). Perhaps there is a vision of the community of the new age, of the rule of God, in whatever fragments of Jesus' preaching can be discerned. It is a vision that is eschatological, albeit often expressed in words that must be classified as wisdom sayings. It is a vision that reckons with God's coming, a coming that begins to be realized in the community of those who dare to follow him. And it is a universalistic vision of a banquet in which privileges of status, wealth, and religious heritage are no longer relevant. But there is no guarantee that such sayings or the inaugural sermon of Q (Luke [Q] 6:27-49) represent the preaching of the historical Jesus. Moreover, it is interesting that sayings of highly charged mythical content are rarely assigned to this Jesus by modern interpreters. In any case, the fragmentary character of these texts, even if some sayings originate with the historical Jesus, does not permit the writing of the story of his life and message—not to speak of a "reconstruction" of the historical Jesus. Such an attempt only reveals once more the preoccupation with the search for the great human personality. It may bypass the real challenge that arises from early Christian texts, namely, to understand our world on the basis of criteria

---

33. J. M. Robinson has demonstrated that Paul's description of the experiences of the ministry of the apostles in 2 Corinthians may correspond very closely to the preaching of Jesus, although there is no direct reference to any "historical" words of Jesus (*A New Quest*, 124-25).

34. Käsemann, "The 'Jesus of History' Controversy," 44.

35. Mark 10:42-44 may be an original saying of Jesus; however, Mark 10:45 ("the Son of man has come to give his life as a ransom for many") must be assigned to the later community.

36. If Jesus was a teacher of secular wisdom, this saying is an invitation to bankruptcy.

that have their origin in the proclamation of Jesus the victim. We have enough talk about great personalities of religious traditions. After Jesus died, his followers recognized that Jesus as a great human person would mean nothing, but that the kingdom of God had to be proclaimed as the utopia of a new community, a new political order, and indeed a new world.

Social Class as an Analytic and Hermeneutical Category in Biblical Studies*

Norman K. Gottwald
New York Theological Seminary

It has long been recognized that differentials in wealth and power figure prominently in biblical texts and traditions. Although the presence of the rich and the powerful within the Bible—shadowed by their poor and powerless counterparts—is widely noted and commented on, the formative dynamics and far-reaching effects of grossly unequal concentrations of wealth and power have seldom been conceptualized in a fashion empirical and systematic enough to yield sustained exegetical and hermeneutical insights.

This theoretical lag in analyzing and explaining wealth and power in the Bible follows from three sources which reinforce one another. The first is the traditional hegemony of religious and theological categories in biblical studies, which stubbornly resists sociology as a threat to the religious integrity and authority of scripture. The second source is the controversy within the social sciences themselves over whether wealth and power should be understood principally along structural-functional or conflictual lines.[1] The third source is the embedment of biblical studies in a pervasive capitalist ethos that blunts or denies the existence of significant structural divisions in society. Together these factors discourage and inhibit efforts to understand wealth and power in the Bible as historically generated and reproduced phenomena. Extremes of wealth and power tend to make their appearance in biblical studies—as in popular opinion about contemporary society—as if they are given "facts of nature," requiring no further explanation. The customary strategies are to view inequalities in wealth and power as the result either of random idiosyncratic personal differences of ability or industry, on the one hand, or the inordinate greed and moral corruption of particular individuals,

---

* The presidential address delivered 21 November 1992 at the annual meeting of the Society of Biblical Literature held at the Hilton Hotel, San Francisco, California.

1. Anthony Giddens and David Held, eds., *Classes, Power, and Conflict: Classical and Contemporary Debates* (Berkeley/Los Angeles: University of California Press, 1982).

on the other.[2] The key analytic tool that could cut through our shallow positivism and moralism about wealth and power in biblical societies is the concept of social class.

I. What Is Social Class?

In my judgment, the most illuminating way to understand wealth and power in the Bible—as in all societies—is to understand the relation of groups of people to the process of production of basic goods, which generates and replenishes human society in the perpetual flow of daily life. Social classes may be said to exist whenever one social group is able to appropriate a part of the surplus labor product of other groups. In such a situation of exploitation, wealth and power accrue disproportionately to those who are able to claim and dispose of what others produce. Those who have this power of economic disposal tend also to have political predominance and ideological hegemony.

On this understanding, it is to be emphasized that social class is a dynamic relational term. Social production brings people together and, amid their interaction, the criterion that establishes the presence of social class is whether or not there are those who can dispose of the production of others de jure or de facto. At base, then, when class is operative there are two classes conjoined in distinctive ways that are mutually conditioning: the exploiters and the exploited, the dominators and the dominated, the ideologically superior and the ideologically inferior. In practice, however, the exploiters and the exploited are usually diversified in sub-classes or class fractions, chiefly according to the degree and manner in which surplus labor value is extracted and distributed in the society. Sub-class differentiation among exploiters and exploited may produce all manner of political coalitions and ideological alignments from situation to situation. Classes are less to be thought of as strata laid down in layers, one on top of the other, than as contending forces in a common field of ever-shifting action seeking to secure their vital interests as they understand them, the dominant class clearly being "one up" in its command over surplus labor value, political power, and ideological supremacy.

The degree to which people in similar or related positions relative to production are conscious of their commonality and pursue joint action differs markedly from society to society and over time within any single society. Classes may be more or less economically, politically, or ideologically active on their own behalf. Action based on common interests may enlist few, many, or most members of a class. The goals pursued may be narrower or broader. The important thing in class analysis is to look for how the social relations of production create groups

---

2. Benjamin DeMott, *The Imperial Middle: Why Americans Can't Think Straight About Class* (New York: Morrow, 1992).

who participate differentially in goods, services, and ideas, and then to examine how they interact in maintaining and advancing their interests. In short, always to ask some version of Gerhard Lenski's deceptively simple-looking question, "Who Gets What and Why?"[3] This kind of analysis, while conceptually applicable to all class societies, yields diverse configurations over space and time, no two of which are exactly alike. Consequently, social class analysis is eminently compatible with historical methodology that respects change and variety in the human story.[4]

II. Social Class in Biblical Societies

What then are the social classes disclosed in the Bible, and how does a recognition of these classes contribute to literary and historical exegesis?

The productive processes that generate wealth and power in the biblical world centered on land and were precapitalist. The vast majority of people produced food and other life necessities from the earth, working in household or village teams. Since technology and transport were not sufficiently developed to create a large consumer market for manufactured goods, the route to concentrating wealth and power in such circumstances was to gain control over agrarian and pastoral products, which the appropriators could themselves consume or assign to retainers at their discretion or convert into other valuables through trade and acquisition of land. This had been achieved in the ancient Near East by the so-called dawn of civilization, distinguished by the emergence of strong centralized states that siphoned off agrarian and pastoral surpluses through taxation, spawned landholding and merchant groups who profited from peasant indebtedness and high-level international trade, and engaged in warfare and conquest of neighboring lands.

This has been called a Tributary Mode of Production (hereafter TMP) in that, while leaving the work relations of the great majority of people largely unchanged, it laid heavy tribute on the fruits of their labor.[5] Developments in the western Mediterranean and Aegean areas appear to have been broadly similar to those in

---

3. Gerhard Lenski, *Power and Privilege: A Theory of Social Stratification* (Chapel Hill/London: University of North Carolina Press, 1984), title of chap. 1.

4. For methodologically sophisticated uses of social class analysis in the studies of three widely separated historical periods, see G. E. M. de Ste. Croix, *The Class Struggle in the Ancient Greek World from the Archaic Age to the Arab Conquests* (Ithaca, NY: Cornell University Press, 1981) 4–98; Eric R. Wolf, *Europe and the People Without History* (Berkeley/Los Angeles: University of California Press, 1982) 3–23; and Gerald M. Sider, *Culture and Class in Anthropology and History: A Newfoundland Illustration* (Cambridge/New York: Cambridge University Press, 1986) 3–11. I have cited the pagination of the methodological discussions in the above references.

5. Samir Amin, *Class and Nation, Historically and in the Present Crisis* (New York/London: Monthly Review, 1980) 46–70. "Tributary" is a more descriptive term for this mode of production than the older label "Asiatic," which, in employing the name of the continent where it has most often appeared, fails to characterize the nature of the mode of production as such.

the immediate biblical world, although by Greco-Roman times slave labor began to produce the critical mass of surplus labor value. Nonetheless, tributary relations of production imposed on the agrarian multitudes continued among much of the populace dominated by Rome, since in the long run slave production did not prove successful in agriculture. Private ownership of immovable property was also legally enshrined in the classical world on a scale and with a rigor unfamiliar to the ancient Near East, but it appears that, even under Roman rule, Jewish Palestine continued to follow the traditional pattern of customary use holdings that could be lost over time through indebtedness.

The social classes visible in biblical societies may be phrased in such a way as to take account of Israel's history in all periods, within which we can identify shifts in the class configurations that were integral to changing economic, political, and ideological developments.[6]

A Synchronic Social Class Typology

On the one hand, *the dominant tribute-imposing class* consisted of the political elite—native and/or foreign—and their administrative, religious, and military retainers, together with the landholding, merchant, and small manufacturing elites who benefited from state power. All these subsections of the dominant class extracted—or attempted to extract—surplus from the mass of agrarian and pastoral producers, as well as other smaller occupational groups (named below). This extraction of surplus was accomplished by a variety of mechanisms, including imperial tribute, domestic taxation, commercial imposts, corvée, slave labor, rent, or debt servicing.

On the other hand, *the dominated tribute-bearing class* consisted of peasants, pastoralists, artisans, priests, slaves, and unskilled workers—all those who did not draw surplus from any other workers but who were structurally subject to their own surplus being taken by members of the dominant class, or who were themselves dependent wage laborers.

Weakness in the dominant class, coupled with resistance or avoidance strategies by the dominated, could reduce the intensity of the exploitation and even, on rare occasions, open up a brief period of relief from all—or most—surplus extraction. Normally this temporary relief was no more than a precarious transition between the fall of one group of exploiters and the rise of another. The peculiarity of earliest Israel is that it enjoyed the longest stretch of tribute-free communal life known to us from any ancient Near Eastern sources.

---

6. For elaboration of these social class shifts in correlation with the customary periodization of biblical history, see my "Sociology of Ancient Israel" in *The Anchor Bible Dictionary* (6 vols.; New York: Doubleday, 1992) 6. 79–89.

DIACHRONIC SOCIAL CLASS DEVELOPMENTS

Communitarian mode of production. In pre-state Israel we meet the anomaly of a period of about two centuries when the grip of Canaanite city-state tributary control over the mountainous hinterland was broken and the previously dominated agrarian and pastoral populace was largely free of surplus extraction. The primary productive units were extended or multifamily households, linked in lineages or protective associations and in tribes. In these farming-herding households, which in some cases included indebted or indentured servants and resident aliens, men and women divided certain tasks and shared others. All members of the household enjoyed the fruit of their arduous collective labor. There remain still unresolved questions about the status and extent of indebted laborers and about the role of chiefs in this society, and exactly how to conceptualize them in relation to class.[7]

In contrast to the Tributary Mode of Production, we might appropriately say that tribal Israel practiced a Household Mode of Production. I prefer, however, to speak of a Communitarian Mode of Production (hereafter CMP), because the success of this tribute-free venture hinged on broad alliances among free producers, formed at the intertribal level, to defend themselves militarily and to grant communally legitimated use holdings to the respective households who assisted one another in aspects of agrarian labor and in the granting of aid to households in need. This was a very particular kind of equality among households, not to be confused with strict equivalence in family organization, size of holdings, or amount of production, and, in particular, not to be understood along the lines of modern individualistic notions of egalitarianism developed since the French Revolution and predicated on doctrines of inalienable human rights. Thus, all attempts to evaluate this Communitarian Mode of Production by modern egalitarian criteria, whether of democracy, anarchism, socialism, or feminism, will inevitably falsify the historically specific situation of early Israel,[8] whereas anthropological analogies of confederated pre-state societies offer more illuminating comparison. Nonetheless, on balance, the CMP provided its practitioners with

---

7. A nuanced social structural understanding of debt servitude and sojourner residency in tribal Israel depends greatly on two debated issues: (1) which provisions of the monarchic redaction of the Covenant Code of Exod 20:22–23:19 are believed to reflect premonarchic conditions; (2) the mix of biological and social processes envisioned in the formation of early Israelite households.

8. Carol Meyers, making use of an abundance of archaeological and anthropological—as well as textual—data, characterizes the place of women in the wider premonarchic society *(Discovering Eve: Ancient Israelite Women in Context* [New York/Oxford: Oxford University Press, 1988]). She wisely cautions against positive or negative prejudgments on early Israelite society based on modern notions that ignore the ancient context.

a more materially, socially, and ideologically satisfying life than they observed among the tribute-burdened producers in their environment.[9]

Native tributary mode of production. Ironically, with the introduction of social classes at the emergence of the monarchy, Israel entered into the very TMP it had struggled free from at its inception and had resisted for decades. Surplus was extracted from producers by state taxation and corvée, by elites who exacted interest on debt and imposed rental fees, and by foreign powers whose demands for tribute and indemnity were passed on to the Israelite producers in the form of higher taxes. Over the course of monarchic history, we detect rising and falling sequences of state power, both in its relation to foreign powers and in its relation to native nongovernmental elites. These shifting balances of power in the dominant elites meant that their subjects were exploited variously by native rulers, foreign rulers, and domestic landholders and merchants. Since the exploited populace faced diversified exploiters who did not have identical interests and whose varied forms of domination differed in severity from period to period, it was in the interests of the exploited to use what power they had to diminish the intensity of domination by throwing their support to what they perceived at any given moment as the lesser—or least—of evils among their contending exploiters. This of course raises questions about varying kinds of self-interest among the exploited, the extent to which they were class-conscious, and the channels available to them for gaining political leverage.[10]

Foreign tributary mode of production. With the eclipse of both Israelite states, a significant shift within the TMP occurred: the dominance in imposing tribute passed decisively to foreign rulers, although the native elite in restored Judah had considerable leeway to operate as long as they remained loyal, preserved domestic order, and delivered tribute to the imperial power. The imperial dominators preferred to stay at arm's length and govern through the native elite, although under the Hellenistic and Roman regimes, they took a more direct hand in ruling Palestine. In effect, the exploited sub-classes were now continuously subject to two levels of surplus labor extraction: by foreign rulers and by native elites. The

---

9. For modification and nuancing of my concepts and conclusions about premonarchic Israel as a society, subsequent to *The Tribes of Yahweh*, see "How My Mind Has Changed or Remained the Same," in *The Hebrew Bible in Its Social World and in Ours* (SemeiaSt, forthcoming).

10. For elaboration of this reconstruction of social classes in monarchic Israel, see my essay "A Hypothesis about Social Class in Monarchic Israel in the Light of Contemporary Studies of Social Class and Social Stratification," in *The Hebrew Bible in Its Social World and in Ours*.

domestic tribute was increasingly garnered through the Temple establishment in the form of tithes and offerings.[11]

Religion, ethnicity, and the tributary mode of production. When early Judaism emerged as a distinctive religiocultural social body that could thrive with minimal political support, religious and ethnic identities became important ways of viewing and articulating class divisions. Consequently, native Jewish elites and their exploited subjects might unite in opposition to foreign domination but with different social programs in view and with different understandings of the social import of their shared religion. In contradictory ways, the temple complex of economic, political, and religious institutions served both to give a solidary identity to Jews and to function as the conduit for the extraction of their surpluses.[12]

The correlate of these observations about shifting class dynamics in biblical history is that the internal perceptions and interests of both the dominant and dominated classes varied in clarity and cohesiveness. There was no unrelieved warfare between two solid social blocs, but a long tug-of-war, with momentary truces and skirmishes, breaking out at times into sharp confrontation and crisis. On occasion, members of the dominant class could take action on behalf of—even make common cause with—the exploited, to lessen their grievances when it was felt that their own social survival depended on it. Similarly, members of the dominated classes could be cooperative with—and not merely sullenly resigned to—programs put forward by their dominators when they saw some marginal advantage in doing so. This "fudging" of class lines in the rough and tumble of actual social history is of great importance to a nuanced reading of the social dimensions of biblical texts.[13]

III. Social Class in Biblical Texts

On the ideological plane, which of course included religion, the ideas produced by state officials and their clients claimed that their superior wealth and power were justified by the improved production, domestic peace, freedom from foreign aggression, and blessings of the gods that the state and its client elites provided.

---

11. Daniel L. Smith, "The Politics of Ezra: Sociological Indicators of Postexilic Judaean Society," in *Second Temple Studies 1. Persian Period* (ed. P. R. Davies; JSOTSup 117; Sheffield: JSOT Press, 1991) 73–97.

12. Joseph Blenkinsopp, "Temple and Society in Achaemenid Judah," in *Second Temple Studies 1*, ed. Davies, 22–53.

13. For a particularly instructive account of how Israelite ruling classes at times acted—or promised to act—on behalf of their exploited subjects in order to solidify political control over them, see Marvin L. Chaney, "Debt Easement in Israelite History and Tradition," in *The Bible and the Politics of Exegesis: Essays in Honor of Norman K. Gottwald on His Sixty-Fifth Birthday* (ed. D. Jobling, P. L. Day, and G. T. Sheppard; Cleveland: Pilgrim, 1991) 127–39.

These ideas are the dominant ones in the literature of the ancient Near East, produced as it was largely under the auspices of the TMP ruling class. These ruling-class ideas are also articulated in the Hebrew Bible, particularly in royal texts and in some of the wisdom literature, as also in the NT, in Gospel redactions and in second- and third-generation epistolary literature. The counterideas of many subjects of the state were far less sanguine, marked by suspicion or outright accusation that their rulers were in fact parasitic, bringing no long-lasting benefits to the immediate producers, providing illusory social harmony that masked injustices, engaging in wars of expansion that were largely irrelevant—and often damaging—to the interests of the general populace and, through it all, falsely claiming approval by the gods. These "dark" views of the ruling class are only marginally visible in ancient Near Eastern literature but rather amply represented within the Hebrew Bible, under the initial impetus of the CMP, particularly in early poems and laws and in prophets and some wisdom literature, and likewise within the NT, especially in the earliest layers of the Gospels and in James and Revelation.

Granted a sharp class edge in much of the Bible, it is nonetheless true that there are large tracts of biblical literature where the class lineaments are obscure or scrambled for various reasons: because of the nature of the topics treated, or because of the terseness of treatment, or because conflicting class outlooks are joined in the text, or because the social strategy of the text is to try to blur or cross class lines. An important service of a sociological reading of the Bible is to plot the contours of class consciousness and class strategy—when and how they are expressed, ignored, or suppressed—in order to give a convincing social context to the diversities of biblical texts and religious developments. In this task, all of the existing methods of biblical criticism are indispensable aids. The way in which a combination of methods can illuminate the functioning of social class in biblical history is best shown in particular instances. For illustrative purposes, I offer three groups of texts of varying ages and genres: narrative, prophetic speech, and parable. In these texts, considerations of genre criticism and redaction criticism, illuminated by comparative social scientific method, intertwine to disclose social class dynamics that are routinely overlooked by exegetes.

Social Class in Hebrew Bible Narratives

Fortunately, there are narratives in the Hebrew Bible where a fair amount of social historical context and data are given. Narrative genres would seem to be "naturals" for revealing social class, but not uniformly so. In some of these texts, opposing social class perspectives are vividly evident, while, in others, conflicting class outlooks are concealed. The methods of redaction evidently played a key role in censoring the flow of social information and in determining what meaning, if any, the textual frame would assign to the data reported. I give two examples, one in which social class is easier to locate and the other in which it is more veiled even as it is powerfully present.

Secession of the northern tribes. The rebellion of Jeroboam and the secession of the northern tribes are reported in 1 Kings 11–12 with a social realism that stands in acute dissonance with what is said earlier in the book about Solomon's governmental policies.[14] The accounts of the Solomonic economic program of redistricting, heavy taxation, and forced labor in 1 Kings 4–10 are surrounded with an aura of benign wisdom that induces Solomon's subjects to welcome these harsh measures enthusiastically.[15] At one point, the text—sensitive to some disquiet in the audience—goes out of its way to insist that the corvée was not imposed on Israelites but only on Canaanites (1 Kgs 9:20–22). To the contrary, Jeroboam is introduced as the one appointed by Solomon "over all the forced labor of the house of Joseph" (1 Kgs 11:28). The immediate occasion of Jeroboam's abortive revolt is said to have been Solomon's building projects in Jerusalem which presumably enlisted north Israelite drafted labor that Jeroboam was expected to muster and direct, but against which he recoiled (1 Kgs 11:27).

Years later, when the north Israelite delegation met Rehoboam at Shechem to negotiate the terms on which his succession to the monarchy might be acceptable, the crucial concession demanded was a lightening or lifting of the corvée (1 Kgs 12:3–4). This onerous form of surplus extraction, coupled with taxation in kind, had become a widespread class grievance on which the united monarchy foundered and then split when the Judahite ruling class failed to modify the policy. Although we have no certain social information for the immediately following decades, it is likely that for some time the northern monarchy relinquished use of the corvée, at least on the scale Solomon had practiced it, until presumably it was reintroduced by Omri as he sought to ape the Davidic dynasty's accomplishments.

It is noteworthy that the Deuteronomistic editor attributes the breakup of Solomon's kingdom to the unbridled sexuality and idolatry of the king's old age, whereas the narrative of the schism, oblivious to these judgments, lays the responsibility squarely on the monarch's abusive forced labor policy. Ideologically, Jeroboam ensured religious legitimacy for the new kingdom he was chosen to head by reconstructing the cult of Yahweh on northern territory, completely severed from the priesthood and festival schedule at Jerusalem. By approving places of worship throughout his kingdom, in addition to the royal shrines at Dan and Bethel, Jeroboam honored the wishes of his subjects for local practices of religion that from their perspective were more properly Yahwistic than Jerusalem's

---

14. For a sociopolitical scenario of Jeroboam's program and the constituencies supporting it, see Robert B. Coote, *In Defense of Revolution: The Elohist History* (Minneapolis: Fortress, 1991) 61–69.

15. David Jobling, "The Commodification of Wisdom in 1 Kings 3–10" (paper presented to the Narrative Research on the Hebrew Bible Group, SBL annual meeting, 1987), revised as "'Forced Labor': Solomon's Golden Age and the Question of Literary Representation," *Semeia* 54 (1992) 57–76.

tribute-laden cultic practices (1 Kgs 12:31). The Deuteronomist's anachronistic "theological" explanation of the schism is altogether out of touch with the social class conflict informing the politics so concretely expressed in the Jeroboam tradition. To be sure, some aspects of the schism remain obscure. Ahijah, the prophet who encourages Jeroboam to rebel, is made to speak almost exclusively in terms of the Deuteronomistic ideology; it is likely, however, that as a Shilonite he was sensitive to the peasant grievances that moved Jeroboam. Absent from the story are Judahite peasants, because they had been exempted from the corvée, or because the Deuteronomist did not want to disclose any Judahite resistance to the rule of Rehoboam, or simply because the story of the assembly at Shechem (because it was North Israelite) did not have the populace of Judah in view.

Josiah's reformation. Josiah's reformation, described largely in religious terms in 2 Kings 22–23, has escaped careful class analysis in favor of more literary and theological concerns, such as the relation of the reform to the Deuteronomic law code and the overt religious aims of the reformers. Often the discussion proceeds as though the law code in and of itself was the cause of the reform and its formulators the sole proponents of reform. Above all, the religious dimensions of the reform are abstracted from its social class matrix. In undertaking a social class reading of the situation behind 2 Kings 22–23, we do not have two sharply contradictory points of view as in 1 Kings 4–12, so we have to bring together more textual sources to get a larger reading of the conjunction of social historical circumstances at that watershed moment.

Judah had been a shrunken vassal kingdom of Assyria for seventy-five years, reduced in size, with its ruling class members—both those in and out of government—pushed to wring all they could out of the peasant economic base in order to survive and prosper marginally. Simultaneously, this ruling class was drawn into adopting Assyrian high culture to solidify its precarious political position, further alienating its members from those they exploited. The rapid dissolution of the Assyrian imperial rule in Syria-Palestine early in the reign of Josiah completely altered the class balance of power in Palestine. The political rulers in Jerusalem saw that it might now be possible not only to solidify their hold on Judah but to expand their dominion over the territory and populace of the former northern kingdom of Israel, which no longer functioned as Assyrian provinces. This expansion would open up new economic resources for the crown and for the landholding and merchant elites of Judah.

Given the goals and the resources, what would it take to bring off this ambitious project? It would certainly necessitate concerted military and bureaucratic efforts over a very large area and in the face of a hostile populace to prosecute this program. But in order to enlist, train, and motivate the necessary troops and lesser officials, expanded revenues and a loyal and committed Judahite populace were indispensable. The firm base of the reformation proponents consisted of the king and his court officials, army commanders, priests and prophets attached to

Jerusalem, and landowners and merchants of Judah, who had a stake in seeing greater wealth and power flow to Jerusalem.[16] But could the tribute-laden populace of Judah be reliably enlisted in the cause?

Since there was no way for Josiah to proceed that did not require more revenues from his subjects, his first approach was to rally Judahites with a twin appeal to patriotic fervor and religious purity. The nationalist religious ideology of the Deuteronomists was broadcast in the hopes of building a strong "popular front" in the cause of Israel's God against Assyrian foreigners and apostate Israelites, north and south. In short, Josiah and his regime aspired to restore the territorial conquests and embody the religious loyalties of Joshua and David. The reform's bold move to outlaw all Yahwistic worship outside of Jerusalem served both to enhance the authority of the capital and to finance the conquest of the north from the tithes and offerings flowing into the city and from increased trading revenues derived from the obligatory festival pilgrimages.[17] The diversion of funds and religious activities to Jerusalem also devalued local culture and religion, and the effect of Deuteronomic legislation on family life further undercut the autonomy and integrity of the households that still survived in many rural areas.[18] Especially radical was the uprooting of the Passover observance from its longstanding household milieu and its restrictive relocation to Jerusalem.[19] In return for an increase in tribute, service in the army, and the eviscerating of local religious culture, the reforms offered some debt relief and public charity to the needy.

So how did Josiah's "bread and circuses" policies fare with the great majority of the tribute-obligated populace? Not very well. To begin with, most of the populace of the former northern kingdom had long been alienated from the Davidic dynasty in Jerusalem. They deeply resented the compulsory payments and long pilgrimages to Jerusalem and were appalled at the brutal violence that Josiah visited on their cult centers. In Judah, reception of the reforms was doubtless more mixed outside elite circles. Some resonated with the hope of reviving the glorious days of the Davidic empire. Some were attracted to the promise of debt relief. Peasants living close enough to Jerusalem to make easy pilgrimage might be pleased at the convenience, but the violent suppression of Judahite cult sites

---

16. Typical of the present trend to trace a coalition of professional elites behind the Deuteronomic reform, rather than a single faction, is Patricia Dutcher-Walls, "The Social Location of the Deuteronomists: A Sociological Study of Factional Politics in Late Pre-exilic Judah," *JSOT* 52 (1991) 77–94.

17. The primacy of fiscal goals in Josiah's reforms was astutely argued by W. Eugene Claburn, "The Fiscal Basis of Josiah's Reforms," *JBL* 92 (1973) 11–22, but his insights have been largely ignored until Nakanose's recent study (see n. 19).

18. Naomi Steinberg, "The Deuteronomic Law Code and the Politics of State Centralization," in *The Bible and the Politics of Exegesis*, ed. Jobling et al., 161–70.

19. Shigeyuki Nakanose convincingly reconstructs Josiah's revamped Passover festival as a key factor in radically centralizing the political economy (*Josiah's Passover: Sociology and the Liberating Bible* [Maryknoll, NY: Orbis Books, forthcoming]).

outside Jerusalem was alienating to many. The rural priests, respected in their communities, were defrocked and angered. The increased revenues to Jerusalem were irritating for some and onerous for many. The measures that struck at local loyalties and threatened household culture and religion were resented. Consequently, it is reasonable to conclude that a large majority of the Judahite peasantry fell along a spectrum ranging from indifference to open hostility toward the reforms. By contrast, it is likely that the biggest supporters of the reforms among the exploited sub-classes were day laborers who were descended from refugees of the northern kingdom in 722 BCE or who came off farms in Judah that they had lost to indebtedness. This rootless group, often unemployed, would profit from increased work in military preparations, in public construction, and in service jobs occasioned by the pilgrimage trade. Living in and around Jerusalem, they also stood to gain more from public charity than peasants scattered in the countryside.[20]

Here then was a draconian reconstitution of government and cult from above, drastically extracting surplus and severely disrupting culture in all major areas of the common life. Stripped to its central point, the reformers offered a trade-off between a more powerful centralized government and cult, on the one hand, and improved living conditions for the general populace, on the other. All in all, the strident reform effort probably did not win over a very sizable base of support, rooted as it was in the dominant class in Jerusalem, resisted almost unanimously in the north, and precariously supported by only a minority of the Judahite exploited class. It could only succeed by immediate force of arms, with the hope of securing conditions for a longer-term revival and expansion of the economic base by incorporating the more fertile northern territories into a political economy orchestrated from Judah. It was hoped that nationalist religious fervor, symbolically and institutionally anchored to the Jerusalem Temple, would provide the ideological sustaining power needed for this monumental endeavor.

As it turned out, the ambitious reform project was cut short in less than twenty years. The freedom from foreign intervention did not last long. Initially Egypt, and then Neo-Babylonia, extended imperial control over Judah. Regrettably, we know very little about how extensively or intensively the reforms were actually carried out, especially the economic, social, and juridical measures in Deuteronomy that are not mentioned in 2 Kings 22–23. Judging from Jeremiah and Ezekiel, who wrote some years after Josiah's death, the prestige of the Jerusalem cult was enhanced, but with a virtual superstitious sanctity and without many of the religious purifications that Deuteronomy had mandated. Social injustice and judicial corruption are heavily scored by these prophets, while the sole evidence we possess of social reforms actually having been instituted is one

---

20. This contention of Nakanose that wage laborers alone among the exploited Judahite subclasses stood to gain measurable advantages from the reforms (*Josiah's Passover*) is preferable to Claburn's claim that the reforms were rooted in a peasant movement for national liberation.

oracle of Jeremiah that praises Josiah for having "judged the cause of the poor and needy" (Jer 21:13-17), which may actually be a reference to wage laborers on royal construction projects who replaced corvee, and who were the one group of the depressed populace that profited from the reforms.

SOCIAL CLASS IN HEBREW BIBLE PROPHETIC TEXTS

An abundance of prophetic poetic texts presupposes social conflict, and, as with the narratives, they both conceal and reveal social class. In some cases redaction criticism, using social class criteria, is able to uncover the fault lines of social conflict in the text. In other instances we have to work with inferences drawn from what is omitted or avoided in a basically seamless text. Figurative and metaphorical speech, socially and politically innocent at first glance, may be highly charged with social class assumptions and judgments. As with the narratives, I have chosen one instance where the social class situation is recoverable along intertextual and redactional lines, and another where, given the text's position in a known historical trajectory, we can infer social class from stylistic tone and failure to treat certain expected topics highly relevant to the subject matter.

Isaiah on the spoliation of the vineyard. The present text of Isaiah contains two versions of the ruination of the vineyard as a metaphor for the destruction of Israel. By far the better known is the elegant Song of the Vineyard (Isa 5:1–7), which, in spite of the difficulty in determining the precise meaning of its opening references to "my beloved," appears to be a straightforward parable. The surface teaching of the parable is that a social entity variously identified as Israel, Judah, and Jerusalem is corporately responsible for its imminent self-destruction because of injustice and unrighteousness, underscored by the vivid terms "bloodshed" and "outcry." For our purposes, we may pass by the inconsonance in the analogy that pictures a vineyard as bearing moral responsibility for being infertile. Such metaphorical license is typical enough in the Bible to put Isaiah's device within accepted literary practice. The chief point I would make is that, taken alone, the parable does not obviously premise social class conflict in the society, but suggests rather a breakdown in social order reflected in a soaring crime rate.

It so happens, however, that the Song of the Vineyard does not stand alone, since in 3:13–15 the image of Israel as vineyard is repeated with an emphatic class content. "Yahweh enters into judgment with the elders and princes of his people: 'It is you who have devoured the vineyard. The spoil of the poor is in your houses. What do you mean by crushing my people, by grinding the face of the poor?'" On this reading of events, it is the exploiters of the poor who are responsible for the destruction of the whole society. Moreover, it is highly probable that these verses are a redactionally relocated fragment of the original Song of the Vineyard, which, like the parables of Nathan (2 Sam 12:1–15) and the woman of Tekoa (2 Sam 14:1–20) addressed to David, was a self-incriminating juridical parable, in this case addressed to the dominant class and probably targeting their appropriation of indebted property,[21] although it might equally refer to the whole cluster of abuses that contributed to systemic poverty, including excessive taxation, corrupt courts, and fraudulent business practices. In the absence of this telltale social class specifier, the Song of the Vineyard loses much of its original punch and can be read as an indiscriminate moralizing attack on society from top to bottom. The dilution of the class content in the Song of the Vineyard is yet another instance of the tendency of the redactors of prophetic books to smooth off the jagged edges of class conflict as has been argued in other cases, notably in the so-called "B" and "C" levels of tradition in the books of Amos and Micah.[22]

Deutero-Isaiah on the leadership of restored Judah. Information from the book of Kings, coupled with the known deportation policies of ancient Near Eastern empires, makes it clear that the Babylonian exiles addressed by Deutero-Isaiah were members and descendants of the former Judahite political elite. The prophet's ornate rhetoric is devoted to convincing them that they should prepare themselves for immanent return to Judah, since Cyrus was about to overthrow Babylonian rule and authorize a reconstituted Judahite community. It is striking, however, that the prophet has nothing to say about the Jews who remained in Palestine. They are not expected to play any role in the leadership of restored Judah, but appear only as a welcoming chorus at the good news of the return of the exiles. Moreover, instead of a restored Davidic dynasty, the political functions of a native Jewish king are redistributed between Cyrus as emperor and the body of restored exiles conceived as a kind of theocratic oligarchy. The pervasive assumption of the prophet is that the previously disgraced and discredited exiled leaders have been purified by the experience of exile and will rule with justice and equity over a passively receptive Palestinian citizenr. The social class addressed by the prophet is conceived as a reformed and purged political elite with professional competency and a renewed sense of mission, which it can successfully carry out if it is willing to follow Deutero-Isaiah's lead.[23] While the text's

---

21. Gerald T. Sheppard, "The Anti-Assyrian Redaction and the Canonical Context of Isaiah 1–39," *JBL* 104 (1985): 204–11. Employing a different tack, Marvin L. Chaney, "The Song of the Vineyard: Reading Isa 5:1–7 in the Context of Eighth-Century Political Economy" (paper presented in the Social Sciences and the Interpretation of the Hebrew Scriptures Section, SBL annual meeting, 1992) uncovers clear signs of the prophet's condemnation of the exploiting class within 5:1–7 proper that do not necessitate the restoration of 3:13–15 to the body of the song.

22. For Amos, see Robert B. Coote, *Amos Among the Prophets: Composition and Theology* (Philadelphia: Fortress, 1981) 46–134. For Micah, see Itumeleng J. Mosala, *Biblical Hermeneutics and Black Theology in South Africa* (Grand Rapids: Eerdmans, 1989) 101–53.

23. Norman K. Gottwald, "Social Class and Ideology in Isaiah 40–55: An Eagletonian Reading," in *Semeia* (vol. on Ideological Criticism of Biblical Texts, ed. D. Jobling and T. Pippin, forthcoming).

manner of expression is idiosyncratic, and its hopefulness extreme, it is rooted in the social experience of those who once ruled Judah and who can envision ruling it again.

In short, the elitist mentality of Deutero-Isaiah is truly "prophetic" of the self-assurance and elan of those Jewish leaders who, returning from exile, took charge of the rebuilding of Judahite society and religion. In Deutero-Isaiah, we see in bold signature the indestructible commitment to a mission that drove the restored leaders to persist in their efforts to rebuild Judah. Equally clearly revealed is their assumed moral right to leadership, since just punishment and excess of suffering in exile had purified them of their sullied past. The corollary of their right to lead is their certainty that they know what is best for the compliant majority of Jews who had remained in Judah and who would surely follow their lead. This potent social class ideology sustained the restoration project through difficult times, but it also sowed the dragon's teeth of discord in the restored community that bore bitterly opposed factions—evident in Trito-Isaiah and Malachi—and that finally necessitated radical reform measures by Nehemiah, one of their own number, who a century later was able to see that this elite's blindness to the needs and feelings of the subject class would undermine the community disastrously if it were not corrected forthwith. Needless to say, the passionately committed architects of reconstructed Judah depended on the Persian imperial tributary structures to carry out their local program of native tributary rule based on Temple economy and religion.

Social Class in the Parables of Jesus

Social class in the Jesus traditions. Lastly, there is an assortment of Jesus traditions of various genres which only recently has been adequately scrutinized from the perspective of Jesus' location in the social class conflict of his day.[24] Heretofore, for the most part, the social interrogation of these traditions has been lopsidedly focused on whether Jesus was violent or nonviolent, usually with the naïve assumption that if Jesus did not advocate or lead a violent movement he could not have been involved in social struggle or political activity. The exposure of this non sequitur has opened the way to new paths of social critical study of the Jesus traditions.

An array of repeated themes in the Jesus traditions speaks overwhelmingly for his deliberate participation in social conflict: his focus on the destitute and marginalized elements of the populace, his open table fellowship, his severe strictures on wealth, his cavalier attitude toward the legitimacy of Roman and Temple

---

24. David A. Fiensy, against the backdrop of a society torn by conflict, focuses on the effect of changing land tenure on the lives of peasants (*The Social History of Palestine in the Herodian Period: The Land Is Mine* [Studies in the Bible and Early Christianity 20; Lewiston/Queenston/Lampeter: Edwin Mellen, 1991]).

taxes, his symbolic attack on the Temple economy, his healing of sickness and demon possession as symptoms of social oppression, and his rejection of the ideology that the personal sin of the victims was the cause of all or most of the social misery he encountered.[25] On the other hand, these socially confrontational traditions are now enclosed in redactions primarily interested in interpreting Jesus theologically and in toning down the harshness of Jesus' sociopolitical critique of the Jewish and Roman authorities who stood at the pinnacle of his society. The general failure to pursue this discrepancy probably follows from the fact that redaction critics more nearly share the social class perspective of the Gospel redactors than they do the social class perspective of Jesus.

Among the social class criteria now being honed is the test of how particular reported teachings of Jesus would have been heard by his primarily Palestinian peasant audience struggling under the burden of multilayered surplus extraction through tribute to Rome, taxes to Herodian client rulers, tithes and offerings to the Temple, rent payments to landlords, and debt payments to creditors. The reasoning behind this strategy is sound, namely, that the way the teachings of Jesus were likely to have been construed by his peasant audiences gives a more reliable index to what Jesus had in mind than the construals of redactors in urban Christian communities some decades later. The parables of Jesus provide an intriguing test case of this methodology.

Parables of Jesus and economic exploitation. Among the parables attributed to Jesus there is a considerable number whose plots are built up around familiar social class conflicts, especially involving economic exploitation. One thinks immediately of the laborers in the vineyard who receive identical wages for unequal work (Matt 20:1–15), of the traveling man of means who entrusts huge amounts of money to his servants while he is away (Matt 25:14–28 // Luke 19:11–25), of the rebellious tenants who try to seize the absentee landlord's property (Mark 12:1–9 // Matt 21:33–41 // Luke 20:9–16), of a rich man's steward about to lose his job who improves his prospects by reducing the amounts owed by his master's debtors (Luke 16:1–8a), of the rich man and Lazarus, whose fortunes are reversed in the afterlife (Luke 16:19–26), of the insistent widow who presses her case at law until even an unjust judge gives her satisfaction (Luke 18:1–8a), and we could go on with other examples.

The Gospel redactors often clearly label these stories as parables of the kingdom, and, even in instances where they do not, the predominant exegetical tradition has assumed them to be so. Jesus is understood to be using these

---

25. John Dominic Crossan (*The Historical Jesus: The Life of a Mediterranean Peasant* [San Francisco: Harper, 1991] 227–416) and Ediberto Lopez ("The Earliest Traditions About Jesus and Social Stratification" [Ph.D. diss., Drew University, 1992]) exegete a broad range of Jesus traditions with the tools of social class analysis, producing perceptive alternatives to many socially diluted traditional interpretations.

social conflict paradigms as examples of what God is like in dealing with humans. The result in a number of instances produces a portrait of God as a monarch, merchant, or landlord who high-handedly, even cruelly, exhibits the very social practices, goals, and values that Jesus elsewhere rejects or condemns. Either as redacted or as interpreted over the centuries, these same parables invite—or appear implicitly to commend—compliant and approving attitudes toward authority figures who behave in oppressive and arbitrary ways contrary to Jesus' nonparabolic teaching. So we are compelled to ask: Was Jesus meaning to say that this kind of manipulation of people for purposes of gaining wealth and power is condemnable in humans but praiseworthy in God? And, if so, would his peasant audience have accepted this interpretation and looked forward to the establishment of the sort of divine kingdom thus described or implied? There is ample cause for a second look at the presumed kingdom orientation of many of these parables. I shall only indicate a few first steps in rethinking these parables within an alternative hermeneutic to the mainstream of parable scholarship.[26]

It is completely clear to begin with that in some of these parables God is emphatically not represented by any of the characters in the parable. The unjust judge, for example, is said to entertain "no fear of God and no respect of anyone" (Luke 18:4), and in the story of the rich man and Lazarus, God is represented only by proxy in the person of "Father Abraham," and in the afterlife at that (Luke 16:24). Thus, even as redacted, the characters in the parables are not homogeneously descriptive of how God acts in human affairs. The unjust judge and the rich man who ignores Lazarus are simply human figures who wield social class power over others, and they are judged to be in the wrong for doing so. It is appropriate to inquire if the same might have been true in other parables as they were originally framed by Jesus.

At this point, it seems to me critical to apply the test of audience reception among Palestinians drawn to Jesus' teaching. For instance, is it not probable that peasants or wage laborers, on hearing that one servant harbored the money entrusted to him instead of risking it to make profit, would instantly have identified with his blunt reply to the master, "I knew that you were a harsh man, reaping where you did not sow, and gathering where you did not scatter seed; so I was afraid..." (Matt 25:24–25). This is a vivid colloquial description of the exploitation of surplus labor value at the heart of the class conflict in Palestine, and Jesus'

---

26. I am particularly indebted to William R. Herzog II (*Parables as Subversive Speech: Jesus as Pedagogue of the Oppressed* [Louisville: Westminster/John Knox, forthcoming]) for orally providing the key hermeneutical perspective, and many of the exegetical details, for this social class reading of a number of the parables, although the proposal to construe them as wisdom example stories is my own.

audience would have felt the sting of it, being little surprised at the undeserved fate of a rash subordinate who had the audacity to "tell off" his master.[27]

Or, consider another parable, in which the social class superior is customarily thought to be presented in praiseworthy terms. Is it not likely that Jesus' hearers would have smelled sarcastic condescension and hypocritical self-congratulation in the retort of the vineyard owner to his laborers who objected to equal pay for unequal labor, "Am I not allowed to do what I choose with what belongs to me? Or are you envious because I am generous?" (Matt 20:15)? Would they not be familiar with such self-trumpeted "generosity" that humiliated and dismissed them as contemptible for daring to speak up in their own interests? From bitter experience they would note that the owner desperately needed the last-minute workers, for whom he was willing to pay a daily subsistence wage only because he had gotten himself "in a jam" by miscalculating his labor needs at the start of the day. They would also observe that he deliberately shamed the laborers who had worked all day by paying them last in front of the others, taunting their powerlessness, laying his stinginess on them—all with the aim of confusing and dividing the work force by putting them at the mercy of his whims and at one another's throats. And would they not have snorted—if not loudly guffawed—over the owner's nasty crack at the expense of the last batch of workers who had been waiting in vain for an employment offer, "Why are you standing around here idle all day?" (Matt 20:6)? Jesus' listeners knew the owner's ideology all to well: Yes, indeed, that's exactly what we are in the exploiter's eyes: selfish ingrates when we do work, and listless idlers when we can't find work! We could easily cite other details in this family of parables that the exploited audience of Jesus would not readily have found acceptable, either as models of divine or human behavior or as counsel about how to regard God and their social class superiors.

All this considered, the outline of an alternative hypothesis suggests itself. It seems probable that a fair number of these parables were not at all intended by Jesus as paradigms of the kingdom, but as negative example stories in the wisdom tradition,[28] exposing and clarifying the way things are in a capriciously unjust society, subject to the power and pride of those able to exercise their social class dominance at will. To see in them the genre of a provocative negative wisdom story, aimed at raising the consciousness of the hearers, would be to invert or overthrow much of the moral and theological teaching we have attributed to these stories. Later redactors, in part because they lacked rural Palestinian social class experience and in part because they wanted to be socially and politically

---

27. Richard L. Rohrbaugh offers a similar "reverse reading" of this parable ("A Text of Terror? The Parable of the Talents" [paper delivered at a conference on The Bible in a New Context, Orlando, Florida, 4 January 1992]).

28. Roland E. Murphy, *Wisdom Literature: Job, Proverbs, Ruth, Canticles, Ecclesiastes, Esther* (FOTL 13; Grand Rapids: Eerdmans, 1981) 130, 176.

palatable to pagan authorities, elided much of the original social class thrust of these wisdom parables.

If this seems dubious on first consideration, we need to recall that this is precisely the way we view eschatology and ecclesiology as differentiating criteria for discerning redactional activity. We recognize that the eschatology of Jesus was considerably different from the eschatology of the redactors, as we also discern that Jesus' notion of the kingdom of God and of his circle of followers differed from the ecclesiology of the redactors. In principle, therefore, it should not surprise us if the social class perspective of Jesus differed from the social class perspective of the redactors. What is surprising, I think, is that we should have delayed so long to establish methodological and hermeneutical parity among the redactional criteria of eschatology, ecclesiology, and social class.

IV. Social Class as Fate and Gift

My particular social class readings of the foregoing texts are of course partial, open-ended, and debatable. What I have tried to illustrate is a procedure that focuses the input of all relevant methods on the social relations described or implied in texts. Our analysis of a text is never complete until we pose questions about social class, the answers to which will be more or less substantial or persuasive from case to case, as is true of any method. We ask about the economic, political, and ideological aspects of the mode of production exhibited in texts with dizzying combinations and configurations of genre and redaction, without knowing in advance what we will find. We ask these social class questions of the various textual voices, both of speakers identified on the same axis in a story or a poem and of authors and redactors whose messages, more or less openly stated, may be positioned on different axes in a text that has accumulated meanings in passing through various social contexts. To add to the challenge, some of these voices may not want us to know anything about their social conditioning, and we shall have to insist until their identity is revealed. Throughout we are aiming to build up a textured history of the interaction of social classes as disclosed in the efforts of biblical writers to produce textual meanings that signify, validate, defend, and commend varying social practices. Only as we explore the social contents, correlates, and implications of biblical texts do we begin to grasp their full-bodied witness to what mattered to the people who produced, distributed, and consumed them.

In the end, what is probably most exciting and disturbing about trying to do a social class analysis of biblical texts is that to do so adequately we have to acknowledge and take responsibility for our own social class location. This is extraordinarily difficult for North American scholars to do, for all the reasons stated at the beginning of this address, but especially because we do not like the vulnerability that comes with full ownership of social class partiality. Admission of social class may make us anxious, defensive, guilty, or combative, hardly the best attitudes and dispositions for good scholarly work. Moreover, if we have to face up to conflicting class stances both in the biblical world and in our own, we may begin to feel the Bible slipping away as a determinative cultural or religious point of reference.

As long as social class stands as a category external to our interpreting selves, it can only foster hermeneutical heartburn. But once we grasp social class as one of our most significant ways of being in the world, affecting all that we do, including our biblical interpretation, we gain an unexpected resource. As we frankly embrace our own social class advantages and disadvantages—including our pain that humans should be divided in this way—the anguish and the grandeur of the biblical record dawns upon us with previously unexperienced power. Across the very cultural and social chasms that careful social class analysis opens up between us and the biblical world, we establish a bond with those ancients: we, no less than they, are fragile social creatures, not as much in control as we sometimes fancy but much more graced with possibilities for personal and social transformation than we often dare accept. What begins as fate becomes ultimately a gift.

Antiquity and Christianity*

Hans Dieter Betz
University of Chicago

Let me begin, if I may, with some personal remarks. The fact that I have been honored to be president of the Society of Biblical Literature is far from self-explanatory. When I came to this country in 1963, I was an unknown young immigrant from a country that not even twenty years earlier had been at war with the United States. In that same year, when James Robinson introduced me to the Society, I was welcomed as if this was the place where I belonged. I still see before me the faces of Henry Cadbury, Paul Schubert, Amos Wilder, John Knox (the president of that year), and Kendrick Grobel (the secretary), as they sat in the audience to listen to my first public lecture in English.

Nobody at that time told me, to be sure, that some day I would be president of this Society, although that possibility was certainly implied in being received as a member. Yet I may be forgiven, perhaps, if there are moments when I wonder whether all this is a dream or reality. There can be no doubt, however, about my deep gratitude for this great honor bestowed on me.

Dream or reality? This is also a question the Society might ask itself. When I joined the Society of Biblical Literature, its membership included a few hundred people. The annual meetings took place at Union Theological Seminary in New York, in whose dormitory rooms we all stayed and in whose refectory we all ate our meals. All those who attended listened to all the papers, the list of which was mimeographed on a few sheets of paper. Hardly anybody beyond the premises of Union Theological Seminary took notice of the meetings or the subject matters with which they dealt.

In 1997 membership stands at more than seven thousand who paid their annual dues. The programs for the annual meetings with hundreds of lectures and discussions have the size of a book, and there is only a limited number of

---

* Presidential address given at the 1997 Annual Meeting of the Society of Biblical Literature in San Francisco, California. The footnotes were added later. See also my forthcoming article "Antike und Christentum," *RGG* 1 (4th ed.).

convention hotels in the country large enough to provide rooms and facilities adequate for these annual meetings. I am passing over comments on the size of the annual budget, the respectable investment capital, and the numerous research and publication projects that this Society is undertaking. We have every reason to be proud of our Society and to be grateful to those who contribute to its programs in so many ways. The evidence speaks for itself.

The fact that we have this fine Society should, however, not detract us from asking some tough questions. What are the real reasons that can explain the phenomenal success that this Society is enjoying? Or are we like fools simply taking advantage of the boom, fashion, or fad, as long as it lasts? Is our work undergirded by human seriousness as well as intellectual and social foundations that support the astonishing enthusiasm and interest in studying the biblical literature at this time in history? Can this Society articulate its mission and purpose in ways that make sense to those wondering what it all means? It is my view that the time has come that we give some serious thoughts to the questions concerning the intellectual foundations of our many activities and the aims and purposes that this Society pursues.

While there may be many viewpoints concerning the aims and purposes of the Society of Biblical Literature, there are some official statements that we all agree on. Let us begin with them:[1]

The purpose of this not-for-profit organization is to:
— stimulate the critical investigation of biblical literature;
— illuminate the religions, histories, and literatures of the ancient Near East and Mediterranean regions;
— provide a wide range of support for students and educators of the Bible;
— widen the conversation partners of all interested in biblical literature.

These statements, however, regulate already existing interests and activities. Indeed, on the surface this Society provides a framework and space within which critical inquiry can take place, a space that has been created and is maintained by the membership. It is to be kept free from external interference by religious institutions, power politics, ideological warfare, and commercial exploitation.

These agreements, however, do not address the issues underlying biblical scholarship, such as: What are the subterranean forces that create and maintain our interest in biblical studies in all its aspects? What is it that enables the mind to be critical and that builds the scientific ethos without which the results of scholarship cannot have any validity?

One of the primary issues that to this day keeps this NT scholar excited and productive is summed up by the words "antiquity and Christianity." As evidence

---

1. Cited according to the 1996 program, p. 31.

I can refer to the paper I delivered at that 1963 meeting of the SBL mentioned above; it had the title "The Problem of the Relation between Antiquity and Christianity in the Acts of the Apostles."[2] Further evidence is my long involvement in the international research project *Corpus Hellenisticum Novi Testamenti*.[3] In my address tonight I would like to summarize why even after forty years I regard this topic to be of fundamental importance for our fields of study. I do not intend, however, to make everyone happy with a complete, finely balanced and absolutely unbiased survey of the concept of antiquity and Christianity in the history of its application. What I will do is highlight a number of historical events and periods when this concept became manifest in a decisive way.

I. Antiquity and Christianity: A Heuristic Concept

Since Franz Joseph Dölger (1879–1940), the great patristic scholar and historian of religion,[4] the theme of "antiquity and Christianity" has established itself in scholarship as a heuristic concept.[5] It is closely affiliated with the complex of

---

2. The 1963 meeting took place at Union Theological Seminary in New York City, January 1–2, 1964. The paper was not published.

3. For survey and bibliography, see my article "Hellenismus," *TRE* 15.19–35, esp. 23–24; also Pieter W. van der Horst, "Corpus Hellenisticum Novi Testamenti," *ABD* 1.1157–61; *Neuer Wettstein: Texte zum Neuen Testament aus Griechentum und Hellenismus*, vol. II/1–2 (ed. Udo Schnelle; Berlin: de Gruyter, 1996), with the "Einführung" by Gerald Seelig (pp. ix–xxiii).

4. See Theodor Klauser, *Franz Joseph Dölger, 1879–1940: Sein Leben und sein Forschungsprogramm "Antike und Christentum"* (JAC, Ergänzungsband 7; Münster: Aschendorff, 1980); Georg Schöllgen, "Franz Joseph Dölger und die Entstehung seines Forschungsprogramms 'Antike und Christentum,'" *JAC* 36 (1993 [1994]) 7–23.

5. The bibliography on this topic is immense. See Carl Clemen, *Religionsgeschichtliche Erklärung des Neuen Testaments: Die Abhängigkeit des ältesten Christentums von nichtjüdischen Religionen und philosophischen Systemen* (Giessen: Töpelmann, 1909; 4th ed., 1924) esp. 1–18; Leopold Zscharnack, "Antike und Christentum (Nachleben der Antike im Christentum)," *RGG* 1.378–90 (2d ed., 1927); Rudolf Bultmann, "Zum Thema Christentum und Antike," *TR* 16 (1944) 1–20; Carl Andresen, "Antike und Christentum," *TRE* 3.50–99; Wolfgang Fauth, "Philosophische Tradition und geistige Begegnung mit der Antike im Schrifttum der Patristik," *Göttingische Gelehrte Anzeigen* 230 (1978) 69–120; Edwin A. Judge, "'Antike und Christentum': Towards a Definition of the Field; a Bibliographical Survey," *ANRW* 2.23.1 (1979) 3–58; Alfred Schindler, "Antike und Christentum," in *Antike und europäische Welt: Aspekte der Auseinandersetzung mit der Antike* (ed. Maja Svilar and Stefan Kunze; Bern/Frankfurt/New York: Lang, 1984) 85–101; for the history of research, see the articles assembled in *Patristique et Antiquité tardive en Allemagne et en France de 1870 à 1930: Actes du Colloque franco-allemand de Chantilly (25–27 octobre 1991)* (ed. Jacques Fontaines et al.; Paris: Institut d'études Augustiniennes, 1992) esp. 3–19: Gerhard May, "Das Konzept Antike und Christentum in der Patristik von 1870 bis 1930"; Walter Burkert, *Klassisches Altertum und antikes Christentum: Probleme einer übergreifenden Religionswissenschaft* (Hans-Lietzmann-Vorlesungen 1; Berlin/New York: de Gruyter, 1996).

problems known as Hellenism,[6] but more specifically it designates the contentious relationship between the culture of antiquity and emerging Christianity. In this respect, "antiquity," a notion encompassing ancient historical, cultural, and religious phenomena generally,[7] relates these to "Christianity" as a special entity. What Dölger meant is indicated by the subtitle of the *Reallexikon für Antike und Christentum*, which aptly describes it as a comprehensive process of the "Auseinandersetzung des Christentums mit der antiken Welt."[8] Dölger, however, never formulated his ideas in a systematic way, so that further clarification is needed at this point.[9] Most importantly, this process did not begin only after the NT but included it. It even reaches back into the history prior to the rise of Christianity and comprises the entire environment with its political, social, economic, cultural, and religious phenomena. After the period we call antiquity came to its end in the sixth century,[10] the process continued under different circumstances and in a multitude of different expressions until the present day. As we shall see later, in this process "antiquity" and "Christianity" do not simply stand in opposition to each other as monolithic blocks but as entities subject to mutual historical change. As Jacques Fontaine has pointed out in an important article, the continuous impact these entities have on each other occurs not only as *Auseinandersetzung*, that is, as opposition and confrontation between the culture of the Greco-Roman world and Christianity, but also as their *Ineinandersetzung*, that is, as "intraposition," integration, and new creation.[11] One does well to realize, however, that this approach is implicitly opposed to the radically alternative views, still influential after more than a century, by Friedrich Nietzsche and Franz Overbeck.[12]

---

6. See my article "Hellenism," *ABD* 3.127–35, with further bibliography; also my *Hellenismus und Urchristentum: Gesammelte Aufsätze I* (Tübingen: Mohr-Siebeck, 1990); Hans-Joachim Gehrke, *Geschichte des Hellenismus* (Oldenbourgs Grundriß der Geschichte 1A; Munich: Oldenbourg, 1990).

7. On the concept of "antiquity," see W. Rüegg, A. Reckermann, A. Müller, "Antike," *Historisches Wörterbuch der Philosophie* 1 (1971) 385–92; Hubert Cancik, "Antike I–III," *RGG* (4th ed., 1998), forthcoming.

8. Vol. 1 of the lexicon appeared in 1950. See Ernst Dassmann, ed., *Das Reallexikon für Antike und Christentum und das F. J. Dölger-Institut in Bonn, Mit Registern der Stichwörter A bis Ianus sowie der Autoren, Bände 1–16* (Stuttgart: Hiersemann, 1994).

9. See the pertinent remarks by Albrecht Dihle, "Antike und Christentum," in *Forschung in der Bundesrepublik Deutschland: Beispiele, Kritik, Vorschläge* (ed. Christoph Schneider; Weinheim: Verlag Chemie, 1983) 31–37.

10. For a comprehensive survey, see Alexander Demandt, *Die Spätantike: Römische Geschichte von Diokletian bis Justinian 284–565 n. Chr.* (Handbuch der Klassischen Altertumswissenschaft, Abt. 3, T. 3, Bd. 6; Munich: Beck, 1989).

11. Jacques Fontaine, "Christentum ist auch Antike," *JAC* 25 (1982) 5–27, esp. 9.

12. See Paul Valadier, *Nietzsche et la critique du christianisme* (Paris: Cerf, 1974); Heinrich Kutzner, "Friedrich Nietzsches Antichristentum und Neuheidentum: Zu ihrer psychohistorischen Dimension," in *Die Restauration der Götter: Antike Religion und Neo-Paganismus* (ed. Richard Faber and Renate Schlesier; Würzburg: Königshausen & Neumann, 1986) 88–104. See

According to them, Christianity ended with the death of Jesus, and any present claims to continuity by Christian churches are without foundation.[13] Nietzsche dreamed of a revival of classical Hellenic antiquity, excluding Christianity.[14] Present scholarship is guided, rather, by the complexities of history. Accordingly, the phenomena covered by the concept of "antiquity and Christianity" appear during the course of history as ever-changing configurations of discontinuity and continuity, destruction and conservation, and retroversion and progress. The thesis I am going to pursue in this lecture is that in this tumultuous course of history certain phases can be distinguished; these phases are marked by highly intense encounters between antiquity and Christianity, followed by high points of cultural renewal.

II. The New Testament

The theme of antiquity and Christianity permeates early Christian literature from its beginnings in all of its aspects. Christianity originated from within antiquity, but as a new phenomenon. More precisely, what became Christianity had its origins indirectly in the confrontation between Judaism and Hellenism, first in Hellenistic Judaism, and then through Paul directly in the confrontation with pagan polytheism. Thus, the earliest version of "antiquity and Christianity" occurs as part of the Jewish conflict with Hellenism and its imposition of Greek standards of culture and religion. The actual circumstances are mostly inaccessible to the historian, either because of the lack of reliable data, or even because of the dynamics intrinsic to history.[15] It is clear from the extant sources that what

---

the reedition of Overbeck's work *Ueber die Christlichkeit unserer heutigen Theologie 1873, 1903*, with introduction, commentary, and bibliography in Franz Overbeck, *Werke und Nachlaß*, vol. 1, *Schriften bis 1873* (ed. Ekkehard W. Stegemann and Niklaus Peter; Stuttgart/Weimar: Metzler, 1994). For important essays, see *Franz Overbecks unerledigte Anfragen an das Christentum* (ed. Rudolf Brändle and Ekkehard W. Stegemann; Munich: Kaiser, 1988); Niklaus Peter, *Im Schatten der Modernität: Franz Overbecks Weg zur 'Christlichkeit unserer heutigen Theologie'* (Stuttgart/ Weimar: Metzler, 1992).

13. See also my articles "The Birth of Christianity as a Hellenistic Religion," *JR* 74 (1994) 1–25, esp. 15–24; and "Jesus and the Cynics: Survey and Analysis of a Hypothesis," *JR* 74 (1994) 453–75.

14. See Hubert Cancik, *Nietzsches Antike: Vorlesung* (Stuttgart/Weimar: Metzler, 1995) esp. 134–49. For a post-Nietzschean statement regarding the legacy of Greek culture, see Bernard Williams, *Shame and Necessity* (Sather Classical Lectures 57; Berkeley/Los Angeles: University of California Press, 1993) esp. chap. 1: "The Liberation of Antiquity."

15. Cf. Goethe's comment on the beginnings of the Royal Society of London in the early seventeenth century (*Geschichte der Farbenlehre*, 6. Abt., in *Werke* [Hamburger Ausgabe, ed. Erich Trunz, vol. 14, 7th ed.; Munich: Beck, 1982] 133): "Der Ursprung wichtiger Begebenheiten und Erzeugnisse tritt sehr oft in eine undurchdringliche mythologische Nacht zurück. Die Anfänge sind unscheinbar und unbemerkt und bleiben dem künftigen Forscher verborgen" ("The origin of important events or inventions very often withdraws into an impenetrable

later became Christianity began with John the Baptist and Jesus of Nazareth. They were Jews[16] concerned about the theological and practical integrity of obedience toward the will of God as revealed in the Torah, concerns heightened in view of the external and internal provocations and challenges by the Hellenistic culture in the heartland of the Jews. As far as Jesus is concerned, his teachings and activities occurred as his response to the question of how the kingdom of God could be manifest in the midst of the Roman occupation and under the influence of pagan life in Palestine.[17] This question was crucial among all Jews at the time, and a variety of answers was given by different Jewish groups. At this stage, therefore, it was a Jewish problem, not a Christian one, because Christianity as an identifiable entity did not yet exist.

Yet, while the sources agree that Jesus was a Jew, they also affirm that what later was labeled Christianity came into existence with him. The way the sources present the matter is that Jesus was not simply the bearer of a new message; his message largely agreed with that of John the Baptist, his mentor and teacher. Rather, the *Ursprung* was Jesus himself, his *persona*, not anything detachable from him.[18] Clearly, Jesus was opposed to Hellenistic culture and its influences,[19] although the Gospel narratives, being of Hellenistic origin themselves, have managed to tone down his anti-Hellenistic hostility and to shift the focus toward Jesus' disputes with the Jewish leadership. This shift creates the impression that Jesus was opposed to Judaism and implicitly friendly to Hellenism. However, it seems clear that his confrontation, as well as John the Baptist's, with the Jewish leadership grew out of the fact that they both saw the Jewish religion under the control of these leaders as having been corrupted by their assimilation to Greco-Roman culture.[20] There is, however, a deep-seated ambiguity as well, contained in stories admitting a strange openness on the part of Jesus toward Jews not living up to the standards and even toward non-Jews. At any rate, the immediate confrontations ended in John's and Jesus' defeat and death.

---

mythological night. The beginnings are inconspicuous and unnoticed and remain hidden to the future researcher" [trans. mine.]).

16. See my article "Wellhausen's Dictum 'Jesus was not a Christian, but a Jew' in Light of Present Scholarship," *ST* 45 (1991) 83–110.

17. A pivotal incident illustrating the problem was the story of the so-called Cleansing of the Temple, for which see my article "Jesus and the Purity of the Temple (Mark 11:15–18): A Comparative Religion Approach," *JBL* 116 (1997) 455–72.

18. See on this point my *Paulinische Studien: Gesammelte Aufsätze III* (Tübingen: Mohr-Siebeck, 1994) 281–85.

19. Note the polemics against assimilation to the ways of the Gentiles in early sources such as Matt 5:47; 6:7, 32; 10:5, 18; see my commentary *The Sermon on the Mount, Including the Sermon on the Plain (Matthew 5:3–7:27; Luke 6:20–49)* (Hermeneia; Minneapolis: Fortress, 1995) 320, 363–67, 480–81.

20. See on this point my essay "Jesus and the Purity of the Temple," 469, with reference to the so-called Herodians.

How matters developed after Jesus' death is to a large degree obscured by the lack of unbiased source material. Jesus' opposition to Hellenism seems to have been continued, albeit ambiguously, by his disciples. Sources report about a mission to Jews under the leadership of Peter going beyond the Jewish heartland (Gal 2:1–10). Other sources contain evidence of opposition against contact with non-Jews (Matt 10:5–6; Gal 2:11–14; 2 Cor 6:14–7:1). John the Baptist, Jesus, and his disciples clearly were on the side of the Jewish opposition against the representatives of Hellenism among the Jewish leadership and the Roman military, but they seem to have pursued unconventional approaches in dealing with the loss of Jewish integrity due to the impact of Greco-Roman culture.

The apostle Paul and, later, the Gospels, however, legitimated Gentile Christianity by deriving its origins from the epiphanies of the crucified Jesus before his disciples (Gal 1:16; 1 Cor 15:3–8; Mark 16 parr.). From these epiphanies they drew the conclusion that Jesus had been raised from the dead and that he was alive. The debates about the interpretation of the death and the visions experienced by the disciples, however, immediately confronted them not only with Hellenistic-Jewish but also with Greco-Roman religious concepts regarding postmortem existence. Was the image of Jesus the disciples had seen in their visions the ghost of the dead master?[21] Or had he been transferred to the heavenly realm like the pagan heroes and divine men (θεῖοι ἄνδρες)?[22] These options, however, were rejected in favor of the older Jewish eschatological concept of the resurrection of the dead: Jesus was assumed to be the proleptic first instance of the general resurrection of the dead (1 Cor 15:4, 12, 20, 23) and to be enthroned in heaven "son of God" and κύριος (1 Thess 1:3; Phil 2:11; Rom 1:4; 10:9–10).

It remains doubtful whether the early appearances of the risen Jesus to Cephas, James, and others (1 Cor 15:5–7) revealed anything related to the questions of Hellenism or mission.[23] In this regard, Jesus' appearance to Paul was a complete novelty in that Paul received the commission to preach the Christ and the gospel to the non-Jews: ἵνα εὐαγγελίζωμαι αὐτὸν ἐν τοῖς ἔθνεσιν (Gal 1:16; 2:7; Rom 1:5, 13–14; 11:13). The clear implication of this commission was that the Greco-Roman world was to be won over by the conversion of the Gentiles (cf.

---

21. For the following, see my article "Die Auferstehung Jesu im Lichte der griechischen magischen Papyri," in *Hellenismus und Urchristentum,* 230–61, esp. 247–53.

22. On this point see my contribution "Heroenverehrung und Christusglaube: Religionsgeschichtliche Beobachtungen zu Philostrats *Heroicus,*" in *Geschichte—Tradition—Reflexion: Festschrift für Martin Hengel zum 70. Geburtstag* (ed. Hubert Cancik, Hermann Lichtenberger, and Peter Schäfer; Tübingen: Mohr-Siebeck, 1996) 2.1–21, esp. 18–21.

23. This is true for the vision reports by Paul in 1 Cor 15:5–7, but not for the later revelation in Gal 2:1–3, which has to do with mission, and so do the postresurrection appearances of Jesus in Matt 28:16–20; Luke 24:47–48; John 20:21; Mark 16:14–18. In Acts (1:8; 9:10, 15; 10:3, 9–48, etc.) appearances of Jesus and of angels have to do with mission as well as with issues concerning paganism.

Rom 15:15–24). The early mission kerygma cited by Paul in 1 Thess 1:9–10 stipulates the terms: the converts were to turn their backs on the pagan idols, to cease worshiping them, that is, to turn away from polytheism to the service of the one and only true God and to await the eschatological *parousia* of Christ.

The goal of Paul's mission to the Gentiles was not, however, to make them converts to (Christian) Judaism. As described in Gal 2:1–10 the conference of the Christian leaders in Jerusalem settled that issue after heated debates, especially with a minority opposition. The decision of the majority was that the Christian converts of the Pauline mission would constitute a new entity that was on the one hand a secondary extension of the Jewish-Christian mission to the Jews, while on the other hand not a part of the Jewish religion. This agreement had two consequences. First, Paul and his collaborators were now left with the task of developing new structures for the Gentile-Christian churches located between paganism and Judaism ("neither Jew nor Greek" [Gal 3:28; cf. 1 Cor 12:13]). These Gentile Christians remained culturally Greco-Roman, but ceased religiously being pagan polytheists. This position required the development of a new religious and cultural identity, including theological doctrines, rituals, and codes of behavior and ethics, which would establish and maintain their special place in the ancient world as a corporate entity (the ἐκκλησία τοῦ θεοῦ). Second, this result also clarified that Jewish converts to Peter's mission were not to return simply to "conventional" Judaism but to a new entity within Judaism, a Christian-Jewish reform Judaism, perhaps called by Paul "the Israel of God" (Gal 6:16). As far as this world is concerned, therefore, both mission enterprises were culture-specific, but under an eschatological perspective they were both part of the one salvation of the world by the one God (Gal 2:8; Phil 2:11; Rom 11:25–36).

The authors of the Gospels reflect the religious struggle concerning antiquity and Christianity each in his own way. This comes to expression in the terms by which they make sense of the life and death of Jesus. The Gospel of Mark is the first attempt to compose a variety of sources into a biography of Jesus as both a human being and a divine redeemer.[24] The work boldly places Jesus in the center between Judaism, paganism, and in some sense even Christianity. He is shown to have emerged out of Judaism, appearing as a strange figure even to his closest relatives and disciples, dispensing revelatory wisdom and performing miracles

---

24. In several studies Adela Yarbro Collins has rightly argued that the Gospel of Mark does not fit the genre of typical ancient biographies (*The Beginning of the Gospel: Probings of Mark in Context* [Minneapolis: Fortress, 1992]; eadem, "Rulers, Divine Men, and Walking on the Water (Mark 6:45–52)," in *Religious Propaganda and Missionary Competition in the New Testament World: Essays Honoring Dieter Georgi* [ed. Lukas Bormann, Kelly del Tredici, Angela Standhartinger; Leiden/New York/Cologne: Brill, 1994] 207–27; eadem, "From Noble Death to Crucified Messiah," *NTS* 40 [1994] 481–503).

like a Hellenistic θεῖος ἀνήρ,[25] his true identity as Messiah hidden except for the demons and angels, and his role as the first Christian becoming apparent only in hindsight. Mark's Gospel proved intriguing and provoked revisions and further developments involving the search for the appropriate literary genre, the literary arrangement of disparate sources, clarifications regarding Christology, the transition of the gospel from the Jewish to the Gentile world, and the mission of the church. Only in Luke-Acts are the problems of facing not only Judaism but also pagan polytheism and philosophy, in connection with the expansion of Christianity, made major themes.[26]

III. The Patristic Period

The Apologists

While the New Testament writings and those of the apostolic fathers are preoccupied with the formation of Christianity, from the second century onward the church presupposes the existence of Christianity. The so-called apologists continue to discuss many of the issues raised by the New Testament writings, but they do so in a new context and with different purposes.[27] The main problem concerning antiquity and Christianity that the patristic theologians had to solve was to secure a legitimate space for Christianity in the Greco-Roman society and culture. At the beginning, Christianity, much like Judaism earlier, found itself in the position of a minority regarded with suspicion. As the name "apologists" indicates, these authors attempted to demonstrate the injustice and unfairness of persecuting the new religion, and they did so in writings explaining Christian teachings to outsiders, in particular to the rulers, as compatible with the ancient culture at large. The dilemma was that Christianity refused to be simply integrated into pagan antiquity as just another cult. The apologists justified the Christian rejection of pagan polytheism by endorsing and exploiting the critique of polytheistic religion that had been part of Greek and Roman philosophy since classical times. Positively, the apologists proclaimed Christianity as a new religion, which, however, they described in terms and concepts current and acceptable at

---

25. See, also for bibliography, Bernd Kollmann, *Jesus und die Christen als Wundertäter: Studien zu Magie, Medizin und Schamanismus in Antike und Christentum* (FRLANT 170; Göttingen: Vandenhoeck & Ruprecht, 1996).

26. See Hans-Josef Klauck, *Magie und Heidentum in der Apostelgeschichte des Lukas* (SBS 167; Stuttgart: Katholisches Bibelwerk, 1996), where further bibliography is provided.

27. See Leslie W. Barnard, "Apologetik I: Alte Kirche," *TRE* 3.371–411; Robert M. Grant, *Greek Apologists of the Second Century* (Philadelphia: Westminster, 1988); Reinhart Herzog, *Restauration und Erneuerung: Die lateinische Literatur von 284 bis 374 n. Chr.* (Handbuch der Klassischen Altertumswissenschaft, Abt. 8, Bd. 5; Munich: Beck, 1989) 11, 363–407; Oskar Skarsaune, "Apologetik, IV. 1: Alte Kirche," *RGG* 1 (4th ed.), forthcoming.

the time. Whatever their immediate success may have been, the main result of these enormous efforts in the second to the fourth century was that comprehensive theologies were worked out in competition with the philosophical schools of thought. While some of these theologies opposed the philosophical systems, others were adapted to or merged with them. In this process, so-called Middle Platonism proved especially useful.

THE GNOSTICS

A very different course was pursued by Christian Gnosticism, a kind of intellectual movement that entered into religions and philosophies at the time of nascent Christianity.[28] While not originating in Christianity, its early influences can be detected in some New Testament texts, such as the Pauline and the Johannine writings. Based on a radical dualism, Gnosticism rejected the ancient world in its entirety as the realm of evil, including the Christian *Großkirche*. Their stance was, therefore: Neither antiquity nor world-related Christianity.

THE CHURCH FATHERS

The Christian theologians of the patristic period in turn challenged non-Christian thinkers to come up with new and pointedly pagan conceptions. "Antiquity and Christianity" in this period meant a theological and philosophical contest that in the end decided where the Greco-Roman world was going to go. The extensive writings of the Hermetica and of Neoplatonism contain, in fact, pagan theologies combining older traditions of Egyptian theology and forms of Platonism. While prominent philosophical authors like Celsus, Porphyry, or the emperor Julian openly attacked Christian theology, others simply ignored it but worked ardently at the renewal of Greek and Roman culture and religion. A turning point was reached when in the year 325 the emperor Constantine made Christianity the official religion of the Roman Empire. Thereafter, paganism was deprived of its official status and privileges of support, and it declined rather rapidly. When Augustine wrote his *De civitate Dei libri XXII* in the years 413–426,[29] it repre-

---

28. For survey and bibliography, see Kurt Rudolph, "Gnosticism," *ABD* 2.1033–40.

29. For commentary, see Heinrich Scholz, *Glaube und Unglaube in der Weltgeschichte: Ein Kommentar zu Augustins De civitate dei* (Leipzig: Hinrichs, 1911); Ernst Troeltsch, *Augustin, die christliche Antike und das Mittelalter* (Historische Bibliothek 36; Munich/Berlin: Oldenbourg, 1915); Wilhelm Kamlah, *Christentum und Geschichtlichkeit: Untersuchungen zur Entstehung des Christentums und zu Augustins "Bürgerschaft Gottes"* (2d ed.; Stuttgart/Cologne: Kohlhammer, 1951) 133–340; for more recent discussion and bibliography, see Peter Brown, *Augustine of Hippo: A Biography* (Berkeley: University of California Press, 1967); Robert A. Markus, *Saeculum: History and Society in the Society of St Augustine* (Cambridge: Cambridge University Press, 1970); Klaus Thraede, "Das antike Rom in Augustins De civitate dei: Recht und Grenzen eines

sented the climax of the confrontation of Christian theology with pagan antiquity, but in the many towns and villages of the empire the battle had been decided much earlier. The conquest of the city of Rome by Alaric in 410 and the charge by pagans that this was the fault of Christianity[30] moved Augustine to his final reckoning of the struggle against pagan antiquity. To a large extent Augustine's work also laid the intellectual foundations for the history of the Latin West until the Middle Ages.

IV. THE CULTURE OF BYZANTIUM

After the victory of Christianity and the relocation of the capital from Rome to Byzantium (Constantinople),[31] what we call the Byzantine culture developed in the eastern parts of the empire.[32] The more this culture flourished, the more different it became from the Latin West. Regarding "antiquity and Christianity," Byzantium not only preserved much of the Greek heritage, whether Christian or non-Christian, but it also transformed it into a new symbiosis. In one sense, the Byzantine authors looked back on antiquity as their pagan past, but in another sense they allowed their Greek heritage to play an active role in the formation of the culture. Especially in the christological controversies, Byzantine theology consisted of Christian adaptations of Neoplatonic ideas, notwithstanding the official condemnation of Neoplatonism by the Council of Constantinople of 553.[33] Scholars like the Patriarch Photios (ca. 810–893/4),[34] Michael Psellos (1018–1096/7),[35] Barlaam of Calabria (ca. 1290–1348),[36] and Bessarion of Nicaea

---

verjährten Themas," *JAC* 20 (1977) 90–148; John M. Rist, *Augustine: Ancient Thought Baptized* (Cambridge: Cambridge University Press, 1994).

30. See on this issue Alexander Demandt, *Der Fall Roms: Die Auflösung des römischen Reiches im Urteil der Nachwelt* (Munich: Beck, 1984); idem, *Die Spätantike*, 471–92.

31. See Demandt, *Die Spätantike*, 75–76,391–99.

32. For comprehensive surveys and bibliography, see Hans-Georg Beck, *Kirche und theologische Literatur im byzantinischen Reich* (Handbuch der Klassischen Altertumswissenschaft, Abt. 12, T. 2, Bd. 1 [Byzantinisches Handbuch 2.1]; Munich: Beck, 1959); idem, *Geschichte der orthodoxen Kirche im byzantinischen Reich*, in *Die Kirche in ihrer Geschichte* (vol. 1, Lieferung D 1; Göttingen: Vandenhoeck & Ruprecht, 1980); John Meyendorff, "Byzanz," *TRE* 7.500–531; Demandt, *Die Spätantike*, 75–76, 391–99.

33. See Gerhard Podskalsky, *Theologie und Philosophie in Byzanz: Der Streit um die theologische Methodik in der spätbyzantinischen Geistesgeschichte (14./15. Jh.), seine systematischen Grundlagen und seine historische Entwicklung* (Byzantinisches Archiv 15; Munich: Beck, 1977); Herbert Hunger, *Die hochsprachliche profane Literatur der Byzantiner* (2 vols.; Handbuch der Klassischen Altertumswissenschaft, Abt. 12, T. 5, Bd. 1–2 [Byzantinisches Handbuch 5.1–2]; Munich: Beck, 1978) 1.4–58; Meyendorff, "Byzanz," 517–19.

34. See Franz Tinnefeld, "Photius," *TRE* 26.586–89 (bibliography).

35. See Emmanuel Kriaras, "Psellos," *PWSup* 11 (1968) 1124–82.

36. See Franz Tinnefeld, "Barlaam von Calabrien," *TRE* 5.212–15 (bibliography).

(1403-1472)[37] consciously cultivated the intellectual heritage of Hellenism. Even shortly before the collapse of the empire, the influential Georgios Gemistos Plethon (1355-1452)[38] established in Mistra on the Peloponnesos a new state that was based on Plato's political ideas and also reestablished Greek religion. The activities by the Byzantine scholars as well as the transfer to Italy of their immensely valuable libraries of ancient Greek and Latin literature proved to be a decisive factor in the emergence of the Italian Renaissance, in particular the creation of the Platonic Academy in Florence (1474).[39]

V. RENAISSANCE, HUMANISM, REFORMATION

The tensions between antiquity and Christianity shaped also the humanism of the Renaissance and the Reformation.[40] Again, the result was a fundamental cultural renewal. The decisive turn from the Middle Ages to the Renaissance in the fourteenth century is associated with the names of Francesco Petrarca, Dante Alighieri, and Giovanni Boccaccio. It was their rediscovery of famous Latin literary works that led to the revival of Roman cultural ideals, followed by a renewed interest in Greek literature, philosophy, and language, and as a consequence of it, a new appreciation of the patristic literature. With the cultural and religious institutions of paganism gone, the cultural revolutions of the fifteenth century took place within the institutional structures of the church. This fact is all the more noteworthy, though it is sometimes overlooked, because the renewed interest in antiquity included the so-called occult sciences (alchemy, astrology, magic, and miracles) as well.[41] The leading minds of the time, men

---

37. See Ludwig Mohler, *Kardinal Bessarion als Theologe, Humanist und Staatsmann* (3 vols.; Paderborn: Schöningh, 1923-40); Joseph Gill, "Bessarion," *TRE* 5.725-30 (bibliography).

38. See also, for texts and bibliography, C. M. Woodhouse, *George Gemistos Plethon: The Last of the Hellenes* (Oxford: Clarendon, 1986); Norbert Wokart, "'Hellenische Theologie': Die Religionsform des Georgios Gemistos Plethon," in *Die Restauration der Götter: Antike Religion und Neo-Paganismus* (ed. Richard Faber and Renate Schlesier; Würzburg: Königshausen & Neumann, 1986) 183-97; Wilhelm Blum, *Georgios Gemistos Plethon: Politik, Philosophie und Rhetorik im spätbyzantinischen Reich (1355-1452)* (Bibliothek der griechischen Literatur 25; Stuttgart: Hiersemann, 1988).

39. For the later developments, see Gerhard Podskalsky, *Griechische Theologie in der Zeit der Türkenherrschaft (1453-1821): Die Orthodoxie im Spannungsfeld der nachreformatorischen Konfessionen des Westens* (Munich: Beck, 1988).

40. For a survey of humanism and rich bibliography, see Lewis W. Spitz, "Humanismus/ Humanismusforschung," *TRE* 15.639-61.

41. See the essays and bibliographies in *Hermeticism and the Renaissance: Intellectual History and the Occult in Early Modern Europe* (ed. Ingrid Merkel and Allen G. Debus; London/ Toronto: Associated University Presses; Washington: The Folger Shakespeare Library, 1988); *Occult and Scientific Mentalities in the Renaissance* (ed. Brian Vickers; Cambridge: Cambridge University Press, 1984); *Die okkulten Wissenschaften in der Renaissance* (ed. August Buck; Wolfenbütteler Mitteilungen zur Renaissanceforschung 12; Wiesbaden: Harrassowitz, 1992).

like Nicolaus Cusanus,[42] Marsilio Ficino,[43] and Giovanni Pico della Mirandola[44] intended nothing but a new synthesis of Christian faith and Platonism (i.e., Neoplatonism). The title of Ficino's main work *Theologia Platonica*, written 1469–1474, indicates programmatically what the result of the synthesis was: Christian faith and Platonic love were to melt into a new reality altogether. It took a figure like Laurentius Valla to point out that ancient Platonism and Christianity presented fundamental alternatives between which choices had to be made. While Valla's work *On the Free Will* (*De libero arbitrio*)[45] pointed to the central problem, the world-historical controversy in the years 1524–1525 between Desiderius Erasmus (*De libero arbitrio*) and Martin Luther (*De servo arbitrio*) exposed the full extent of the conflict.[46]

Although the Reformers did not repudiate the Renaissance and humanism, in which they all were deeply rooted, the Reformation marked for them the historical event in which under Luther's leadership they saw the rediscovery and revival of what was the *proprium* in Christianity, the *viva vox evangelii*.[47] To some extent, it can be argued, the Reformation appears to be simply another step in the course of the Renaissance. In reality, however, the Reformation opened up a new era with a wide variety of new configurations of "antiquity and Christianity." Important for the translation of the Bible became the Reformers' study of Hebrew, Greek, and Latin philology and literature (Johannes Reuchlin [1455–

---

42. For Nicolaus's idea about an "oecumene of religions," agreeing on monotheism while tolerating variety in observing rituals, see Michael Seidlmayer, "'Una religio in rituum varietate': Zur Religionsauffassung des Nikolaus von Kues," *Archiv für Kulturgeschichte* 36 (1954) 145–207; Wolfgang Heinemann, *Einheit in Verschiedenheit: Das Konzept eines intellektuellen Religionsfriedens in der Schrift "De pace fidei" des Nikolaus von Kues* (Altenberge: Christlich-Islamisches Schrifttum, 1987). On Nicolaus and for bibliography, see Hans Gerhard Senger, "Nikolaus von Kues (Nicolaus de Cusa, Nicolaus Cusanus) (1401–1664)," TRE 24.554–64.

43. See Paul Oskar Kristeller, *The Philosophy of Marsilio Ficino* (New York: Columbia University Press, 1943); idem, *Die Philosophie des Marsilio Ficino* (Frankfurt a. M.: Klostermann, 1972); Ilana Klutstein, *Marsilio Ficino et la théologie ancienne: Oracles chaldaïques—Hymnes Orphiques—Hymnes de Proclus* (Istituto nazionale di studi sul rinascimento 5; [Florence]: Olschki, 1987); Josef Nolte, "Ficino, Marsilio (1433–1499)," TRE 11.171–75; Gian Carlo Garfagnini, *Marsilio Ficino e il Ritorno di Platone: Studi e documenti* (2 vols.; Istituto nazionale di studi sul rinascimento: studi e testi 15; Florence: Olschki, 1986).

44. For current scholarship and bibliography, see *Pico, Poliziano e l'Umanesimo di fine Quattrocento: Biblioteca Medicea Laurenziana 4 novembre–31 dicembre 1994* (ed. Paolo Viti; Centro internazionale di cultura 'Giovanni Pico della Mirandola': studi Pichiani 2; Florence: Olschki,1994); Gian Carlo Garfagnini, "Pico della Mirandola, Giovanni," TRE 26.602–6.

45. *Laurentius Valla, De libero arbitrio* (ed. Maria Anfossi; Florence: Olschki, 1934).

46. See Gerhard Ebeling, "Luthers Kampf gegen die Moralisierung des Christlichen," in his *Lutherstudien* (Tübingen: Mohr-Siebeck, 1985) 3.44–73, esp. 63–70: "Die Auseinandersetzung mit Erasmus."

47. See Gerhard Ebeling, "Luther und der Anbruch der Neuzeit," in his *Wort und Glaube* (Tübingen: Mohr-Siebeck, 1975) 3.29–59.

1522], Philipp Melanchthon [1497–1560]), because these interests opened the door to the scholarly investigation of the Bible.

Only the so-called left wing of the Reformation understood the Reformation to imply an apocalyptic repudiation of all ancient history, culture, and forms of Christianity, and the call to return to the New Testament with its plain and uncorrupted gospel of Jesus. Destroyed by military defeat or forced into emigration, the left wing of the Reformation had little influence on the predominant direction of European culture.

The major changes in the post-Reformation period came with the social and cultural emergence of a new profession, the university-related scholar largely independent of the church and its dogmas. In many different ways, "antiquity and Christianity" became the subject of scholarly and scientific study or of artistic and literary representations.

VI. Enlightenment and Rationalism

One result of the Reformation was that henceforth no further attempts were made to harmonize antiquity and Christianity. The Enlightenment[48] cast the relationship between the two within elaborate categories of historical periodization.[49] In this respect, the most important thinkers were Hermann Samuel Reimarus (1694–1768),[50] Gotthold Ephraim Lessing (1729–1781),[51] and Johann Gottfried Herder (1744–1803).[52] Instead of juxtaposing antiquity and Christianity, both were divided into historical epochs. Classical antiquity was distinguished, on the one side, from the so-called prehistoric times (*Urgeschichte*)

---

48. For an overview and rich bibliographies, see Rainer Piepmeier, Martin Schmidt, Hermann Greive, "Aufklärung I–III," *TRE* 4.575–615; Horst Stuke, "Aufklärung," in *Geschichtliche Grundbegriffe: Historisches Lexikon zur politisch-sozialen Sprache in Deutschland* (ed. Otto Brunner, Werner Conze, Reinhart Koselleck; Stuttgart: Klett, 1972) 1.243–342. For important essays, see *Historische Kritik und biblischer Kanon in der deutschen Aufklärung* (ed. Henning Graf Reventlow, Walter Sparn, John Woodbridge; Wolfenbütteler Forschungen 41; Wiesbaden: Harrassowitz, 1988).

49. See Reinhart Koselleck, "Fortschritt," in *Geschichtliche Grundbegriffe* 2 (1975) 351–423; Christian Meier, Odilo Engels, Horst Günther, "Geschichte," ibid., 593–717; Karl Löwith, *Weltgeschichte und Heilsgeschehen: Zur Kritik der Geschichtsphilosophie*, in his *Sämtliche Schriften* (Stuttgart: Metzler, 1983) vol. 2.

50. Hermann Samuel Reimarus, *Apologie oder Schutzschrift für die vernünftigen Verehrer Gottes* (ed. Gerhard Alexander; 2 vols.; Frankfurt: Insel, 1972).

51. See Karl Aner, *Theologie der Lessingzeit* (Halle: Niemeyer, 1929); Leopold Zscharnack, *Lessing und Sender: Ein Beitrag zur Entstehungsgeschichte des Rationalismus und der kritischen Theologie* (Giessen: Töpelmann, 1905); R. F. Merkel, "Lessing und Herder als Religionshistoriker," *Theologisch Tijdschrift* 25 (1936) 129–44.

52. See Johann Gottfried Herder, *Ideen zur Philosophie der Geschichte der Menschheit*, in *Johann Gottfried Herder, Werke in zehn Bänden* (ed. Martin Bollacher; Frankfurt a. M.: Deutscher Klassiker Verlag, 1989) vol. 6.

and the ancient Orient, and, on the other side, from Hellenism, Romanism, and the ethnic religions of the Germans, Celts, Slavs, and so on. Within Christianity, the period of the historical Jesus[53] was distinguished from primitive Christianity (*Urchristentum*)[54] that included both Jewish and Gentile Christianity. The idea that hellenized Christianity began with Paul also originated in the eighteenth century.[55] As exemplified by the works of Siegmund Jakob Baumgarten (1706–1757),[56] his student Johann Salomo Semler (1725–1791),[57] and Johann Jakob Wettstein (1693–1754),[58] mere juxtaposition of antiquity and Christianity was now changed to religio-historical comparison between them. This approach resulted in a relativizing of both antiquity and Christianity in that they were distinguished from a primordial, purely natural *Urreligion* of reason. A special place in that history was attributed to Socrates and Jesus by identifying the natural religion of reason with both these preeminent teachers.[59] By contrast, later Christian dogma and Hellenistic philosophy were both seen as showing the marks of decline from the master.

---

53. For the origin of the juxtaposition of Jesus and Paul since Reimarus and Lessing, see Friedemann Regner, *"Paulus und Jesus" im neunzehnten Jahrhundert: Beiträge zur Geschichte des Themas "Paulus und Jesus" in der neutestamentlichen Theologie* (Studien zur Theologie- und Geistesgeschichte des Neunzehnten Jahrhunderts 30; Göttingen: Vandenhoeck & Ruprecht, 1977). For a review of this important work, see Otto Merk, *TLZ* 115 (1990) 350–51.

54. See Stefan Alkier, *Urchristentum: Zur Geschichte und Theologie einer exegetischen Disziplin* (BHT 83; Tübingen: Mohr-Siebeck, 1993).

55. For the origins of Paulinism and anti-Paulinism, see Regner, *"Paulus und Jesus,"* 74ff., 103ff.

56. For a comprehensive overview of the literature of the sixteenth to eighteenth century regarding the "religious parties" (including atheists, pagans, Jews, Muslims, Christian heretics and denominations), see Siegmund Jakob Baumgarten, *Geschichte der Religionsparteyen* (ed. Johann Salomo Semler; Halle: Gebauer, 1766; reprint, Hildesheim: Olms, 1966); on Baumgarten, with further bibliography, see Martin Schloemann, *Siegmund Jacob Baumgarten: System und Geschichte in der Theologie des Übergangs zum Neuprotestantismus* (Forschungen zur Kirchen- und Dogmengeschichte 26; Göttingen: Vandenhoeck & Ruprecht, 1974).

57. Semler was one of the first to look at the history of religions comparatively. He proposed that from the beginning Christianity existed in several varieties, all going back to the historical Jesus. See his self-apology, *Joh[ann] Sal[omo] Semlers Versuch einer freieren theologischen Lehrart, zur Bestätigung und Erläuterung seines lateinischen Buches* (Halle: Hemmerde, 1777). On Semler, see Hartmut H. R. Schulz, *Johann Salomo Senders Wesensbestimmung des Christentums: Ein Beitrag zur Erforschung der Theologie Semlers* (Würzburg: Königshausen & Neumann, 1988); Alkier, *Urchristentum*, 34–44.

58. For introduction and bibliography, see C. L. Hulbert-Powell, *John James Wettstein 1693–1754: An Account of his Life, Work and Some of His Contemporaries* (London: SPCK, 1937 [1938]); *Neuer Wettstein: Texte zum Neuen Testament aus Griechentum und Hellenismus*, Band II/1-2, *Texte zur Briefliteratur und zur Johannesapokalypse* (ed. Georg Strecker and Udo Schnelle; Berlin: de Gruyter, 1996).

59. See Benno Böhm, *Sokrates im 18. Jahrhundert: Studien zum Werdegang des modernen Persönlichkeitsbewußtseins* (2d ed.; Neumünster: Wachholtz, 1966).

VII. The New Humanism

These views were soon to be contested. Against the devaluation of Greek and Roman antiquity arose a thoroughgoing revaluation of Greek art and culture in the eighteenth century, begun by Johann Joachim Winckelmann[60] and elevated to prominence by Johann Wolfgang von Goethe, Friedrich von Schiller, and Friedrich Hölderlin. The discovery of antique art works (*Antiken*)[61] in Italy was taken as evidence that antiquity was by no means extinct and gone, but that it was a present and living reality, a splendid foundation for the renewal of an emerging European culture.[62] Idealizing classical antiquity and articulating its literary and philosophical values as a new humanism (*Neuhumanismus*)[63] were consciously positioned against the Christian churches and their culture. While Herder as *Generalsuperintendent* still acted as an official of Protestantism, Winckelmann and Goethe proudly but ambiguously declared themselves to be "pagans" (*Heiden*).[64] This kind of humanistic neopaganism became popular especially among educated Protestants, the very people whom Friedrich Schleiermacher addressed as the "*cultured* among the despisers" in his *Über die Religion: Reden an die Gebildeten unter ihren Verächtern*.[65] Such efforts by Schleiermacher and, in a different way, by

---

60. Of great influence was Goethe's essay "Winckelmann"; see *Johann Wolfgang von Goethe, Werke* (ed. Erich Trunz; Hamburger Ausgabe; 11th ed.; Munich: Beck, 1989) 12.96–129; further, *Johann Joachim Winckelmann (1717–1768)* (ed. Thomas W. Gaethgens; Studien zum 18. Jahrhundert 7; Hamburg: Meiner, 1986).

61. For the origin of the concept of *Antike*, see Walter Müri, "Die Antike: Untersuchung über den Ursprung und die Entwicklung einer geschichtlichen Epoche," *Antike und Abendland* 7 (1958) 745.

62. So Goethe's interpretation ("Winckelmann," 100–101).

63. See Klaus Prange, "Neuhumanismus," *TRE* 24.315–18.

64. Goethe points to Winckelmann's "paganism" as well as his Lutheran piety ("Winckelmann," 101, 120). On Winckelmann's and Goethe's "paganism," see Peter Meinhold, *Goethe zur Geschichte des Christentums* (Freiburg/Munich: Albig, 1958) esp. 238–46; Jörg Baur, "'Alles Vereinzelte ist verwerflich': Überlegungen zu Goethe," *Neue Zeitschrift für Systematische Theologie* 33(1991) 152–66.

65. Friedrich Schleiermacher, *Ueber die Religion: Reden an die Gebildeten unter ihren Verächtern* (Berlin: Unger, 1799; reprinted in Friedrich Daniel Ernst Schleiermacher, *Schriften aus der Berliner Zeit 1800–1802* [ed. Günter Meckenstock; Kritische Gesamtausgabe 1/3; Berlin/New York: de Gruyter, 1988]; Eng. trans. Friedrich Schleiermacher, *On Religion: Speeches to Its Cultured Despisers* [Introduction, translation and notes by Richard Crouter; Cambridge: Cambridge University Press, 1988]). On Schleiermacher, see esp. Gerhard Ebeling, "Frömmigkeit und Bildung," in his *Wort und Glaube* (Tübingen: Mohr-Siebeck, 1975) 3.60–95; idem, "Zum Religionsbegriff Schleiermachers," in *Wort und Glaube*, vol. 4, *Theologie in den Gegensätzen des Lebens* (Tübingen: Mohr-Siebeck, 1995) 55–75; Markus Schröder, *Die kritische Identität des neuzeitlichen Christentums: Schleiermachers Wesensbestimmung der christlichen Religion* (BHT 96; Tübingen: Mohr-Siebeck, 1996).

Georg Friedrich Wilhelm Hegel[66] could not prevent the new humanistic ideal of being a cultured person (*Gebildeter*),[67] contemptuous of Christian religion, from becoming part of the mentality of the nineteenth and twentieth centuries.[68] Characteristically, this mentality consists of wavering loyalties. In many ways, Goethe was a prototype of what was then imitated by many; for instance, he is reported to have described himself thus: "in the natural sciences and philosophy he is an atheist, in art a pagan, and in his intuitive feelings a Christian."[69] This mentality was soon to be coopted by political ideologies that also moved toward implementing the consequences of these commitments for the political, cultural, and religious institutions.[70] Most influential in these developments were Karl Marx, Bruno Bauer, Arthur Schopenhauer, Friedrich Nietzsche,[71] and Franz Overbeck.[72] On the Christian side, Adolf von Harnack tried to meet the challenge with his thesis concerning the "Hellenization of Christianity"[73] and his inaugural lectures in Berlin, published under the title "The Essence of Christianity" (*Das Wesen des*

---

66. See the summary of Hegel's philosophy of history by Erich Weichel, "Hegels Geschichtsphilosophie," *Neue Zeitschrift für Systematische Theologie* 33 (1991) 23–43.

67. See on the concept of "Bildung" ("culturedness") Ebeling, "Frömmigkeit und Bildung," 76–95.

68. On the developments from Schleiermacher to Albrecht Ritschl, see Franz Courth, *Das Wesen des Christentums in der Liberalen Theologie, dargestellt am Werk Friedrich Schleiermachers, Ferdinand Christian Baurs und Albrecht Ritschls* (Theologie im Übergang 3; Frankfurt/Bern/Las Vegas: Lang, 1977); Berthold Lannert, *Die Wiederentdeckung der neutestamentlichen Eschatologie durch Johannes Weiß* (Texte und Arbeiten zum neutestamentlichen Zeitalter 2; Tübingen: Francke, 1989).

69. Reported by Dorothea von Schlegel: "Goethe hat einem Durchreisenden offenbart, er sei in der Naturkunde und Philosophy ein Atheist, in der Kunst eine Heide und dem Gefühl nach ein Christ!—Jetzt wissen wir es also ganz naiv von ihm selber, wie so er es nirgends zur Wahrheit bringt. Der arme Mann! mich dauert er sehr" (Dorothea von Schlegel, 18th November 1817, cited according to *Dorothea v. Schlegel geb. Mendelssohn und deren Söhne Johannes und Philipp Veit: Briefwechsel* [ed. J. M. Reich; Mainz: Kirchheim, 1881] 2.452; trans. mine). Dorothea was the second daughter of Moses Mendelssohn; she was swept up in the early romanticists' wave of conversions, first to Protestant Pietism, then to Roman Catholicism, to all of which Goethe was fiercely opposed.

70. For important essays dealing with these problems, see *Philologie und Hermeneutik im 19. Jahrhundert: Zur Geschichte und Methodologie der Geisteswissenschaften* (ed. Hellmut Flashar, Karlfried Gründer, Axel Horstmann; Göttingen: Vandenhoeck & Ruprecht, 1979).

71. See Heinrich Kutzner, "Friedrich Nietzsches Antichristentum und Neuheidentum: Zu ihrer psychohistorischen Dimension," in *Die Restauration der Götter*, 88–104. See also nn. 13, 14 above.

72. See n. 12 above.

73. For this hypothesis, its historical background and bibliography, see Walther Glawe, *Die Hellenisierung des Christentums in der Geschichte der Theologie von Luther bis auf die Gegenwart* (Neue Studien zur Geschichte der Theologie und der Kirche 15; Berlin: Trowitzsch, 1912); E. P. Meijering, *Die Hellenisierung des Christentums im Urteil Adolf von Harnacks* (Verhandelingen der Koninklijke Nederlandse Akademie van Wetenschappen, Afd. Letterkunde, Nieuwe Reeks,

Christentums).[74] He argued for a critical distinction to be made between the simple and undogmatic gospel of Jesus and hellenized Christianity, qualified negatively because of its institutionalized dogmatism. In opposition to the goals of the *Religionsgeschichtliche Schule* Harnack argued vigorously against secular departments of religious studies, as we would call them, and for the retaining of the traditional faculties of theology.[75] At the same time, his colleague at the Humboldt University in Berlin, the influential classicist Ulrich von Wilamowitz-Moellendorff wanted to institute the idealized values of Greek culture as the foundation for the modem educational system.[76] On this point, Wilamowitz agreed even with Nietzsche,[77] although the latter was different from the former because of his eschatological expectation that after the end of Christianity there would occur a rebirth of the ancient Hellenic culture, and it would be under the sign of Dionysos.[78]

---

deel 128; Amsterdam: North Holland, 1985); idem, "Adolf von Harnack und das Problem des Platonismus," in *Patristique et Antiquité tardive*, 155-64.

74. Adolf von Harnack, *Das Wesen des Christentums* (Leipzig: Hinrichs, 1900; republished by Rudolf Bultmann; Stuttgart: Klotz, 1950); Eng. trans. *What Is Christianity?* (New York: Harper, 1957). For the history and background, see Hans Wagenhammer, *Das Wesen des Christentums: Eine begriffsgeschichtliche Untersuchung* (Mainz: Grünewald, 1972); Johanna Jantsch, *Die Entstehung des Christentums bei Adolf von Harnack und Eduard Meyer* (Bonn: Habelt, 1990); Schröder, *Die kritische Identität*, 1-11, 158-59, 231.

75. Adolf Harnack, "Die Aufgabe der theologischen Fakultaten und die allgemeine Religionsgeschichte: Nebst einem Nachwort," in his *Reden und Aufsätze* (2d ed.; Giessen: Töpelmann, 1906) 2.159-87; see also Karl Holl, "Urchristentum und Religionsgeschichte," in his *Gesammelte* Aufsätze (Tübingen: Mohr-Siebeck, 1928) 2.1-32.

76. The role and significance of Wilamowitz has recently been investigated in a number of important contributions. See, also for bibliography, Manfred Landfester, "Ulrich von Wilamowitz-Moellendorff und die hermeneutische Tradition des 19. Jahrhunderts," in Flashar, *Philologie und Hermeneutik*, 156-80; *Wilamowitz nach 50 Jahren* (ed William M. Calder III, Hellmut Flashar, and Theodor Lindken; Darmstadt: Wissenschaftliche Buchgesellschaft, 1985), esp. Albert Henrichs, "'Der Glaube der Hellenen': Religionsgeschichte als Glaubensbekenntnis und Kulturkritik" (pp. 263-305); Luciano Canfora, "Wilamowitz und die Schulreform: Das 'Griechische Lesebuch'" (pp. 632-48). Important are further contributions by Bernhard vom Brocke, "'Von des attischen Reiches Herrlichkeit' oder die 'Modernisierung' der Antike im Zeitalter des Nationalstaates: Mit einem Exkurs über die Zerschlagung der Wilamowitz-Schule durch den Nationalsozialismus," *Historische Zeitschrift* 243 (1986) 101-36; Rudolf Kassel, review of William M. Calder, *Wilamowitz nach 50 Jahren*, in *Göttingische Gelehrte Anzeigen* 239 (1987) 188-228; Araldo Momigliano, *New Paths of Classicism in the Nineteenth Century* (History and Theory 21:4; Middletown, CT: Wesleyan University Press, 1982).

77. Wilamowitz's disavowal of Christianity and his dedication to Plato's religion was revealed in an unpublished autobiography. See William Calder III, "Ulrich von Wilamowitz-Moellendorff: An Unpublished Latin Autobiography," *Antike und Abendland* 27 (1981) 34-51; idem, *Studies in the Modern History of Classical Scholarship* (Antiqua 27; Naples: Jovene Editore, 1984), esp. part 2, "Wilamowitziana."

78. On "neopaganism" in the twentieth century, see the essays assembled in the volume edited by Richard Faber and Renate Schlesier, *Die Restauration der Götter*.

VIII. The Twentieth Century

These ideals and utopias collapsed as a result of the catastrophes of two World Wars and the aftermath of social and political revolutions inside and outside of Europe. Institutionally, the established churches survived the catastrophes as well as the unprecedented anti-Christian propaganda and repression campaigns by the quasi-religious ideologies of National Socialism and Marxism-Leninism. Yet it took a series of comprehensive new theologies worked out by leading Protestants like Karl Barth, Rudolf Bultmann, Friedrich Gogarten, Dietrich Bonhoeffer, and Paul Tillich to renew possibilities of credibility for Christian faith and life.

These theologians no longer argued in confrontation with classical antiquity and its humanistic interpretations of the eighteenth and nineteenth centuries, but against the political ideologies and new beliefs based on the progress made by science, medicine, and technology. Apparently, after World War II the heritage of classical antiquity was finally lost.[79] The attempts at a "Third Humanism" by Werner Jaeger, and in different ways by the leading philosophers Jean Paul Sartre and Martin Heidegger, to legitimate existentialist philosophy as a humanism had no chance of a lasting success.[80] The combined forces of ideological criticism inspired by Marxism, popular modernism of a society oriented toward consumerism, and new directions in art and literature seemed to have extinguished any enthusiasm for antiquity.[81] By implication, classical antiquity was declared totally antiquated.[82]

---

79. See the provocative inaugural lecture by Manfred Fuhrmann, *Die Antike und ihre Vermittler: Bemerkungen zur gegenwärtigen Situation der Klassischen Philologie* (Konstanz Universitätsverlag, 1969); cf. the review by Wolfgang Schmid (*Gnomon* 42 [1970] 507–14) and the debate between Manfred Fuhrmann and Hermann Tränkle, *Wie klassisch ist die Antike?* (Zurich/Stuttgart: Artemis, 1970).

80. See esp. Werner Jaeger, *Humanistische Reden und Vorträge* (Berlin: de Gruyter, 1937; 2d ed., 1960); Jean Paul Sartre, L'Existentialisme est un humanisme (Collection Pensées; Paris: Nagel, 1946); Eng. trans. *Existentialism and Humanism* (Brooklyn: Haskell House, 1977); Martin Heidegger, "Brief über den Humanismus" [1947], in his *Wegmarken* (2d ed.; Frankfurt a. M.: Klostermann, 1978) 311–60; see Robert Henri Cousineau, *Humanism and Ethics: An Introduction to Heidegger's Letter on Humanism, with a Critical Bibliography* (Louvain: Nauwelaerts, 1972).

81. See Heidegger, "Brief über den Humanismus," 318: "Der Humanismus von Marx bedarf keines Rückgangs zur Antike, ebensowenig der Humanismus, als welchen Sartre den Existenzialismus begreift" ("The humanism advocated by Marx has no need for a recourse to antiquity, just as little as the humanism Sartre understands existentialism to be" [trans. mine]).

82. Also for Heidegger ("Brief über den Humanismus," 341) the word humanism has lost its meaning ("dieses Wort [hat] seinen Sinn verloren"). "Es hat ihn verloren durch die Einsicht, daß das Wesen des Humanismus metaphysisch ist und das heißt jetzt, daß die Metaphysik die Frage nach der Wahrheit des Seins nicht nur nicht stellt, sonder verbaut, insofer die Metaphysik in der Seinsvergessenheit verharrt" ("It lost its meaning because of the insight, that the essence of humanism is metaphysical, and this now means that metaphysics not only fails to raise the quest for the truth of being but precludes it, insofar as metaphysics remains in the state of for-

Not so for Bultmann, however![83] For him the dialogue between antiquity and Christianity constituted the heart of the historical and cultural debate between the present and the past.[84] In a memorandum from 1946 concerning the reorganization of German universities after World War II, Bultmann declared: "The question of the *relationship of the university to antiquity and Christianity* for the most part coincides with the question of the *unity of the university.* Is our university only a random collection of specialized scientific enterprises, or is it truly a 'universitas,' a unity, the parts of which-the specialized scientific enterprises-belong together as the members of an organism?"[85]

At the end of the twentieth century, the situation appears to be changing again. The postmodern world is characterized by deep-seated disillusionment. The promises of political-social ideologies and utopias of progressivism have turned out to be mostly fabricated myths and illusions of the credulous masses. This disenchantment has laid bare the ills of an impoverished quality of life, in particular inner emptiness, purposeless activism, breakdown of ethical and social values, and cultural deterioration. Barbarity, supposedly eradicated by a mature civilization, was back. The older mentality of progressive optimism has given way to a cynical pessimism concerning the possibilities of human fulfillment and to a gloomy prospect of apocalyptic cataclysm in the future.

This description, however, reflects only the most conspicuous side of present public mentality. There are other factors, the strength of which can hardly escape the alert observer. Information about the ancient world and access to it have expanded in a breadth and depth unimaginable only a few decades ago. Public interest and participation in archaeological discoveries, visits to museum exhibitions of ancient art, and tourists traveling to ancient sites and monuments are at

---

getfulness of being"). This is, of course, not Heidegger's last word. See also Karl Jaspers, *Über Bedingungen und Möglichkeiten eines neuen Humanismus* (1951; reprint, Stuttgart: Reclam, 1962).

83. See Bultmann's *Das Urchristentum im Rahmen der antiken Religionen* (Zurich: Artemis, 1949); Eng. trans. *Primitive Christianity in Its Contemporary Setting* (New York: Meridian, 1959). The theme "antiquity and Christianity" continuously occurs in titles of his publications; see the bibliography in his *Exegetica: Aufsätze zur Erforschung des Neuen Testaments* (ed. Erich Dinkler; Tübingen: Mohr-Siebeck, 1967) 483–507.

84. This was rightly emphasized by Erich Dinkler in his lecture in memory of Bultmann, given on November 16, 1976, "Die christliche Wahrheitsfrage und die Unabgeschlossenheit der Theologie als Wissenschaft: Bemerkungen zum wissenschaftlichen Werk Rudolf Bultmanns." The lecture was published in *Gedenken an Rudolf Bultmann* (Tübingen: Mohr-Siebeck, 1977) 15–40, esp. 35–40.

85. Cited according to Dinkler, "Die Wahrheitsfrage," 37 n. 28: "Die Frage nach dem *Verhältnis der Universität zu Antike und Christentum* fällt weithin zusammen mit der Frage nach der *Einheit der Universität.* Ist unsere Universität nur eine Sammelstätte für alle möglichen Einzelwissenschaften, oder ist sie eine wirkliche 'Universitas,' eine Einheit, deren Teile—die Einzelwissenschaften—als die Glieder eines Organismus zusammengehören?"

an all-time high. The number of scholars involved in the many fields of research on antiquity as well as the volume and quality of scholarly publications have never been larger and better than they are in the present generation. Stimulated by the awareness of the worldwide pluralism of cultures and religions past and present, the study of antiquity and Christianity has apparently entered into a new phase. Given this new awareness of a global symbiosis of religious cultures, seen in their historical, social, and cultural dimensions, one can reasonably hope that the study of antiquity and Christianity may again provide criteria of interpretation and conduct for a world that is in danger of losing all meaning and measure.

PRESIDENTIAL ADDRESS

by

CAROLYN OSIEK

President of the Society of Biblical Literature 2005
Annual Meeting of the Society of Biblical Literature
November 19, 2005
Philadelphia, Pennsylvania

*Introduction given by Robert A. Kraft,
Vice President, Society of Biblical Literature*

It would perhaps be enough simply to read or summarize for you what is printed on p. 11 of the program book—that Lyn Osiek is Charles Fischer Catholic Professor of New Testament at Brite Divinity School of Texas Christian University, having relocated in 2003 from the Catholic Theological Union in Chicago, where she had served for a quarter of a century as Professor of New Testament. She has already been president of the Catholic Biblical Association (ten years ago, 1994–95) and is currently on the executive council of the Studiorum Novi Testamenti Societas, while also performing editorial and other scholarly functions for both of those organizations and for the North American Patristics Society. And she has published a lot, including NT commentaries, thematic studies on families and women in early Christianity, and even a commentary on the second-century *Shepherd of Hermas* in the Hermeneia series (1999), following up on her 1978 Th.D. dissertation at Harvard Divinity School (directed by Helmut Koester), *Rich and Poor in the Shepherd of Hermas* (CBQMS 15; 1983).*[1]

But we are surrounded here with scholars, many of whom also can boast of long bibliographies and impressive academic accomplishments. I'd like to put a more human face on Lyn, by telling you some things about her that few here

---

*For a more complete bibliography (and her picture), the interested reader should visit the Brite Divinity School Web site: http://www.brite.tcu.edu/directory/osiek/index.htm. For more details on her professional accomplishments, see also http://studentorg.cua.edu/cbib/cnop.cfm.

would know—perhaps some that even she herself doesn't know. Calling up her name in its various permutations (including the middle initial A., which I imagined might perhaps be for her paternal grandmother Achepohl, but she has just informed me that it stands for Ann—a disappointment for us genealogists) on a Web searcher such as Google produces more than fifteen hundred hits of various sorts.

Lyn's family name, Osiek (Ohsiek), seems to be Eastern European (Polish or Czech)—I'm sure she is asked about it more than a little—but the family genealogists who are represented on the Internet trace her immediate family back to late-eighteenth-century Germany, and her great-great-grandfather Caspar Heinrich Osiek in the northwest part of that country. The Osiek ancestors came to America in the mid-1800s and settled in Missouri (appropriately St. Charles county), where Lyn was born and bred—and where she happily mastered the skills of horseback riding. She's an only child with a strong Lutheran as well as Catholic family heritage. She has even done some family history writing herself, in the *St. Charles County Heritage* magazine 21, no. 4 (2003), "Recollections of Omar Henry Osiek (1906–1986)" [her father].

Lyn has traveled widely, and as recently as spring 2001 taught at a seminary in West Africa. Interestingly, the only detail about her that is mentioned in the online genealogy, beyond her birthdate (which I'll let you find for yourselves), is that she is a "member of Catholic Theological Union," information that certainly needs to be updated. She is also designated elsewhere on Google as "Sr" (Sister) and more cryptically as "RSCJ" (Religieuse du Sacre Coeur de Jesus— http://www.rscj.org, which translates as "Religious of the Sacred Heart")—not "RSJC" as in some Web entries. Those Internet ascriptions perhaps can serve well here as appropriate transitions to her presidential address. She is the fourth woman and the eighth Catholic to preside over the SBL. She speaks to us now on the subject "Catholic or catholic? Biblical Scholarship at the Center." Carolyn A. Osiek.

Catholic or catholic?
Biblical Scholarship at the Center*

Carolyn Osiek
Brite Divinity School, Texas Christian University

Sometime in the first decade of the second century, Ignatius, bishop of Antioch in Syria, was condemned to death *ad bestias*, that is, by wild animals in the amphitheater. He was sent under guard with other prisoners to Rome for the games there, probably in the Flavian Amphitheater, what today we call the Colosseum. As his party made its way up the western coast of Asia Minor, he wrote to a string of Christian communities there after he had received visits from their envoys. When writing to the Christians of Smyrna, he remarks that the Eucharist should be celebrated only by the bishop or someone he delegates, for "wherever the bishop appears, let the whole community be gathered, just as wherever Jesus Christ is, there is ἡ καθολικὴ ἐκκλησία (*Smyrn*. 8.2). A generation later, in the same city, old bishop Polycarp was about to be martyred in the amphitheater. But the narrator of his martyrdom reports that when the police came to arrest him in a country house where he had taken refuge, since it was dinnertime, he ordered food and drink to be set out for them, while he went aside and prayed aloud for two hours. In his prayer, he remembered everyone he had ever encountered and ἡ καθολικὴ ἐκκλησία throughout the world. The narrator finished the report of Polycarp's martyrdom by concluding that now Polycarp is enjoying the glory of God and Jesus Christ, shepherd of ἡ καθολικὴ ἐκκλησία throughout the world (*Mart. Pol.* 8.1; 19.2).

The word καθολικός was in general use in Hellenistic Greek, meaning "general" or "universal." Thus Iamblichus (*Life of Pythagoras* 15.65) speaks of "universal harmony" and Epictetus speaks of οἱ καθολικοί as general principles or standards (4.4.29; 2.12.7). Indeed, today we are accustomed to calling the NT Letters of James, Jude, 1–2 Peter and John the "catholic epistles," mostly because we really do not have a clue whence they came or whither they were destined.

---

* Presidential Address delivered on November 19, 2005, at the annual meeting of the Society of Biblical Literature in Philadelphia, Pennsylvania.

Similarly, the fourth-century Christian historian Eusebius, quoting the anti-Montanist Apollonius, recalls a Montanist writer Themisto, who wrote an ἐπιστολή καθολική "in imitation of the apostle" (*Hist. eccl.* 5.18.5). By the fourth century, the word was taking on a more specific meaning of orthodox Christianity, as when Constantine, quoted in Eusebius, refers to the church represented by Eusebius as the καθολική θρεσκεία, perhaps best translated as the catholic religion (*Hist. eccl.* 10.6.1).

The *Oxford Dictionary of the Christian Church* gives five definitions of the word "catholic": (1) universal, not local; (2) orthodox, not heretical; (3) the undivided church before 1054; (4) from 1054 to the sixteenth century, not Orthodox; (5) Western, not Protestant. This is a handy resume of the mutations in meaning acquired by this simple little word over the centuries, and it is ironic to note that this word, meant to be all-inclusive, in every case but one (the undivided church before 1054) is defined over against something else. While Ignatius and Polycarp back in the second century sound as if they mean the whole church, in effect they probably really mean that network of many local churches that profess roughly the same faith and are in communion with each other. Ignatius had some harsh things to say about those who disagreed with him about how to live the Christian life. They would probably not be included when he thinks about his universal church.

So the irony is that a word and an idea meant to include everyone have historically been used most often to delineate some against others. Most of us when reciting the Apostles' Creed say that we believe in the "holy catholic church," with small *c* or capital *C,* depending on our situation, but in this context it is intended to be restored to its original meaning of "universal." Yet the Catholic Church with capital *C,* more commonly known as the Roman Catholic Church, is in many respects universal and in some aspects quite particular. It is found in nearly every country in the world. With the changes of Vatican Council II, many Catholics lamented the loss of the Latin liturgy, which had become a universally recognized ritual, at least in the West. It was said that a Catholic could walk into a Catholic Church anywhere in the West and understand the progression of the ritual. Today the Roman Catholic Church is creeping slowly toward the particularity of truly indigenous liturgical traditions and practices, with the attendant losses and gains that this change implies.

It is the play on catholic with capital *C* and small *c* that forms the foundation for what I wish to explore this evening: biblical scholarship that arises from the traditions of the capital *C* but is at the service of the small *c*. Today, Roman Catholic biblical scholars are in a number of key posts in major university programs in biblical studies, in a position to influence significantly the next generations of biblical scholars. How will that influence play out? What contributions have been made and are being made by Roman Catholic biblical scholars to the wider field of biblical scholarship? How does this work and how might it work in the future?

First of all, what makes biblical interpretation Catholic (with capital C)? That it is done by someone who professes adherence to the Roman Catholic Church? And its teachings? By someone who has grown up with a Catholic cultural heritage? By someone who expressly and consciously holds in mind the major church documents of the last two centuries on biblical interpretation? By someone who simply interprets out of one's own academic and religious identity, the unarticulated "pre-understanding"? Several attempts have been made recently to describe or characterize Catholic biblical interpretation, and we will consider them in due time. First, some background.

The quality of Roman Catholic biblical scholarship in the past and present generation needs no special pleading to those acquainted with names of past SBL presidents such as John L. McKenzie (1967), Raymond E. Brown (1977), Joseph A. Fitzmyer (1979), Roland E. Murphy (1984), Elisabeth Schüssler Fiorenza (1987), Harry Attridge (2001), and John J. Collins (2002). Roman Catholic biblical scholarship is founded on the rich tradition of patristic and medieval exegesis, yet also embraces historical criticism. One sometimes sees histories of biblical interpretation that give minimal attention, if any, to patristic and medieval traditions in a meager introduction, then go on to develop the "real stuff" in the sixteenth, seventeenth, or even eighteenth centuries, as if nothing happened between the writing of the biblical texts and the rise of modern biblical criticism, or at least between Augustine and Luther.

It is certainly true that institutional Roman Catholicism was not the first to embrace "higher criticism," and in fact condemned it in the otherwise progressive encyclical of Leo XIII in 1893, *Providentissimus Deus,* on biblical interpretation. The Catholic Church, however, was soon dragged into it kicking and screaming by the persuasive arguments of German Protestant scholarship in the nineteenth century on such questions as the authorship of the Pentateuch and the interrelationships of the Synoptic Gospels. But once the church accepted the new criticism, it grabbed on with a bulldog grip, so much so that the 1993 document of the Pontifical Biblical Commission, *The Interpretation of the Bible in the Church,* declared historical criticism to be "the indispensable method for the scientific study of the meaning of ancient texts," to the chagrin both of those who think the whole enterprise of historical criticism was a terrible mistake in the first place and would return to patristic exegesis as the norm, and of the postmodernists, who would declare historical criticism passé. The document goes on to say that Scripture, being the Word of God in human language, "has been composed by human authors in all its various parts and in all the sources that lie behind them. Because of this, its proper understanding not only admits the use of this method but actually requires it" (I.A, p. 35).

How did we get from there to here? The interest of Catholic theologians in modern biblical study began earlier than one might have thought. Already the Council of Trent in 1546 stated that its purpose was "that in the Church errors be removed and the purity of the gospel be preserved." It underlined the importance of proper training of Scripture teachers and specified Jerome's Latin Vulgate as the standard text, but never required that all translations be made from it.[1]

Contrary to some popular images, the Roman Catholic Church from the time of the Reformation was never against biblical research or the reading of the Bible by the faithful. What it opposed was *private* interpretation contrary to the common understanding of the church. Both Catholics and Protestants often interpreted the prohibition of private interpretation as a prohibition of Bible reading, but such was not the case. For instance, some of the first American Catholic bishops were eager to get an approved translation into the hands of their people.

The standard Catholic translation at that time was the Douay Bible, which had been done by a group of Oxford-trained exiled English Catholics at the English College in Flanders, then at Rheims, France, from 1568 to 1582. It was finally published as a whole in 1609–10, just before the first publication of the King James Bible in 1611.

The Douay Rheims translation had undergone five revisions by 1728. The most extensive revision was done by Bishop Challoner of London in 1749–52, so that it came to be called the Douay-Rheims-Challoner Bible.

In 1757, Rome decreed that all Bible translations should include "notes drawn from the holy fathers of the Church, or from learned Catholics," in other words, an annotated Bible.[2] In 1789, Bishop John Carroll of Baltimore urged a Catholic publisher in Philadelphia, Matthew Carey, to publish the Douay-Rheims-Challoner Bible, so that it could be placed "in the hands of our people, instead of those translations, which they purchase in stores & from Booksellers in the Country." The competition, of course, was the King James Version, generally recognized as an excellent translation by all who studied it. Carey published editions of this Douay-Rheims-Challoner Bible in 1790 and again in 1805.[3]

Meanwhile, in Brussels and Paris, the Catholic physician Jean Astruc (1684– 1766) wrote a number of medical treatises, especially on midwifery, but is remembered for none of them. Rather, he is remembered for one anonymous publication of 1753, "Conjectures on the original Memoirs which it appears that Moses used to write the book of Genesis."[4] Because of it, he is considered by many to be the father of modern biblical criticism. His method was simple: he divided

---

1. Dean P. Béchard, ed. and trans., *The Scripture Documents: An Anthology of Official Catholic Teachings* (Collegeville, MN: Liturgical Press, 2002), 3, 6–10.

2. Gerald P. Fogarty, S.J., *American Catholic Biblical Scholarship: A History from the Early Republic to Vatican II* (New York: Harper & Row, 1989), 6.

3. Ibid., 3.

4. *Conjectures sur les Mémoires originaux dont il paroit que Moyse s'est servi pour composer le livre de la Génèse* (Brussels: Fricx, 1753); critical edition with introduction and notes, Pierre Gibert, *Conjectures sur la Génèse* (Paris: Noesis, 1999). For context, see Ana M. Acosta, "Conjectures and Speculations: Jean Astruc, Obstetrics, and Biblical Criticism in Eighteenth-Century France," *Eighteenth Century Studies* 35, no. 2 (2002): 256–66.

those texts in Genesis that call God Elohim from those that call God Yahweh and reasoned to two sources upon which Moses had drawn. A predecessor, the Oratorian priest Richard Simon (1638–1712), had published in several editions in the 1680s critical histories of Old and New Testaments, arguing that Moses could not be the author of the Pentateuch. Astruc, on the other hand, was conservative in both his medical and his religious views and did not mean to suggest that Moses was not the author of Genesis, but his work would later be picked up in German Protestant scholarship as the documentary hypothesis.

Francis P. Kenrick, priest and theologian, later to become successively archbishop of Philadelphia (1842–51) and Baltimore (1851–63), published the first edition of his *Theologia Dogmatica* in 1839. It is clear that he had been reading the biblical scholarship of the day, for he wrote that the Scriptures "cannot be referred to the age of Christ, nor to the beginning of the apostolic preaching: for it is evident that many years elapsed before anything was consigned to writing. The apostolic writings are not known to have been collected together until the second century; and some were not recognized by some churches for another four centuries."[5]

Between 1849 and 1860, Kenrick did a complete revision of the Douay-Rheims-Challoner Bible, comparing the translation to the King James, and comparing the Latin Vulgate to the Greek and Hebrew. He acknowledged the many advances made by Protestant scholarship and cited Protestant as well as Catholic authors in the notes, considering that more unity of thinking could only serve the common cause of Christianity. He took conservative positions on questions of authorship while noting the reasons behind contrary arguments; for example, since Moses did not know science, he can be excused for speaking of creation in six days, which not all the patristic authors understood literally, and thus a diversity of views was legitimate.[6] How timely for today!

Kenrick's version enjoyed wide popularity, but was not without its critics. For instance, Martin Spalding, bishop of Louisville, objected in 1858 to the critical note explaining the Greek word βαπτίζω as immersion, complaining that "the Baptists out there have been exulting over it too much." Orestes Brownson, philosopher and Catholic convert, championed Kenrick's cause, noting that St. Jerome studied Hebrew with Jewish scholars and Cicero was a master of Latin. So too, Protestants could be just as good as Catholics at grammar, philology, geography, history, or "the natural productions of the Holy Land."[7]

The Second Plenary Council of American Catholic bishops in 1866, three years after Kenrick's death, came close to endorsing his translation as the official one of the American Catholic Church. A committee appointed to study the question made this recommendation, but Kenrick's own brother Peter, bishop of St.

---

5. *Theologia Dogmatica*, 292-83; quoted in Fogarty, *Catholic Biblical Scholarship*, 8.
6. Fogarty, *Catholic Biblical Scholarship*, 8, 15, 23–25.
7. Ibid., 28, 26.

Louis, strenuously objected. Ultimately, they fell back on the Douay-Rheims-Challoner version without making any new recommendation.

Meanwhile, in Palestine Marie-Joseph Lagrange (1855–1938) had been sent from France by his Dominican superiors to found the École Practique d'Études Bibliques in Jerusalem, which would emphasize study of the Bible in the physical and cultural context in which it had been written. In 1920, it became the national archaeological school of France, changing its name to École Biblique et Archéologique Française. The faculty that Lagrange assembled there included such names as the Arabic ethnographer Antonin Janssen (1871–1962), the preeminent Palestinian archaeologist Louis-Hugues Vincent (1872–1960), and Semitic epigrapher Antoine Raphael Savignac (1874–1951). Later eminent faculty included Felix-Marie Abel (1878–1953), Bernard Couroyer (1900–1992), Roland de Vaux (1903–1971), Pierre Benoît (1906–1987), Marie-Émile Boismard (1916–2004), and Jerome Murphy-O'Connor. In the first fifty years of its existence, the École Biblique produced forty-two major books, 682 scientific articles, and over 6,200 book reviews. Its flagship journal, *Revue biblique*, founded in 1892, continues to be a leader in scientific biblical research. The school's major translation project was the *Jerusalem Bible*, first published in French in 1956, and subsequently in most major languages.[8]

In 1892, the progressive Archbishop John Ireland of St. Paul, Minnesota, wrote to the first rector of the newly founded Catholic University of America that he should educate his professors and hang onto them, "making bishops only of those who are not worth keeping as professors."[9]

In 1893, the encyclical *Providentissimus Deus* of Pope Leo XIII on the study of Sacred Scripture reaffirmed that professors of Scripture must use the Latin Vulgate, sanctioned by the Council of Trent, but it also encouraged the learning and use of the original languages and the use of methods of scientific criticism. It declared, on the authority of Augustine (*De Genesi ad litteram* 1.21), a foundational principle that is still affirmed today, and importantly so in light of recent issues of Creationism and Intelligent Design: that there cannot be any real discrepancy between theology and the natural sciences, as long as each remains true to its own language and discipline (39). If an apparent contradiction arises, every effort must be put to its solution. "Even if the difficulty is after all not cleared up and the discrepancy seems to remain, the contest must not be abandoned. Truth cannot contradict truth, and we may be sure that some mistake has been made either in the interpretation of the sacred words or in the polemical discussion itself. If no such mistake can be detected, we must then suspend judgment for the time being" (45).[10] What is most interesting in the previous statement is that

---

8. Http://www.op.org/ebaf/index-eng.htm.

9. Fogarty, *Catholic Biblical Scholarship*, 38–39.

10. Béchard, *Scripture Documents*, 57. All translations of church documents are taken from this book. In general, see also Gerald P. Fogarty, "Scriptural Authority (Roman Catholicism)," *ABD* 5:1023–26.

mistakes may be attributed to biblical interpretation and discussion but not to science.

At the same time, the encyclical condemned the so-called higher criticism as tainted with "false philosophy and rationalism" for its attempt to alter traditional understandings of the authorship and origins of biblical books. The pope's letter was sufficiently ambiguous for both sides of the controversy, progressives and conservatives, to find something that would bolster their cause. Father Lagrange and his companions in Jerusalem took it as confirmation for what they were doing. Others took a different view.

The openness and optimism of the mid-nineteenth century were giving way to an oppressive reaction. The opponents of change were gathering force. In 1890, Alfred Loisy at the Institut Catholique in Paris was recognized by Denis J. O'Connell, rector of American College in Rome as the best biblical scholar in the church.[11] Three years later, he had been forced out of his academic position and was to become embroiled in the controversy over modernism. The enemies of Father Lagrange succeeded in having him removed from Jerusalem for one year, 1912, but he was never formally condemned.[12]

The uncertainties of the times and the condemnation in 1899 of "Americanism," a vague heresy never quite defined, led to the establishment of the Pontifical Biblical Commission in 1902 to ride herd on error in biblical study. Some of the responses of the Pontifical Biblical Commission in its early years seriously impeded progress in scholarship. In the words of Roland Murphy, the commission "has had a topsy-turvy career in the century of its existence, but it can safely be said that it is now constituted by a broad band of international scholars ... [who] have displayed a reasonable openness to various approaches to the biblical text that have emerged in modern times."[13]

The Pontifical Biblical Institute was established by Pope Pius X in 1909 as a Roman center for higher studies in Scripture and entrusted to the Jesuits. Originally it was an organ of the Pontifical Biblical Commission; its purpose was to

---

11. Fogarty, *Catholic Biblical Scholarship*, 39.

12. Restored to Jerusalem, he continued there until ill health forced his return to France, where he died in 1938, at the age of eighty-three. In 1967 his body was brought back to Jerusalem to be interred in the center of the choir of the Basilica of St. Stephen, where it rests today (www.op.org/op/ ebaf/index-eng.htm).

13. Roland E. Murphy, "What Is Catholic about Catholic Biblical Scholarship—Revisited," *BTB* 28 (1998): 112–19, here 117. On July 3, 1907, came a list of condemned modernist propositions in a decree aptly titled *Lamentabili*, published by the Holy Office (known today as the Congregation for the Doctrine of the Faith), and on September 8 of the same year, the encyclical *Pascendi Dominici Gregis*, condemning modernism as heresy. Neither so-called Americanism nor modernism directly concerned biblical study but, more generally, the philosophical preunderstanding with which one approaches the texts. They were more directly involved with political questions of separation of church and state. The waves of rationalism and empiricism had washed over the Bible as well as the rest of theology and Christian life.

exercise control over biblical studies and prepare students for its examinations. But by 1916, the Pontifical Biblical Institute granted the licentiate degree, and by 1930 it was independent of the PBC and was granting doctoral degrees. Today, with its added house of study in Jerusalem, it is a respected center for biblical studies and educates students from some sixty countries.[14]

By 1936, there was full realization of the limits of the standard Catholic English translation, the Douay-Rheims-Challoner, and of the use of the Vulgate as the foundational text. Bishop Edwin O'Hara of Great Falls, Montana, episcopal chair of the Confraternity of Christian Doctrine,[15] called a meeting in Washington of prominent Catholic biblical scholars. This meeting would give rise not only to a new translation of the NT but also to the founding of the Catholic Biblical Association of America in 1937 and the *Catholic Biblical Quarterly* in 1939. The *CBQ* was to be "both technical and practical" to appeal to scholar, priest, and educated laity, a stretch that was eventually to prove impossible, so that in 1962 *The Bible Today* was founded to fulfill the pastoral function, allowing the *CBQ* to become the respected scholarly journal that it is today.

The Catholic Biblical Association was in the early years totally composed of priests, and before the outbreak of World War II, all Catholic professors of Scripture were supposed to have degrees from the pontifical faculties in Rome. The war made this impossible and was the occasion for the first Catholic priests to begin their studies at Johns Hopkins University in Baltimore with the renowned William Foxwell Albright.

At the 1944 meeting of the Catholic Biblical Association, Albright was invited to deliver a paper, accompanied by his Catholic wife, who, it was rumored, would make up for his reticence with her vivacity. At that meeting, Albright (without his wife) was elected to honorary lifetime membership, the first non-Catholic member.[16] In 1947, Sister Kathryn Sullivan, R.S.C.J., professor of history at Manhattanville College, tutored and self-taught in Scripture because no Catholic faculty at the time would have admitted a woman, became the first woman elected to membership. She was elected vice-president in 1958, an office from which she would normally have succeeded to the presidency, had they dared at the time to elect a woman as president. The first woman president of the CBA was not to come until 1986, Pheme Perkins, predating by a year the first woman president of SBL. Today the CBA counts more than fifteen hundred members, including a number of Protestants and Jews.

The watershed moment came with the publication of the encyclical *Divino Afflante Spiritu* by Pius XII in 1943. It seemed to reverse all the hesitancies that had plagued Catholic biblical scholarship in the years since the modernist

---

14. www.pib.urbe.it.
15. An organization founded in Rome in 1562 for the purpose of coordinating religious instruction.
16. Fogarty, *Catholic Biblical Scholarship*, 241.

crisis. It called for use of the original biblical languages, saying that the special "authenticity" granted the Vulgate was not for its critical quality but because of its venerable history of use through the centuries. It called for the use of historical methods and every scientific means at the disposal of exegetes. It declared that apparent contradictions and historical inaccuracies were due to ancient ways of speaking, written by authors who could not have known anything about science. The key to interpretation, it said, was to go back to the extent possible to the original context, using history, archaeology, ethnology, and whatever other tools were available. The fear of modernism was over and historical criticism was in.

The encyclical was dated September 30, 1943; however, because of the war, it did not reach the United States until February 1944. It was at the next meeting of the CBA that Albright gave his aforementioned address and was elected an honorary lifetime member.

Just when Catholic biblical scholars thought it was safe to go back in the water, however, came another encyclical by the same Pope Pius XII in 1950, *Humani Generis,* aimed not at biblical studies but at the so-called New Theology coming out of France that tended to gloss over ecumenical differences and blur the distinction between nature and grace. But it also warned against polygenism, the evolutionary theory of multiple human origins, as being incompatible with revelation as given in Genesis. Once again, an authoritative document was open to the kind of ambiguity in which ideological opponents can take potshots at each other. This situation was to last until the promulgation of the Dogmatic Constitution on Divine Revelation (*Dei Verbum*) at the fourth session of Vatican Council II in September 1965.

Dei Verbum confirmed the progressive movement of *Divino Afflante Spiritu* in 1943, setting the theological context and the tone for further development. At issue here especially was the role of Tradition with regard to the Bible. In Catholic theology, Tradition has always been considered a privileged source of theological reflection alongside Scripture. But how are the two related? Rejecting the idea of two sources of revelation, the Vatican document declared: "Sacred Tradition and sacred Scripture make up a single sacred deposit of the Word of God, which is entrusted to the Church" (10) to be authentically interpreted by the Magisterium.

"Yet this Magisterium is not superior to the Word of God, but is its servant." Thus according to the plan of God, "sacred Tradition, sacred Scripture and the Magisterium of the Church are so connected and associated that one of them cannot stand without the others" (10). Scripture teaches authoritatively only those things necessary for salvation. "Since, therefore, all that the inspired authors ... affirm should be regarded as affirmed by the Holy Spirit, we must acknowledge that the books of Scripture, firmly, faithfully and without error, teach that truth which God, for the sake of our salvation, wished to see confided to the sacred Scriptures" (11). Since God speaks through human means in the

Bible, all helpful methods must be used for ascertaining the meaning intended by God (12).[17]

These statements, taken together, constitute something of a recognition of the scope and limits of biblical research. It is fully recognized that the Word of God is delivered in human language, and thus all helpful human methods of interpretation must be brought into play, both scientific and literary. At the same time, interpretation is grounded in Tradition and thus is rooted in the ongoing history of interpretation and stands on its shoulders. It affirms the application to biblical interpretation of the profound theological reality already begun in 1943 with *Divino Afflante Spiritu* and present throughout many documents of Vatican II: the incarnational principle, that because the Word became flesh in a particular and specific time and place, in a specific human person, faith is inevitably incarnated in historical process; and therefore all possible human tools are to be used to attempt to understand its full meaning.

That position was reiterated in 1993 in *The Interpretation of the Bible in the Church*. As stated earlier, that document reaffirmed in the face of biblical fundamentalism that the historical sciences and ascertaining of historical levels of meaning remain basic and necessary to the enterprise of biblical interpretation, while other literary, linguistic, and analytical methods are also valuable and to be encouraged. This document has become widely recognized as a modern manifesto of the significant contributions of the historical-critical method and the ways in which other newer methods can be seen as complements to it rather than threats.

All of this positive thinking is not to say that there have not been victims along the way, victims of authoritarianism, of fear of change, of enemies in high places, of in-house politics, of reactionism, and of the historical process itself. Names like Alfred Loisy, George Tyrell, Henry A. Poels, and Edward Siegman come to mind, scholars whose reputations and teaching positions were sacrificed to institutional fear of new ways of thinking. Many others are known, and many remain nameless.

The function of religious teaching authority is to say what has been, not what will be. It has been said that being Catholic means learning to think in centuries[18] It also means thinking universally as well as in the local particular. The burning issues of one part of the world are not those of another. Each generation in each specific cultural context must resist the temptation to make of itself the center of the universe or of the historical process. That is why appropriation of apocalyptic symbolism with reference to ourselves—that the end times are happening

---

17. Béchard, *Scripture Documents*, 23–25. On the understanding of tradition in biblical interpretation, see Sandra Schneiders, *The Revelatory Text: Interpreting the New Testament as Sacred Scripture* (Collegeville, MN: Liturgical Press, 1999), 64–90, passim.

18. Otto Maduro, in discussion after the Borderlands lecture, Brite Divinity School, October 11, 2005.

now— has always struck me as not so much naïve as arrogant. History moves slowly, and the principle that truth will prevail offers no promises that there will not be victims along the way. Every generation builds on the breakthroughs, the mistakes, and the tragedies of those who went before.

A case in point is the welcoming of newer players and newer forms of biblical interpretation. Continuing fear of liberation and feminist hermeneutics remains in many academic and ecclesiastical minds. In the 1993 document of the Pontifical Biblical Commission, *Interpretation of the Bible in the Church*, besides fundamentalism, only these two approaches receive warnings about possible dangers involved, and only feminist interpretation receives a slap on the wrist about confusing power with service, a paragraph that received a very divided vote in the com mission (par. I E.2).[19] Postcolonial interpretation is not yet mentioned.

At the annual meeting of the Catholic Biblical Association of America in 1997, Luke Timothy Johnson caused a stir with his paper, "What's Catholic about Catholic Biblical Scholarship?" presented in revised form in 2002 as the lead chapter in his book co-authored with William S. Kurz, *The Future of Catholic Biblical Scholarship: A Constructive Conversation*. Johnson argues that "what is distinctively 'catholic' about Catholic biblical interpretation (scholarship) is to be found in its instinct for the both/and, and in its conviction that critical scholarship is not merely a matter of separating and opposing, but also of testing and reconnecting."[20] I think Johnson has said here in other words what was said in 1993 in *Interpretation of the Bible in the Church*, in its chapter entitled "The Characteristics of Catholic Interpretation," largely based on *Dei Verbum* and on the earlier papal encyclical *Divino Afflante Spiritu*.[21] One passage from that document is worth quoting at length:

> Catholic exegesis actively contributes to the development of new methods and to the progress of research.
>
> What characterizes Catholic exegesis is that it deliberately places itself within the living tradition of the Church, whose first concern is fidelity to the revelation attested by the Bible. Modern hermeneutics has made clear ... the impossibility of interpreting a text without starting from a "pre-understanding"

---

19. This is the only paragraph in the entire document in which the vote was recorded in the notes: eleven in favor, four opposed, and four abstentions. Those opposed asked that the result be noted in the text (Béchard, *Scripture Documents*, 273).

20. Luke Timothy Johnson and William S. Kurz, S.J., *The Future of Catholic Biblical Scholarship: A Constructive Conversation* (Grand Rapids: Eerdmans, 2002), 19.

21. Helpful background on the document is provided by Joseph A. Fitzmyer, *The Biblical Commission's Document: "The Interpretation of the Bible in the Church" Text and Commentary* (Subsidia Biblica 18; Rome: Pontifical Biblical Institute, 1995), and by Peter S. Williamson, "Catholic Principles for Interpreting Scripture," *CBQ* 65 (2003): 327–49. Implications of biblical research for interreligious dialogue as presented in the document are discussed in Jean l'Hour, "Pour une lecture Catholique' de la Bible," *BibInt* 5 (1997): 113–32.

of one type or another. Catholic exegetes approach the biblical text with a preunderstanding which holds closely together modern scientific culture and the religious tradition emanating from Israel and from the early Christian community. Their interpretation stands thereby in continuity with a dynamic pattern of interpretation that is found within the Bible itself and continues in the life of the Church. This dynamic pattern corresponds to the requirement that there be a lived affinity between the interpreter and the object, an affinity which constitutes, in fact, one of the conditions that makes the entire exegetical enterprise possible. (*Interpretation of the Bible in the Church*, introduction)[22]

Johnson makes some valid points about the spirit of Protestantism as characterized by "either/or" and embedded as preunderstanding in some historical-critical exegesis, forcing an either/or interpretation (e.g., interpretation of the parables either historically or allegorically, with one judged to be superior to the other).[23]

Another way of answering the question, "What's Catholic about Catholic biblical interpretation?" was taken up by Roland E. Murphy in 1998, the year following Johnson's first presentation. He tackled the assumption on the part of many opponents of historical criticism that it cannot yield results of theological value or have anything important to say to present life. Murphy claims that it is unfair to blame the method

> for not delivering what it has never promised.... Many subjective and hypothetical studies often overshadow the reasonable insights of historical criticism, but the method itself is not to be identified with abuses. A very important role of the method is to recognize what can*not* be answered, to admit to what is insoluble, at least for the present. Whatever happened to that expressive Latin phrase, *non liquet* (no clear answer?)?[24]

Murphy goes on to show that sometimes the literal meaning of a text is directly theological, as in the case of some of the prayers of the Psalms, for example, or recitation of the Shema (Deut 6:4).[25]

---

22. Béchard, *Scripture Documents*, 284. A good introduction for the general reader is Daniel J. Harrington, *How Do Catholics Read the Bible?* (Lanham, MD: Rowman & Littlefield, 2005).

23. Johnson and Kurz, *Future of Catholic Biblical Scholarship*, 3–19. I am not persuaded, however, that the alternatives are quite as pronounced as Johnson puts them. I am even less persuaded by his assessment of his (and my) third generation of Catholic biblical scholars who find ourselves graduates of the best schools, teaching in them, and now wondering if it was all worth it (p. 13). It would seem that Johnson has set up his own "either/or" alternatives in such a way as to force a wedge between what is characteristically Catholic and characteristically Protestant, a problem that he himself acknowledges (p. 5).

24. Murphy, "What Is Catholic," 113.

25. Also recognized in *Interpretation of the Bible in the Church* II.B.2 (Béchard, *Scripture Documents*, 282).

Recent critics of historical criticism and of historical critics have not been kind. Murphy quotes Christopher Seitz, who claims that "historical criticism plays no positive theological role whatsoever. Its only proper role is negative. It establishes the genre, form, possible setting, and historical and intellectual background of the individual text."[26] Another notes: "Instead of being based on God's Word, it (historical-critical theology) had its foundations in philosophies which made bold to define truth so that God's Word was excluded as the source of truth."[27] For another: "The sheer amount of scholarship is part of the crisis.... There is much product, indeed much admirable product, but is there any point to the production? The present generation approaches the state of *idiot savants,* people who know everything about some small aspect of the Bible, but nothing about the Bible as a whole, or its good and destructive uses."[28] Yet another:

> ... there is no innocent reading of the Bible, no reading that is not already ideological. But to read the Bible in the traditional scholarly manner has all too often meant reading it, whether deliberately or not, in ways that reify and ratify the status quo—providing warrant for the subjugation of women (whether in the church, the academy, or society at large), justifying colonialism and enslavement, rationalizing homophobia, or otherwise legitimizing the power of hegemonic classes of people.[29]

Much of the rejection of historical criticism as voiced today, in what I will call the ahistorical paradigm, parallels the phenomenon of Creationism and Intelligent Design, two related theories that have become surprisingly accepted today. It is astounding that a recent poll conducted by a respected research center indicates that 42 percent of Americans believe that "[l]ife has existed in its present form since the beginning of time."[30] Both Creationism/Intelligent Design and rejection of historical criticism are reactions, in the first order, against the mindset of scientism, which makes inappropriate totalitarian claims, as replacement for theology and philosophy, and the failure to retain an appropriate distinction between science and theology. The parallel in the case of historical criticism is the

---

26. Christopher Seitz, *Word without End: The Old Testament as Abiding Theological Witness* (Grand Rapids: Eerdmans, 1998), 97, as quoted in Murphy, "What Is Catholic," 112.
27. Eta Linnemann, *Historical Criticism of the Bible: Methodology or Ideology?* (Grand Rapids: Baker, 1990), 17–18.
28. Johnson and Kurz, *Future of Catholic Biblical Scholarship,* 37–38.
29. George Aichele et al., *The Postmodern Bible* (New Haven: Yale University Press, 1995), 4.
30. Pew Research Center, Forum on Religion and Public Life. Poll conducted on two thousand participants July 7–17, 2005. Forty-eight percent said that life evolved over time; of that 48 percent, 18 percent chose the further option, "guided by a supreme being," 26 percent through natural selection, and 4 percent did not know how. The remaining 10 percent of the poll indicated "Don't know." See http://pewforum.org/docs/index.php?DocID=115 (accessed October 20, 2005).

inappropriate claim to have a method that will yield convincing results that can be verified by independent researchers, *and* that these results are the only ones that matter.

In both cases, *inappropriate* use of a scientific tool leads to claims to be able to answer all questions, scientific, historical, philosophical, or theological, and imposes its paradigm as the only viable way of thinking. Scientism limits the questions worth asking to those that can be answered by scientific methods, and overemphasis on historical criticism limits the questions worth asking to those that can be answered with the methods of historical criticism. In the physical sciences, an empirical and materialist worldview is imposed, while philosophical and spiritual interpretations of physical reality are excluded. When this happens, science does not respect its own proper limits. In biblical interpretation, historical criticism was incorrectly presented as the foolproof method (which we now know not to be fool-proof) for reaching the literal level of the text.

Sometimes historical-critical interpreters have been too naïve about the implications of their methods. As noted by Wayne Meeks in his presidential address to the Society for New Testament Studies in 2004, "the science of history was a weapon of liberation ... from lazy credulity, from dogmatic abstractions, from venomous prejudices, from authoritarian structures ... (but) our practice of writing history was never innocent. It was a means of power.... Those failings demonstrated that interest does not have to be conscious in order to serve privilege."[31]

I have already called attention to the description of Catholic biblical scholarship given by the 1993 document of the Pontifical Biblical Commission, with which I am in agreement:

> What characterizes Catholic exegesis is that it deliberately places itself within the living tradition of the Church, whose first concern is fidelity to the revelation attested by the Bible.... Catholic exegetes approach the biblical text with a pre-understanding which holds closely together modern scientific culture and the religious tradition emanating from Israel and from the early Christian community. Their interpretation stands thereby in continuity with a dynamic pattern of interpretation that is found within the Bible itself and continues in the life of the Church. This dynamic pattern corresponds to the requirement that there be a lived affinity between the interpreter and the object, an affinity which constitutes, in fact, one of the conditions that makes the entire exegetical enterprise possible. (*Interpretation of the Bible in the Church*, introduction)[32]

Now I wish to focus from the above statement on the "pre-understanding which holds closely together modern scientific culture and the religious tradition" of Israel and the early church. This is the "both/and" rather than the "either/or."

---

31. Wayne A. Meeks, "Why Study the New Testament?" *NTS* 51 (2005): 155-70, here 157, 160.

32. Béchard, *Scripture Documents*, 284.

This is the center point from which Catholic biblical scholarship can especially contribute to our common enterprise of interpretation, to the catholic endeavor, with small *c*. This is the principle that enables biblical scholarship to be open to a variety of levels of meaning, beginning always from the historical level but ongoing from there.

Many will be familiar with the thirteenth-century formula of Augustine of Denmark:

Littera gesta docet, quid credas allegoria,
moralis quid agas, quid speras anagogia.

For those whose Latin is a little rusty, I give Roland Murphy's translation: "The letter (or literal sense) teaches facts; the allegorical, what we are to believe; the moral, what we are to do; the anagogical, what we are to hope for."[33] As Murphy goes on to note, it does not always work this way. Sometimes the literal sense teaches what we are to believe or even hope for, and spiritual meaning cannot be limited to allegory. While Jewish and Christian interpreters might agree on the literal sense of a text, the Jewish interpreter might have a different understanding from that of the Christian on other levels. It is doubtful that an adequate moral or spiritual sense could be retrieved today, for example, from prescriptions that slaves obey their masters, as found in the household codes of the NT. Allegory was the patristic and medieval way of avoiding literalism and fundamentalism. Today, historical criticism plays that role in part. If today we are uncomfortable with some of the ways in which previous generations used allegory, perhaps we need to come to a new understanding of how metaphor, imagery, and even allegory continue to inform the very heart of biblical interpretation in its arena of greatest use, the worshiping community.

The mistake of some misuses of historical criticism was an assumption that a text can have only one meaning, but contemporary language theory recalls us to the reality that in fact all human communication is open to many possible levels of meaning. Biblical texts, too, have the potential for multiple levels of meaning, however complex the interplay among them and however complex the process of sorting them out and evaluating what is to be retained and what discarded.

There are simpler ways than that of Augustine of Denmark to characterize levels of meaning as used by Christians. One traditional and helpful one is suggested in *Interpretation of the Bible in the Church*. It is threefold: literal, spiritual, and the so-called fuller sense. For Christians, the "spiritual sense" according to this understanding, is "the meaning expressed by the biblical texts when read, under the influence of the Holy Spirit, in the context of the paschal mystery of

---

33. Murphy, "What Is Catholic," 116; see also *Interpretation of the Bible in the Church*, II.B (Béchard, *Scripture Documents*, 279; Joseph A. Fitzmyer, "The Sense of Scripture Today," *ITQ* 62 (1996–97): 101–16.

Christ, and of the new life that flows from it."[34] "And of the new life that flows from it"; this new life did not cease at the end of the biblical period, but continues to flow through the patristic, medieval, and modern eras, into our own age. Institutional documents are rarely prophetic; for the most part, they summarize what has been up to the time of writing, but rarely point beyond.

In light of this, I would expand on the understanding of the "spiritual sense" to include many newer methods and perspectives that are informed by the desire to have us live more authentically the new life that flows from the paschal mystery. I am speaking of those methods born out of the hermeneutic of suspicion, for example, liberation, feminist/womanist/mujerista, and postcolonial interpretation, which probe the implications of the paschal mystery in ways not envisioned in previous centuries. Even if they challenge established power bases—or precisely because they do—they are new manifestations of the same inspiration that led earlier interpreters to ask of the biblical text the question: But what does this have to do with life today? Earlier answers included various forms of metaphor and allegory arising from contemporary preunderstanding. Today's preunderstanding requires analysis of how power is used. If the paschal mystery is about deliverance from death to life, then without the hermeneutic of suspicion, we risk being diminished, not by the text but by earlier preunderstandings that are not yet open to a wider and more inclusive way of living and loving. Just as historical criticism asked the hard analytical questions a century ago and was suspect by many for that reason, so too does the hermeneutic of suspicion today ask the critical questions of our time, and is suspect on the part of many for the same reasons.

The 1993 *Interpretation of the Bible in the Church* stresses that spiritual interpretation is not to be confused with subjective imagination. "Spiritual interpretation, whether in community or in private, will discover the authentic spiritual sense only to the extent that it is kept within these perspectives. One then holds together three levels of reality: the biblical text, the paschal mystery, and the present circumstances of life in the Spirit."[35] I believe that this is where these newer methods fit into the common endeavor, as part of the expanded spiritual sense in which we bring our own new understandings to the task, out of our own new questions, and discover new levels of meaning as participants in the ongoing flow of interpretive tradition.

The Bible belongs to the church. It does not belong to theologians, denominational committees, bishops, or biblical scholars. Therefore, biblical scholarship and interpretation must be in some way oriented to the nourishment and growth of the community. This is not in any way to impede the necessary freedom, integrity, and autonomy that scholars must have to engage in research for its own sake.

---

34. *Interpretation of the Bible in the Church*, II.B.2 (Béchard, *Scripture Documents*, 281–82).
35. Ibid.

Scholars have the responsibility to seek truth even if it seems to contradict consensus, popular ideas, or ecclesiastical politics. But one eye of the Roman Catholic biblical scholar must be kept on the good of the community. Sometimes upholding that good upholds and underpins consensus; sometimes it must dissent from the consensus in the interest of that new life that flows from the paschal mystery.

There is a third, rather obscure and debated level of meaning discussed in *Interpretation of the Bible in the Church*, the "fuller sense," or *sensus plenior*.[36] The term was first used in 1925 and was extensively discussed until about 1970. *Interpretation of the Bible in the Church* revives it but without a great deal of enthusiasm. It defines the "fuller sense" as "a deeper meaning of the text, intended by God but not clearly expressed by the human author. Its existence in the biblical text comes to be known when one studies the text in the light of other biblical texts which utilize it or in its relationship with the internal development of revelation."[37] This "fuller sense" "brings out fresh possibilities of meaning that had lain hidden in the original context."[38]

Hidden indeed. It is not clear, even in *Interpretation of the Bible in the Church* or commentaries on it, how this differs from the spiritual sense.[39] Indeed, it may be another form of the spiritual sense. The definition, remember, is a meaning "intended by God, but not clearly expressed by the human author." What is intended by God, I cannot say. If there is a difference between the spiritual and the "fuller" sense, I propose that it lies in this: not only that the meaning is "not clearly expressed by the human author" but that it is not at all in the mind of the human author, both "distinct from the internal thought of the writer and capable of an increment in meaning which transcends his conscious intent."[40] It is a meaning that is theologically comprehensible at a later point in the unfolding of tradition. I suggest further that two very different hermeneutical methods might be illustrative of this: canonical and psychological interpretation.

While some biblical authors were certainly aware of the biblical tradition in which they were writing (e.g., the author of Daniel or the author of Revelation), it is unlikely that any of them intended to write in the context of the whole bibli-

---

36. For a history of understanding of the term, see Raymond E. Brown, "The History and Development of the Theory of a *Sensus Plenior*," *CBQ* 15 (1953): 141-62; idem, *The Sensus Plenior of Sacred Scripture* (Baltimore: St. Mary's University, 1955); idem, "The *Sensus Plenior* in the Last Ten Years," *CBQ* 25 (1963): 262-85; idem, *JBC* 71:56-70; *NJBC* 71:49-51. Brown noted in 1963: "Fortunately, the misconception that the theory of a SP is an attempt to circumvent scientific exegesis or to let piety run riot is gradually disappearing" ("*Sensus Plenior* in the Last Ten Years," 262).

37. The first part of the definition appears as well in *NJBC* (71:49) and probably originates with Raymond Brown.

38. *Interpretation of the Bible in the Church*, II.B.3 (Béchard, *Scripture Documents*, 283).

39. See, e.g., Fitzmyer, *Biblical Commission's Document*, 130-31.

40. Brown, "*Sensus Plenior* in the Last Ten Years," 269; Brown preferred to say that the consciousness of this meaning on the part of the human author is not necessary (pp. 267–69).

cal canon, be it Hebrew or Greek, as we have it today. Yet when their writings are read today in light of the canonical process and context, new theological insights emerge and new and richer meanings are acquired by the text.

Likewise, biblical writers were psychological beings, but psychology is intensely influenced by social factors. They wrote with conscious intent to portray not psychological dynamics and relationships but rather social and theological ones. Yet in light of modern understandings of the dynamics of unconscious forces, the symbols and relationships in the biblical text can be reread to give expanded meanings to profound human experiences.

Our understandings of the spiritual senses of Scripture should lead us not only backwards to a new appreciation of what has enriched our tradition but also forward to a fuller and richer appreciation of how the Bible speaks to our own world with its proper questions and exigencies. In the Society of Biblical Literature, no one particular confessional stance or methodological stance can be imposed, and some would prefer none at all. I am suggesting ways in which the heritage of Roman Catholic biblical scholarship can continue to contribute to and enrich our common effort. I suggest that it is precisely the challenge of holding together ancient text, ongoing history of interpretation, modern science, and postmodern insights, within a conscious participation in a living tradition, that has enabled and can continue to enable Roman Catholic biblical scholarship to make its contribution, so that it can take an important part in the common catholic (small *c*) tradition of biblical interpretation. In this way, catholic can truly mean universal, open to all.

Recently I read something in the area of religious conflicts that argued that religious tolerance is not the goal, but a bare minimum of "live and let live"; rather, the goal is inter-understanding, a lively appreciation of the other for what the other is, all the while affirming one's adherence to one's own religious tradition. Analogously, can we not at this point in the biblical guild produce not a cacophony but a symphony of our various methods and not only *tolerate* a diversity of methods, but begin to see how they complement each other, can be integrated with each other, and can together form a rich network of interpretations?

In the words of someone familiar to all of us: "I do not consider that I have made it my own; but this one thing I do: forgetting what lies behind and straining forward to what lies ahead, I press on toward the goal" (Phil 3:13–14 NRSV).

Appendix 1
SBL Presidents and Presidential Addresses[†]

The following list of SBL presidents includes the titles of, publication data for, and relevant information pertaining to presidential addresses delivered to the Society since its founding in 1880 and the establishment of the annual presidential address in 1889.[1] An asterisk (*) indicates a year in which no address was delivered or for which no information can be located in Society records or other contemporary sources. In a few instances, there is a record of the title but no evidence that the address ever appeared in published form.

1880–1887   Daniel Raynes Goodwin*
1887–1889   Frederic Gardiner*
1889–1890   Francis Brown*
1890–1891   Charles A. Briggs*
1891–1892   Talbot W. Chambers. The minutes of the December 1892 meeting note that Chambers "delivered an opening address on the Function of the Prophet." It is not clear whether this was the title of the address, and there is no record that the address subsequently appeared in print. Frank K. Sanders reports that the address was on "Prophets and Prophecy."[2]
1893   Talbot W. Chambers. Owing to his absence from the June meeting (the only meeting held in 1893), Chambers did not deliver a presidential address.[3]

[†] Adapted from Patrick Gray, "Presidential Addresses of the Society of Biblical Literature: A Quasquicentennial Review," *JBL* 125 (2006): 172–77

1. Article 5 of the amended 1889 Constitution reads: "The Society shall meet at least once a year, at such time and place as the Council may determine. On the first day of the annual meeting the President, or some other member appointed by the Council for the purpose, shall deliver an address to the Society."

2. See further Sanders, "Exploration and Discovery," *The Biblical World* 1 (1892): 134.

3. Since presidential addresses were typically presented at the December meeting, one might suspect that Chambers would have delivered a presidential address, had a meeting been held in December 1893.

1894	Talbot W. Chambers and J. Henry Thayer each served as president for a portion of 1894, but the minutes of the meetings contain no mention of a presidential address.[4]
1895	J. Henry Thayer, "The Historical Element in the New Testament," *JBL* 14 (1895): 1–18.
1896	Francis Brown, "Old Testament Problems," *JBL* 15 (1896): 63–74.
1897	Edward T. Bartlett. Neither Bartlett not Vice-President Milton S. Terry attended the December meeting, so no presidential address was delivered.[5]
1898	George Foot Moore, "Jewish Historical Literature"
1899	George Foot Moore, "The Age of the Jewish Canon of Hagiographa"
1900	John P. Peters, "The Religion of Moses," *JBL* 20 (1901): 101–28.
1901	Edward Y. Hincks, "Some Tendencies and Results of Recent New Testament Study"
1902	Benjamin W. Bacon, "Ultimate Problems of Biblical Science," *JBL* 21 (1903): 1–14.
1903	Richard J. H. Gottheil, "Some Early Jewish Bible Criticism," *JBL* 22 (1904): 1–12.
1904	Willis J. Beecher, "'Torah': A Word-Study in the Old Testament," *JBL* 23 (1905): 1–16.
1905	William Rainey Harper. Due to an illness, Harper did not attend the meeting. Consequently, Paul Haupt presented "the address of the Vice-President," an expanded version of which was published as *Purim: Address Delivered at the Annual Meeting of the Society of Biblical Literature and Exegesis, New York, December 27, 1905* (Beiträge zur Assyriologie und semitischen Sprachwissenschaft 6.2; Leipzig: Hinrichs; Baltimore: Johns Hopkins University Press, 1906).
1906	Paul Haupt, "The Book of Nahum," *JBL* 25 (1907): 1–53.
1907	James Hardy Ropes, "The Epistle to the Hebrews"
1908	Frank Chamberlain Porter, "The Bearing of Historical Studies on the Religious Use of the Bible," *HTR* 2 (1909): 253–76.

---

4. The records for the December meeting note that "President Thayer" presented a paper, later published as Σὺ εἶπας, Σὺ λέγεις, in the Answers of Jesus" (*JBL* 13 [1894]: 40–49), but neither the minutes nor the article itself gives any indication that it was a presidential address. One should note that in December 1894 the SBLE met jointly with six other "philological associations" (American Oriental Society, American Philological Association, Modern Lanuage Association of America, American Dialect Society, Spelling Reform Association, Archaeological Institute of America), in large part to honor the memory of the recently deceased William Dwight Whitney of Yale. It may be that the decision not to present a presidential address was a necessity, given the reduced program available to SBLE-specific papers and the desire to devote significant time to joint sessions with the other societies.

5. Beginning in 1897, the Society abandoned the practice of meeting semiannually and restricted itself to a single December meeting each year.

1909	Henry Preserved Smith, "Old Testament Ideals," *JBL* 29 (1910): 1–26.
1910	David G. Lyon, "On the Archaeological Exploration of Palestine," *JBL* 30 (1911): 1–17.
1911	Ernest de Witt Burton, "Some Phases of the Synoptic Problem," *JBL* 31 (1912): 95–113.
1912	Lewis B. Paton, "Israel's Conquest of Canaan," *JBL* 32 (1913): 1–53.
1913	George A. Barton, "The Hermeneutic Canon 'Interpreted Historically' in the Light of Modern Research," *JBL* 33 (1914): 56–77.
1914	Nathaniel Schmidt, "The Story of the Flood and the Growth of the Pentateuch"
1915	Charles Cutler Torrey, "The Need of a New Edition of the Hebrew Bible"
1916	Morris Jastrow Jr., "Constructive Elements in the Critical Study of the Old Testament," *JBL* 36 (1917): 1–20.
1917	Warren J. Moulton, "The Dating of the Synoptic Gospels," *JBL* 37 (1918): 1–19.
1918	James A. Montgomery, "Present Tasks of American Biblical Scholarship," *JBL* 38 (1919): 1–14.
1919	Edgar J. Goodspeed, "The Origin of Acts," *JBL* 39 (1920): 83–101.
1920	Albert T. Clay, "A Recent Journey through Babylonia and Assyria"
1921	Kemper Fullerton, "Viewpoints in the Discussion of Isaiah's Hopes for the Future," *JBL* 41 (1922): 1–101.
1922	William R. Arnold, "Observations on the Origin of Holy Scripture," *JBL* 42 (1923): 1–21.
1923	Max L. Margolis, "Our Own Future: Forecast and a Programme," *JBL* 43 (1924): 1–8.
1924	Clayton R. Bowen, "Why Eschatology?" *JBL* (1925): 1–9.
1925	Julius A. Bewer, "The Hellenistic Mystery Religions and the Old Testament," *JBL* 45 (1926): 1–13.
1926	Shirley Jackson Case, "The Alleged Messianic Consciousness of Jesus," *JBL* 46 (1927): 1–19.
1927	Irving F. Wood, "The Contribution of the Bible to the History of Religion," *JBL* 47 (1928): 1–19.
1928	Loring Woart Batten, "Hosea's Message and Marriage," *JBL* 48 (1929): 257–73.
1929	James E. Frame, "Paul's Idea of Deliverance," *JBL* 49 (1930): 1–12.
1930	William Frederic Badè, "Ceramics and History in Palestine," *JBL* 50 (1931): 1–19.
1931	Burton Scott Easton, "New Testament Ethical Lists," *JBL* 51 (1932): 1–12.
1932	J. M. Powis Smith, "The Character of King David," *JBL* 52 (1933): 1–11. Due to the untimely death of Smith a few months before the meeting, W. C. Graham read the paper in his place.

1933	James Moffatt, "The Sacred Book in Religion," *JBL* 53 (1934): 1–12.
1934	Frederick C. Grant, "The Spiritual Christ," *JBL* 54 (1935): 1–15.
1935	Elihu Grant, "The Philistines," *JBL* 55 (1936): 175–94.
1936	Henry J. Cadbury, "Motives of Biblical Scholarship," *JBL* 56 (1937): 1–16.
1937	George Dahl, "The Messianic Expectation in the Psalter," *JBL* 57 (1938): 1–12.
1938	William Henry Paine Hatch, "The Primitive Christian Message," *JBL* 58 (1939): 1–13.
1939	W. F. Albright, "The Ancient Near East and the Religion of Israel," *JBL* 59 (1940): 85–112.
1940	Chester C. McCown, "Gospel Geography: Fiction, Fact, and Truth," *JBL* 60 (1941): 1–25.
1941	Julian Morgenstern, "The Society of Biblical Literature and Exegesis," *JBL* 61 (1942): 1–10. The original title of the address was "The Task of the Society of Biblical Literature and Exegesis."
1942	Kirsopp Lake. No address was delivered, due to to Lake's absence.
1943	Kirsopp Lake. No address was delivered, due to to Lake's absence.
1944	Theophile James Meek, "The Syntax of the Sentence in Hebrew," *JBL* 64 (1945): 1–13.
1945	Morton Scott Enslin, "The Future of Biblical Studies," *JBL* 65 (1946): 1–12.
1946	Leroy Waterman, "Biblical Studies in a New Setting," *JBL* 66 (1947): 1–14.
1947	Ernest Cadman Colwell, "Biblical Criticism: Lower and Higher," *JBL* 67 (1948): 1–12.
1948	John W. Flight. "The Presidential Address was omitted, since Professor Flight was prevented by illness from being present."[6]
1949	Floyd V. Filson, "Method in Studying Biblical History," *JBL* 69 (1950): 1–18.
1950	Robert H. Pfeiffer, "Facts and Faith in Biblical History," *JBL* 70 (1951): 1–14.
1951	Erwin R. Goodenough, "The Inspiration of New Testament Research," *JBL* 71 (1952): 1–9.
1952	Sheldon H. Blank, "Men Against God: The Promethean Element in Biblical Prayer," *JBL* 72 (1953): 1–13.
1953	S. Vernon McCasland, "The Unity of the Scriptures," *JBL* 73 (1954): 1–10.
1954	Millar Burrows, "Thy Kingdom Come," *JBL* 74 (1955): 1–8.

---

6. "Proceedings, December 28th to 30th, 1948," *JBL* 68 (1949): v.

1955	Amos N. Wilder, "Scholars, Theologians, and Ancient Rhetoric," *JBL* 75 (1956): 1–11.
1956	J. Philip Hyatt, "The Dead Sea Discoveries: Retrospect and Challenge," *JBL* 76 (1957): 1–12.
1957	Sherman E. Johnson, "Early Christianity in Asia Minor," *JBL* 77 (1958): 1–17.
1958	William A. Irwin, "A Still Small Voice … Said, What Are You Doing Here?" *JBL* 78 (1959): 1–12.
1959	Robert M. Grant, "Two Gnostic Gospels," *JBL* 79 (1960): 1–11.
1960	R. B. Y. Scott, "Priesthood, Prophecy, Wisdom, and the Knowledge of God," *JBL* 80 (1961): 1–15.
1961	Samuel Sandmel, "Parallelomania," *JBL* 81 (1962): 1–13.
1962	Herbert G. May, "Cosmological Reference in the Qumran Doctrine of the Two Spirits and in Old Testament Imagery," *JBL* 82 (1963): 1–14.
1963	John Knox, "Romans 15:14–33 and Paul's Conception of His Apostolic Mission," *JBL* 83 (1964): 1–11.
1964	Frederick V. Winnett, "Re-examining the Foundations," *JBL* 84 (1965): 1–19.
1965	Kenneth W. Clark, "The Theological Relevance of Textual Variation in Current Criticism of the Greek New Testament," *JBL* 85 (1966): 1–16.
1966	John L. McKenzie, "Reflections on Wisdom," *JBL* 86 (1967): 1–9.
1967	Paul Schubert, "The Final Cycle of Speeches in the Book of Acts," *JBL* 87 (1968): 1–16.
1968	James Muilenburg, "Form Criticism and Beyond," *JBL* 88 (1969): 1–18.
1969	Frank W. Beare, "The Mission of the Disciples and the Mission Charge: Matthew 10 and Parallels," *JBL* 89 (1970): 1–13.
1970	Harry M. Orlinsky, "Whither Biblical Research?" *JBL* 90 (1971): 1–14. The title of the address originally bore the subtitle "The Problem of 'Sin' as a Case in Point."
1971	Bruce M. Metzger, "Literary Forgeries and Canonical Pseudepigrapha," *JBL* 91 (1972): 3–24.
1972	Walter J. Harrelson. The 1972 annual meeting was held in Los Angeles in conjunction with the International Congress of Learned Societies in the Field of Religion. It was to that point the largest meeting of the Society, with over 2,500 attending. So as not to add to an already crowded program, Harrelson chose not to deliver a presidential address.
1973	Norman Perrin, "Eschatology and Hermeneutics: Reflections on Method in the Interpretation of the New Testament," *JBL* 93 (1974): 3–14.

1974	Frank M. Cross, Jr., "A Reconstruction of the Judean Restoration," *JBL* 94 (1975): 4–18.
1975	Robert W. Funk, "The Watershed of the American Biblical Tradition: The Chicago School, First Phase, 1892–1920," *JBL* 95 (1976): 4–22.
1976	David Noel Freedman, "Pottery, Poetry, and Prophecy: An Essay on Biblical Poetry," *JBL* 96 (1977): 5–26.
1977	Raymond E. Brown, "'Other Sheep Not of This Fold': The Johannine Perspective on Christian Diversity in the Late First Century," *JBL* 97 (1978): 5–22.
1978	James A. Sanders, "Text and Canon: Concepts and Method," *JBL* 98 (1979): 5–29.
1979	Joseph A. Fitzmyer, "The Aramaic Language and the Study of the New Testament," *JBL* 99 (1980): 5–21.
1980	Bernhard Anderson, "Tradition and Scripture in the Community of Faith," *JBL* 100 (1981): 5–21.
1981	James M. Robinson, "Jesus from Easter to Valentinus (or to the Apostle's Creed)," *JBL* 101 (1982): 5–37.
1982	Lou H. Silberman, "Listening to the Text," *JBL* 102 (1983): 3–26.
1983	Krister Stendahl, "The Bible as a Classic and the Bible as Holy Scripture," *JBL* 103 (1984): 3–10.
1984	Roland E. Murphy, "Wisdom and Creation," *JBL* 104 (1984): 3–11.
1985	Wayne A. Meeks, "Understanding Early Christian Ethics," *JBL* 105 (1986): 3–11.
1986	James L. Mays, "The Place of the Torah-Psalms in the Psalter," *JBL* 106 (1987): 3–12.
1987	Elisabeth Schüssler Fiorenza, "The Ethics of Interpretation: De-Centering Biblical Scholarship," *JBL* 107 (1988): 3–17.
1988	Philip J. King, "The Eighth, the Greatest of Centuries?" *JBL* 108 (1989): 3–15.
1989	Paul J. Achtemeier, "*Omne verbum sonat*: The New Testament and the Oral Environment of Late Western Antiquity," *JBL* 109 (1990): 3–27.
1990	Walter Brueggemann, "At the Mercy of Babylon: A Subversive Rereading of the Empire," *JBL* 110 (1991): 3–22.
1991	Helmut Koester, "Jesus the Victim," *JBL* 111 (1992): 3–15.
1992	Norman K. Gottwald, "Social Class as an Analytic and Hermeneutical Category in Biblical Studies," *JBL* 112 (1993): 3–22.
1993	Victor P. Furnish, "On Putting Paul in His Place," *JBL* 113 (1994): 3–17.
1994	Phyllis Trible, "Exegesis for Storytellers and Other Strangers," *JBL* 114 (1995): 3–19.

1995	Leander E. Keck, "Rethinking 'New Testament Ethics,'" *JBL* 115 (1996): 3–16.
1996	Gene M. Tucker, "Rain on a Land Where No One Lives: The Hebrew Bible and the Environment," *JBL* 116 (1997): 3–17.
1997	Hans Dieter Betz, "Antiquity and Christianity," *JBL* 117 (1998): 3–22.
1998	Patrick D. Miller, "Deuteronomy and Psalms: Evoking a Biblical Conversation," *JBL* 118 (1999): 3–18.
1999	D. Moody Smith, "When Did the Gospels Become Scripture?" *JBL* 119 (2000): 3–20.
2000	Adele Berlin, "The Book of Esther and Ancient Storytelling," *JBL* 120 (2001): 3–14.
2001	Harold W. Attridge, "Genre Bending in the Fourth Gospel," *JBL* 121 (2002): 3–21.
2002	John J. Collins, "The Zeal of Phinehas: The Bible and the Legitimation of Violence," *JBL* 122 (2003): 3–21.
2003	Eldon Jay Epp, "The Oxyrhynchus New Testament Papyri: 'Not Without Honor Except in Their Hometown'?" *JBL* 123 (2004): 5–55.
2004	David L. Petersen, "Genesis and Family Values," *JBL* 124 (2005): 5–23.
2005	Carolyn Osiek, "Catholic or catholic? Biblical Scholarship at the Center," *JBL* 125 (2006): 5–22.

Appendix 2
Editors of the *Journal of Biblical Literature*†

1880–1883	Frederic Gardiner
1883–1889	Hinckley G. Mitchell
1889–1894	George Foot Moore
1894–1900	David G. Lyon
1901–1904	Lewis B. Paton
1905–1906	James Hardy Ropes
1907	Benjamin W. Bacon
1908–1909	Julius A. Bewer
1910–1913	James A. Montgomery
1914–1921	Max L. Margolis
1922–1929	George Dahl
1930–1933	Carl H. Kraeling
1934	George Dahl
1935–1942	Erwin R. Goodenough
1943–1947	Robert H. Pfeiffer
1948–1950	J. Philip Hyatt
1951–1954	Robert C. Dentan
1955–1959	David Noel Freedman
1960–1969	Morton S. Enslin
1970	John Reumann
1971–1976	Joseph A. Fitzmyer
1977–1982	John H. Hayes
1983–1988	Victor Paul Furnish
1989–1994	John J. Collins
1995–1999	Jouette M. Bassler
2000–2005	Gail R. O'Day
2006–	James C. VanderKam

† The title "editor" has been used since 1938. Prior to that the secretary or corresponding secretary fulfilled editorial responsibilities.

www.ingramcontent.com/pod-product-compliance
Lightning Source LLC
Chambersburg PA
CBHW020638300426
44112CB00007B/154